ECONOMISTS AND SOCIETY

ECONOMISTS AND SOCIETY

THE DEVELOPMENT OF ECONOMIC THOUGHT FROM AQUINAS TO KEYNES

Second edition

JOSEPH FINKELSTEIN
UNION COLLEGE

ALFRED L. THIMM
UNION COLLEGE

1981

UNION COLLEGE PRESS
Schenectady, New York

To Nadia and Pat

Economists and Society: The Development of Economic Thought from Aquinas to Keynes. Second edition

Copyright © 1973 by Joseph Finkelstein and Alfred L. Thimm

Printed in the United States of America. All rights reserved. No part of this book may be used or reproduced in any manner whatsoever without written permission except in the case of brief quotations embodied in critical articles and reviews. For information address Union College Press, Union College, Schenectady, New York 12308

Published by Union College Press, Schenectady, New York 12308, U.S.A.

Distributed by Syracuse University Press, Syracuse, New York 13210, U.S.A.

Standard Book Number: 06-046599-9

Library of Congress Catalog Card Number: 81-51797

CONTENTS

PREFACE

The new revised paperback edition of *Economists and Society* is meant to satisfy the demand for an up-to-date, readable yet sophisticated account of the development of economic thought and economic history; moreover, the renewed interest in the intellectual history of economic thought in the economics curricula of American colleges encouraged us to provide a book that would be used not only as a text but also as inexpensive supplementary reading in a variety of economics and management courses. Since the hard cover edition was well received by college students and "intelligent laymen" we hope that the new paperback version will reach an even wider audience.

In our first edition, we did not give sufficient attention to Friedman's work in monetary theory. The problems of inflation and stagflation were neglected during the 1950s and 1960s, but have become enormous burdens in the post-war world; these problems needed exposition and analysis. The easy extrapolations of the Phillips' curve, which seemed so comfortable in the 1960s, needed redefinition in the light of experience, and the work of Duesenberry, Simon, Drucker, and others called for inclusion to place the superficial analysis of the "Affluent School" of economists of the recent pre-O.P.E.C. past in its proper perspective. We believe that these changes and inclusions are important and deserve study.

The new edition retains the quite original attempt to emphasize the connection between economic history and economic thought, but adds new material on post-Keynesian economics, and the economic history of the last fifteen years. The second edition brings the reader to the threshold of exciting developments in economics and economic theory. We hope that all our readers will share our discoveries.

J.F.
A.L.T.

Acknowledgements

We should like to thank many friends—colleagues, students, and administrators who have been most helpful: especially Miss Ruth Anne Evans, Librarian, colleagues in the History and Economics departments, and several thousand graduate students in Economics 212, *Controlling Forces in American Economic Development*, which both of us have had the pleasure of teaching.

Two people deserve our special thanks: Mrs. Elinor Lambert, who typed and nurtured our manuscript, and Dr. Artur Klausberger, our former research assistant.

INTRODUCTION

Contemporary Economic Problems in the Western World

The great economists concerned themselves with the wealth and poverty of nations, economic development and stagnation, national priorities and full employment, business cycles and inflation; these are, however, the issues of the day and of tomorrow. We shall briefly sketch the most important contemporary problems to give us a framework for considering the works of the great economists and their impact on policy. The last thirty years have brought an amazing rise in the level of living of the people in the Western world. In America the comforts and even luxuries enjoyed by large segments of the population prompted John Kenneth Galbraith to refer to America as the "affluent society" where nearly 55 percent of all families earned over $15,000 in 1978,[1] where, by the standards of the rest of the world,

[1]*Statistical Abstracts of the United States*, 1979, U.S. Department of Commerce, Table No. 735, p. 449.

even relief recipients seem outwardly to be affluent.[2] Truly, for such a society, Galbraith claimed, the traditional concern of economists with the allocation of scarce resources is no longer entirely germane.

Unfortunately, the actual picture is not quite as cosy. True, the family income in current dollars increased from an average income of $2335 in 1929[3] to a median income of $16,009 in 1978.[4] The proportion of "poor" families (under $3000 a year), furthermore, was reduced from 68.3 percent in 1935-1936[5] to 3.6 percent in 1978.[6] The number of well-off families (above $7000) increased from 7 percent in 1935-1936[7] to 86 percent in 1978.[8] Yet, there remain serious economic and social problems, which are especially disturbing because they affect large but isolated segments in our population—the old, the unemployable, the black, and the other "enclave" groups. The isolation of these Americans increases precisely because they represent poverty in an affluent society. Thus poverty remains a grave social problem even in our society.

UNEMPLOYMENT

Two different types of unemployment, technological and cyclical, concern Americans today. Traditionally, classical and neoclassical economists have been little concerned with technological unemployment. They reasoned that in the long run those unemployed by technological change would be eventually reabsorbed into the economy. It is quite doubtful whether any unemployed individual ever felt particularly consoled by the assurance that in the long run he would be reemployed, but this kind of thinking did assuage the conscience of the middle class, especially because the economists seem to have been generally correct.

Cyclical unemployment, on the other hand, has been one of the prime characteristics of a capitalistic society, and remains one of the

[2]Gabriel Kolko, *Wealth and Power in America* (New York: Praeger, 1961), p. 123. Even Kolko admits that in 1961 a quarter of the very poorest people owned their own automobiles (today this percentage is much higher); perhaps no other example could illustrate better the material wealth of our society.
[3]*Historical Statistics of the U.S. Colonial Times to 1957*, U.S. Department of Commerce, Bureau of the Census, Table G118-130, p. 166.
[4]*Statistical Abstracts of the U.S.*, Table 735, p. 449.
[5]*Poverty and Deprivation in the U.S.*, Conference on Economic Progress, (Washington, D.C., 1962), p. 26.
[6]*Statistical Abstracts of the U.S.*, Table 735, p. 449.
[7]*Poverty and Deprivation*, p. 34.
[8]*Statistical Abstracts of the U.S.*, Table 735, p. 449.

major areas of interest and study for modern Western economists. This interest was heightened during the worldwide depression of the 1930s, and the emergence of noncapitalistic and planned economies in the post-World War II period has added new relevance and vigor to intensive studies. No matter how abundant the merits of a capitalistic society, not many economists believe that it could survive another "great" depression. Still, the modern economists' concern with business cycles and mass unemployment is rather recent. Until the depression of the 1930s, respectable economists accepted, at least implicitly, Say's law, which sternly maintains that unemployment and depression are impossible because people produce only to consume, save only to invest. Except for Joseph Schumpeter, the institutionalists, and a few monetary theorists, only the economic "underworld" of Marx, LaSalle, Sismondi, Hobson, and Major Douglas studied business cycles and unemployment before 1930.[9]

Clearly, not all respectable neoclassical economists refused to admit the existence of depression in the face of historical experience. Before the 1930s, however, most of the academic Anglo-American economists failed to look for the fundamental causes of depressions and prosperities but rather tried to find the remedy to the problem in sterile analyses and criticisms of the financial superstructure of capitalism. The reforms advocated by these early "monetary" economists led to certain achievements such as the establishment of the Federal Reserve System in the United States, and the "autonomous" compensatory monetary policy, as practiced by the monetary authorities in the West, but fell far short of dealing with the real causes of cyclical fluctuations.

Monetary policy proved to be completely inadequate to prevent the inflations and depressions of the post-World War I period, and everywhere monetary policy broke down completely in the 1930s.[10] Mass unemployment and the breakdown of neoclassical economics

[9]The institutionalists Veblen, Mitchell, and the National Bureau of Economic Research provided the necessary data; the "monetary"economists Hawtrey, Robertson, and von Hayek developed business cycle theories which were generally compatible with both neoclassical economics and laissez faire policy. Contemporary monetary economists at the universities of Chicago and Virginia have been particularly influenced by von Hayek.

[10]It should be added that contemporary monetary economists such as Milton Friedman believe that the breakdown of monetary policy in the 1930s was due to incorrect and vacillating decisions made by the monetary authorities in Washington and London, rather than to the inadequacy of monetary policy per se.

set the stage for Keynes' *General Theory* and the Keynesian revolution in economic theory and policy. In the decade of the 1930s, deficiency in demand (under-consumption) became widely accepted as the major cause of depressions and unemployment. Governments could no longer afford to be neutral but had to take the necessary steps to provide employment.

The impact on the American public of the Keynesian revolution can be judged by two important events. In 1946, the U.S. Congress almost unanimously passed the so-called Full Employment Act. While of little practical importance, this act is historically of great significance. For the first time in American history Congress clearly stated that maintaining full employment was the responsibility of the government. This triumph of the Keynesian revolution was sealed seven years later during the recession of 1953. Faced with a serious rise in unemployment, President Eisenhower and Secretary of the Treasury George Humphrey took the necessary Keynesian steps of fighting deficiencies in demand by increasing government expenditures and by intentionally incurring a large deficit. Eisenhower and Humphrey were the dominant members of the last Administration that had ideological ties to a version of neoclassical thought.

The very fact that the difference between the economic policies of the Republican Eisenhower-Nixon-Ford Administrations and the Democratic Truman-Kennedy-Johnson-Carter Administrations was primarily one of rhetoric rather than of action emphasized the broad agreement that existed until the late '70s among economists and decision makers concerning policies dealing with business cycles, depressions and unemployment.[11] The differences that remained were invariably differences of degree rather than of kind. Thus everybody was for full employment and against inflation, but because full employment and price stability did not necessarily go hand in hand, the controversies of the 1970s centered around how much inflation should be risked in order to maintain full employment and vice versa. Thus the Democratic party by and large had and has been willing to risk increases in the price level in order to maintain full employment, whereas the Rupublican party has been more likely to risk a small increase in unemployment in the hope that it might help maintain price stability.

---

[11]John Kenneth Galbraith, *Economics and the Art of Controversy, passim* (New York, Vintage Books), 1959.

Unfortunately, both sides in this political debate tended to overlook the fact that the real question was no longer the amount of unemployment but its composition. The issues overlooked in the 1970s have emerged as the real problems of the 1980s. An unemployment rate of five percent of the labor force might be bearable if the unemployed, on the average, can expect to find employment in three to four months. If out of five million unemployed, three million are permanently unemployed, and if this percentage grows steadily, then a critical problem exists. If the unemployed, moreover, belong to special groups—the old, the young, the minorities, and so forth—then it may take a long time before either the public or economists become aware that traditional fiscal policies fail to remedy the problem.

Interestingly enough, although "mainstream" economists in the past generally failed to consider cyclical unemployment, they had been very much concerned with poverty, the concomitant of underemployment, and chronic unemployment. In spite of their interest, traditional economists did not find a solution to this problem. On the other hand, Keynesian economists, who believed that they had solved the unemployment problem at least theoretically, had not been concerned with the problem of poverty per se. They either believed with Galbraith that this was no longer an economic but rather a caseworker problem, or they believed with Keyserling and Heller, the advisers of Truman and Kennedy, that a faster growth rate of the national economy would solve the entire problem of chronic unemployment and poverty. The high growth rate enjoyed by the United States during the middle 1960s reduced industrial unemployment virtually to the vanishing point, but did not have a similar impact on the poverty groups that existed outside our technological society. The fact that during a period of unprecedented growth and prosperity the welfare rolls continued to grow indicated that Galbraith may have been correct; the groups that live in poverty in the United States today are too insulated from economic activity to be touched by conventional economic policy. The elimination of poverty in the United States seems to be essentially a question of social policy and social therapy.

The slow rate of growth of the American economy during the 1950s and early 1960s became one of the major issues in the Nixon-Kennedy election campaign of 1960. The press and interested laymen discussed for the first time the esoteric economic topic of optimum growth and the consequences of insufficient growth. The rapid economic growth experienced by the United States during the Johnson Administration ended for nearly ten years the public concern with "insufficient growth" and restored this topic briefly to professional economists. The major philosophical question that dominated the period 1968-1975 was the contribution of excessive growth and affluence to inflation and pollution. The quality of economic life rather than the rate of production became a key issue. Only a few present-day economists, such as Galbraith and Boulding, had continued to be concerned primarily with the qualitative nature of our society and with the qualitative composition of our GNP. A rapid increase in the GNP due to vast additional expenditures on billboards, roadside stands, TV commercials, and cosmetics had been greatly deplored by these writers, no matter what their impact on employment and personal income might have been. Neither the quality of our society nor its military strength could gain from such an increase. Galbraith maintained that it was shortsighted to glorify production for production's sake, to weigh the accomplishments of a society merely by the size of its GNP.

Today, the persistent and accelerating inflation, accompanied by falling productivity, the highest unemployment since the 1930s, growth in government bureaucracy and sharp deterioration in public services, has become a worldwide phenomenon; the crises of the Western welfare states have been paralleled by a critical breakdown in the Eastern European command economies. The supply-side economics in the West and the search for "economic reforms" that permit the market to decentralize economic decision-making represent a return to the concerns of the classical economists that give the study of Adam Smith, Ricardo, Malthus and Marx fresh importance.

1

THE CULTURAL FRAMEWORK OF ECONOMIC LIFE

Economics as a science is not much more than two centuries old, yet within this comparatively short time it has both provoked wide-ranging and often bitter controversy and amassed a body of literature truly monumental in quantity, if not always exceptional in quality. In freeing itself from superstitions, taboos, and magic, it has produced new superstitions and new magic. Dogmas more rigid than those of the scholastics have been promulgated by new scholastics who proclaim their economics the true salvation. Marx, that bushy-browed omniscience of the midnineteenth century, looms largest today, but he does not stand alone. For each writer of the scope and generous nature of Adam Smith, there are, generation after generation, the Ricardos—professional Cassandras blinded by self-constructed projections of disaster.

The science of economics is useful. It helps us understand phenomena that make life more difficult and less pleasant—the nature of rent and wages, the nineteenth-century market economy, and the implications of twentieth-century growth, unemployment, and fiscal policy, to name but a few. The more insightful our analysis of such phenomena, the more competent we are to deal with their social implications. Furthermore, we must never forget that the knowledge we have at present is small compared to the annual growth in data and skills. Today, particularly, the well-being of millions depends on decisions based on economics.

Two closely connected problems face the economist. First, there must be closer contact, and greater mutual respect, between professional economists and policy makers. In Keynes's famous phrase, "madmen in authority who hear voices in the air are distilling their frenzy from some academic scribbler of a few years back."[1] Writers such as Schumpeter, Heilbroner, and Samuelson have pioneered in making economics understandable. Others must turn to this work. Much more is known than is being utilized, and "common-sense" economics is largely inaccurate, harmful, and costly.

The second problem has to do with the cultural nature of economics. If economics consists of a body of scientific knowledge and is scientific in its handling and solution of problems, economists nevertheless are culturally contained (even when they are revolutionary), and the problems they are concerned with are culturally defined. Culture sets the entire environment in which discussion takes place, and the premises of a culture are long-lived. They survive all kinds of catastrophic political change and emerge as vestigial but powerful intellectual remnants decades or even centuries later. The mercantilism of the sixteenth century and the neomercantilism of the twentieth have more in common than title. They reflect the relatedness of problem and policy, which was the concern of government leaders in both periods.

Medieval Economics

The discussion of economic thought can begin at any stage. We choose the religious-intellectual framework of the Middle Ages (c. 1100-1400) because it sets standards and values that influenced economic life and thinking that still affect the ideas of Western society. In fact, so strong is this residue that it would be foolhardy to omit the topic.

Consider the economic world of St. Godric of Finchale, who might be considered the Horatio Alger of the twelfth century.[2] The chronicler tells us that the "Making of a Merchant" was a slow and

---

[1]John Maynard Keynes, *The General Theory of Employment, Interest and Money* (London: Macmillan, 1946), p. 383.

[2]G. G. Coulton, *Social Life in Britain: From the Conquest to the Reformation* (Cambridge: Cambridge University Press, 1919), pp. 415-420.

happenchance career, and fraught with great perils, more spiritual than temporal, but he also reassures us that success was attainable (indeed, one might even become a saint as Godric did). Although born of godly and virtuous parents, Godric chose not to become a husbandman (farmer) but to aspire to be a merchant. First he was a chapman (peddler) and wandered around neighboring villages and farmsteads. Obviously he was successful, and showed real entrepreneurial ability, for soon he joined a group of city merchants and extended his market. Through towns and boroughs, fortresses, cities, and fairs, Godric made his way "with simplicity." Then he branched out into overseas trade, more perilous but also more profitable.

For he labored not only as a merchant but also as a shipman—to Denmark and Flanders and Scotland; in all which lands he found certain rare, and, therefore, more precious wares, which he carried to other parts wherein he knew them to be least familiar, and coveted by the inhabitants beyond the price of gold itself; wherefore he exchanged the wares for others coveted by men of other lands; and thus he chaffered [traded] most freely and assiduously. Hence he made great profit in all his bargains, and gathered much wealth in the sweat of his brow; for he sold dear in one place the wares which he had bought elsewhere at a small price.[3]

After sixteen years as a merchant, Godric "began to think of spending on charity, to God's honor and service, the goods which he had so laboriously acquired."[4] First, he took the cross as a pilgrim to Jerusalem, but eventually visited St. James of Compostella, St. Gilles, and twice Rome, the latter time barefoot and carrying his aged mother on his shoulders. But this was still not enough: "Wherefore, that he might follow Christ the more freely, he sold all his possessions and distributed them among the poor."[5] Finally he became a hermit and a saint. Thus, the self-fulfilling prophecy of the twelfth century.

Altogether too much has been made of the Church's blanket hostility toward economic life during these centuries. Goods were scarce —all goods—and economic activity was essential, as it is essential in some form to every society, but it was perilous to the soul because its pleasures and rewards could become ends in themselves, and lead not

[3]*Ibid.,* p. 418.
[4]*Ibid.,* p. 419.
[5]*Ibid.,* p. 420.

toward but away from salvation. A society chainbound to scarcity could not praise material acquisition unless this economic activity contributed to the larger end. That end was spiritual, and economic life, successful or unsuccessful, had to bend to those values. Such was the background of Christian thought, and so long as economic inequality exists and distribution is inequitable, there must remain this sense of guilt and unease. These values are not phantoms of the twelfth century alone, but the prickling nature of Judeo-Christian ideas, which either breaks out in harshness even against the poor as a projection of the anxieties of the rich, or in the constant reminder of charity and philanthropy. This bent toward humanitarianism, toward universality, toward equalitarianism again and again injects itself into the sternness and rationality of everyday life. Whether as religious value, or current secular belief, "caritas" underpins Godric of Finchale and Henry Ford. Neither the Newtonian revolution of the eighteenth century nor the Social Darwinism of the nineteenth has obliterated the deep-rooted ideals of Christian asceticism and Christian obligation.

A second example from the medieval world is provided by Iris Origo's the *Merchant of Prato*,[6] biography of one Francesco Datini, a taverner's son who became a great merchant. Datini did not achieve sainthood. Indeed he feared he might be accused of usury as he amassed his fortune, which he willed to charity. For us he left bales of letters, which tell much of economic life within this Christian value structure. Hard-working, shrewd, and lusty, Datini turned every economic opportunity to his advantage. The great woolen and silk industries of Florence and Prato and the fantastic burgeoning of trade, with northern Italy as its center, provided him his chance. From second-hand weaponry to religious art, Datini turned his hand to making money. To what end? Although neither ascetic nor prodigal, he lived well and enjoyed most of life (he worried constantly over the operations of his branches and his relatives who managed them), but he saw himself as a good Christian and as one who might be deserving of salvation. Datini represents a new scale of economic activity—a broader market, a wider skill, a more aggressive aspiration. Life is not gain, but gain is to be used for life's ends—a jeweled collar for the bishop's dog, fine wines, and even a concubine—but in the end all he has goes to charity. The bishops of northern Italy were trying to work out new

---

[6]Iris Origo, *The Merchant of Prato* (New York: Knopf, 1957).

definitions of interest and new perimeters of justifiable economic activity as the Datinis and Medicis and others "pulled the rug" out from under them. The cities and merchants of northern Italy carried on big business, and carried it on well, but it was not capitalism as we know it. The intellectual resolution of what they were doing came neither from St. Godric's Norfolk nor Datini's Prato, but from the intellectual heart of Christendom, the University of Paris.

Western Europe of the thirteenth century was not the brutal chaos of the tenth or even the eleventh century. In practice as well as thought, economic activity had spread widely along with urbanization and political security. Of all the questions the Schoolmen faced, none seemed more crucial than to explain material gain. Within and without the Church, critics were increasingly aware of the growing dangers and threats. The unfortunate Abelard had warned the Church that unless she surrendered her material riches she stood in danger of losing Christ. But Abelard was too erratic, too volatile a personality, and his solution impossible even in the twelfth century.

Although his writings were condemned at one point, Aquinas emerged as the most convenient reconciler of religious and secular ideological conflicts. Aquinas was not interested primarily, or even secondarily, in economics. He was concerned with God and the relation of society to God and to salvation. But how to avoid economics— ever growing, ever waxing, ever threatening to pull down the whole structure of faith and obligations of daily life and religious works? We will return to Aquinas after briefly examining some of this economic activity.

Some forty years ago, R. H. Tawney set out to battle with Max Weber and brilliantly showed that economics and social changes acted powerfully on religion not only in the sixteenth century and after, but even earlier in the Middle Ages. Tawney's brief opening chapter remains one of the most sensitive and perceptive analyses of the "Medieval Background."[7] He suggests that society was conceived as a "social organism," akin to the human body, composed of many members, each having different functions but complementing each other in an overall harmony. Overarching all individuals was the unifying sense of purpose, the same goal for all those who inhabit Christendom: "The

[7]R. H. Tawney, *Religion and the Rise of Capitalism* (New York: Harcourt Brace Jovanovich), pp. 3-61 ; Max Weber, *The Protestant Ethic and the Spirit of Capitalism,* trans. Talcott Parsons (New York: Scribner, 1958).

perfect happiness of man cannot be other than the vision of the divine essence."[8]

Otherwise, there was little uniformity either in time, place, or function. Between the tenth and fifteenth centuries, the entire pattern of life in its outward modes changed greatly. The serf of the early period gives place to the "businessman" farmer of the later century—true, not everywhere, but in more situations than was ordinarily recognized. But if change were characteristic of time, it was endemic of place and function. Northern Italy was ever a forerunner of new economic devices and mercantile aggressiveness. Great cities and great families struck out into new areas. Venice bought the destruction of its commercial rival, the Dalmatian city of Zara, in the Fourth Crusade, and the Arsenal of Venice was a highly integrated economic and military organization. Effectively run and powerfully organized, the Arsenal played no small role in guaranteeing long superiority to the city of canals and swamps at the head of the Adriatic. The great families spread across the Mediterranean—the Medicis and the Datinis set up their kinsmen in "fattore" (branch outposts) and included God as a shareholder on a percentage basis in any profits they might make. The Antonio of Shakespeare's *Merchant of Venice* is a sorry businessman; the shrewd businessman had long been hedging against loss by purchasing sea insurance, which was readily available on the Rialto. Somewhere, deeply but vaguely, within this environment, the concept of corporate business activity came into being as a standard device for large risky undertakings.

The fairs of France abounded with commercial vitality. Every student of medieval history knows the role Champagne played in the international commerce of the twelfth century. Goods were wholesaled here, and a law merchant practiced. Champagne was only one place of contact. Between North and South, the lines of trade crossed and interlocked; East and West they also ran, and even to the far outposts of northern England the range of economic activity put its mark. To escape the world of corruption, a band of Cistercians settled in the Yorkshire wilds. They cleared the land, and brought in sheep, and built an abbey for religious contemplation. "Fountains" not only

---

[8]Aquinas, *Summa Theologica*, 2ª 2ᵃᵉ, div. I, Q. iii, art. VIII, quoted in Tawney, *Religion and the Rise of Capitalism*, p. 25.

became the greatest religious center of the North, but also was famed for its wool and wealth. Abbots mortgaged the wool clip four years in advance to raise church and dwellings. With ease that would shock Barclay's Bank, monies crossed from Lombard bankers to England to pay for those undertakings. Thus if manor and guild existed everywhere, so there was also incredible economic vitality throughout Western lands.

This energy, in fact, had to be channeled within the framework of religious design. The sin of avarice was no figmentary creature of the preachers; it was a living threat to the body social. The reconciliation of reality and theory was not singularly successful. We might say that there were three different approaches to the problem — compliance, intellectual reconciliation, and institutional mechanism.

DOCTRINE OF ACCEPTANCE

Least successful overall, but with some amazing peaks of strength, was the resort to compliance. Largely an outgrowth of the agricultural base of society, and most easily fitted into Catholic religious teaching, the doctrine of acceptance and conformity was widely stressed. Not gain nor striving, but grateful compliance with the position and role in which one found oneself placed was preached. It must have taken a tremendous amount of ever-constant teaching to make this view of society meaningful, but it did have important repercussions. The ideas fitted well into the metaphor of a social-biological organism, which John of Salisbury and others elaborated so picturesquely in the twelfth century:

Those are called the feet who discharge the humbler offices, and by whose services the members of the whole commonwealth walk upon solid earth. Among these are to be counted the husbandmen, who always cleave to the soil, busied about their ploughlands or vineyards or pastures or flower-gardens. To these must be added the many species of cloth-making, and the mechanic arts, which work in wood, iron, bronze, and the different metals; also the menial occupations, and the manifold forms of getting a livelihood and sustaining life, or increasing household property, all of which, while they do not pertain to the authority of the governing power, are yet in the highest degree useful and profitable to the corporate whole of the commonwealth . . . . For inferiors owe it to their superiors to provide them with service. Just as the superiors in their turn owe it to their inferiors to provide them with all things needful for their protection and succour.[9]

INTELLECTUAL RECONCILIATION: AQUINAS

Aquinas contributed the intellectual reconciliation of economic reality, and Christian doctrine found in him its most effective spokesman. The University of Paris and its faculty was the ideological center of Christian Europe. Whatever Paris lacked in intellectual originality, it made up in authority. Aquinas, of course, reached the pinnacle of this structure eventually by reconciling Aristotle with modern life—that is, the thirteenth century. Aristotle, however, had written no books on political economy, and Aquinas certainly must have viewed these problems, nagging though they were, as at best secondary. However much we may admire Aquinas' genius, there is not very much that is original with him, particularly in the area of economic ideas. In the main, he is intellectually conventional, though there are glimmerings of the disquieting intricacy of economic matters in the knotty differences he is forced to raise concerning value. Fundamentally, Aquinas added nothing to the medieval idea of wealth and industry. Wealth was an act of fortuitous circumstance, which the recipient was to accept calmly and dispose of as quickly as possible in good works and charity. Too frequent or too intimate contact with material prosperity was living dangerously, and a good Christian saw to it that he did not needlessly imperil his soul. Industry or labor, however, represented a positive good. Man must labor with the sweat of his face—the Bible had decreed—and hard work combined both religious and social values. If this world provided boot-camp training for the world of eternity, that training had to be sufficiently rigorous to condition weak human beings for the future. None of this was original, but Aquinas preached it convincingly. But what of the more difficult situations, which increasing trade (the most perilous of all the medieval occupations) was bringing? In thirteenth century Paris there were more than 100 guilds, more than 5000 masters and journeymen. For all of these, a wider explanation was needed, and the explanation most richly lauded by the Church was justice. The just price and its counterpart, the just wage, were meant to contain such bitter enemies as the goose-roasters

---

[9]*The Portable Medieval Reader,* assembled and illuminated by J. B. Ross and M. M. McLaughlin (New York: Viking, 1949), Part One: The Body Social, pp. 129-130, From *Policraticus,* trans. J. Dickinson.

and poulterers, and the feuds between the secondhand clothes dealers and tailors. The just price, the measure of exchange value, was composed of the simple costs of production plus an amount—just wage— able to maintain the producer in that station of life in which he had been placed.[10] Obviously, the just price and the just wage were not entirely removed from a market concept. However, neither supply nor effective demand nor the producer himself was meant to control price, but equity placed within a religious framework. Price then was closely connected with labor cost, which in turn, was directly connected with a person's status. But Aquinas knew that other situations did exist in the exchange of commodities for money. "Is it acceptable to sell a good for more money than one paid?" If the question arose out of a simple straightforward transaction, the answer was an unqualified "no," but there might be exceptions. If the goods were of special value to the holder, then an additional amount might be added to compensate the seller. If the owner added to the value of the good either intrinsically or extrinsically, a higher price would be charged. If the producer would suffer any loss because of being deprived of the good, then he could ask the purchaser additional recompense, or if the owner had suffered some risk, he might be assuaged by an added factor.[11] There is thus considerable flexibility in Aquinas, and producers did indeed manage to live within these broad categories, or to evade them without feeling great guilt (probably more of the latter than the former, if the records of offense for forestalling, engrossing, and regrating are taken into account and if we examine in detail the range of economic activity). No doctrine was more outmoded by the thirteenth century than the traditional Church view of interest, but there was no way around it. Christ had ordered: "datum, nihil inde sperantes" ["Give, hoping for nothing in return"]. Aristotle, a weak economist at best, had declared that money was barren and could not increase itself; thus to demand payment for its use was unjust. Civil law made money a "consumptible"—there could be no loan without outright sale. "To take usury for a loan of money," Aquinas wrote, "is in itself unjust; for it is to sell what does not exist, which is an inequality and therefore, an injustice."[12] Money he compares to wine—"to use the article is to

[10]Raymond de Roover, "The Concept of the Just Price: Theory and Economic Policy," *Journal of Economic History,* 18 (1958), pp. 418-434.
[11]W. J. Ashley, *An Introduction to English Economic History and Theory. Part I, The Middle Ages* (New York: Putnam, 1910), pp. 133-154.
[12]*Ibid,* p. 153.

consume it. In articles of this kind [consumptibles], therefore, the use of the thing must not be reckoned separately from the thing itself; he who is given the use is thereby given the thing. And accordingly in lending a thing of this kind, all the rights of ownership are handed over."[13] To the modern view this is unfortunate nonsense, but Aquinas, tied to his Aristotle, had no way to go but backward. The wine metaphor persists, and thus he who lends is seeking two rewards: The restitution of an equal amount of the article and also a payment for its use, called usury. "Wherefore he would be manifestly committing injustice and sinning."[14]

Although we can fully understand the hatred of the usurer in a society so close to the margin of subsistence, the doctrine itself was not enlightened. In practice, it was increasingly avoided. First those outside the religious bond—Jews and Syrians, for example—were allowed to take interest. And then others. Datini told his executor in his will to make restitution if any claims were to arise after his death. The threat of not being buried in consecrated ground for a manifest usurer was a formidable one, but usually not keenly felt by the merchant until life was spent. Economic life had just too much aggressiveness to accept and stay within these guidelines.

INSTITUTIONAL MECHANISM: THE GUILDS

We see the same historical process in the development and evolution of the guilds, the third approach to the problem of medieval economic life. These quasireligious, quasieconomic combinations were the best urban institutional arrangements devised to carry out economic life within this religious framework. Wherever we find merchant and craft guilds we meet exclusiveness, monopoly, and bitter infighting. For the in-group membership, there were welfare benefits such as sickness payments, medical aid conventions, and burial rights. The guilds did contribute to religious foundations, but the major purpose was economic gain by and for members. Masterships became property—an old German drinking song tells young men to have a rollicking good time, for if they want to get ahead in life, they must marry an old widow, one who had inherited her husband's mastership. That reality diverged from economic fact is evident in the modifications in church doctrine the schoolmen were making in the fourteenth and fifteenth centuries, but to update Aquinas was no easy task.

[13]*Ibid,* p. 153.
[14]*Ibid,* p. 153.

Aquinas himself had left open conditions: Where a loss occurred because of a loan, or a gain was missed, a sum of restitution might be demanded of the borrower. Tawney suggests that later church writers noted the subjective elements in the religious formulation of the just price. They held that a free contract in which both parties expressed satisfaction, since the transaction was completed, might be a more adequate measure of fairness. Obviously one need only comment that a completed transaction is not always recognition of justice. St. Antonino, an Italian bishop of the fifteenth century, Tawney tells us, tried to reconcile a highly developed commercial civilization with outmoded doctrine. Within traditional bounds, which had to be observed, it was necessary to give some play to economic consideration. Because a "just price" might vary with individuals and circumstances, Antonino suggested that price be considered a range rather than an absolute. The price of an article might then be religious, fair, or uncompromising. Only after the seller exceeded the fixed price by more than 50 percent did he get into difficulty. The seller, if deliberately guilty, must make restitution. The operation of a market structure with fluctuating prices, without the danger of either buyer or seller incurring sin, was gropingly approached.

It is now fashionable (as it was once most unfashionable) to credit the medieval schoolmen with intellectual virtues and insights which would solve all our present needs. In the realm of economic thought, nothing would be more misleading and uncomplimentary. To a man, they saw themselves as religious thinkers, never as economists, and they would have been most horrified to be viewed as being concerned in any primary sense with secular problems. What they had in mind was an overview of society, a broad religious canopy under which all human institutions, including the economic, were to be gathered in and made to work harmoniously. This was both natural and according to God's plan. This Christian Commonwealth was never more than an abstract dream—here and there put into practice briefly. But it was a great dream. It makes all the later attempts, from Utopianism to Marxist Communism, seem puny by comparison. Essentially, however, and this is the real point, it could never really be concerned with economic activity as such, and we look in vain and mistakenly for hidden signs of future analytical concepts. All societies have an economic life, but only after Western society fragmented its religious uniformities could economic activity achieve a respectable place, and even this was still defined largely in religious terms for many future centuries.

Precisely because these religious writers and these centuries of medieval life took such an arcane view of economic matters are they fruitful. This medieval view gives us not only a sense of historical continuity and insight into what happened, but also a real basis for comparisons. Only by looking intensely at the medieval framework of economic life can we understand fully the immensity of change that has occurred in economic thinking. Many people would emphasize the changes in technology as the great difference, but between the twelfth and the twentieth centuries, technological changes are a modest alteration compared to the alteration of the view of society—from a world of harmonies within a harmonious universe to a world of Faustian competition. Modern views of economc determinism would have been thoroughly and utterly incomprehensible to the past age.

The medieval writer had almost none of our modern kit of concepts or tools. Reluctantly he came to see the difference between a natural market of barter and agricultural exchange and an exchange market of commercial importance. He was, as we have suggested, thoroughly bogged down in a welter of inability to distinguish between interest and usury; the churchmen missed an opportunity to have a voice in the burgeoning commercial activity of these centuries. Beyond a simple labor concept of value, they broke no new ground, and the just price and just wage are more fruitful as social concepts than they are in economic analysis. Not production or distribution or unemployment, but justice, was the key and goal of pre-modern theorists.

We owe the churchmen only this much; we owe a larger debt to their society. History does not view this period as stationary. No bonds would contain the vigor of its activity. From the eleventh century, western Europe regained the offensive and began a long period of expansion which would end in the world domination of the eighteenth century. New lands were brought into cultivation, and older lands brought into higher productivity. Constant warfare produced continuous demand for weaponry and military goods. And millions of human beings produced growing demands for luxuries and necessities. The mighty lords, secular and religious, lived prodigally. If Edward I imported $100,000 of wine for his household for a three-year period, princes of the Church raised cathedrals and abbeys. Wine from France, woolens from Flanders, fish from the Baltic, silks from Florence, many items, including spices and jewels, from the East—these products streamed in to supply the needs and wishes of the population, which could not be contained. Wise men feared that these appetites would turn men from the contemplation of God and the need for salvation. They were not wrong. It may be that every age has its chance to remain in the Garden of Eden, but chooses the uncertainty and dynamics of expulsion. Economic thought arose out of life in this society of growth and speculation. Practical businesses in this age pushed out the potential of profitmaking; the hesitant intellectuals followed.

Mercantilism

Many histories of economic thought are satisfied to treat the mercantilists as forerunners of the science of economics rather than as deserving a place of their own. We think this is a wrong approach, for the mercantilists made real contributions to *political* economy, which the twentieth century has more than recognized, even if the nineteenth century had only disregard for their doctrines. Mercantilist thought was not homogeneous either in time or place; it ranged from the simple bullionist approach to trade to the sophisticated political economy of Thomas Mun, a director of the East India Co. and a writer on economic policy. Its real essence was neither trade nor economic strength, but *power.* The aggrandizement of power to a state authority emerged from the fragmented political authority of the Middle Ages. This concept of public—that is, royal—authority binds together the mercantilists. Colbert, Louis XIV's minister, and Joseph II, Holy Roman Emperor, shared this common concern, but because power arose in different contexts out of different historical pasts, mercantilist doctrine emphasized different elements in different national contexts. Essentially, there were three major types: English, French, and Germanic. The English theorists and English practices seem to us the most advanced and most perceptive. English writers contributed significant and permanent ideas concerning money, international trade, and comparative advantage. French mercantilism emphasized, in particular, state subsidization of industry and the interlinkage of economic and military power. The Germanic mercantilists contributed important ideas concerning state finance and bureaucratic organization. Let us look more closely at the evolution of mercantilist thought.

RISE OF STATE POWER

The most amazing fact about Europe from the fifteenth century on was its vitality. In every area, there seemed to be outpourings of tremendous energies. William Langer suggests that the passing of the great plagues, which had decimated European population in earlier centuries, gave rise, in part, to a new sense of psychological optimism and security, which made life more positive and more creative.[15] In retrospect, many factors must have contributed: More political security; more intellectual controversy and experimentation; better standards of living beyond famine and subsistence levels; the existence of a considerable body of social overhead capital, which made larger economic developments possible; religious fervor and personal disquietude—a permanent dynamic within Western culture; great successes already achieved, which fed the ego of European man; and a sense of largeness, which spurred experimentation at home and abroad. All of these factors and the many more that might be added loom large in the new sense of strength emerging in this tiny peninsular land area jutting out from the Eurasian land mass. Intertwined and overarching every development was the rise of state power. The feudality had been crushed in western Europe, or was so completely on the defensive that princes could look confidently to their own plans for strengthening royal authority. From the Elbe to the Atlantic shoreline, national power as a concept dominated educated thinking. Even in the crisis of the religious revolts of the sixteenth century, the final outcome was everywhere decided along political boundaries and state power rather than by personal religious beliefs. "Cuius regio eius religio" ("The religion of the prince determines the religion of the realm") applied not only to the settlement in the German lands; it applied as well in England, France, and the Austrian possessions.

THE "NEW WORLD"

Of all the changes, the most dramatic perhaps was the discovery of the nature and extent of the earth. Within the briefest period, some fifty years, not only was the globe circumnavigated, but also a whole range of new data and impressions were borne into a Europe already rich in its own strivings. It is no accident that Thomas More opens his account of *Utopia* with a conversation between himself and a sailor, Raphael Hythloday, just returned from a voyage to the New World. In hard economic terms, too, the new discoveries and their exploitation were to have immense repercussions and implications in every corner of Europe and for every policymaking official.

[15]William Langer, "The Next Assignment," *American Historical Review,* (January 1958), pp. 283-304.

Consider what happened: Land—some twenty times the amount of land known to the Europeans—came under their control. Bullion—some ten to fifteen times the amount of existing specie—flowed into Europe over the next century and a half in one of the most massive and long-run inflations ever known. Jean Bodin is rightfully famous for recognizing the cause of this inflation.[16] The discoveries expanded greatly European tastes, from new foods such as potatoes to new vices such as tobacco. To the Turks, Europe owes the introduction of coffee, but one could name many products from East and West that became necessities of life for the European. People—over the next three centuries some 20 million blacks—were to be forcefully transported; during the same period, at least an equivalent number of Europeans were more or less voluntarily to remove themselves (in the nineteenth century, the outmigration of Europeans may have numbered as much as 100 million people). Such vast changes produced a revolution in men's thinking. Europeans accepted relativity in space and time, and with this an expansion of physical and mental horizons to match the vast canvas unfolding before them. New ideas of control and command, of politics and government, had to be worked out. Everywhere challenges and opportunities emerged, which individuals and states would then seize to their immense advantage. Not one generation but a dozen generations worked in vain to control these shifts of power. In all of this ferment, economic life and thought played its part.

Before considering the schools of English, French, and German mercantilism, let us look briefly at those ideas the three generally shared. Without doubt, they agreed that the state should be powerful at home and abroad,[17] and they unquestioningly approved the supersession of national royal power over local power. Policies that contributed to state power were on the whole desirable. And although pre-Darwinian, they saw power as antagonistic and exclusive. Internal barriers to control were to be eliminated by force, by edict, or by reform; external power was to be built by treaty, by war, or by deliberate policy. Colbert, for example, for the first time made central France a free trade area; externally he advocated the war against the Dutch as an opportunity to break their mercantile power. He noted in a memorandum that the commerce of Europe was carried on by

---

[16]Jean Bodin was the adviser to the French King, a brilliant political strategist and a perceptive economic observer.

[17]Jacob Viner, "Power versus plenty as Objectives of Foreign Policy in the Seventeenth and Eighteenth Centuries," *World Politics,* 1 (October 1948), pp. 1-29.

20,000 ships, that the Dutch had 15,000 to 16,000 ships, the English 3,000 to 4,000, and the French only 500 to 600. Destroying a sizable portion of the Dutch fleet, he suggested, would make an agreeable contribution to France's economic strength.

Too much has been made of mercantilist confusion between wealth and money. According to their premises, there was a close connection between the two. Specie, gold and silver, played roles in the sixteenth, seventeenth, and eighteenth centuries they no longer play (although the magic of specie holdings is not entirely lost even today). Consider the rudimentary nature of banking, taxation, and credit, and it is not hard to understand the value the mercantilist placed on the acquisition of bullion. Remember that national armies were just emerging and that gold could augment national strength by buying mercenaries or allies. The English front lines lay in the Low Countries during the wars of the late seventeenth and early eighteenth centuries, and these lines were held together as much by bullion as by allegiance. Power was closely linked to the possession of hard currency. Did not the vast influence of treasure play a large part in holding a decadent Spanish monarchy together for so long a time?

Some mercantilists did confuse wealth and bullion, but in macro terms they were more right than wrong. A large and favorable trade was desirable and would add to the national strength. Trade was the major subject of discussion of mercantilist writing, as power was the underlying premise. The extension, control and manipulation of trade, both foreign and domestic, could fill the deficiencies and augment the royal coffers with the means of wealth. Without mineral wealth, what other alternatives were there? Sheep, however, could be turned into gold, and wine into silver by a simple alchemy. If one sold more than one bought, the difference would be made up in bullion payment. A favorable balance of trade served then two visible purposes. It served as a fruitful mechanism to increase continually one's own store of metal and consequently to weaken one's enemy. In the state of power politics of seventeenth- and eighteenth-century Europe, trade was considered more a weapon of statecraft than a means to increase the real income of nationals.

Mercantilist theory also held that the amount of trade was relatively fixed; therefore, it also followed that any action that benefited one's own trading position must have harmed one's adversary. Only Mun offers a broader perception and a recognition of the difference between a balance of trade and a balance of payments, but then the distinction is a modern one, for to the mercantilist the object of trade was different from the present-day view.[18] Only in these terms can we better understand the vast amount of legislative concern with trading activity from the control over exports and imports to the Navigation Acts of the English Parliament. Foreign trade was an outgrowth of foreign policy, which was, in turn, a measure of political power. Internal or domestic trade was ideologically less significant than foreign trade, though by no means was it to be neglected.

Three aspects of policy seem important to consider in this context. First, the national state was enforcing its power over residual local power authorities—for example, provinces, towns, guilds—and thus the regulation of economic life was an important instrument to effect this control. The imposition of minute domestic regulation of manufacturing and commerce was designed to demonstrate to everyone that national power had come to supplant local authority everywhere. Second, a domestic economy flourishing in every aspect could contribute to overall national strength. The mercantilist was concerned with neither individual nor collective well-being. Hobbes's *Leviathan,* although a gross exaggeration of the mercantilist view, did at least echo many elements of this thinking. Finally, internal economic health could play an important role in the more important area of foreign trade. Large home manufacturers could supply the flow of goods essential to capture that favorable balance of trade. A healthy internal economy could guarantee an increasing growth in population, which was basic to providing artisans and peasants for production, sailors for the navy and marine, soldiers for the army, and colonists for possessions that could furnish raw materials and goods that could not be produced at home. Although some saw colonies as markets for goods, the thrust of colonialism was exploitative.

Rightfully, the American colonist resented the autarchic English trade policy. He was treated as a cog—the "hewer of wood and drawer of water." His function was to furnish spars and masts, tobacco, cotton, furs—goods that could not be easily or cheaply produced in England. The French colonies fared even worse; they were never allowed to develop to a political stage at which they might contemplate revolt.

---

[18]Thomas Mun, *England's Treasure by Foreign Trade 1664* (New York and London: n.p., 1895).

To summarize briefly, mercantilism developed literally an enormous body of minute and intricate economic controls over both internal domestic and external foreign trade as a means to build state power.[19] It utilized every device of control—coercion, regulation of guilds, grants of monopoly power, administration of tolls, tariffs and taxes, subsidies and prohibitions. How successful was it? Theoretically, it added only a small amount to economic knowledge and that largely arose over the controversy of acquiring or losing bullion and its relation to trade policy. Practically, it is more difficult to evaluate. Adam Smith wrote over two hundred pages condemning the restrictive and emprisoning effects of mercantilism on economic life, but by 1776 not much good could be said about an outmoded and impossible structure. In France, mercantilism as a policy probably must be accounted a failure. All of the trading companies established by Colbert failed, either for economic or political-military reasons. The pattern of high-cost luxury goods manufacture established in France has had a continuous life, though partially at the price of not developing healthier attitudes toward mass-produced goods. In Russia, the brutal mercantilist program of Peter the Great brought this backward country into the purview of Western society but at a price of two million people. Prussian mercantilism turned an impoverished wasteland area into a productive state capable of withstanding the disastrous wars of the mideighteenth century and of emerging as a great power in the nineteenth century. Austrian mercantilism drowned in politics and had little economic success. Everywhere mercantilism as an economic program must be judged highly restrictive and imprisoning; but as an economic program whose aim was more political, mercantilism did succeed. The state emerged in absolute control at home, though at a heavy price. Not even the English could hold onto their colonies, and in England and France this absolute state itself was relatively short-lived.

ENGLISH MERCANTILISM: THOMAS MUN

Let us examine more specifically aspects of mercantilist theory. Thomas Mun, whom we have already mentioned, was a member of the establishment. Born in 1571, the son of a London merchant, he was raised and educated to a position of importance. His early mer-

[19]Eli F. Heckscher, *Mercantilism,* trans. M. Shapiro, 2 vols. (London: Allen and Unwin, 1935).

cantile career was spent in the Mediterranean, largely in Italy and the Levant. That he was highly thought of was shown by the fact that Ferdinand I, grand duke of Tuscany, lent him 40,000 crowns, interest free, for business activities in Turkey. In 1615, he was elected a member of the East India Company, and it was in connection with his duties that Mun wrote his two celebrated books. The first, *A Discourse of Trade, from England unto the East-Indies,answering to diverse Objections which are usually made against the same,* was published in 1621.[20] The object of this work was a very political one. It had become necessary for the East India Company to export bullion in order to carry on its trading activities in the East. To many this was tantamount to treason, and the government of James I was less than sympathetic because it had legally prohibited the exporting of specie and had attempted further regulation of international transactions. Public fervor was also aroused against the company when one of its ships carrying bullion was wrecked in 1613. Mun's defense of the company was direct. He modified the bullionist position one step. To the bullionist charge that trade was desirable only if it increased the amount of bullion England had, Mun argued that this was, in fact, the outcome of the company's activities in the long run. The East India trade was both desirable and profitable. Yes, the company was forced to export bullion in the short run if it was to carry on this trade, but in exchange it bought goods cheap which it later largely reexported. The end result of its activities was not a loss of bullion but a net gain; government policy and the public opposition were ill-advised. If the company were not performing these functions, England would be buying these Eastern wares from others, and in this situation the country would be losing gold, exactly the situation that the bullionists like Gerard de Malynes, an assay master at the English mint, feared.

Mun's second book, published after his death, *England's Treasure by Foreign Trade, or the Balance of our Foreign Trade Is the Rule of our Treasure,* is a much richer work, though not nearly as radical as some writers have contended. Mun extended his early position concerning the freedom and importance of trade as a means of earning bullion, but he went no further.

---

[20]Thomas Mun, *A Discourse of Trade. From England unto the East-Indies 1621* (New York: The Facsimile Text Society, 1930).

Although a Kingdom may be enriched by gifts received, or by purchase taken from some other nations, yet there are things uncertain and of small consideration when they happen. The ordinary means, therefore, to increase our wealth and treasure is by *Forraign Trade* wherein we must ever observe this rule; to sell more to strangers yearly than we consume of theirs in value. For suppose that when this Kingdom is plentifully served with the Cloth, Lead, Tin, Iron, Fish and other native commodities, we do yearly export the overplus to foreign countries to the value of twenty two hundred thousand pounds; by which means we are enabled beyond the Seas to buy and bring in foreign wares for our use and consumptions, to the value of twenty hundred thousand pounds; by this order duly kept in our trading, we may rest assured that the Kingdom shall be enriched yearly two hundred thousand pounds, which must be brought to us in so much Treasure; because that part of our stock which is not returned to us in wares must necessarily be brought home in treasure.[21]

In all other areas, Mun remained the creature of his society, culture-bound by the economic beliefs of his day. The kingdom is as "the estate of a private man" and should be governed by the same principles of private parsimony and frugality.

Mun was not the first macrotheorist, but he is interesting for the breadth of his knowledge concerning foreign trade. Exports might be increased by better utilization of waste areas to provide items such as hemp, flax, cordage, and tobacco, which were currently imported, though he is not continental enough to suggest that these new industries should be subsidized. He objected loudly against the "excessive consumption of foreign wares in our diet and raiment,"[22] vices whose correction would diminish imports. He had some idea of what we call the concept of "value added" for he urged his countrymen to sell finished goods so that "we may (besides the rent of Materials) gain so much of the manufacture as we can, and also endeavor to sell them dear, so far forth as the high price cause not a less rent in the quantity."[23] His praise of an extensive shipping and carrying trade in domestic bottoms is within the orthodox mercantilist framework, as is his commendation of fishing and of the establishment of plantations (colo-

[21]Mun, *England 's Treasure, pp. 7-8.*
[22]*Ibid.* p. 10.
[23]*Ibid,* p. 10.

nies) and staples abroad. Still he is refreshing when he counsels his government to allow goods manufactured of foreign materials to be exported custom-free, and not to make native commodities with too heavy export duties lest they be made too expensive and their sale hindered. But above all, he urged his countrymen to accept a broadly conceived trading program and thus to overcome the prejudice that wares only, not money, should be exported. For by foreign trade three agents may gain, the commonwealth, the merchant, and the king. Mun's experience had taught him that their interests are not harmonious, but even if commonwealth and merchant might lose, the king ever stands to gain.

The sum of all that hath been spoken, concerning the enriching of the Kingdom, and the increase of our treasure by commerce with strangers, is briefly thus. That it is a certain rule in our foreign trade, in those places where our commodities exported are overbalanced in value by foreign wares brought into this Realm, there our money is undervalued in exchange; and where the contrary of this is performed, there our money is overvalued. But let the Merchants exchange be at a high rate or at a low rate, or at the *Par pro pari* or put down altogether; Let Foreign Princes enhance their Coins, or debate their Standards, and let His Majesty do the like, or keep them constant as they now stand; Let Foreign Coins pass current here in all payments at higher rates than they are worth at the Mint; Let the Statute for employments by Strangers stand in force or be repealed; Let the mere Exchanger do his worst; Let Princes oppress, Lawyers extort, Usurers bite, Prodigals waste, and lastly let Merchants carry out what money they shall have occasion to use in traffic. Yet all these actions can work no other effects in the course of trade than is declared in this discourse. For so much Treasure only will be brought in or carried out of a Commonwealth, as the Foreign Trade doth over or under-balance in value. And this must come to pass by a Necessity beyond all resistance. So that all other courses (which tend not to this end) howsoever they may seem to force money into a Kingdom for a time, yet are they (in the end) not only fruitless but also hurtful; they are like to violent floods which bear down their banks, and suddenly remain dry again for want of waters.

Behold then the true form and worth of foreign trade, which is, *The great Revenue of the King, The Honour of the Kingdom, The Noble profession of the Merchant, The School of our Arts, The supply of our wants, The employment of our poor, The improvement of our Lands, The Nurcery of our*

Mariners, The walls of the Kingdoms, The Means of our Treasure, The Sinnews of our wars, The terror of our Enemies.[24]

Mun laid down the pattern of multilateral trade that England was to follow for more than three centuries. Note also that he ends his analysis on a note of power.

FRENCH MERCANTILISM: COLBERTISM

French mercantilism is so closely connected with the personal career of Louis XIV's Minister of Finance, Jean Baptiste Colbert, that it is not infrequently referred to as Colbertism. Sometimes the term statism is used, but that is even less helpful. One basic policy runs through Colbert's broad program to enhance the power of his absolute sovereign: to manage economic life in such a way that France would become self-sufficient at home and possessed of such economic resources that she could carry on military and diplomatic action against neighboring states. Colbert stands for the aggrandizement of France, and he ranks with the Marshal Vauban as the architect of French power in the seventeenth century.

Although there are trading and commercial aspects in Colbert's policies (he founded half a dozen overseas trading companies), his major programs were political. Not until the present century, however, has there been anything similar in scope to his managed economy. Fortunately, Colbert had neither the theoretical nor the technical knowledge to make his grandiose schemes effective. And he was limited too by his strong dislike for businessmen and the business community. He failed as an economic planner except for his efforts to remove internal tolls and tariffs and to standardize weights and measures in France. In other aspects, almost all of his regulations were similar in content and arbitrariness—and consequence—to those of the guilds, which had hamstrung medieval production.

Even less successful, but of significance, was his attempt to stimulate manufactures. Colbert sought to supplant the high cost of foreign imported luxury goods by establishing state-supported factories within France. He imported craftsmen and liberally subsidized plants for the production of fine tapestry, glass, china, and other items of aristocratic consumption. The costs were heavy, and imports were reduced only minimally. A few of these enterprises succeeded, although they

[24]*Ibid.,* pp. 118-119.

established a pattern of high priced, high quality luxury goods.[25] Overseas, Colbert fared even worse. Within a few decades, all that had been invested in the French Levant Company, the French East India Company, and the rest had come to naught, and by the mideighteenth century, France indeed had lost much of her physical and commercial empire.

France was a country at war during most of this period, and we must keep this in mind in evaluating Colbert's policies. Aggressive war and civil strife caused by the king's bigoted religious views twisted every economic issue and distorted the entire national orientation. Colbert's genius lay more in channeling the resources of the state toward grandiose wars than in constructing a healthy economy for peace. Materialistic and aristocratic in his views, he forged no link between merchant, producer, and state. He distrusted them; they feared him. Colbert demonstrated the new extent of power in the modern state. By coercion he improved such things as roads and bridges; by royal appropriation he built the Languedoc canal, which joined the Atlantic and the Mediterranean. But France, a wealthy country, grew successively poorer; the burden of twenty-five years of war was too much to bear.

In economic theory, there was little advance. Where Colbert deviated from overall mercantilist thought, he looked backward. His view of the business community was outmoded even then. His distinction between productive and unproductive individuals was meaningless. Priests, lawyers, and officials were idlers. He treated the poor harshly and contemptuously. His attempts to increase population by offering tax benefits to large families was openly abused and quickly repealed. He did little to reform tax collection, and state management of revenues remained a fiction under Louis XIV. He particularly lacked any understanding of the real factors that make a country wealthy. Colbert was a man of great gifts who served a difficult master. French economic theory had to wait for the Physiocrats.

GERMAN MERCANTILISM: KAMERALISM

In some ways, German Kameralism is even more interesting for us than French Colbertism, though in certain respects it resembled it closely. Under four rulers, the Great Elector Frederick William, Fred-

[25]Professor Cole's studies of Colbert and French mercantilism fully demonstrated all the difficulties and inefficiencies of this artificial program. Charles W. Cole, *Colbert and A Century of French Mercantilism* (New York: Columbia University Press, 1939).

erick I, Frederick William I, and Frederick II the Great, the small
state of Prussia instituted a full-scale policy to increase wealth by
aiding the growth of industries and manufactures. Liberal edicts of all
kinds encouraged the movement to the cities and cut back the power
of the guilds. Religious freedom and grants of asylum made Prussia a
haven for the displaced person of the late seventeenth and eighteenth
centuries. Frederick the Great is credited with bringing 30,000 immigrants into the province of Silesia. Gustav Schmoller lists a wide
range of industries that evolved from Frederick's state policies.[26]
Mining in Silesia, iron manufacturing and machine making, silk
weaving in Crefold, textile plants and bleaching establishments—even
a partial list tells much of the difference between French and German
"models." Prussian producers and artisans also labored under heavy
regulatory mechanism, but their accomplishments were highly regarded by the state. Small tradesmen were aided in obtaining credit;
exemption from taxation for special workmen such as cotton spinners
fostered the growth of new industry. Some regulations were onerous
and useless—for example, soldiers were ordered to spin. On the whole,
a small but utilitarian productive structure was established.

Kameralist theory originally was concerned with the problems of
royal finance, taxation, and spending. Partially because of the overwhelming importance of the royal economy in the Austrian and
German lands, continental mercantilism came to include all economic
questions. Never, however, did it lose its primary concern nor its
absolutist and authoritarian political tendencies. In no country where
Kameralism succeeded, did real democratic institutions develop.
There is a clear line of progeny from the Kameralism of the sixteenth
century to the rejection of classical laissez-faire economics in the
nineteenth. Not only the economic backwardness of central Europe,
but also its political framework set the pattern for a protectionist and
institutional evolution of economic theory and action.

Two writers may serve as illustrators of the continuity and separate-
ness of Kameralist thinking, Philipp Wilhelm von Hornig and Johannes
von Justi. In *Oesterreich uber alles, wenn es nur will* (Austria Over
All If Only She Wants To) Hornig laid down nine rules, which fall well
within the mercantilist spectrum: (1) The nation's resources should
be scientifically surveyed, particularly the mineral potential of gold

[26]Gustav von Schmoller, *The Mercantile System and Its Historical Significance* (New
York and London: Macmillan, 1897).

and silver sources; (2) raw materials as far as possible should be made into manufactured goods; (3) the state should encourage the training of individuals for useful occupations, even bringing foreign teachers into the country if necessary; (4) gold and silver should be kept constantly circulating in useful productive occupations; (5) Austrians should forbear from foreign luxuries; (6) essential imports should be paid for with domestic goods not specie; (7) imports should be kept to raw materials and/or semimanufactured goods and worked up at home; (8) foreign markets should be encouraged "even to the ends of the earth"; and (9) if the State has a surplus of a good, it must not be imported.[27]

Everywhere in Hornig's work, one senses the political implications of his thought, though the best definition of Kameralism came from Joachim Daries in his *First Principles of Kameral Sciences:* "The capital or fund of the princely income is the wealth of the state and the subjects."[28]

Two decades before Adam Smith, Johannes Heinrich Gottlob von Justi published his *Political Economy, or a Systematic Treatise on all Economic and Kameral Sciences, which are necessary for the administration of a country.* Here we have one of the most complete early statements of government taxation, the real concern of the Kameralist. Although in many areas Justi's approach to trade was narrowly mercantilist, his views on taxation were remarkably broad. He argued that taxes should fulfill six criteria: (1) They should be so levied that the taxpayer will not try to avoid payment; (2) they should not be oppressive, either to industry or to individuals; (3) they should be levied fairly and equally; (4) they should be certain and definite; (5) the cost of collection should be minimal; (6) they should be payable at times convenient to the taxpayer, and in appropriate amounts.[29]

Kameralist thought is important. In practical terms it appeared less pragmatic in its approach than French and English mercantilism. It drew largely from law and jurisprudence and was much influenced by the difficult struggle for unified political power in central Europe. If it placed less emphasis on trade and commerce, it gave new insight into the encouragement of economic growth in these underdeveloped areas. Above all, Kameralism provided the most advanced

[27]Lewis H. Haney, *History of Economic Thought,* 4th ed. (New York: Macmillan, 1949), p. 155.
[28]*Ibid.* p. 157.
[29]*Ibid.,* pp. 160-161.

explanations of fiscal policy, the management of state finances under war conditions, and the development of a centralized bureaucracy to handle financial and tax policies. Although Kameralism was essentially antidemocratic, both individually and socially, it was nevertheless concerned with fundamental economic issues.

In summary, mercantilism whether English, French, or German, stands well within the framework of modern times. The mercantilists and the Physiocrats are the heralds of economic science.

The Physiocrats

Adam Smith and Karl Marx agreed in overall judgment of the Physiocrats. Marx recognized that their analysis of capital, despite its bourgeois horizon, made a real contribution by placing the origin of surplus value in the sphere of direct production. Despite their concentration on the exclusive productivity of agricultural labor, and their emphasis on the landowner's role, the Physiocrats perceived the predominant elements inherent in modern production: competition, large-scale enterprise, and capitalistic organization.

Agriculture is carried on capitalistically, that is to say, it is the enterprise of a capitalist farmer on a large scale; the direct cultivator of the soil is the wage laborer. Production creates not only articles of use but also their value; its compelling nature is the procurement of surplus value, whose birthplace is the sphere of production, not of circulation.[30]

Marx, who was much concerned with the Physiocrats, drew a number of extremely important concepts from their work. Adam Smith, who knew some of the Physiocrats personally, referred to their system as "ingenious."

That system, which represents the produce of land as the sole source of the revenue and wealth of every country has, so far as I know, never been adopted by any nation, and it at present exists only in the speculations of a few men of great learning and ingenuity in France. It would not, surely, be worthwhile to examine at great length the errors of a system, which never has done, and probably never will do, any harm in any part of the world.[31]

[30]Karl Marx, *Capital,* ed. Friedrich Engels (Moscow: Foreign Languages Publishing House, 1957), vol. 2, p. 360.
[31]Adam Smith, *An Inquiry into the Nature and Causes of the Wealth of Nations,* (New York: Random House, 1937), book 4, chap. 9, p. 627.

TABLEAU ECONOMIQUE

In the history of thought, the Physiocrats individually, and the physiocratic ideas generally, form part of the great intellectual movement of the eighteenth century, the Enlightenment. They shared, therefore, certain overall beliefs, which are essential in understanding their economic doctrine. They believed in science. Of all the influences on this century none was greater than Newtonian physics—the majestic sense of a handful of great laws governing the cosmos impersonally, mathematically. Every social thinker "knew"—and hoped—that he might be the great discoverer of the laws of social physics. If we today smile at the naïveté of this early sociology, we should not minimize either the certitude or the intensity of those investigators. Because they believed in a natural order, they opposed what they considered the harmful regulations society had accumulated haphazardly. Not accidentally did a Physiocrat coin the phrase "laissez faire, laissez passer." Until proper order could be imposed on society, it was better to allow perfect freedom. In any event, a good deal of underbrush clearing had to take place. If they conceived of the order of things as natural, both cosmic and social, they also conceived of the mechanism of this order as deterministic, either mechanical or biological. Francoise Quesnay, one of the leading Physiocrats, himself was a physician, and the operation of the model presented in his *Tableau Economique* is cast in terms very similar to the eighteenth-century conception of the human circulatory system.[32] In this case, the impact of general ideas was fruitful because Quesnay's model presents the first dynamic explanation of general equilibrium analysis, an approach that will be emphasized throughout this work. Other contemporaries led the Physiocrats deeply into error. "Natural" became romantically translated into "nature." The many examples of this—from Rousseau's *Emile* to Marie Antoinette's milking parlor—led to a preposterous and somewhat silly overemphasis on rural life. Bucolic virtue and the pure simple life of the peasant were widely exaggerated in Enlightenment literature. Some writers have stressed the thesis that the Physiocrats' emphasis on agriculture as society's only productive force was a reaction to, a rejection of, Colbert's urban-oriented policies. Their outlook was strongly reinforced by the general intellectual current of the Enlightenment, which

[32]For a brilliant and thorough discussion of Quesnay, see Joseph Schumpeter, *History of Economic Analysis* (New York: Oxford University Press, 1954), pp. 223-242; also Haney, *History of Economic Thought*, pp. 171-192.

defined rural life as the noblest life. In several other ways, Physiocratic thought linked up with the Enlightenment: It was optimistic, positive, simplistic, and "creatively destructive."

What did the Physiocrats stand for? Adam Smith's careful outline can serve us as a guide through their general ideas. The Physiocrats divided society into three categories: (1) proprietors of land, who serve an important function for society though they are not themselves productive; (2) farmers and country laborers, who are the truly productive element in any society; (3) the remaining occupations of workmen, manufacturers, and merchants who make up the "barren or unproductive" class. What persuaded the Physiocrats to err? They went astray in trying to answer the central question in economics: "What creates wealth?" The mercantilists had answered it in bullionistic terms; the classical economists were to evolve a general labor theory. The Physiocrats focused on agriculture. The process of wealth creation in farming is more obvious than in other economic processes. The farmer cultivates his land and plants seed, and the amount he harvests in any efficient agricultural system is many times greater than the amount he directly consumes. That obvious excess is, of course, a surplus, a surplus directly created by the agriculturist.

It was not difficult for Smith and Ricardo to demonstrate that a surplus can also be created by other economic processes, but Quesnay, and others, never reached this level. He saw in the productive process of agriculture the source of the elusive "net product"; he had found one source, one explanation of economic process. How did the *Tableaux Economique* operate? Assume a gross national product of 5 billion. Two billion in kind, say, are to be deducted as the necessary costs of production in the next cycle (food for the agricultural producer, seed, etc.). The residual "net product" is 3 billion in kind of which 2 billion consists of food, and 1 billion of raw materials of manufacture. Further, the farmers hold 2 billion, the nation's total money supply. The landowners, the proprietors, start at zero but have rent claims on the farmers' first 2 billion, and the sterile or unproductive class holds goods worth 2 billion manufactured in the preceding period. The dynamics of the cycle now commence. Farmers pay the landowners the 2 billion they owe them in rent but, in turn, the landowners return to them half this amount in purchases of food; the other half comes back via the circular route of the proprietors who buy 1 billion of manufactured goods from the sterile class who, in turn, give this back to the farmers for food and raw materials. Thus the cycle comes again full circle and the farmers have 2 billion in money to start the next productive round. Everything adds up nicely. Proprietors and the members of the unproductive class have taken the food surplus of the "net product" while the raw materials fund has gone only to the "sterile" sector. The manufactured or produced goods have been divided between farmers and proprietors, and the "sterile" sector has received 1 billion in food to sustain them, and 1 billion in raw material goods with which they will produce their 2 billion's worth of manufactured goods next turn around.

Our own views of economic life are so highly colored by the impact and processes of industrialization that it is difficult to give the *Tableau Economique* its just due. Quesnay paid little attention to the problem of costs. Again and again, his sole emphasis on agriculture as the only productive sector strikes us as being a retrograde not a creative step, but this is not entirely true. Three concepts emerge as the major contribution of the Physiocrats. First, they recognized that economic life is one of process. Not until the general equilibrium school will we get as helpful an approach to dynamic economics. Second, they provided a macroview of production. Third, they grasped the concept of circular flow: They discovered the "net product," broke it into distributive shares, and then showed how these segments came together again to form the next cycle.

Compared to these significant contributions, their limitations were minimal, considering their time. Let us return again to Adam Smith's evaluation of their doctrine. The landowner is accorded a surprisingly significant role in their scheme. The improvement of the land, buildings, drains, enclosures, or other outlays that produce a greater surplus are included as the productive contribution of this group. These capital expenses on the land *(dépenses foncières)* yield to the proprietor a greater rental return, which is his (the landowner's) interest or profit on the capital he has employed for durable improvements. The advanced (prepaid) rent, which in the Physiocrats' model the landowner gets from his land, should be subject neither to tithe nor tax because in their view this would be inequitable, and these impositions would serve only to discourage further improvements. The rental the landlord receives is his due only after all the necessary expenses, which must be previously paid to the cultivator, have been distributed. The cultivator makes his contribution to the net annual produce by expending outlays for "original and annual expenses" *(dépenses primitive et dépenses annuelles).* These consist of cattle, seed, and the costs of maintaining the farmer's family, servants, and cattle until the return from the land can make some contribution for them. Annual expenses, of course, are seed, depreciation of machinery, equipment, and labor costs. The farmer employs then two bundles of capital, which must be completely restored to him plus a reasonable profit, or opportunity costs would compel him to leave agriculture for other occupations. (One might ask what other occupation the Physiocrats would have accepted?) The return to the cultivator, after his payment of rent to the landlord, must remain sufficient to repay all of his original and annual expenses, plus a reasonable return on both his fixed and circulating capital.

Against all of this productive and creative effort stand the artificers and manufacturers. Their labor replaces only the capital that employs them plus a reasonable profit. This capital includes the materials, tools, and wages their employer advances for their maintenance, and the profits of this endeavor serve to sustain only him. The capital employed in agriculture bears two crops; that in manufacturing only one.

The expence, therefore, laid out in employing and maintaining artificers and manufacturers does no more than continue, if one may say so, the existence of its own value, and does not produce any new value. It is, therefore, altogether a barren and unproductive expence.[33]

Capital employed in trade and commerce is equally barren and unproductive. Only by depriving themselves of part of the fund set aside for their subsistence can these unproductive classes contribute anything to the wealth of their society. The Physiocrats did not completely consider this a likely happening; they saw these unproductive groups as subsidized heavily by the proprietors and cultivators. These classes, however, were by no means useless. The positive contributions of the sterile classes enabled the productive classes to buy foreign and domestic goods at a cheaper price—if the unproductive classes were industriously efficient and competitive. Proprietors and cultivators should never restrain or discourage the industry and

[33]Smith, *Wealth of Nations,* p. 631.

liberty of merchants and manufacturers, and in like manner, the unproductive class should never oppress the more productive members of society.

The establishment of perfect justice, of perfect liberty, and of perfect equality, is the very simple secret which most effectually secures the highest degree of prosperity to all the three classes.[34]

The recognition of these facts is, however, more than the concern of particular classes or individuals; it determines the inner consistency of the nation.

Nations, therefore, which, like France or England, consist in a great measure of proprietors and cultivators, can be enriched by industry and enjoyment. Nations, on the contrary, which, like Holland and Hamburgh, are composed chiefly of merchants, artificers and manufacturers, can grow rich only through parsimony and privation. As the interest of nations so dIfferently circumstanced, is very different, so is likewise the common character of the people. In those of the former kind, liberality, frankness, and good fellowship, naturally make a part of that common character. In the latter, narrowness, meanness, and a selfish disposition, averse to all social pleasure and enjoyment.[35]

For Smith, the capital error of the Physiocrats was their premise that artificers, manufacturers, and merchants are completely barren and unproductive. Marx rightly pointed out that England, a country of industrial capitalists, could never accept so narrow a definition.[36] Even for France, this overemphasis on the agricultural source of surplus value was unfortunate. Marx, however, wrote critically, that Smith lumped together several different forms of capital, and that "this is a big step back compared to the physiocrats."[37] Goods command value because of the social labor put into them through the mechanism of the exchange system.

Smith considered the physiocratic system important enough to examine it thoroughly.[38] In the first place, Smith said, even if one accepted their idea that the class of artificers, manufacturers, and

---

[34]*Ibid.,* book 4, chap. 9, p. 634.
[35]*Ibid.,* book 4, chap. 9, pp. 632-633.
[36]Marx, *Capital,* vol. 2, p. 367.
[37]*Ibid.,* p. 192.
[38]Smith, *Wealth of Nations,* book 4, chap. 9, pp. 627-643.

merchants reproduced annually only the value of what they consumed, and a reasonable return on the capital they utilized, this in itself denies the thesis that they were totally unproductive. At most, they were less productive. Second, Smith believed that it was wrong to place them in the same category as menial servants. Smith himself considered artificers, manufacturers, and merchants as productive, but servants and the like as unproductive. Third, the Physiocrats distorted the truth when they said that the "barren" class added no increase to the real revenue of the society because it consumed exactly equal to what it produced. Only by misconceiving the nature of the surplus this class produced could the Physiocrats have arrived at this conclusion, not by empirical observation. Fourth, the demand of parsimony and frugality concerned every member of society, barren and productive. Abstinence from consumption is enjoined on culti-vator as well as merchant.

The annual produce of the land and labor of any society can be augmented only in two ways; either, first, by some improvement in the productive powers of the useful labor actually maintained within it; or, secondly, by some increase in the quantity of that labor.[39]

Finally, the Physiocrats were wrong again in insisting that a country's revenue consists of the quantity of subsistence it produces—for exam-ple, agriculture and mining. The case of England alone demonstrates the contrary.

By means of trade and manufactures, a greater quantity of subsistence can be annually imported into a particular country than what its own lands, in the actual state of cultivation, could afford . . . . It is thus that Holland draws a great part of its subsistence from other countries; live cattle from Holstein and Jutland, and corn from almost all the different countries of Europe. A small quantity of manufactured produce purchases a great quantity of rude produce.[40]

Bound within the perimeters of the *Tableau Economique,* the Phys-iocrats never developed the distinction between use-value and ex-change value; thus the circularity of their system and its rigidity. Had

[39]*Ibid.,* book 4, chap. 9, pp. 640-641.
[40]*Ibid.* book 4, chap. 9, pp. 641-642.

they recognized the value created in exchange, their contribution to economic science would have been even greater. Smith concluded:

With all its imperfections, this system . . . is, perhaps, the nearest approximation to the truth that has yet been published upon the subject of political economy, and is upon that account well worth the consideration of every man who wishes to examine with attention the principles of that very important science.[41]

The Physiocrats, in Smith's opinion, had broken the chains by which the mercantilists had fettered society; they, the Physiocrats, had produced a definition of wealth which, although too narrow, was based on the consumable goods annually produced by the labor of society rather than on the "unconsumable riches of money." In proclaiming perfect liberty the only means of furthering this reproduction, they had made a frontal attack on mercantilist restraints and regulations. Adam Smith saw this as a noble contribution.

Marx was another vigorous, though sympathetic, critic of the Physiocrats. Although many of Marx's strictures against the Physiocrats are historically inaccurate, some of what he said is extremely interesting and perceptive. Essentially, Marx saw the Physiocrats as important rationalizers of a historic period—that is, that period when feudal society was becoming bourgeois society through the introduction of capitalistic means of production. "Quesnay himself and his immediate disciples believed in their feudal shop-sign . . . . But, as a matter of fact, the system of the physiocrats is the first systematic conception of capitalist production."[42] For Marx, the specific greatness of the Physiocrats was their derivation of value and surplus value from production, and their specific limitation was their definition of surplus value as a gift of nature.

In the world of affairs, physiocratic ideas made a powerful impact on French eighteenth-century society. Quesnay himself was court physician of Louis XV and The Marquise de Pompadour. Supposedly it was for the king of France that he composed the celebrated *Tableau Economique*. Vincent de Gournay, an inspector of goods and the author of the phrase "laissez faire, laissez passer," was converted to the system of free trade, though he held a high position in the

[41]*Ibid.,* book 4, chap. 9, p. 642.
[42]Marx, *Capital,* vol. 2, p. 359.

mercantilist bureaucracy. Mirabeau the elder, as well as a number of the old aristocracy, favored the Physiocrats. Mirabeau considered the *Tableau Economique*, writing and money as three inventions which have given stability to political societies.

TURGOT

At least two Physiocrats were Intendants. Mercier de la Riviere, who wrote *The Natural and Essential Order of Political Societies*, was Intendant of Martinique, and Anne Robert Jacques Turgot was Intendant of Limoges before he became Louis XVI's controller general of finance in 1774. Turgot valiantly tried to save the French monarchy from economic disaster. His widespread reform included abolition of the corvée and many mercantilistic regulations. He decreed internal free trade in grain, abolished guilds and privileged trading companies, and imposed taxes on landowners. All this proved too much for the vested interests, including the queen. Turgot was dismissed in 1776, and France drifted without any economic program toward revolution.

Schumpeter, in his *History of Economic Analysis,* has wonderful things to say about Turgot. Although a certain portion of Turgot's *Reflections on the Formation and Distribution of Wealth* is "splashed" with physiocratic arguments, Turgot's thinking had advanced well beyond Quesnay's. Schumpeter goes so far as to state that Turgot's theoretical skeleton is "distinctly superior to the theoretical skeleton of the *Wealth of Nations,*"[43] though it was a mere outline of a system of economic theory compared with Adam Smith's finished work. Both in England and in France, perceptive individuals were breaking new ground and constructing new systems of economic theory far more original and sophisticated than anything done previously. Turgot's career was almost entirely bureaucratic and he had little time for extensive scholarly work, though he parallels Smith in his concern with many of the same problems. "It is not too much to say," Schumpeter commented, "that analytic economics took a century to get where it could have got in twenty years after the publication of Turgot's treatise had its content been properly understood and absorbed by an alert profession."[44]

Turgot soon abandoned the narrow land-based conflicts of the Phys-

---

[43]Schumpeter, *History of Economic Analysis,* p. 248.
[44]*Ibid.,* p. 249.

iocrats. He saw the totality of economics in capitalistic terms. Of particular importance was his explanation of interest. He was one of the first to differentiate between the "value of money" as a measure of exchange value and as a measure of loan value. Although Turgot was well versed in Church teaching (he had studied first for the clergy), he refused to be trapped by any sterile outdated arguments over the barrenness of money. The price of money—that is, interest—is determined by the forces of supply and demand in the marketplace, and is related to time and opportunity costs. Money emerges clearly as savings to be utilized by entrepreneurs who are willing to give the capitalist, or supplier of funds, a portion of their entrepreneurial success, or profit. The rate of interest is the thermometer of the relative plenty (or shortage) of investment funds, and a measure of the extent to which production will be carried on.

A good deal of this formulation will remain virtually intact until late in the nineteenth century. Schumpeter himself was influenced by Turgot's views on the role of interest and its effect on both entrepreneurs and capitalists (cf. idea of interest as an agio).[45] Schumpeter is Turgot's most generous interpreter; other writers find him more closely limited to traditional eighteenth-century economic beliefs. Turgot did have trouble freeing himself from the preoccupation with land, and he was overly concerned with the taxation of land as the only proper source of revenue; furthermore, Turgot's opening chapters on the origins of property in land and the formation of different classes were almost entirely defined in eighteenth-century terms. His reputation will suffer little from acknowledgment that on occasion he went astray in following the conventional wisdom of his day. When he pursued his own ideas, his contributions were rich. In *Reflections on the Formation and Distribution of Wealth,* Turgot treated incisively the division of labor, the origin and use of money, the improvement of agriculture, the nature of capital and its different uses, and the legitimacy of interest.

Turgot also presented an early version of the law of diminishing returns as it applied to agriculture.

The earth's fertility resembles a spring that is being pressed downwards by the addition of successive weights. If the weight is small and the spring not very flexible, the first attempts will leave no results. But when the weight is

[45]"Agio" is a premium because time has value for people.

enough to overcome the first resistance, then it will give to the pressure. After yielding a certain amount, it will again begin to resist the extra force put upon it, and weights that formerly would have caused a depression of an inch or more will now scarcely move it by a hair's breadth. And so the effect of additional weights will gradually diminish.[46]

This quotation does not present the law of diminishing returns in a modern way, but it clearly demonstrates how sentient and perceptive Turgot's analysis had become.

[46]A. R. J. Turgot, "Observations sur le Memoire de M. De. Saint-Perary," *Oeuveres de Turgot,* ed. M. Eugene Daire (Paris: Guillaumin, 1844), vol. 1, p. 420. This translation appears in Jacob Oser's *The Evolution of Economic Thought* (New York: Harcourt Brace Jovanovich, 1963), p. 33.

2

THE WORLD OF ADAM SMITH

Life and Works

Adam Smith was the first great professor of economics, and his *Wealth of Nations* is an academic masterpiece in the best sense of that term.[1] In that one work, Smith contributed (1) a massive summary and integration of eighteenth-century economic thought; (2) a devastating political tract, the death blow to English mercantilism; (3) a brilliant economic policy statement for the future; and (4) a genuine attempt to deal scientifically, carefully, and disinterestedly with all the major economic problems, from value and division of labor to rent and taxation. Smith did not discuss unemployment or business cycles because

[1]The impression has often been created that Smith was the "first" economist, or at least the "first" postmercantilist economist. This is entirely incorrect. Smith synthesized the rich Anglo-French postmercantilistic tradition, and was especially influenced by Turgot, Quesnay, Hume, Cantillon, and the Italian Galiani. In several specific respects, especially monetary and value theory, he may even suffer by comparison with his predecessors; none of them, however, had his breadth and vision to build an economic system.

they were not pertinent to his time. The *Wealth of Nations* was a large fresh pool from which flowed a century of stimulating and impressive economic investigations of the market system. Even his inconsistencies have been fruitful and his theoretical shortcomings productive.

Again and again, one finds it easier and more desirable to let Smith speak. If you do not have the time to read *An Inquiry Into the Nature and Causes of the Wealth of Nations,* then at least you should be familiar with Smith's example of the pin factory—probably the most famous passage in all economic literature.

To take an example, therefore, from a very trifling manufacture; but one in which the division of labour has been very often taken notice of, the trade of the pin-maker; a workman not educated to this business (which the division of labour has rendered a distinct trade), nor acquainted with the use of machinery employed in it (to the invention of which the same division of labour has probably given occasion), could scarce, perhaps, with his utmost industry, make one pin in a day, and certainly could not make twenty. But in the way in which this business is now carried on, not only the whole work is a peculiar trade, but it is divided into a number of branches, of which the greater part are likewise peculiar trades. One man draws out the wire, another straights it, a third cuts it, a fourth points it, a fifth grinds it at the top for receiving the head; to make the head requires two or three distinct operations; to put it on, is a peculiar business, to whiten the pins is another; it is even a trade by itself to put them into the paper; and the important business of making a pin is, in the manner, divided into about eighteen distinct operations, which, in some manufactories, are all performed by distinct hand, though in others the same man will sometimes perform two or three of them. I have seen a small manufactory of this kind where ten men only were employed, and where some of them consequently performed two or three distinct operations. But though they were very poor, and therefore but indifferently accommodated with the necessary machinery, they could, when they exerted themselves, make among them about twelve pounds of pins in a day. There are in a pound upwards of four thousand pins of a middling size. Those ten persons, therefore, could make among them upwards of forty-eight thousand pins in a day. Each person, therefore, making a tenth part of forty-eight thousand pins might be considered as making four thousand eight hundred pins in a day. But if they had all wrought separately and independently, and without any of them having been educated to this peculiar business, they certainly could not each of them have made twenty, perhaps not one pin in a day; that is, certainly, not the two hundred and fortieth, perhaps not the four thousand eight hundredth part of what they are at present capable of performing, in consequence of a proper dlvision and combination of their different operations.[2]

Adam Smith was born in Kirkcaldy, a somber Scottish seaport town of 1500 people, in 1723, one year after the Scots burned their last witch. His father was controller of customs at Kirkcaldy and private secretary to Hugh Campbell, third Earl of Loudon. Two months before Smith was born, his father died. Smith was raised by hls mother, with whom he had a close relationship. We know that during his childhood he was extremely delicate and frail, already subject to fits of absentmindedness, which was to be a life-long characteristic. (One may add parenthetically that frailness was not unusual during this century. Edward Gibbon, the historian, was the sixth Edward in his family and was not expected to survive an early age, and Richard Cantillon (1680-1734), who wrote the *Essay on the Nature of Commerce in General,* assumed a mortality rate of 50 percent for children.)

At the age of seventeen, Adam Smith left for Oxford. Obviously, he was sufficiently gifted to make the journey and wealthy enough to bear the costs. He stayed at Oxford six years, concentrating apparently on Greek and Latin literature and on improving his French. Contemporary opinion suggests that he worked too hard and kept to himself. Oxford boasted few scholar-students at the time. Smith was a serious student destined to become a serious scholar. Later, he studied moral philosophy at the University of Glasgow under Francis Hutcheson, a great teacher to whom Smith did acknowledge his lasting indebtedness. The "never-to-be-forgotten" Hutcheson gave him that deep insight and concern for "natural liberty" which formed the basic premise in Smith's mature work. For three years, from 1748 to 1751, Smith lectured on English literature and logic at Edinburgh, but in 1751, he was unanimously elected to a chair of logic at Glasgow University. Smith had initially served as the substitute for the Professor of Moral Phllosophy who was ill. In 1752, he was offered the chair. His lectures on moral philosophy dealt with four themes: natural theology, ethics, jurisprudence, and politics. His lectures on ethics were incorporated in his first book, *The Theory of Moral Sentiments* (1759), which stressed sympathy, rather than mere utility, as

---

[2]Adam Smith, *Wealth of Nations,* Modern Library ed. (New York: Random House, 1937), book 1, chap. 1, pp. 4-5.

the basis of morals.[3] The lectures on the political institutions based on expediency were to influence his thinking in the *Wealth of Nations*. He promised, but never wrote, a book on the political institutions founded on justice.

The Theory of Moral Sentiments insured its author a lifetime of scholarly leisure. He was soon a famous public person and much-sought lecturer. Four years after the book's publication, Charles Townshend, stepfather of Henry Scott, Third Duke of Buccleuch, engaged him as tutor to the young aristocrat. Smith was to receive £300 a year plus traveling expenses for the duration of the tutorship and a £300 pension for life—a princely sum in an age when one could get "dead drunk for a penny." Smith's European tour had a broadening impact on him, though already at Glasgow he had emerged as a striking personality. Within a half dozen years of his university appointment, he had become one of its leading figures; he was treasurer of the university from 1758 to 1764, dean of faculty from 1760 to 1762, and vice-rector from 1762 on. His obligations ranged from presiding at college meetings to being in charge of "chambers let to students." He was also the patron of James Watt, who, with university help, was established as a mathematical instrument maker at Glasgow. Smith himself belonged to a group devoted to the discussion of trade; as early as the late 1750s, he was attempting to convert members to free trade, in particular to free trade in wheat.

At age thirty-eight, Smith paid his first visit to London, met the great Dr. Johnson, and received fulsome tributes to his scholarship from London society. In February 1764, Smith and Scott left on their grand tour. They traveled with David Hume, Smith's friend for more than a decade. They met Voltaire, Turgot, Condorcet, and others, but we know very little about their conversations. In October 1766, the tour abruptly ended when Scott's younger brother was found murdered on the streets of Paris. Smith returned to Kirkcaldy on a generous pension and began work on the *Wealth of Nations*. The book had long been in his thoughts, and was to occupy him for the remainder of his life.

Hume wrote that Smith was "cutting himself off entirely from human society." In 1772, he was recommended to the directors of the East

---

[3]*The Theory of Moral Sentiments* had the important subtitle *An Essay Towards an Analysis of the Principles by Which Men Naturally Judge Concerning Conduct and Character First of Their Neighbour and Afterwards of Themselves,* which represented the framework of Smith's body of thought.

India Company to lead a commission of inquiry to India, but nothing came of it.

WEALTH OF NATIONS

By the spring of 1773, however, the *Wealth of Nations* had been "completed," but constant revision delayed publication until March 1776. The book was an immediate and lasting success. The first edition was sold out in six months, and Smith received £500; on later editions, he received one-half the profits. The initial impact of the book was on economic policy rather than on economic thought or theory. In 1777, Smith was appointed commissioner of customs because of his analysis of taxation. Lord North, the prime minister, to whom Gibbon's *Decline and Fall* was dedicated, was greatly influenced by the *Wealth of Nations*. Pitt the Younger studied the book, and Smith's policies on free trade may first have been applied in the Eden-Rayneval treaty of 1786 between England and France. At a dinner party in April 1787, Pitt invited Smith to "be seated first for we are all your scholars." In introducing his budget in 1792, Pitt spoke of the *Wealth of Nations* with veneration.

The Wealth of Nations was a large tome; it was originally published as two volumes which Smith divided into five books. In this particular case, we wish to outline for the reader the content of the first economic "text." Smith laid out virtually all the economic problems that were to concern economists and policy makers for the next two hundred years.

Book I was entitled "Of the Causes of Improvement in the productive Powers of Labour, and of the Order according to which its Produce is naturally distributed among the different Ranks of the People." It is no rhetorical device that the *Wealth of Nations* opening problem was the source of economic wealth:

The annual labour of every nation is the fund which originally supplies it with all the necessaries and conveniences of life which it annually consumes, and which consist always either in the immediate produce of that labour, or in what is purchased with that produce from other nations.[4]

Book II (Of the Nature, Accumulation, and Employment of Stock) was a further analysis of capital:

[4]Smith, *Wealth of Nations,* book 1, Introduction, p. 1vii. We shall return later to the specific implications of this labor theory of value.

As the accumulation of stock |capital| must, in the nature of things, be previous to the division of labour, so labour can be more and more subdivided in proportion only as stock is previously more and more accumulated . . . . The quantity of industry, therefore, not only increases in every country with the increase of the stock which employs it, but, in consequence of that increase, the same quantity of industry produces a much greater quantity of work.[5]

Book III (Of the Different Progress of Opulence in Different Nations) was a historical introduction to the two final books of the treatise, in which Smith analyzed how different commercial policies had aided or distorted the "natural progress of opulence," and twice referred to the developing conflict with the American colonies as an example of the effect of erroneous mercantilist policy. We know that Smith discussed the North American colonies with Benjamin Franklin when he was revising the manuscript for publication. Economists have always wished that Smith had expanded his ideas on commercial policy because he had the beginnings of a comparative study of economic history, which he never carried through.

Book IV (Of Systems of Political Economy) delivered less than it promised, but it contains nevertheless some of the most famous sections of the *Wealth of Nations:* Of the Principle of the Commercial or Mercantile System; Of Restraints upon the Importation from Foreign Countries; Conclusion of the Mercantile System; Of the Agricultural Systems. Book IV (Of Systems of Political Economy) is justly famous. In it, we have the complete, devastating, and final indictment of mercantilism, a fine review of the ideas of the Physiocrats, two interesting self-contained historical essays on Banks of Deposit and the Corn Trade, and an excellent section on Colonies. Finally, Book V (Of the Revenue of the Sovereign or Commonwealth), with its two divisions—Of the Expenses of the Sovereign or Commonwealth and Of the Sources of the General or Public Revenue of the Society—contained Smith's famous comments on taxation.

The impact of the *Wealth of Nations* was striking. By 1800, it had run to nine English editions, and had been widely dispersed throughout western Europe in translation—Danish, Dutch, German, Italian, Spanish, and Russian (1802-1806). Smith's treatise dominated all serious discussions of economics and permeated expressions of economic

[5]*Ibid.,* book 2, introduction, p. 260.

policy by European statesmen in the first quarter of the nineteenth century. Ordinarily statesmen do not read two-volume economic treatises, either in 1800 or 1980.

However, the *Wealth of Nations* was an impressive political policy statement as well as a scientific investigation of a new discipline. The statesmen were impressed by the work's political relevance, while the philosophers pondered its economic implications.

Let us look more closely and in some detail at these two areas of economic policy and economic science which Smith knit together in the *Wealth of Nations.*

Every student knows that Adam Smith should be linked with the doctrine of laissez faire (the phrase itself was borrowed from Gournay), but laissez faire sums up none of the breadth and wisdom of the policies Smith was advocating. Smith discussed all the major economic questions of his day, from psychology of motivation to the equity of taxation. Naturally, some topics were developed more completely than others and some were only briefly mentioned, but Smith has been mined so deeply because his book is such a rich ore-yielding vein.

From both the *Theory of Moral Sentiments* and the *Wealth of Nations,* we can draw some picture of human nature. Smith was deeply influenced by the psychological assumptions of his age, particularly those of Locke, Hume, and his teacher, Hutcheson. His approach was largely empirical, in the footsteps of the "associational" school of psychology. Smith concentrated on ethics as a "theory of people's judgments about behavior," and used a relative approach to values rather than a normative one. He defined "natural" as psychologically normal. Utility thus was conceived as an integral part of esthetic, ethical, and social judgments. In this sense, Smith was more sensible and more tolerant than either Bentham or Veblen.

People do not merely strive for the necessities of nature. The real happiness of human life, the ease of body and peace of mind are open to all the different ranks . . . and the beggar, who suns himself by the side of the highway, possesses that security which kings are fighting for. It is the vanity, not the ease or the pleasure, which interests us. The rich man glories in his riches, because he feels that they naturally draw upon him the attention of the world. . . . It is the deception which rouses and keeps in continual motion the industry of mankind. It is this which first prompted them to cultivate the ground, to build houses, to found cities and commonwealths, and to invent and improve all the sciences and arts, which ennoble and embellish human life, which have entirely changed the whole face of the globe, have turned the rude forests of nature into agreeable and fertile plains, and have made the trackless and barren ocean a new fund of subsistence, and the great highroad of communication to the different nations of the earth.[6]

Smith, the kindly but dour Scot, could not be expected to perceive play as a source of creative action, but he could appreciate the broad differences among human beings. There was surely no bitterness in Smith, only deep humor and human sympathy. It was really unfortunate that economists lost this breadth of vision, understanding, and treatment in the nineteenth century. Conduct, human conduct, was viewed by Smith optimistically, though man was motivated by realistic self-love.

It is not from the benevolence of the butcher, the brewer, or the baker that we expect our dinner, but from their regard to their interest. We address ourselves, not to their humanity, but to their self-love, and never talk to them of our own necessities but of their advantages.[7]

Nowhere, however, did this lead Smith to the brutal view of society that Marx sought and found. If Smith was too optimistic, Marx was surely even less accurate, for only in Dickens' *Oliver Twist* did English life really become sordid, though the industrial revolution produced great hardship. In Kirkcaldy it remained pretty solid. Sympathy —the ability of each of us to place ourselves in the place and thoughts of the other party—was the second pillar of Smith's house. The desire to be free, linked with a sense of property, was the third; and the propensity to truck, barter, exchange, and labor, the fourth. If this view of human nature will not satisfy the Freudian complexities of the twentieth century, Smith was nevertheless wholesome, sound, and quite practical for his time.

Man was a complex dignified being, but never reduced either to a population statistic as in Malthus or to a proletarian slave as in Marx. Smith's view of human nature is the key to understanding his view of society and of economics. He was no social revolutionary; he struck

---

[6]Smith, *The Theory of Moral Sentiments* (London: Cadell and Davies, 1804), book 1, p. 384, pp. 373-406.
[7]Smith, *Wealth of Nations,* book 1, chap. 2, p. 14.

out at neither capitalist nor landlord. He was perfectly content to accept the distribution rewards and mechanism of his society. By our standards, he was insensitive to the problems of social welfare. His views of the proper activity of government as a regulator of those few functions that private interests could not profitably provide has always shocked the radicals of succeeding decades.

One does not need to excuse Smith; there is always sufficient vigor in his social comments to satisfy even the most critical. This was no scholar devoid of human feeling!

It is but equity, besides, that they who feed, cloath, and lodge the whole body of the people, should have such a share of the produce of their own labour as to be themselves tolerably well fed, cloathed and lodged.[8]

And again,

Servants, labourers, and workmen of different kinds make up the far greater part of every great political society. But what improves the circumstances of the greater part can never be regarded as an inconveniency to the whole. No society can surely be flourshing and happy, of which the far greater part of the members are poor and miserable.[9]

In that natural order of which the cosmos, man, and society were a part, each man was the best judge of his own interests, and should as far as possible be allowed to pursue these interests. "I have never known," he wrote, "much good done by those who affected to trade for the public good."[10] Again, however, these individual interests are not exclusive, nor ruthless. Self-love was joined with human sympathy and because these interests were connected, each individual is "led by an invisible hand to promote an end which was no part of his intention."[11] The very essence of Smith's ideology was that motives do not have to be intentional; overall harmony arises out of the spontaneous functioning of human personality.

Government interference was the greatest barrier to this spontaneity. Everywhere government had intervened, Smith stated, the outcome was less effective than if it had remained aloof. Only a few

[8]*Ibid.*, book 1, chap. 8, p. 78.
[9]*Ibid.*, pp. 78-79.
[10]*Ibid.*, book 4, chap. 2, p. 423.
[11]*Ibid.*, book 4, chap. 2, p. 423.

duties "plain and intelligible to common understanding" were the definite exceptions Smith recognized. The first two, defense and justice, were obvious prerequisites of sovereign power; the third duty of government was more ambiguous.

The third and last duty of the sovereign or commonwealth is that of erecting and maintaining those public institutions and those public works, which, though they may be in the highest degree advantageous to a great society, are, however, of such a nature, that the profit could never repay the expence to any individual or small number of individuals, and which it therefore cannot be expected that any individual or small number of individuals should erect or maintain.[12]

The post office was "perhaps the only mercantile project which has been successfully managed by, I believe, every sort of government."[13] The worst example of government control was the operation of the East India Company: "no two characters seem more inconsistent than those of trader and sovereign."[14] Smith had abundant contemporary evidence for his feelings about the Company.

But though the profusion of government must, undoubtedly, have retarded the natural progress of England towards wealth and improvement, it has not been able to stop it . . . . It is the highest impertinence and presumption, therefore, in kings and ministers, to pretend to watch over the economy of private people, and to restrain their expense, either by sumptuary laws, or by prohibiting the importation of foreign luxuries. They are themselves always, and without exception, the greatest spendthrifts in the society. Let them look well after their own expense, and they may safely trust private people with theirs. If their own extravagance does not ruin the state, that of their subjects never will.[15]

However, despite Smith's personal inclination, his comments about the proper role of government are sufficiently broad to justify a wide range of modern activities. He recommended not only the building of roads, bridges, canals, and harbors by the government, but even wider

---

[12]*Ibid.*, book 5, chap. 1, part 3, p. 681.
[13]*Ibid.*, book 5, chap. 2, part 1, p. 770.
[14]*Ibid.*, book 5, chap. 2, part 1, p. 771.
[15]*Ibid.*, book 2, chap. 3, pp. 328-329.

activities such as education, licensing of professions, and control over bank note issue. As in other portions of the *Wealth of Nations,* the conventional wisdom of the century clashed head on with Scotch empiricism.

Smith viewed the businessman with equal realism: "People of the same trade seldom meet together, even for merriment and diversion, but the conversation ends in a conspiracy against the public, or in some contrivance to raise prices."[16] Smith was not the dogmatic champion of a cause, but a true scholar, searching disinterestedly for insight, ever fair and cultivated.

VALUE, PROFIT, RENT

We have tried to present the tone and philosophical framework of the *Wealth of Nations* before discussing Smith's major contribution to economic science, his descriptive model of a self-adjusting market system. For expository reasons, we must, however, first examine Smith's approach to the philosophical foundations of eighteenth-century economics—value, profit, and rent.

In economic thought, no concept has produced more circular reasoning than the search for the lodestone of value. What constitutes value? Every economic writer immediately spotted that portion of value contributed by total utility, but it was obvious that this was an insufficient explanation. Some theorists attempted to derive crude anthropological explanations for the origins of value, but neither their imagination nor their anthropology was adequate. We have already seen how a Christian society tried to place value partially within the confines of a moral-ethical system, but with only modest success, though even today the Christian definitions have great historical significance. The mercantilist determined value through bullion and foreign trade, and the Physiocrats pushed this further into a generalized system of agricultural production.

It was the Calvinist Smith who adopted the concept that, in principle, labor was the source of all value.

In that early and rude state of society which precedes both the accumulation of stock and the appropriation of land, the proportions between the quantities of labour necessary for acquiring different objects seems to be the only circumstance which can afford any rule for exchanging them for one another.[17]

[16]*Ibid.,* book 1, chap. 10, part 2, p. 128.
[17]*Ibid.,* book 1, chap. 6, p. 47.

When Smith discovered that in a more complex society this concept could be reconciled neither with observed price phenomena nor the price mechanism of his market system, he promptly dropped the labor theory of value and adopted a cost of production theory in which payments to capital, land, and labor determined "value" in the long run. Similarly, Smith started with an implicit acceptance of the mercantilist subsistence theory, rejected its pessimistic implications, which did not reflect his view of the world, and modified his wage theory until it fitted into his price-determined model.[18]

Smith was never fully at ease with his modified labor theory of value; even his more general cost of production theory did not account for exchange and use values. Smith could not see why diamonds, which had scarcely any use at all, should command more value than water! The solution to the diamond-water problem was, of course, the concept of marginal utility, which escaped Smith, although he provided the foundation for marginal analysis in his discussion of rent. The philosophical problem of "intrinsic value," however, was not really germane to Smith's system, especially because a modified "cost of production" value theory fitted well into the logical need of a dynamic model that emphasized a long-run view.

Profits, Smith defined generally as the return to the capitalist after the primary deductions of wages and rent.[19] As wealth increased in a developing country, and competition ensued, the rate of profit tended to fall, moving in the opposite direction from wages, thus making it possible for countries with higher wage rates to compete in foreign trade with countries whose wage rates might be lower but whose cost of capital was higher. Although Smith foresaw a declining rate of profit, nevertheless profits had to take into account the risks of loss and leave a net gain for the capitalist. Gross profit minus compensation for risk equalled net profit, which the capitalist appropriated. Profits varied greatly from country to country and time to time; the best clue to what was happening to profits was to follow the rate of

---

[18]This was typical of Smith's pragmatism. Though he accepted the labor theory of value ideologically, it did not fit into his model analytically. Compare this flexibility with the involved efforts Marx and Ricardo made throughout their lives to fit the labor theory into their systems. Neither succeeded, as we shall see. Marx, toward the end of his life, practically repudiated the labor theory of value in Volume 3 of his *Capital,* and Ricardo similarly admitted before his death his failure to reconcile the labor theory of value with reality.

[19]Smith's discussion of profit is often contradictory, and is scattered throughout Books 1 and 2 of the *Wealth of Nations.*

interest of money. Interest, or the cost of money, would rise or fall with profits. In order to induce the capitalist to borrow, the rate of interest had to be lower than his net profit. Similarly, in order for the capitalist to lend, the rate of interest had to be higher than the risk of loss. As Smith said, the minimum "must be something more than sufficient to compensate the occasional losses to which lending, even with tolerable prudence, is exposed."[20]

Smith's treatment of rent is more interesting from a historical *rather* than from a theoretical point of view because his discussion represented a transition from Hume's definition of rent as a "scarcity payment" to Ricardo's view of rent as a price-determined differential surplus. Initially (Book I, chapters 6 and 9), Smith considered rent to arise when all the free land had been appropriated by landlords. From this point on, the farmer must pay the landowners a part of his harvest to compensate for the use of land. This rent payment made up the "third component part" of price.

In his formal chapter on rent (Book I, chapter 11), Smith explored further the implication of the landlord's monopoly position, and arrived, after some difficulty, at a differential surplus theory:

High or low wages and profit are the causes of high or low price; high or low rent is the effect of it. It is because high or low wages and profit must be paid, in order to bring a particular commodity to market, that its price is high or low. But it is because its price is high or low . . . that it affords a high rent or a low rent.[21]

Even though the owner may contribute nothing, he demands and succeeds in obtaining a monopoly price, the highest price the tenant could afford to pay over and above wages and profits. This monopoly rent varied with the quality and location of the land. High prices yielded high rents, low prices low rents. The framework of the Ricardian rent theory, and even the rudiments of a marginal productivity theory, began to take shape, though Smith never quite explained how a price-determining monopoly could become a price-determined residual which would disappear if the price were merely high enough to pay wages and interest.

[20]*Ibid.,* book 1, chap. 11, p. 96.
[21]*Ibid.,* book 1, chap. 11, p. 146.

The diffuse and often contradictory nature of Smith's discussion of rent has led to widely differing evaluation of his rent theory. Eric Roll, for instance, considered that "in some respects Smith's analysis (of rent) is even superior to that of Ricardo,"[22] while Schumpeter referred to Smith's efforts as a "muddled argument," and suggested that Ricardo's rent theory "*might* have emerged from an effort to put logical order into the Smithian jumble."[23] The point should be made, however, that the theory of rent really played no essential role in Smith's market mechanism and had, therefore, only secondary importance for his system.

The Smithian Model

Smith's market system was a highly interdependent model that showed the interactions of prices, wages, profit, and rent. The market automatically decided through the price mechanism the basic questions of "what," "how," and "for whom" to produce. But the price mechanism operated through the "invisible hand" of self-interest, which directed the entrepreneur into those endeavors where profits were largest, while labor would seek those jobs that offered the highest wages — that is, where society most appreciated their efforts. This self-interest was held in check by competition, which urged other entrepreneurs to imitate the efforts of the most profitable firms, thereby reducing to "normal" proportions the high short-term profits earned by successful entrepreneurs or specially skilled "mechanics." Self-interest (profit incentive), competition, and the price mechanism were thus fully entwined, and represented the essence of the Smithian system.

By considering demand and supply as specific data at a point in time, Smith's system portrayed especially well the immediate or short-run effects of the price mechanism. But Smith distinguished quite carefully between short-run market fluctuations and the natural (long-run) price. This natural price is loosely related to the cost of production, and it is through this relationship that the price mechanism effects long-run changes in the economy.

The long-run, or "natural," price of a commodity is determined by the cost of its production. In "civilized" society, this cost of produc-

---

[22]Eric Roll, *The History of Economic Thought,* 3d ed. (Englewood Cliffs, N.J.: Prentice-Hall, 1957), p. 166.

[23]Schumpeter, *History of Economic Analysis* (New York: Oxford University Press, 1954), p. 191

tion consists of payments for interest, wages, and rent to reward the three factors of production, capital, labor, and land.

In every society, the price of every commodity finally resolves itself into some one or other, or all of those three parts [interest, wages, rent] ; and in every improved society, all the three enter more or less, as component parts, into the price of the far greater part of the commodities.[24]

The natural price, therefore, is equal to the cost of production; but due to fluctuations in demand, the actual, or market, price will rarely, if ever, coincide with the natural price.

When the price of any commodity is neither more nor less than what is sufficient to pay the rent of land, the wages of the labour, and the profits of the stock [i.e., interest] employed in raising, preparing, and bringing it to market, according to their natural rates, the commodity is then sold for what may be called its natural price.

The commodity is then sold precisely for what it is worth, or for what it really costs the person who brings it to market.[25]

If the market price is above the natural price the entrepreneur is making a profit (a windfall profit); he loses if the natural price is less than the market price. It was through this profit or loss that the price mechanism generates long-run changes. A windfall profit would attract additional firms into producing this particular commodity. They would bid up the price for the existing labor and resources until these higher prices eliminated the profit. Conversely when the market price was less than the natural price, production would be cut back, and the decline in the demand for labor and land would reduce wages and rent payment. This process will continue until the market price approaches the natural price—that is, the cost of production.[26]

The natural price, therefore, is . . . the central price, to which the prices of all commodities are continually gravitating. Different accidents may sometimes keep them suspended a good deal above it, and sometimes force them down

---

[24]Smith, *Wealth of Nations,* book 1, chap. 6, p. 50.
[25]*Ibid.* book 1, chap. 7, p. 55.
[26]Smith used the term *profit* both when referring to "profit of stock," that is, interests, as well as when referring to the windfall profit due to price fluctuations; the latter profit is closer to our modern concept of profit.

even somewhat below it. But whatever may be the obstacles which hinder them from settling . . . they are constantly tending towards it [the natural price].[27]

By equating natural price with the cost of production, Smith extended the price mechanism to the factors of production. This extension of the price system implied a strong materialistic-economic interpretation of history.

Wages, rent, and interest are all determined by demand and supply like a commodity. Again, it was self-interest and competition that made the price system the effective regulator of the economy in the long run. Monopoly was, in the long run, a greater danger to the effectiveness of the price system; monopolists sabotage the effectiveness of the price system and are the enemies of society. A monopoly price is above the natural, cost-determined price and misrepresents the actual market forces. Ordinarily, writers emphasize that Smith's price mechanism is cost determined.[28] This does not seem entirely correct to us. In the long run, price had to cover cost of production, but in the short run, the market price was determined by demand and supply. The short-run profits or losses, due to the divergence of the market price from the natural price, effected, in turn, changes in the demand and supply of the basic components of the cost of production; we actually have a rather sophisticated price system which, anticipating Alfred Marshall by about a hundred years, implicitly conceives of demand and cost of production as two interacting forces, "two blades of a pair of scissors," which determine price. Except for Smith's primitive definition of demand as a single quantity (i.e., a point on a contemporary demand schedule), his explanation of the forces determining price is often very close to that of the neoclassical school.

Smith's price system regulates the use and growth of the supply of capital and labor through the deviations of the market price from the natural price. Now the circle is closed and the size and well-being of the very population whose self-interest drives it into the division of

[27]Smith, *Wealth of Nations,* book 1, chap. 7, p. 58.

[28]Eric Roll, *A History of Economic Thought* (New York: Prentice-Hall, 1946); Robert L. Heilbroner, *The Worldly Philosophers* (New York: Simon and Schuster, 1961); Charles Gide and Charles Rist, *A History of Economic Doctrines,* trans. R. Richards, (Boston: D.C. Heath & Co., n.d.); Eduard Heimann, *History of Economic Doctrines* (Oxford University Press, 1945).

labor, the creation of capital, and the development of the price system are, in turn, regulated by this same system.

If there is a greater demand for labor during a period of labor shortage and hence a higher price for labor is paid, the population (i.e., supply) would increase, while during periods of unemployment (excess labor supply) the price for labor would decline and the population would decrease.

Labour is there [in North America] so well rewarded that a numerous family of children, instead of being a burthen is a source of opulence and prosperity to the parents . . . . The value of children is the greatest of all encouragements to marriage. We cannot, therefore, wonder that the people in North America should generally marry very young. Notwithstanding the great increase occasioned by such early marriages, there is a continual complaint of the scarcity of hands in North America.[29]

If the supply of labor is, therefore, regulated like that of any other commodity by the market price, it would have been only natural that Smith should have, in turn, expected wages to fluctuate also around their natural cost of production level. It probably was Smith's natural optimism that prevented him from accepting the widely endorsed mercantilistic subsistence theory of wages. Rather, he looked at subsistence wages as a minimum level, from which the working class could escape because higher wages tended to increase the efficiency of labor and hence, through increased production, augmented the capital necessary for raising the demand for labor in return.

Some very eminent economists have criticized Smith for letting the cost of the factors of production determine the price of the commodity, and then letting the factor prices (wage, rent, interest) be, in turn, determined by the commodity price.[30] However, we deal with this very problem whenever we solve a set of simultaneous equations, and though during Smith's time economists had not yet developed explicitly general equilibrium models, which represent the economy by a system of "$n \times n$" linear equations, the algebraic solutions of such systems

---

[29]Smith, *Wealth of Nations,* book 1, chap. 8, pp. 70-71.

[30]Of course, once this charge is made, Smith's system can no longer be considered completely cost determined. Thus, most certainly, Smith cannot be accused of both developing a purely cost-determined price system *and* of creating a "vicious circle," where market prices are determined by factor costs and factor costs by the market price of commodities.

Figure **2.1** Dampened Price Oscillations

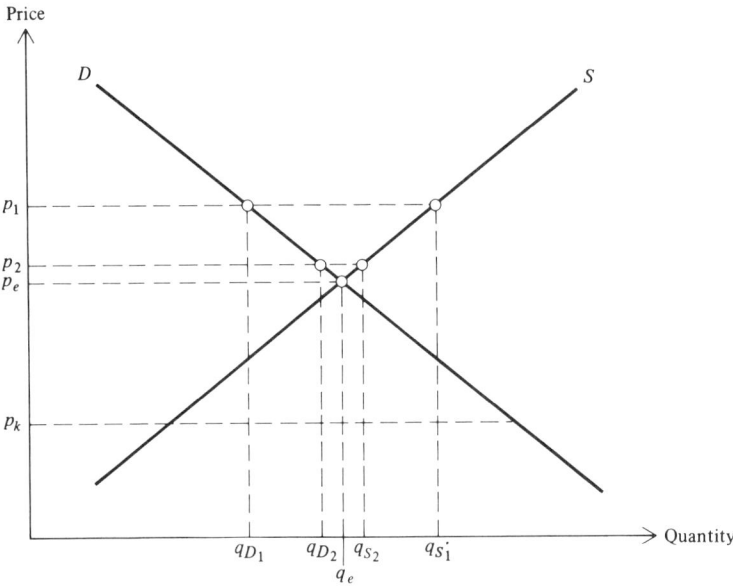

Assuming that for some reason price $p = p_1$, the following converging price variations occur: at p_1, $q_{D_1} < q_{S_1}$ and price drops to p_2, where still $q_{D_2} < q_{S_2}$ and price continues to drop until p_e where $q_{D_e} = q_{S_e} = q_e$ and a new equilibrium has been reached.

Note that $\left| q_{D_1} - q_{S_1} \right| > \left| q_{D_2} - q_{S_2} \right| > \left| q_{D_e} - q_{S_e} \right| = 0$

However, the diagram is merely an illustration, not a proof, of a process which Smith asserted to take place. There is no reason, for instance, why p_1 may not lead to p_k rather than to p_2.

By distinguishing between "Very Short Run," "Short Run," and "Long Run" demand and supply functions, Marshall showed in greater detail how a dynamic equilibrium adjustment could occur.

were certainly known. This mutual interdependence of prices is an essential aspect of Smith's contribution, and it is at the heart of classical, neoclassical, and general equilibrium analysis, even if Smith did not explicitly formulate this concept. J. B. Say, however, who introduced Smith to continental readers, came very close to presenting Smith's market system as an explicit general equilibrium model. It was Say's interpretation of Smith that, in turn, influenced Leon Walras.

A serious defect in Smith's system is, however, his assumption, basic to classical thought, that the haggling of the market place will produce dampened price oscillations, which will ultimately end, if left alone, in equilibrium. These dampened oscillations are ordinarily represented in elementary texts by the diagram shown in Figure 2.1.

However, anyone familiar with differential equations can easily see that oscillations are dampened only under specific circumstances. Economists realized this fully only in the 1930s, and consequently developed a geometric theory, the cobweb theorem,[31] which showed that over several time periods and under certain demand and supply configurations (e.g., no quantity adjustments can be made on the supply side in the short run), the "haggling of the market place" can lead to ever-increasing ("explosive") oscillations rather than to an equilibrium price.[32] (See Figure 2.2.)

A market system, however, which in certain cases is not completely and predictably self-adjusting, violates the philosophical foundations of the Smithian model. There can be no exceptions for a system of natural laws. Although the cobweb theorem points out a serious flaw

Figure **2.2** Explosive Price Oscillation; Cobweb system

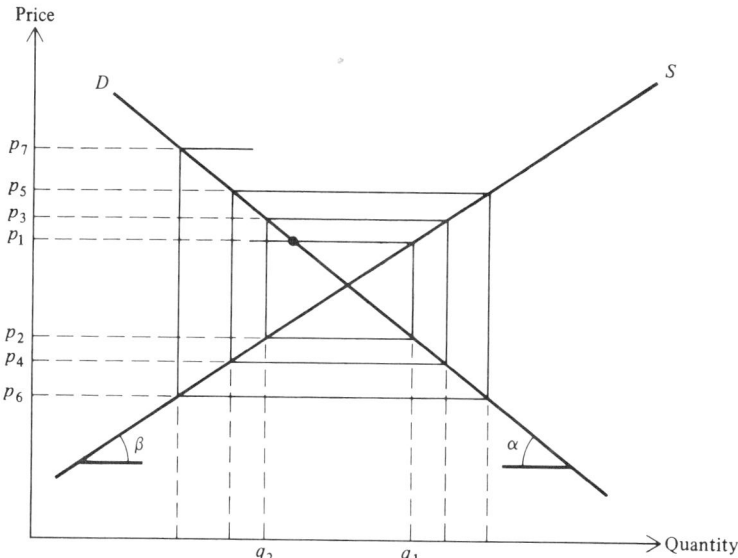

Assume that, for some exogenous reasons, $p = p_1$, and that, in accordance with the cobweb assumptions, *no* short run supply changes can take place. Since at $p = p_1$, $S > D$, sellers must lower their price to $p = p_2$, where in the short run $S = D_1$ However, in the long run at p_2 suppliers are only willing to supply q_2. In the long run $D > S$, and the price rises to p_3, etc. This process continues until the wider and wider price oscillations destroy the system. Note that if S is steeper than D, $(\beta > |\alpha|)$ the cobweb process will converge to an equilibrium.

[31]Cf. Mordecai Ezekiel, "The Cobweb Theorem," *Quarterly Journal of Economics,* *52* (1938), 255-280, for a full discussion of its intellectual history.

[32]In addition to the Smith-Marshallian and the cobweb equilibrium processes, there exist others, such as Walras' "perturbations" *(tatonnement),* Dutch auctions, etc.

in the theory of a self-adjusting market, it is only of little practical value in evaluating Smith's contribution. Smith was not familiar with the concept of demand and supply schedules, and he cannot be criticized for failing to discover the mathematical relationship between converging oscillations and the slopes of the schedules. In practice, during the nineteenth century, the continuous changes in income, tastes, and technology that affected the demand for specific commodities prevented dampened oscillations from converging to an equilibrium, or explosive oscillations from becoming chaotic.

Of much greater significance for the development of economic theory and policy was Smith's capital theory. In developing his capital theory, Smith touched upon such highly sensitive topics as the source of value, the nature of productive and unproductive labor, and the consequences of thrift or wastefulness. These topics are intimately connected with a number of philosophical and political issues, and Smith's frequently offhand comments can be interpreted to strengthen or weaken different ideological positions. His passing pronouncements are of little consequence, however, for appreciating the essential nature of his capital theory as the last component of his system. Smith considered capital a "stock," or accumulation of wealth consisting of the "annual produce" (GNP in our terminology) and goods accumulated but not consumed in previous years. It could be said that Smith had a notion of circulating and fixed capital except that, living before the Industrial Revolution, he conceived of fixed capital as durable commodities such as housing and furnishings not as productive tools of production. His circulating capital was a fund that consisted of the provisions and inventory necessary to maintain labor and production during a production cycle.

Though the whole annual produce of the land and labour of every country, is . . . ultimately destined for supplying the consumption of its inhabitants, and for procuring a revenue to them; yet when it first comes either from the ground, or from the hands of the productive labourers, *it naturally divides itself into two parts.* One of them . . . is destined for replacing a capital, or for renewing the provisions, materials, and finished work, which had been withdrawn from a capital; the other for constituting a revenue either to the owner of this capital, as the profit of his stock [i.e., interest]; or to some other person, as the rent of his land.[33]

[33]Smith, *Wealth of Nations,* book 2, chap. 3, pp. 315-316 (our italics).

Smith was more astute and explicit than many subsequent economists in specifically equating "real" circulating capital—that is, land, inventory, clothing, and so forth—with the money fund necessary to buy the goods.

> . . . money is, as it were, but the deed of assignment, which conveys from one hand to another those capitals which the owners do not care to employ themselves. . . . A capital lent at interest may, in this manner, be considered as an assignment from the lender to the borrower of a certain considerable portion of the annual produce [GNP].[34]

Whenever profit opportunities expanded, the demand for capital (what might be called loanable funds today) increased, and this, in turn, prompted an increase in the interest rate.[35] A rise in interest, according to Smith, brought about an increase in the accumulation of capital because people of means, at least, would be prompted to spend less and save more. Thus the rate of capital accumulation (i.e., savings) is a function of the interest rate, and frugality and thrift promote an increase in the rate of capital formation. It did not occur to Smith that, at best, only among a very frugal race would the men of means be prompted to cut down on their consumption because the interest rate had increased half a point. Nor did Smith consider that such a frugal race might save even more if the interest rate were low, and therefore their income from capital loans less. Lastly, and most importantly, it did not occur to Smith that if a substantial number of families reduced their consumption in order to save more, the entrepreneurs who had expanded their business activities in anticipation of increased sales could not realize their anticipation, and thus might go bankrupt because of overproduction. Overproduction as well as oversavings were inconceivable phenomena to Smith. Thus Smith was responsible for introducing the notion that the rate of saving depends on the interest rate, and that savings are always immediately turned into investment. Say merely paraphrased Smith when he reformulated these theories, which, under the name of Say's law, were to dominate economic thinking and economic policy until the 1930s and still have a strong hold on the ideology of the American

---

[34]*Ibid.,* book 2, chap. 4, pp. 334-335.
[35]"It may be laid down as a maxim that wherever a great deal can be made by the use of money, a great deal will commonly be given for the use of it. . . ." Smith, *Wealth of Nations,* book 1, chap. 9, p. 88.

businessman. There is abundant evidence that the level of the interest rate has only a very slight impact on saving at the very best; similarly, most economists agree today that people generally do not save in order to invest, and even corporate savings are rarely immediately reinvested, and occasionally not at all.

It is possible that among the Presbyterian Scotsmen of Smith's time—who must have served for his model of the "economic man"—the rate of interest actually affected some savings and consumption decisions. There is less excuse for his belief that savings and investment are necessarily identical.[36] Because Quesnay's *Tableau Economique* established the notion of an economic flow, and from a purely analytical point of view, it should have been very easy to imagine that the flow of savings did not necessarily have to equal the flow of investment. From a psychological and philosophical point of view, it is quite clear that it was practically impossible for Smith to conceive of such an event. His system, analogous physically to Newton's mechanistic model and philosophically to Locke's view of a universe governed by natural law, had to be completely self-adjusting. As long as savings equal investments, or as long as savings (i.e., income not spent) are immediately reintroduced into the economic bloodstream by business investments, the total output must always equal the total demand for goods or services by business and individuals. Thus overproduction or underproduction is impossible, unemployment cannot occur and the economy is supremely self-adjusting.

We should reemphasize that the price mechanism, through the interest rate, adjusts the demand and supply for capital, and controls the allocation of the factors of production. If the business community is willing to invest more than society is willing to save, it will, Smith stated, bid up the interest until the society of economic men will cut back their consumption and increase their savings. If savings exceed investment opportunities, a falling interest rate will discourage savings (i.e., encourage consumption) until equilibrium is reestablished.

---

[36]Please note that we are talking here about the amounts (schedules) of money people are *willing to save* and people are *willing to invest.* This should not be confused (but very often is) with the actual amount of money saved and invested, which must be identical; by virtue of the modern definitions of national income, savings and investments are always algebraically equal ($Y = C + I$, and $Y = C + S$, $\therefore S = I$). This is very much the same as the relationship between demand and supply. At any particular point in time, what is bought (demanded) must obviously equal what is sold (supplied). However, the demand (the amount people are willing to buy at a given price) may exceed the supply, may equal supply, or may be less than the supply.

The fluctuation in the market rate of the reward for capital (the interest rate) is affected first by the fluctuations of market prices of commodities. High prices give rise to high profits and high profits increase the demand for capital. An increase in the amount of capital available (i.e., net capital formation) increases the demand for labor, Smith thought, and thus once more the circle is closed, and the long-run cost of the factors of production are again associated with short-run fluctuations; demand and cost are again interdependent.

The demand for those who live by wages, therefore, necessarily increases with the increase of the revenue and stock of every country, and cannot possibly increase without it. The increase of revenue and stock is the increase of national wealth. The demand for those who live by wages, therefore, naturally increases with the increase of national wealth, and cannot possibly increase without it.[37]

Smith's contention that an increase in capital investment will bring about an increase in labor was frequently true in the period before the Industrial Revolution. Additional capital investment need not mean introduction of labor-saving devices, but rather the addition of a spindle or a hand loom requiring additional labor.

Smith's capital *and* population theories not only tie the determination of factor costs to the price mechanism, and once more expose long-run, cost-determined natural price to the impact of short-run market fluctuations; they also lend his model a dynamic quality, which many classical and all neoclassical models lacked.[38] A growth in capital investment raises the demand for labor and hence the wages of labor.[39] Labor, however, will work more efficiently at a higher wage

---

[37]Smith, *Wealth of Nations,* book 1, chap. 8, p. 69.

[38]In economic theory, we distinguish between static and dynamic models. A static model, essentially, does not explain growth or decay over time. A dynamic model contains time as an explicit variable and tries to explain the anticipated changes (growth, decay) in the state of the model over time. An example of non-mathematical dynamic models are, for instance, the theories of capitalistic development of Marx and Schumpeter. For a more detailed discussion of static and dynamic models, see the section on General Systems Analysis in Chapter 11.

[39]Very perceptively, Smith made the rate of capital formation rather than the absolute magnitude of capital the wage determinant. "It is not the actual greatness of national wealth, but its continual increase, which occasions a rise in the wages of labour." Smith, book 1, chap. 8, p. 69. This is a very sophisticated concept that anticipated modern multiplier-accelerator concepts.

(i.e., it will really be "cheaper labor" from the point of view of unit costs), and hence the whole society benefits from a high wage policy. Such a high wage policy, however, would encourage an increase in the population. But this increased labor supply would not depress the wages to a subsistence level (i.e., its natural price) as Mun and Malthus believed. True to the continued division of labor and the increases in productivity that follow from a high wage policy, the total wealth would increase sufficiently fast to promise a continuous rise in the level of living.

Smith, of course, had no analytical tools to prove that the rate of capital formation would exceed the rate of population growth; this was borne out rather by the experience of his time as well as by his own optimistic nature. At a different time, a more pessimistic personality could easily have arrived at a different answer.

Summary and Conclusion

Smith's market system was his major contribution to economic theory, to the developing ideology of classical liberalism, and to the policy decisions that changed the character of British society. One cannot possibly fail to appreciate the majestic concept of the market. The questions of what, how, or for whom to produce are no longer settled by outmoded customs with their roots in the dark pools of irrationality and superstition; nor does society have to rely any longer upon the judgment of planners, corruptible and shortsighted men, exposed to the concerted pressures of vested interest, at the very best prone to let their personal values influence their economic decisions. It is an impersonal mechanism, the market system, that automatically makes all decisions with a perfection and an impersonality no human "planning commission" could ever hope to equal. If, as Smith tried to show, this system was continuously self-adjusting, made its allocating decisions in accordance with the wishes of the consumer, and at all times utilized all resources in an optimum manner, then this was truly one of the marvels of creation, which through its natural laws guided the course of stars and of production with equal impersonal but harmonious regularity.

The rising class of businessmen eagerly grasped the concept that the government that governed least governed best. The bourgeoisie did not have a voice in the government equal to its economic importance, nor did the ruling aristocracy cease to consider them socially far inferior.[40] How wonderfully convenient that it could be shown that the government and the aristocracy were not only unnecessary but were even an obstacle to economic progress. Remove them either with bullets or with ballots, and let the market govern supremely. All that was needed from a government was the enforcement of contracts and the protection of property, two aspects which would assure the dominance of the bourgeoisie.

Thus Smith's market system became an integral part of Western and, above all, American business ideology; any attempt to show that the market system was not completely self-adjusting or did not serve harmoniously the interests of all groups in society was fiercely resented by the bourgeoisie, who adopted Smith as a patron saint without ever realizing Smith's suspicion of the businessman.

There are many other features of Smith that can be of interest to social historians and economists, but they are really not germane to his major contribution—the market system. Economists interested in the history of economic analysis can find numerous and often clashing wage, value, and monetary theories.[41] This is not important because Smith tended to adopt the prevailing theories in these areas and wove them into his market system.

Stripped of all the unessentials, the wonderful sociological analyses, the paraphrasing of accepted economic doctrines, we have left a sparse, self-contained, dynamic model of the economy of considerable sophistication, and probably of considerable validity for Smith's time, especially if we emphasize the long-run aspects of the classical models. His major limitations, the failure to recognize that intended savings and intended investments are not necessarily equal, and that savings do not necessarily follow the interest rate, were probably not as significant in Smith's time as they are today. His failure to recognize that some investments could be of a labor-replacing as well as of a labor-creating nature, and that therefore the interests of capital and labor are not necessarily harmonious, had even less consequence for

---

[40]As a matter of fact, it was the establishment (Tories) that combined with "labor" to pass nineteenth-century social legislation. Disraeli and Bismarck were undoubtedly the founders of the welfare state, the originators of factory legislation and "socialized medicine." France and the United States had a successful bourgeois revolution, and lagged far behind Britain, Germany, and Austria-Hungary in social legislation.

[41]We can find evidence in the *Wealth of Nations* to claim that Smith at one place or another developed wage concepts that can be classified under subsistence, bargaining, wages fund, and productivity theory of labor.

the preindustrial period. Only his inability to develop a more dynamic and realistic theory of money can be held against him, because in this area his friend Hume, and the mercantilists, had already made major contributions.[42] But in spite of these shortcomings, Smith's market system was a contribution of such significance that for the next hundred years the writings of most Anglo-American economists consisted largely of refinements.

Smith's greatest influence, however, was on policy; his work arrived at the proper time. Unlike so many others on whom Fortune did not smile, the *Wealth of Nations* was a Madison Avenue-type success. The treatise was beautifully written—clear, precise, intelligent, urbane, not hard or obscure. Altogether it appealed to the common-sense intelligence of the bourgeoisie, and gave them a policy program which fitted their actions and business environment.

Smith became most renowned for his contribution to the doctrine of free trade adopted as the program of the Manchester Chamber of Commerce, the growing English middle-class industrialists. After 1750, the number and extent of technological and industrial innovations made mercantilistic restraints more anachronistic. The press of realities might have swept mercantilistic regulations away without Smith, but it was infinitely easier to demolish this termite-ridden structure with the *Wealth of Nations* as a guide. In exceptional cases such as saltpeter or shipping necessary for defense, Smith recognized the need for direct control by public authority. He briefly mentions the possibilities of import duties as measures of retaliation against the prior action of other countries if necessary. However, the *Wealth of Nations* provided an outline of a broad panorama of a nation engaged in world trade, free of all encumbrances. This was a vision to stir the heart of the textile manufacturers, the ironmongers, and the pottery makers. Smith's view was almost prophetic, for by 1850 almost everything that had stood in the way of free trade was abolished in England.

On the continent, Smith had many admirers and followers, but nowhere near the impact on government and economic policy he

---

[42]Sir James Steuart's contributions should be mentioned at this time, especially his *Inquiry into the Principles of Political Economy* (1767). Steuart's sophisticated monetary theory led him to the conclusion that a stable, "full employment" level of activity would not necessarily result without government intervention. It was this very interventionism that prompted the unfavorable contemporary reviews. The late 1950s have seen a Steuart "revival." Cf. J. S. R. Sen, *The Economics of Sir James Steuart* (Cambridge, Mass : Harvard University Press, 1957); Douglas Vickers, *Studies in the Theory of Money* (Philadelphia: Chilton, 1959).

exercised at home. France was to flirt with free trade in the Cobden-Chevalier treaty of 1860, but the flirtation was brief and never fully accepted. Germany never accepted "Smithismus." Internal free trade but external protectionism became typical German policy after the Napoleonic Wars. But for more than a century, Smith's great model of a simple market mechanism, adjusting, meliorating, and allocating economic resources with precision and simplicity, dominated British economic thinking. In western Europe, the hundred years that ended in August 1914 saw one of the most massive breakthroughs in economic growth and productivity. Because men believed in free trade and competition and rational liberalism, they achieved unbelievable things. The real income of people rose as they were able to afford cheaper goods. Unfortunately, for the economic history of this period, the most powerful and gifted observer, Karl Marx, was so obsessively hostile to the system that we have taken at face value his view of the miserization of society. One typical example from a letter of Josiah Wedgwood—who had no axe to grind—may suggest some of the improvements that industrialization brought.

I would request you to ask your parents [Wedgwood wrote in 1795] , for a description of the country we inhabit when they first knew it; and they will tell you that the inhabitants bore all the marks of poverty to a much greater degree than they do now. Their houses were miserable huts, the lands poorly cultivated and yielded little of value for the food of man or beast, and these disadvantages, with roads almost impassable, might be said to have cut off our part of the country from the rest of the world, besides rendering it not very comfortable to ourselves. Compare this picture, which I know to be a true one, with the present state of the same country, the workmen earning near double their former wages, their houses mostly new and comfortable, and the lands, roads, and every other circumstance bearing evident marks of the most pleasing and rapid improvements . . . . Industry has been the parent of this happy change.[43]

Smith's major policy contribution was to link the doctrine of natural law and natural rights to bourgeois capitalism and political liber-

---

[43]Josiah Wedgwood, *An Address to the Young Inhabitants of the Pottery,* quoted in Paul Mantoux, *The Industrial Revolution in the Eighteenth Century,* rev. ed., trans. Margery Vernon (London: Cape, 1957), p. 397. Marx falled to appreciate that different segments of the labor force shared differentially in the rewards of industrialization. Not every worker became, in fact, a downtrodden member of the proletariat.

alism. It was a prodigious accomplishment and a magnificent success. This marriage rested not on a materialistic greed, but on a large substructure of romantic altruism. The nineteenth-century midde-class society drew from Smith's investigation a deep faith and com-mitment that the social goals of laissez faire would benefit everyone. Smith was not the narrow spokesman for a single class. His assump-tions, both intellectual and moral, closely tied him to his background and education. Despite the contradictions and lapses within the book, there is an overall economic and social unity. Production, exchange, the invisible hand of the market place, the flexible definitions of government intervention, the course of tax policy—each complements the other.

Smith was so effective not only for reasons already cited, but also because the *Wealth of Nations* was a prognosis of social history directed to the future after the deepest investigation of history. Smith was keenly aware of the existence of social classes in society. There were those who lived off rent, those who worked for wages, and those whose income came from profit; laborers differed from landowners and from businessmen. Each class was bound by the narrowness of its own views, and Smith was highly critical of these parochial interests—that is, the unfeeling monopoly practices of the landlord, the igno-rance and brutish quality of the laborer, the conspiratorial nature of the businessman. The energy of self-interest did not need to end in social fragmentation. Smith believed it could be harnessed for the good of all by recognizing the overall interdependence of society and the application of economic laws.

Smith's definitions of social harmony are unsatisfactory today, as they were unsatisfactory to many thinkers in the nineteenth century. He was too dispassionate, too genteel, too self-assured, and too naïve. Most people were not satisfied with the distributive equity of the market as defined by classical economics. Smith's model of the market never encompassed the full complexities of industrial society. Im-perfect competition, oligopoly power, unemployment of a massive nature—all the economic problems that perplex us today were not yet born.

3

RICARDO AND
THE PROBLEMS
HE RAISED

In Ricardo we meet another giant in the history of economic thought. For over one hundred years his was the preeminent voice in Anglo-American economics. His methodology, even more than his theories, left its mark on English-speaking economists, and has been responsible for the overly static, deductive, and abstract nature of the discipline.[1]

Ricardo's background provides a key to his achievements and shortcomings. His father, a Sephardic Jew, had immigrated to England from Holland. By the time David was born in London in 1772, the father had already become a wealthy and respected stockbroker. The son, in turn, entered business at the age of fourteen. Although he did

---

[1]Note that among the great "systems builders" who mastered the historical and sociological environment of the economic process—Smith, Marx, Pareto, Sombart, Schumpeter, Myrdal—Smith is the only Anglo-Saxon. Note also that among the above at least Pareto, Schumpeter, and Myrdal were competent mathematicians. Thus, analytical competence does not necessarily demand a lack of historical insight.

come from a "cultured" home and read widely as long as he lived, he lacked formal academic schooling and, perhaps most tellingly, the disciplined classical background of an Adam Smith or a John Stuart Mill.

Ricardo changed his religion when he married, was subsequently disowned by his family, and set up his own brokerage firm. He rapidly amassed a huge fortune (reputedly about £2,000,000—an incredible sum for a time when a "gentleman" could live very well on £1,000 a year), and virtually retired from business in his thirties. He acquired an estate, became a member of Parliament (1819), and devoted his life to intellectual pursuits, mainly the study of economics.

As an investment broker, he was, of course, interested in monetary phenomena. In 1810, he published his first essay, *The High Price of Bullion, a Proof of the Depreciation of Banknotes.*[2] A number of brief polemical essays followed. Much of his thinking on value and distribution is stated in his *Essay on the Influence of a Low Price of Corn on the Profits of Stock* (1815).[3] Urged by James Mill to expand and rewrite this essay, Ricardo produced in 1817 his most important work, *The Principles of Political Economy and Taxation.*[4]

This essay, one of the most difficult books a student of economics may encounter, made Ricardo the leading and most popular economist of his day. Moreover, strange as it might seem to a contemporary reader, he managed to glamorize the entire field of economics. Ricardian economics became the fashionable subject in the best salons, and ladies, in hiring a governess, inquired about her competence to teach "political economy." Although *The Principles* was Ricardo's last major work—he died of an earache at age fifty-two—he continued to discuss, refine, and modify his views in his lectures and above all, in his correspondence with James Mill, Malthus, Say, John Ramsay McCulloch, Nassau William Senior, and others. This correspondence is extremely important for an understanding of Ricardo's work, and especially for an understanding of his intellectual integrity. Doctrines that were firmly established in his *Principles* were again and again reexamined, modified, and occasionally abandoned if they no longer seemed adequate to his critical mind.

Ricardo was the first pure theorist. He lacked the historical insight

[2] Cf. *The Works and Correspondence of David Ricardo,* Pierro Sraffa, ed. (Cambridge: Cambridge University Press, 1953), vol. 3.
[3] *Ibid.,* vol. 4.
[4] *Ibid.,* vol. 1.

of Smith, and he did not comprehend the impact of sociological and institutional forces upon economics. Instead, Ricardo's logical mind posed questions. Frequently he took ideas from Smith and Malthus that were not up to his analytical standards and proceeded to build abstract models for further testing. Very much in the manner of the physical scientist, Ricardo attempted to keep his models manageable by holding all variables but one or two constant (the *ceteris paribus* of economic analysis) and then examining the consequences of changes in his remaining variable(s). *Unlike* physical scientists, however, Ricardo neglected actual physical observations; he built his models mainly on the basis of a priori, deductive reasoning.[5] Furthermore, Ricardo often forgot that he had built a model—that is, a simplified picture of reality—and proceeded with both policy recommendations and further analytical examinations as if his abstractions had been identical with the real world. Schumpeter, in discussing Ricardo's policy recommendations, commented perceptively:

In these [Ricardo's policy recommendations] we do miss insight into the motive power of the social process and, in addition, historical sense. . . . I do not think that Ricardo ever did much historical reading. But this is not what I mean. The trouble with him is akin to the trouble I have, in this respect, with my American students, who have plenty of historical material pushed down their throats. But it is to no purpose. They lack the historical *sense* that no amount of factual study can give. This is why it is so much easier to make theorists of them than economists.[6]

Because he overemphasized deductive, a priori reasoning, Ricardo was unable to consider social and institutional forces in his policy recommendations. Unfortunately, these very shortcomings became the prime characteristics of post-Ricardian and neoclassical economics. It was essentially the "Ricardian Vice" that changed political

[5]It is interesting to compare Ricardo with an equally brilliant though less known contemporary, Charles Babbage (1792-1871). The latter, a gifted mathematician and engineer who anticipated the modern electronic computer, was an excellent economist who also anticipated modern value theory. Babbage was primarily interested in applying economic and mathematical analysis to business firms. He analyzed the operations of a pin factory, the printing industry, the postal system, etc. If Ricardo, the first theoretician, and Babbage, the first operational analyst, could have communicated, economics might have advanced much more rapidly.

[6]Joseph Schumpeter, *History of Economic Analysis* (New York: Oxford Univerversity Press, 1954), p. 472.

economics from the *dernier cri* of the fashionable salons into a scholasticism that could look at millions of unemployed in the 1930s and still maintain that unemployment could not persist in a market economy.

While Ricardo's methodology can be held responsible for many of the inadequacies of Anglo-American economics, its power, when properly used, must not be neglected. Much in the writing of Smith, Malthus, and their predecessors was imprecise and vague. These imperfections prompted Ricardo's analytical criticism, and in much of his work he attempted to refine his "forbearers' " imprecise and incomplete concepts.[7] Ricardo made economics analytical instead of literary. After Ricardo, principal economists are all competent analysts, fair mathematicians, and frequently impressive philosophers and historians. Ricardian analysis became the tool kit of all economists. Alone, without the proper historical and social insights, Ricardo's model becomes a sterile, dead-end street; together with the insights of a Pareto or a Schumpeter, it becomes a powerful device, indispensable for the further development of theory.

A Preface to the Ricardian System

Ricardo was above all a toolmaker par excellence. But for a number of reasons it is more difficult to present a definitive, coherent picture of Ricardian economics than it is in the case of the more "literary" economist Smith. First, Ricardo's prose, unlike Smith's, was tortured and obscure (especially in his *Principles,* less in his correspondence). Second, he frequently changed his conditions and modified his thoughts simultaneously. Definitions that appeared in the earlier parts of the *Principles* were in some instances radically changed in subsequent chapters. In other cases, he kept his original terminology, though he changed his concepts. For example, discussion of rent proceeds from a physiocratic definition of rent as scarcity rent—that is, a payment for "the use of the original and indestructible powers of the soil"; subsequently he developed his concept of rent as a differential payment. Yet the original definition remains intact, edition after edition, though clearly inferior to the more sophisticated

[7]While considering the expansion of his essay on the price of corn, he commented, in a letter to his friend Trower (October 29, 1815), on his decision to "concentrate all [his] talents on these topics where [his] opinions" differ from the great authority of Adam Smith and Malthus, "namely the principles of Rent, Profit and Wages," Ricardo, *The Works,* vol. 6, p. 316.

concept of differential rent. Third, his writing was fragmentary, and he anticipated concepts in his earlier chapters that he explained only subsequently. Finally, his writing was on a rarefied level of abstraction; often it is difficult to find the relevance of certain passages among the many assumptions piled upon each other. Essentially what Ricardo did was to write literary mathematics, a style almost impossible to enjoy. If Ricardo had expressed his rigorous models in mathematical terms, he would be more easily read by contemporary students of economics. But had he done so, it is quite likely that he would have failed to make any impact on his time. The major work of the great French economist Antoine Cournot—which appeared about twenty years after Ricardo's *Principles*—was completely unnoticed by his contemporaries because it expressed its original and perceptive analysis in mathematical terminology.[8]

Ricardo's treatment of value and distribution theory in the *Principles* emphasized those aspects about which he disagreed with Smith and Malthus. His book is actually an extended critique, which accounts for its lack of unity. We know from his correspondence with James Mill that at first Ricardo was concerned primarily with distribution theory. He soon found it difficult, however, to reconcile his distribution theory with his notions on price and value.[9] This problem forced him into revising his value theory. By necessity, his value and distribution theories were developed almost simultaneously and represented the bedrock of his economic thinking.

Ricardian value theory had far-reaching ideological implications because Marx based his value and exploitation theory on a logical extension of Ricardo's work. Neoclassical economists, in turn, have attempted to deemphasize the importance of value theory for Ricardian economics, while Marxian economists have stressed Ricardo's contribution to labor value theory at the expense of his other theoret-

---

[8]Cournot, who is discussed below, is accessible to anyone familiar with freshman calculus. Stlll, his contemporaries found him too difficult. This is quite an indictment of the intellectual curiosity of the economists of that period in general, and of the classical economists in particular. "Cournot was not unfavorably placed for getting a hearing. If he failed to get it, this was wholly due to the mathematics in the book. But precisely what sort of a profession was this that laid aside a book because it was a little difficult of access?" Schumpeter, *History of Economic Analysis,* p. 463.

[9]Cf. his "letter of Malthus," May 28, 1816. Ricardo, *The Works,* vol. 3, p. 71; "letter of Mill," *ibid.,* pp. 83-84.

ical contributions.[10] We shall accept the fact that Ricardo's value and distribution theory was highly interdependent and that he tried most strenuously to reconcile one with the other. He failed, just as Marx did not succeed later on, and more than once admitted this defeat to his friends.[11] However, Chapter 1 of his *Principles* starts with a discussion of value, and the labor theory of value is at the heart of Ricardian economics. By the time Ricardo recognized the inadequacies of his value theory, he was no longer a Ricardian. In any event, few Ricardians were aware of Ricardo's ambivalence toward his labor theory.[12] Therefore, in discussing the Ricardian model, we shall disregard his later revisions and begin with the theory of value.

The Ricardian System

Value theory was of central concern to early economists because economics developed as a branch of moral philosophy. Philosophers since Aristotle and Aquinas had analyzed the problem of "value." What made certain commodities more desirable and therefore more expensive than others? The two answers that first suggested themselves were that a commodity's value was the result either of demand (or scarcity, the inverse of demand), or of its production cost. Neither answer was completely acceptable. The subjective nature of demand posed difficulties. Each person valued a commodity for a different, subjective reason. Was there nonetheless measurable "substance" inherent in each commodity? Aristotle was the first to recognize and

[10]For example, we find that Charles Gide and Charles Rist in their delightful *History of Economic Doctrines* [(New York: Heath, n.d., p. 140)], state that "Ricardo did not begin with an elaborate theory of value from which he deduced the laws of distribution, but after having discovered . . . the laws of distribution he attempted to deduce from them a theory of value." Consequently, Ricardo's value theory hardly appears in their discussion. But Eric Roll (*History of Economic Thought*, pp. 187-190) considers Ricardo's value theory his major contribution, and discusses all other aspects of Ricardian economics only in the context of their relation to his value theory.

[11]Discouraged about his inability to reconcile value and price, he wrote to McCulloch on June 13, 1820: "I sometimes think, that if I were to write the chapter on value again . . . I should acknowledge that the relative value of commodities was regulated by two causes instead of by one, namely, by the relative quantity of labour necessary to produce the commodities in question, and by the rate of profit for the time that the capital remained dormant, and until the commodities were brought to market. . . . After all, the great questions of Rent, Wages and Profits must be explained by the proportions in which the whole produce is divided between landlords, capitalists, and laborers, and which are not essentially connected with the doctrine of value." Ricardo, *The Works*, vol. 8, p. 194.

[12]It is difficult to assess how seriously Ricardo's disavowal of the labor theory is to be taken. Thus, his often quoted letter to McCulloch is followed the next year by a new edition, which contains no significant change in his value theory.

define this common substance as "utility," itself a highly subjective concept.[13] Though a particular commodity still contained different amounts of utility for different people, "utility" provided, at least superficially, a common denominator. The value of a commodity, therefore, could be defined by the amount (degree) of utility it possessed for either an individual or a group.

A paradox, which had puzzled Aristotle as it did Smith, prevented the early development of a utility value theory. Why are air and water—which are so "useful that one cannot live without them—so cheap, while gold and silver are so dear?"[14] The simple answer was first given by Fernando Galiani who sketched a rudimentary marginal utility theory in 1750. British economists, however, did not accept a solution to the paradox until the 1870s. In the meantime they were forced to look for the "true" value of a commodity in its cost of production. Unfortunately, this cost consisted of payments in money or kind to the various factors of production—land, labor, and capital, a heterogeneous lot of factors. There had to be some quantity common to all factors, it was reasoned, that made various amounts of labor, capital, and land commensurable! In the labor theory of value, the amount of labor necessary to produce a given commodity was considered the "common denominator"—the cause of value.

LABOR AS CAUSE OF VALUE

The belief that labor is the cause of all value is at least reflected in the writings of Aristotle and Aquinas. Certainly this idea was in line with Thomistic philosophy and the attitude of the Church toward economic activity. To show rigorously that the labor inherent in a commodity determines its value in a market system was much more difficult. The task of the price mechanism is to "evaluate" the commodities exchanged on the market. The intrinsic "value" inherent in a commodity must be defined as its exchange value. Because prices fluctuate in any market, but the quantity of labor inherent in a commodity remains fixed, it was necessary to account for this discrepancy of market price and (exchange) value once the market system became dominant.

[13]We shall note later that the definitive refinement of utility theory had to await the cooperation of John von Neumann and Oskar Morgenstern in the 1940s. It took the joint effort of a great mathematician and an excellent analytical economist to present a utility concept that was truly commensurable.

[14]Adam Smith, *An inquiry into the Nature and Causes of the Wealth of Nations,* (New York: Random House, 1937), book 1. chap. 4, p. 28.

William Petty and John Locke were the first English economists to attempt to develop an analytical foundation for the labor theory of value. Both writers, but especially Locke, reconciled that difference between market price and value by letting market price, the short-run price, fluctuate around the natural, long-run price. This natural price was determined by the quantity of labor necessary to produce a specific commodity.[15]

Smith, who in many respects was greatly influenced by Petty and Locke, was quite willing to accept the labor theory of value because it reflected quite accurately his own outlook. We have already seen that Smith, though a moral philosopher, was much less concerned with the predominantly philosophical question of value than with an explanation of the price mechanism as the director of economic activity.[16] When his labor theory of value failed to explain actual price phenomena, Smith easily dismissed it as applicable only to a primitive society, and adopted a cost of production theory as the determinator of the natural, long-run price.

Ricardo fully accepted Smith's major contribution, the explanation of the price system, but was primarily concerned with distribution and value theory. His logical, analytical mind balked at Smith's cavalier treatment of value theory, especially because it did not fit into Ricardo's distribution theory .

That this [the labor theory of value] is really the foundation of the exchangeable value of all things . . . is a doctrine of the utmost importance in political economy; for from no source do so many errors, and so much difference of opinion in that science proceed, as from the vague ideas which are attracted to the word value.[17]

---

[15]Neither Petty nor Locke stated explicitly that demand-determined market price fluctuated around its cost-determined natural price. Locke, who covered this subject more rigorously than Petty, developed his labor theory of value without reference to market prices in his *Two Treatises of Government*, where he attempted to demonstrate that labor was the cause of all value. In his treatise, *Some Considerations of the Lowering of Interest and Raising the Value of Money* (1691), Locke set forth a demand and supply theory of price. We can reconcile these conflicting views if we assume that Locke concerned himself only with short-run market prices in his *Considerations*, and dealt with the long-run value-determined price in his *Two Treatises*.

[16]In this respect, Smith was remarkably "modern." Most contemporary economists tend to accept price as given, without worrying much about the "intrinsic" determinators of value. Interestingly, the most outspoken critics of this pragmatic attitude are the Marxists on the one hand, and such "right wing" critics of modern economics as Lewis Haney and Ludwig von Mises on the other.

[17]Ricardo, *The Works*, vol. 1, p. 13.

To Ricardo, economics was essentially an analysis of the laws of value and distribution, which operated within the laws of production determined by Smith's market system. For the rest of his life, Ricardo worked on deriving laws of distribution that would be in agreement with a labor theory of value and yet follow logically from the price phenomena of a market economy. As Ricardo developed his distribution and value theory interdependently and progressively, he modified one and then the other to eliminate all possible pitfalls. He did recognize toward the end that he had failed, and we know today that he had to fail.

What then were the fundamental difficulties inherent in a labor theory of value? The first difficulty was presented by the necessity to account for actual or potential differences in price and value (i.e., the amount of labor inherent in a commodity). The second arose because in order to leave labor as the only source of value, land and capital had to be eliminated as independent and necessary factors of production.

There were two possible and not mutually exclusive explanations for the discrepancy between market price and value: (1) Short-run fluctuations in demand cause compensating fluctuations in the market price, which oscillate around the long-run "value" of the commodity — that is, the natural price. This explanation of short-run price fluctuations is found in Locke, as well as in Smith, Ricardo, and Marx. In his chapter on value, Ricardo seemed to accept implicitly Smith's distinction between short-run and long-run prices. Because Ricardo was mainly concerned with long-run phenomena, there was no need to acknowledge market fluctuations explicitly. However the phenomena underlying short-run fluctuations are discussed extensively in his chapter IV, "Of Natural and Market Price."

In making labor the foundation of the value of commodities, and the comparative quantity of labor which is necessary to their production, the rule which determines the respective quantities of goods which shall be given in exchange for each other, we must not be supposed to deny the accidental and temporary deviations of the actual or market price of commodities from this, their primary and natural price.[18]

(2) Long-run discrepancies between price and value result from

[18]*Ibid.,* p. 88.

monopolistic practices. Ricardo took care of such an eventuality by disregarding it—monopoly was not even mentioned by name in his chapter on value[19]—or by defining it away—he permitted only "peculiar wines" and "works of art" to have the capacity to obtain monopoly prices.[20] By disregarding monopoly price, Ricardo really begs the question. The ability of given groups in society to establish monopolistic pricing practices by successful manipulation of institutional devices provides one major source of economic profit (or surplus, or excess profit) independent of the cost of production! Only through his treatment of monopoly price as a special and, in the long run, not significant case of price theory could Ricardo (and Marx) lay the foundation of a theory that equated value with labor.[21] Thus was a pattern set for the next one hundred years. During this period English-speaking economists became thoroughly committed to a model that operated effectively only under the assumption of competition. Their refusal to let empirical realities interfere with their cherished theories prevented the development of useful analyses of the consequences of monopolistic practices until the 1930s. This myopia also prevented the establishment of a theory that could recognize the exploitation of labor by capital as only one and not necessarily the most significant form of exploitation; the exploitation of consumers by monopolistic groups (e.g., oligopolistic corporations, giant unions, guilds in the form of "professional associations" such as the AMA) is until this day not handled too successfully by modern theory.[22]

[19]Ricardo gives the following implicit definition of monopoly:

"There are some commodities, the value of which is determined by their scarcity alone. No labor can increase the quantity of such goods, and therefore their value cannot be lowered by an increased supply. Some rare statues and pictures, scarce books or coins, wines of peculiar quality . . . are all of this description. . . . These commodities, however, form a very small part of the mass of commodities daily exchanged in the market. . . .

In speaking then of commodities, of their exchangeable value, and of the laws which regulate their relative prices, *we mean always such commodities only as can be increased in quantity by |labor|.*" (Our italics.)

Ricardo, *The Works,* vol. 1, p. 12.

[20]*Ibid.,* p. 250.

[21]Note, therefore, that the labor theory of value is thus merely a special case of a general cost of production theory—i.e., a theory that equates value in the long run with the cost of production.

[22]Ricardo's refusal to consider monopoly price as a significant phenomenon had also a lasting indirect effect upon American business ideology, which until today often refused to recognize any form of sellers' monopoly except for cases equivalent to "peculiar" wines and rare pieces of art.

As explained above, Ricardo met the first difficulty inherent in the labor theory of value by virtually disregarding monopoly price and by accepting Smith's distinction between short-run, demand-dictated market price and long-run, cost-determined natural price. Only the natural price expressed the true value of a commodity. An explanation that neglects monopoly pricing is now entirely unacceptable. It should be noted that oligopoly, in the modern sense, was not sufficiently significant during Ricardo's time to cause serious concern or to elicit vigorous criticism for his failure to deal with it.

The second difficulty was far more damaging to Ricardo's theory because he found it impossible to reduce the three costs of production to one. A labor theory adherent must show conclusively that the returns to land or capital either do not constitute payments rewarding necessary contributions to the production process, or are merely indirect payments to labor because these very factors can be reduced to stored-up labor.

Ricardo used both approaches. He was brilliantly successful in developing his theory of "differential rent," which turned the payments to the landlord from a cost of production into an unearned reward for the fortuitous consequences of ownership and population pressure. He was less successful with his vague, unclear, and often modified capital theory, which defined capital as embodied labor and denied it any productivity of its own. Payments to the capitalists are, therefore, either the unmerited reward for ownership or merely equal in value to the amount of labor embodied in capital. Ricardo shied away from the first answer, which would have led him straight into a theory of surplus value and exploitation, but found the second answer equally unsatisfactory.[23] The difficulty of reconciling the postulated nonproductivity of capital with the obvious differences in the profit earned by various firms in accordance with their various capital structures made Ricardo in the end despair of the labor theory of value.

Publicly and professionally, however, the labor theory of value remained an essential part of his system. In his last edition, which appeared two years before his death, we still find his value theory essentially unchanged.

The value of a commodity, or the quantity of any other commodity for which

[23]See again his letter to McCulloch.

it will exchange depends on the relative quantity of labor which is necessary for its production, and not on the greater or less compensation which is paid for that labour.[24]

Once labor had been made the sole denominator of value, there still remained the task of fashioning a yardstick to measure the qualitative and quantitative heterogeneous amounts of labor embodied in a commodity, and furthermore, to make this measure commensurate with the "natural price." Ricardo devoted the first two sections of his chapter on value to this task.

On first glance, the wages paid to labor ought to be an excellent indication of the quantity and quality of labor inherent in a commodity, and hence of its value. This approach was taken by Adam Smith, who simply equated the amount of labor in a commodity with the amount of commodities (i.e., wages) commanded by labor for its "toil and trouble." The difficulty with this approach lies in the fact that wages vary over time and place, and therefore the value of identical commodities would similarly vary. Ricardo recognized the weakness and criticized Smith for failing to note the difference between the value of a commodity determined *by* labor and the value *of* labor, which is just another commodity and whose price—that is, wages—is, of course, subject to short-run market variations.[25]

Is not the value of labor equally variable [as wages]; being not only affected, as all other things are, by the proportion between the supply and demand, which uniformly varies with every change in the condition of the community, but also by the varying price of food . . . on which the wages of labor are expended?[26]

If wages thus did not provide a reliable yardstick of the amount of labor inherent in a commodity, only "time" was left as a straightforward measuring device of the quantity of labor realized in a commodity.[27]

[24]Heading of Chapter 1, section 1, *The Works*, vol. 1, p. 11.

[25]Marx makes this distinction more explicit by distinguishing between the commodity "labor power" (i.e., the ability to work) sold by labor and the "realized amount of labor" in a commodity, which determines its value.

[26]Ricardo, *The Works*, vol. 1, chap. 1, sec. 1, p. 15.

[27]Considering that the recognition of time as a measuring device is fundamental for an understanding of Ricardo's theory, there are amazingly few explicit references to time as the measure of the quantity of labor in his book. In section 1 of Chapter 1 he

If labor time was to measure the amount of labor embodied in a commodity, variations in the speed and skill found among workers had to be accounted for. Ricardo addressed himself to the variations in the quality of labor in the second section of his first chapter:

In speaking, however, of labor, as being the foundation of all value, and the relative quantities of labor as almost exclusively[28] determining the relative value of commodities, it must not be supposed to be inattentive to the different qualities of labor, and the difficulty of comparing an hour's or a day's labor, in one employment, with the same duration of labor in another. The estimation in which different qualities of labor are held, comes soon to be adjusted in the market with sufficient precision for all practical purposes, and depends much on the comparative skill of the laborer, and intensity of the labor performed. . . . If a day's labor of a working jeweler be more valuable than a day's labour of a common laborer, it has long ago been adjusted, and placed in its proper position in the scale of value.[29]

Variations in the quality of labor were recognized by customary, presumably market-determined, wage differentials. Ricardo's extremely vague answer to problems posed by the heterogeneous nature of labor is quite unsatisfactory, as Marx later recognized, but contemporary critics did not object to this particular aspect of Ricardian labor theory.

Of much greater importance was Ricardo's effort to develop the concept of capital as the embodiment of past labor.

---

quotes approvingly a passage of Smith that ends with the sentence: "It is natural that what is usually the produce of two days', or two hours' labor, should be worth double of what is usually the produce of one day's, or one hour's labor." Then Ricardo adds "That this [the above definition] is really the foundation of the exchangeable value of all things, excepting those which cannot be increased by human industry, is a doctrine of the utmost importance in political economy." Ricardo, *The Works*, vol. 1, sec. 1, p. 13. The scarcity of references in Ricardo to time as the critical measuring device is less surprising if we recall once more that Ricardo was concerned chiefly with discussing those aspects of economic theory wherein he disagreed with Smith (or Malthus). Wherever he accepted Smith's writing, he did not believe it necessary to call special attention to his agreement.

[28]The first and second editions do not contain "almost exclusively." This is one of the few acknowledgments in the third edition of his dissatisfaction with the labor theory of value referred to above.

[29]Ricardo, *The Works*, vol. 1, pp. 20-21. Note that Ricardo does not say how the respective value of a skilled jeweler's contribution to the work process will be measured in comparison with the contribution of an unskilled worker. Apparently Ricardo meant that the "proper position on the scales of value" of their respective wages would be adjusted by the market; but this is precisely the position Smith held and it constitutes an abandonment of the labor theory.

Not only the labour applied immediately to commodities affects their value, but the labour also which is bestowed on the implements, tools and buildings, with which such labour is assisted.[30]

Ricardo did not examine the process of creating capital goods, nor did he analyze the institutional nature of the return on capital. Rather, he took the existence of capital as given, and suggested that even in primitive societies capital goods had been used in the productive process. The return on capital, he maintained, was proportional to the amount of labor contained in it.

Suppose the weapon necessary to kill the beaver was constructed with much more labor than that necessary to kill the deer, on account of the greater difficulty of approaching near to the former animal and the consequent necessity of its being more true to its mark; one beaver would naturally be of more value than two deer, and precisely for this reason, that more labour would, on the whole, be necessary to its destruction. . . . All the implements necessary to kill the beaver and deer might belong to one class of men, and the labour employed in their destruction might be furnished by another class; *still, their comparative prices would be in proportion to the actual labour bestowed, both on the formation of the capital, and on the destruction of the animals.*[31]

In a more advanced society, the value of a commodity still varied in accordance with the quantity of labor used up in the creation of the capital goods involved in the production and transportation process, as well as in the actual physical production of the commodity.[32] The only differences in the productive process between a primitive and an "advanced" society lay in the increasingly restricted ownership of fixed capital by one class, the capitalist. Although the value of a commodity is determined by its sole cost factor—labor—capital

---

[30]*The Works,* vol. 1, heading chap. 1, sec. 3, *Ibid.,* p. 22. It should be noted that in his third edition Ricardo omitted a long introductory piece in section 3 of the second edition that criticized Smith for limiting his labor theory of value to "'that early and rude state of society, which precedes both the accumulation of stock and the appropriation of land.'" It is quite likely that by 1821 Ricardo shared at least some of Smith's misgiving regarding the application of the labor theory of value to a capitalistic market economy. (Cf. *The Works,* note 3, p. 22)

[31]*The Works, Ibid.,* pp. 23-24, our italics. Compare this with the beaver-deer example through which Smith advanced his labor theory applicable to primitive periods only.

[32]*Ibid.* pp. 24-25.

receives the payments for "stored-up" labor in the form of profits[33] and labor receives payments for current labor in the form of wages.

This reasoning led Ricardo into a discussion of the rules that govern the distribution of the payments for cost of production between labor and capital, and became part of his distribution theory. He had to anticipate the conclusion reached later in *The Principles* in order to attempt an analytical explanation of the differences in the value of commodities that resulted from the variety of capital structures and the "payback" periods.

Ricardo wrestled unsuccessfully with the problem of distribution based on the labor theory in his chapter on value. He finally admitted that the quantity of labor alone was not a sufficient explanation of value, but that the duration of the investment process[34] as well as the capital structure[35] determine value.

It appears then that the division of capital into different proportions of fixed and circulating capital, employed in different trades, introduces a considerable modification to the rule, [the labor theory of value] which is of universal application when labour [alone] is almost exclusively employed in production. . . .[36]

It appears too, that in proportion to the durability of capital employed in any kind of production, the relative prices of these commodities on which such durable capital is employed, will vary inversely as wages; they will fall as wages rise, and rise as wages fall; and, on the contrary, those which are produced chiefly by labour with less fixed capital, or with fixed capital of a less durable character . . . . will rise as wages rise, and fall as wages fall.[37]

Ricardo's admission that capital is productive and that the quantity of labor does not solely determine value should have signified his abandonment of the labor theory of value, precisely as Smith had discarded this theory at a very similar point in his analysis. Ricardo, however, implied that the impact of the structure and durability of capital on value would balance itself, and that, therefore, the quantity

[33]The classical economists and especially Ricardo did not make any distinction between profit and interest; whenever Ricardo uses the term "profit," contemporary economists would use the term "interest" as signifying "return on capital invested."

[34]Here Ricardo comes very close to the modern capital theory developed by von Bohm-Bawerk.

[35]That is, the ratio of fixed to circulating capital.

[36]Ricardo, *The Works,* vol. 1, pp. 37-38.

[37]*Ibid.,* p. 43. This phenomenon is called today the "Ricardo effect."

of labor embodied in a commodity was at least proportional to its value.[38]

At this point, Ricardo's position is not strong enough for the heavy ideological load the labor theory of value was asked to carry.[39] If capital is productive, then labor has no moral claims on the "full product" and analytical tools must be developed to show exactly what proportion of the value is due to labor. If, furthermore, the time span and depth of capital investment determine its reward, then one can safely anticipate that by lengthening the "roundabout" method of production, the proportion of value due to capital can be increased over time, no matter how small it may have been in Ricardo's time. Clearly, Ricardo, the first rigorous proponent of the labor theory of value, took also the first steps toward burying it.[40]

Ricardo's Distribution Theory

Whereas Smith and Malthus were mainly interested in determining the law of production, Ricardo's main interest concerned the distribution of the national product among the three factors of production. He believed that "to determine the laws which regulate this distribution is the principal problem in political economy."[41] Ricardo turned first to rent because he had to show "whether the appropriation of land, and the consequent creation of rent, will occasion any variation in the relative value of commodities, independently of the quantity of labour necessary to production."[42]

In his usual awkward fashion, Ricardo began his discussion by accepting the physiocratic concept of rent handed down by Smith and Malthus. Rent "is that portion of the produce of the earth which is paid to the landlord for the use of the original and indestructible

---

[38]Schumpeter, who is kinder to Ricardo than we are, maintains that Ricardo thought of his labor theory as merely providing an approximation to the true value of a commodity.

[39]In a recent Russian text, *Material Incentives for Workers in U.S.S.R.*, F. S. Velselkov (Moscow: Gospolitiz das, 1962), the entire section on economic analysis is based upon the labor theory of value.

[40]In a brief note toward the end of his discussion of value, Ricardo actually completely disavowed his labor theory. "Mr. Malthus appears to think that it is a part of my doctrine that *the cost and value of a thing should be the same; it is, if he means by cost 'cost of production' including profits.*" (Our italics.) Ricardo, *The Works,* vol. 1, p. 47. It is rather typical of the struggle over "what Ricardo really meant" that Alfred Marshall took this footnote as the basis for an attempt to "rehabilitate" Ricardo and to infer that Ricardo did not really adhere to a labor theory. Alfred Marshall, *Principles of Economics,* 8th ed. (London: Macmillan, 1946), p. 816, esp. note 1.

[41]Ricardo, *The Works,* vol. 1, p. 5

[42]*Ibid.* p. 67.

powers of the soil."[43] From this definition of rent as "scarcity rent" and thus a cost of production, Ricardo quickly developed the concept of differential rent by applying the law of diminishing returns to the utilization of land.[44]

On the first settling of a country, in which there is abundance of rich and fertile land . . . no one would pay for the use of the land, when there was abundant quantity not yet appropriated, and, therefore, at the disposal of whosoever might choose to cultivate it.[45]

Figure **3.1** The Emergence of Rent

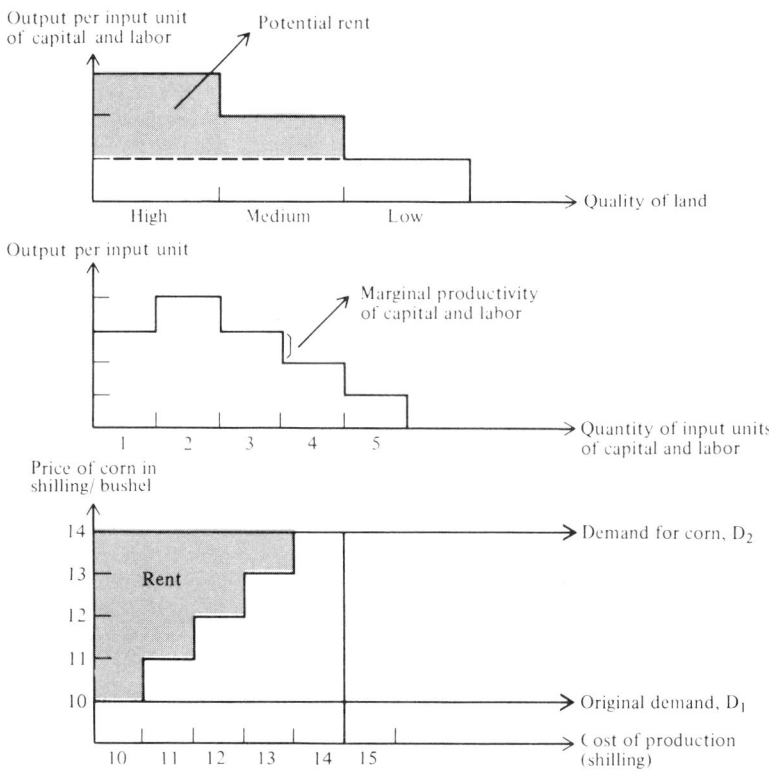

[43]*Ibid.*
[44]Ricardo was not the first to apply the diminishing returns to rent. Malthus, in his *An Inquiry into the Nature and Progress of Rent* (1815), anticipated Ricardo, and Ricardo gave him full credit for it (Ricardo, *The Works,* vol. 1, p. 398). Turgot, of course, anticipated both Ricardo and Malthus, with an exceptionally clear derivation of different rent. The fact that Turgot's name does not appear anywhere in Ricardo's and Malthus' writings is another example of "Anglo-Saxon originality."
[45]Ricardo, *The Works,* vol. 1, p. 69.

As the population increased, however, there was an increasing demand for food, and at the higher price, additional land of lower quality could now be brought into production. This meant, however, that those who produced on land of high quality would incur a surplus, which was appropriated by the landlord in the form of rent.

It is only, then, because land is not unlimited in quantity and uniform in quality, and because . . . land of an inferior quality . . . is called into cultivation, that rent is ever paid for the use of it. . . . When land . . . of [less] fertility is taken into cultivation rent immediately commences on that of the first quality, and the amount of that rent will depend on the difference in quality.[46]

If we let the difference in the quality of land be represented by a homogeneous step function, we can express Ricado's concept by the diagram on page 81. As the demand changes from D_1 to D_2, *we see that rent occurs immediately. This relationship can be expressed in tabular form:*

Table **3.1** COST OF RAISING ONE BUSHEL OF CORN ON LAND OF QUALITY

	I	II	III
PRICE		COST	
	1s	2s	3s
1s	No rent	No production	No production
2s	1s rent	No rent	No production
3s	2s rent	1s rent	No rent

Only the increasing demand for food, along with the variations in the quality and location of the soil generate rent, and only the fact of ownership enables the landlord to appropriate this surplus without any effort of his own.

The variation in the quality and location of fertile land was, however, only one of the factors that enabled the landlord to collect rent from his tenant, the farmer capitalist.[47] The other rent-producing

---

[46]*Ibid.*, p. 70.

[47]Actually, the geographic location of land, which enables farms close to urban areas to transport their goods to the market with little additional cost, was introduced by Ricardo as a separate and original factor. Malthus and others (Sir Edward West, James Anderson) had been approaching a differential rent theory by exclusively considering the heterogeneous nature of land. The German economist J. H. von Thünen,

factor lay in the varying intensity of cultivation open to the farmer as an alternative to bringing poorer soil into production.

It often, and, indeed, commonly happens that before No. 2, 3, 4, or 5 or even inferior lands are cultivated, capital can be employed more productively on those lands which are already in cultivation. It may perhaps be found, that by doubling the original capital employed on No. 1, though the produce will not be doubled . . . it may be increased by eighty-five [percent] . . . .

In such case, capital will be preferably employed on the old land, and will equally create a rent; *for rent is always the difference between the produce obtained by the employment of two equal quantities of capital and labor.* If, with a capital of £1000 a tenant [farmer] obtain 100 quarters of wheat from his land, and by the employment of a second [dose of] capital of £1000 he obtains a further return of eighty-five, his landlord would have the power at the expiration of his lease, of obliging him to pay fifteen quarters [of wheat] . . . for additional rent; for there cannot be two rates of profit. If he is satisfied with a diminution of fifteen quarters in the return for his second £1000, it is because no employment more profitable can be found for it. The common rate of profit would be in that proportion.[48]

This quotation illustrates beautifully to what extent the law of diminishing returns underlies the entire theory of differential rent. The principle of diminishing returns is less explicitly expressed when the consequences of using increasing units of the first factor—heterogeneous land—are analyzed.[49] However, the fact that both rent-producing factors, extensive use of land and extensive use of labor or capital, are subject to the law of diminishing returns can easily be demonstrated by merely substituting units of labor for the units I, II, or III of land. The data remain the same.[50]

Ricardo's contemporary, developed further Ricardo's concept of differential rent due to location. He developed successfully both a complete value and production system based on marginal utility about fifty years before Jevons. His books, however, had little influence in Germany and none at all in Great Britain.

[48]Ricardo, *The Works,* pp. 71-72. (Our italics.)

[49]The very fact that even homogeneous land would give rise to rent, due to the principle of proportionality, was first clearly developed by von Thünen.

[50]One could conceive now of a four-dimensional matrix, similar to the results obtained in a four factor analysis of variance, that could express simultaneously the interdependence of Ricardo's rent theory. If we plot the various qualities of land along the x axis, doses of capital and labor along the y axis, the cost of applying "i" doses on land of quality "j" in the xy plane, and price along the z axis, we obtain a solid. Associated with

From Ricardo's discussion, we can easily understand how the concept of marginal productivity flowed naturally from the principle of diminishing returns. While Ricardo did not fully develop a marginal productivity theory, he developed it sufficiently to appreciate its implication for his value theory. Certainly if identical units of labor produced different volumes of a commodity, then a theory that measured the values of a commodity by the amount of labor embodied in it was apparently in serious analytical difficulties.[51] Though Ricardo had been successful in eliminating rent from the cost of production, this solution now threatened his labor theory from another direction.

every point on our surface is then a specific quantum rent, for example: no rents at points a, b, c; 1s rent at point f; 4s rent at point d; no production at point e.

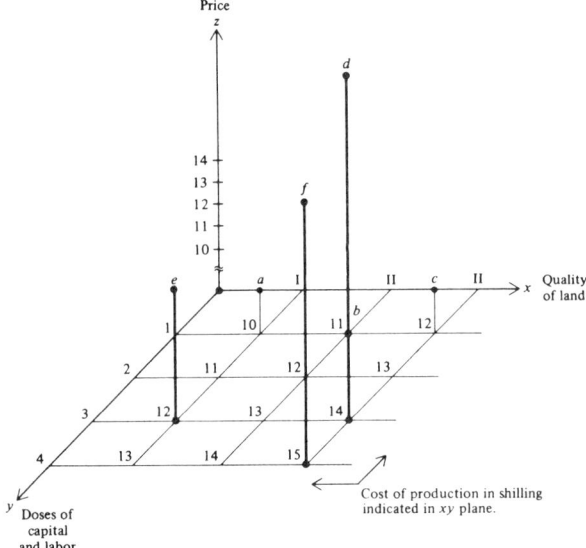

For those who have difficulties with multidimensional diagrams, we can substitute three matrices presenting the relationship between the various factors:

Cost of raising corn on land

Dose of capital and labor	I	II	III	IV
1	10	11	12	13
2	11	12	13	14
3	12			
4	13			
	etc.			

[51]Marx recognized this, but solved the problem by rejecting the principle of diminishing returns. This "solution" has created many problems for Soviet engineers and economists.

Ricardo met this problem by redefining his value theory with respect to the margin of production. Rent ceases to exist only on the margin of production, therefore, and land is no longer a cost factor at this point. Hence only the quantity of labor *on the margin of production* determines value.

The exchangeable value of all commodities *whether they be manufactured, or the produce of the mines, or the produce of the land,* is always regulated, not by the less quantity of labor that will suffice for their production under circumstances highly favorable, and exclusively enjoyed by those who have peculiar facilities of production; but by the greater quantity of labour necessarily bestowed on their production by those who have no such facilities; by those who continue to produce them under the most unfavorable circumstances.[52]

With this Ricardo carried his theory of differential rent far along the lines that ultimately led to the development of the neoclassical marginal productivity theory;[53] Ricardo, at this point, certainly came very close to the Marshallian concept of quasirent. It is not surprising that the unusually generous Marshall insisted that his own contribution to value and rent theory was already implicit in Ricardo.[54] Ricardo, however, in his typical manner, dropped this promising marginal approach at the end of his Chapter 2, and returned to it only sporadically. His theory of rent, his major contribution, is intermittently and at specific instances linked with the rest of his distribution theory.

During his life, high corn prices and high rents were one of the major causes of political controversy. Although Ricardo showed that high rents followed high corn prices rather than having caused them, he also demonstrated that landlords, and only landlords, benefited from the increasing population pressure and from economic development. This argument was political dynamite, and the Ricardian theory of rent became a very practical and powerful tool in the struggle between the rising business class and the landed establishment.

This class struggle only confirmed the implications of Ricardian theory. Smith's "natural order," whereby all classes and individuals

---

[52]Ricardo, *The Works,* vol. 1, p. 73.
[53]See note 47.
[54]Marshall *Principles of Economics,* appendix 1, pp. 813 ff.

gained from the realization of each man's aspiration, was replaced by a more antagonistic society in which the interest of the landlord clashed with the interests of labor and capital. Ricardo himself vigorously took part in this struggle, and his foreign trade theory was actually a very explicit policy proposal to lower food prices and help business and labor at the expense of the landlord.

If the landlords' interests were at odds with those of the rest of society, could labor and capital have common interests? Decidedly not, said Ricardo: Wages and profits were inversely related; however, the limitations imposed upon labor and capital by nature did not give them enough freedom of action to engage in a violent class struggle. His wage theory was a successful marriage of Malthusian population theory and Ricardian rent theory. It provided the basis for later developments in classical and neoclassical wage theory, and it also became an ideological weapon in the hands of businessmen in the struggle against the pressures for social legislation. Business ideology converted the Malthus-Ricardo subsistence theory into a starker and more deterministic philosophy. Ricardo's quantity theory of labor coupled with the Malthusian population theory made reproduction and subsistence of human beings the only cost of production.

Labor, like all other things which are purchased and sold, and which may be increased or diminished in quantity, has its natural and its market price. The natural price of labor is that price which is necessary to enable the laborers, one with another, to subsist and to perpetuate their race, without either increase or diminution.[55]

Thus, the cost of "producing" (Marx called it "reproducing") a worker determined the natural value of labor and hence the average wage level. In the short run, market forces would produce fluctuations of wages around their long-run value in exactly the same manner that market prices of a commodity always oscillate around natural price.

The market price of labor is the price which is really paid for it, from the natural operation of the proportion of the supply to the demand; labor is dear when it is scarce, and cheap when it is plentiful. However much the market price of labor may deviate from its natural price, it has, like commodities, a tendency to conform to it.

[55]Ricardo, *The Works,* vol. 1, p.93.

It is when the market price of labor exceeds its natural price, that the condition of the laborer is flourishing and happy, that he has in his power . . . to rear a healthy and numerous family. When, however, by the encouragement which wages give to the increase of population, the number of laborers is increased, wages again fall to their natural price, and indeed from a reaction sometimes fall below it.

When the market price of labor is below its natural price, the condition of the laborer is most wretched. . . . It is only after their privations have reduced their number . . . that the market price of labor will rise to its natural price, and that the laborer will have the moderate comforts which the natural rate of wages will afford.[56]

The natural price of labor, however, was not necessarily constant over time, nor was it set at the absolute minimum required to keep labor alive. Ricardo, very much like Malthus, left at least the possibility open that, through a chain of fortuitous events, the natural price of labor might increase. [57]

The power of the laborer to support himself . . . does not depend on the quantity of money which he may receive for wages, but on the quantity of food, necessaries, and conveniences become essential to him from habit, which that money will purchase.[58]

Notwithstanding the tendency of wages to conform to their natural rate, their market rate may, in an improving society, for an indefinite period, be constantly above it; for no sooner may the impulse, *which an increased capital gives to a new demand* for labor be obliged, then another increase of capital may produce the same effect; *and thus, if the increase of capital be gradual and constant, the demand for labor* may give a continued stimulus to an increase of people.[59]

A rich society with a high and increasing rate of capital formation could, therefore, contrive to create a demand for labor sufficiently strong to bring about a rising subsistence level for labor. Ricardo, however, did not believe that the long-run forces underlying capitalist

[56]*Ibid., p.94.*

[57]Marx left the same possibility open, although the Marxian mythology had to reject such a development completely.

[58]Ricardo, *The Works,* vol.1, p.93.

[59]*Ibid.,* pp. 94-95. (Our italics.) Note that Ricardo accepted in this passage Smith's view of a growth demand of labor due to an increase in capital.

development would ever permit labor to develop "habits" that would permit wages to rise. As the population increased and less and less fertile land was available, rent and, consequently food prices, increased; the increase in food prices had to lead to an increase in money wages and consequently to a fall in profits because wages and capital were inversely related. The decline in profits would, presumably, lead to a reduced demand for labor.

In the natural advance of society, the wages of labor will have a tendency to fall . . . for the supply of laborers will continue to increase at the same rate, whilst the demand for them will increase at a slower rate. . .. If, then, the money wages of labor should fall whilst every commodity on which the wages of labor were expended rose, the laborer would be doubly affected, and would be soon totally deprived of subsistence. Instead, therefore, of the money wages of labor falling, they would rise, but they would not rise sufficiently to enable the laborer to purchase as many comforts and necessaries as he did before the rise in the price of those commodities. . . .

Notwithstanding, then, that the laborer would be really worse paid, yet this increase in his wage would necessarily diminish the profits of the manufacturer, for his goods would sell at no higher prices, and yet the expense of producing them would be increased.

It appears, then, that the same cause which raises rent, namely, the increasing difficulty of providing an additional quantity of food with the same proportional quantity of labor [i.e., the law of diminishing returns] will also raise [money] wages.[60]

The only way the worker could escape being squeezed between the forces of rising population, rising cost of food production, and declining demand was by restricting the size of his family. Ricardo believed that the English Poor Laws tended to encourage procreation. He advocated, therefore, their elimination ruthlessly in a manner that anticipated many of the arguments of Social Darwinism.[61]

Wage payments, in Ricardian wage theory, constituted essentially the transmission belt through which the rising rent payments would

[60]*Ibid.,* pp. 101-102.
[61]It is of some interest to compare Ricardo's views on social legislation of his time — quite typical of the businessmen and their party — with the views expressed by the Tory Pitt in 1796, whom Ricardo quoted disapprovingly. Pitt considered large families a benefit to the state and, therefore, considered that the state had a moral duty to protect those who "after having enriched their country with a number of children, have a claim upon its assistance for support." (Quoted by Ricardo, *The Works,* vol.1, p.107.)

affect the rate of profit. Although wages and rent were inversely related, labor was merely an innocent bystander in the struggle between landlord and capitalism.

Ricardo, himself the capitalist *par excellence,* failed nevertheless to examine the nature of profit.[62] Rather, he took the institution of profit for granted, and devoted himself to the analysis of "permanent variations in the rate of profit," and to the impact of profit on value. As noted in the discussion of value theory, Ricardo finally was forced to admit that capital added to the value of a commodity, and that profit, therefore, was more than a payment for embodied labor. Profit seemed to be a residual payment to the capitalist after the disbursement of wages and rent.

We have seen that the price [and value] of corn is regulated by the quantity of labor necessary to produce it, with that portion of capital which pays no rent. We have seen, too, that all manufactured commodities rise and fall in price, in proportion as more or less labor becomes necessary to their production. Neither the farmer who cultivates that quality[63] of land; which regulates price, nor the manufacturer . . . sacrifice any portion of the produce for rent. The whole value of their commodities is divided into two portions only: one constitutes the profits of stock, the other the wages of labor.[64]

The wage-profit ratio was affected in the short-run by the variation in the demand and supply of labor, and in the long-run by the changes in the structure of society caused by economic growth and development. Although Ricardo, as all classical economists, was concerned chiefly with the long-run adjustments to economic changes, his analysis was primarily static. He did not consider any changes in the structure of society, but rather expected the long-run trends to manifest themselves under conditions of *ceteris paribus.* The few exceptions to his static approach occur in his discussions on the long-run profit and wage expectations in Chapters 2, 3, and 4.

[62]Let us state again that the term "profit," as used by the classical economists, is identical with the term "interest" used by modern economists. As used by contemporary businessmen, "profit" signifies the excess of bookkeeping resources over cost. This "book profit" may generally contain "interest"—i.e., return on investment, plus other distribution items. As used by Ricardo, the term "interest" referred exclusively to the amount of money businessmen paid to investors.

[63]We have substituted the word "quality" used in the first two editions for "quantity" used in the last edition as more fitting.

[64]Ricardo, *The Works,* vol.1, p.110.

Summary and Conclusion

The dynamic factor in the Ricardian model is entirely Malthusian. It was the growth of population and the law of diminishing returns that determined Ricardo's pessimistic anticipation of increasing population pressure, rising rents, rising money wages, and falling real wages and profits. Technological improvements seemed the only check to this development.

The natural tendency of profits then is to fall; for, in the progress of society and wealth, the additional quantity of food required is obtained by the sacrifice of more and more labor. This tendency . . . is happily checked at repeated intervals by the improvements in machinery . . . as well as by the discoveries in the science of agriculture. . . . The rise in the price of necessaries and in the wages of labor is, however, limited; for as soon as wages should be equal . . . [to] the whole receipts of the farmer [capitalist], there must be an end of accumulation; for no capital can yield any profit whatever, and no additional labor can be demanded. . . . Long indeed before this period, the very low rate of profits will have arrested all accumulation, and almost the whole produce of the country, after paying the laborers, will be the property of the owners of land.[65]

Because capital, both in its circulating and its fixed forms, constituted demand for labor,[66] a declining rate of capital accumulation might have been expected to cause at least short-run unemployment. Ricardo rejected such a notion, however, and relied upon the short-run effect of a falling wage rate and the long-run effect of a halt in the population growth to maintain both employment and the profitability of capital. Because he had, however, accepted the fact of continuous growth in other passages of his book, the foreboding of the doom of

[65]*Ibid.* pp. 120-121.

[66]In his third edition Chapter 31, "On Machinery," Ricardo dropped the Smithian assumption that fixed capital represented demand for labor and accepted instead machinery as a replacement of labor. "I am convinced that the substitution of machinery for human labor is often very injurious to the interest of the class of laborers." From the recognition of capital as a substitute for labor, Ricardo should have approached straightforwardly to a theory of unemployment. As a matter of fact, his analysis of the employment impact of consumer durable expenditures (purchase of luxuries) or service expenditures (hiring of menials) anticipated, if not Keynes, at least Lloyd George. But he did not carry this analysis further, and the whole chapter was pretty much an afterthought, without any organic connection with the rest of the text. Perhaps if he had lived longer, this chapter might have provided a basis for the rejection of Say's Law.

the system short of structural changes (e.g., expropriation of land-lords) was apparent.

It is difficult to understand how readily Ricardo accepted the Smith-Say law of the market. Ricardo, better than anyone else, knew to what extent business activity depended upon speculative profit anticipation. Yet he denied the existence of underconsumption and unemployment, and never included "profit anticipation" in his model.

M. Say has . . . most satisfactorily shown, that there is no amount of capital which may not be employed in a country, because demand is only limited by production. *No man produces, but with a view to consume or sell,* and he never sells, but with an intention to purchase some other commodity. . . . By producing, then, he necessarily becomes either the consumer of his own goods, or the purchaser and consumer of the goods of some other person.[67]

By accepting Say's law and criticizing Malthus' theory of crisis, Ricardo prevented any further development of a theory of economic development. He banished the theory of business crisis to the economic underworld where it stayed, separated from the mainstream of economic development for the next century. Although Ricardo's treatment of the law of the market was, to him at least, one of the less significant aspects of his work, it was his influence that guided Western economics from an analysis of economic development into a sterile preoccupation with value and static distribution theory.

[67]Ricardo, *The Works,* vol. 1, p. 290. (Our italics.)

4

THE
RECONSTRUCTION
OF SOCIETY

No economist is ever entirely removed from his society and his time. However, the link between economic ideology and public policy varies widely. There is no better proof of this general comment than the development in both society and economic thought in the decades following the publication of the *Wealth of Nations*. Many factors contributed to social change. First, there was the Industrial Revolution. Second, there was the cataclysm of the French Revolution and the Napoleonic Wars, which had the most profound consequences for both the economic and the political development of west-central Europe. Third, there was intellectual ferment, ranging from the hypotheses of Malthus to those of Georg Friedrich List and from Jeremy Bentham to Marx. It was a period of exciting social and economic speculation in England and on the continent, to which many others contributed. The roster includes James Mill and his even more gifted son John Stuart, and of course Ricardo, the millionaire friend of Malthus. Across the channel, Say played a significant role as translator of Smith and creator of an atmosphere sympathetic to laissez-faire liberalism.

Despite the intellectual pessimism of much of classical economic thought, a great deal of piecemeal effort, primarily legislative, began slowly to rebuild the social bonds within the community. In asserting this, we are not proclaiming a new bourgeois revisionism, nor are we denying the accuracy or usefulness of those who protested the brutalities of nineteenth-century society. Robert Owen, Marx, and others deserve our continuing respect. Still, in a broad, amorphous, limited way, leaders from every level and social class worked toward a new social synthesls. Every decade of the nineteenth century saw an increasing amount of legislation dealing with social and economic problems. It is easy, but not fair, to measure the shortcomings of this activity by present-day standards. We should remember that "every generation is equidistant from eternity." We should hope to overlook neither the pain of this transformation into modern times nor the efforts to ameliorate these pains, for both are part of the total picture. In all ages in Western history, men have treated each other harshly for the good of their souls.

The Industrial Revolution

Our interpretation of the Industrial Revolution is drawn from many sources, and especially from English history, which furnishes the most complete literature. No one can or should overlook the work of H. L. Beales, Thomas S. Ashton, Phyllis Deane, or the older works of Paul Mantoux, Arnold Toynbee, and John and Barbara Hammond.[1] These writers and others suggest certain broad conclusions we should like to reemphasize. It still is widely believed that a human Garden of Eden existed in the eighteenth century until the industrial takeoff. Then we were "driven out once again to wander in misery, if not in sin." Even Marx was ambivalent about this "original state." Analytically, he had to acknowledge the tremendous contribution of bourgeois production; emotionally, he could see the past only in terms of social exploitation. We know of no place in which Marx indicated concern with the growth of population during the nineteenth century

[1] Hugh L. Beales, *The Industrial Revolution* (London: Cass, 1958); Thomas S. Ashton, *The Industrial Revolution 1760-1830* (New York: Oxford University Press, 1955), Paul Mantoux, *op. cit.*; Arnold Toynbee, *Lectures on the Industrial Revolution* (New York: Humboldt Publishing Co., 1884); John L. and Barbara Hammond, *The Rise of Modern Industry*, 5th ed. (London: Methuen, 1937); Phyllis Deane, *The First Industrial Revolution* (Cambridge: Cambridge University Press, 1965).

or with the fact that the real standard of living ought to have been falling if he were correct. As a matter of fact, the standard of living probably rose in every decade of the century, though of course unevenly, and only if one includes such elements as the rise in health, cleanliness and ease of transportation, all of which were neglected by critics of laissez-faire capitalism.

Most students are immediately conditioned to the social impact of the Industrial Revolution by widely reprinted excerpts from either the Sadler Committee of 1832 or Ashley's Mines Commission Report. Michael Crabtree, the little boy who was beaten in the textile mill, and Patience Kearshaw, the girl of seventeen who worked naked in a coal mine pulling the coal corves by a chain around her waist, are eminently famous. They certainly existed, and the stories they told to the investigating committees are a terrible additional commentary, if one were needed, on man's inhumanity to man. But these horrendous instances should be viewed in context. Even Michael Crabtree admitted that the conditions he told about were those of his youth, and that there had been great improvement since.

In the cotton industry, the force of both technological change and social legislation made the worst of these situations relatively short-lived; it was in industries such as coal mining, chimney sweeping, or piece-rate sewing that conditions were worse than in the new industries and persisted longer. No technological breakthrough of any major consequence freed the coal industry in the nineteenth century from its inhuman reliance on human labor. Traditionally, many of the workers had been serfs and their conditions had changed very little, either in their social status or in their working conditions. Patience Kearshaw was trapped in an industry with little innovation, shortages of capital, and difficult technical conditions to overcome. Zola, in his novel *Germinal,* gives us a similar striking picture of life in the French mines in the latter part of the nineteenth century, where comparable conditions prevailed.

What was the nature of the Industrial Revolution? It has been described as both an industrial and an agricultural revolution, but this is not accurate, for in much of England and western Europe, agriculture remained unchanged. As a result of basic social, political, ideological, psychological, and scientific factors, the rate of technological development and innovation produced a positive feedback after the middle of the eighteenth century. Particularly, these changes clustered in a few areas such as textiles, power, and smelting; the interaction of economic and technical change generated a force that altered significantly the conventional and traditional ways of organizing production. The initial thrust of industrial change carried over into Victorian England, when innovation began to decline. The Industrial Revolution in western Europe followed a similar path, but lagged behind.

AGRICULTURE: GENTLEMAN FARMING

Though much of agriculture remained static, there were some technical advances. The great English agricultural innovators of this period were Thomas Coke, Jethro Tull, and Robert Bakewell. Their achievements are well known. Coke recognized that the crop rotation practiced in the Low Countries was superior to traditional British methods. He introduced turnips into the rotation of his East Anglian estates and made large profits. Tull experimented, entirely empirically, with the drilling and seeding of heavy grains and improved cultivation by advertising the use of simple farm machinery. Bakewell spent most of his life and fortune dramatically illustrating the success of improved breeding methods. All three worked happily in an atmosphere congenial to scientific gentleman farming.

Coke's influence was entirely limited to his immediate Norfolk surroundings, Tull erred on the important question of fertilizer use, and Bakewell had no clear scientific idea of what he was trying to breed. Agricultural science did not emerge until the midnineteenth century, when German chemists achieved breakthroughs in basic knowledge. The English of course, were justly proud of the early work of Rothamstead's experimental station. But the claim of an English agricultural revolution is entirely unsatisfactory. Continuing improvements in food production and in transportation made it possible to raise the standard of living of the English people, but this is far from what we usually designate as revolutionary. Most of the structure of village life remained intact, and agricultural labor is still poorly remunerated even today.

It was both fashionable and frequently profitable to improve one's estates. Many landowners, with steady incomes from urban properties, invested huge sums particularly to drain heavy lands for profitable grain growing. "Improving landlords," however, were a tiny minority, and it took a full century before the best practices of "high farming" were generally accepted. In the decade 1850-1860, when "high farming" was at its height, many counties were still backward; even in the highly developed East Anglian counties much could still be improved, as Scottish farmer-immigrants demonstrated with their new techniques during the Great Depression of the 1880s.[2] The scientific knowledge required to improve agriculture did not yet exist.

INDUSTRY: ENGLAND LEADS THE WAY

When we turn to industry, however, we can understand more readily how the achievements of the eighteenth century appeared revolutionary to the observers of the nineteenth. Consider the textile industry. Within four decades after the introduction of the stocking-frame (a very simple device which probably originated in Italy), a series of machines had altered the semirural nature of textile production, a new conceptual framework of management had been developed and the price of cotton cloth had been cut so substantially that for the first time even the poorest Englishman could afford a change of clothing. The names James Hargreaves, Richard Arkwright, and Samuel Crompton are justly famous, but especially Arkwright. This barely literate barber not only improved the production of thread by a simple but ingenious system of rollers, but also utilized the opportunity to set up factory operations on an extensive scale. He sponsored a new factory discipline and organization and developed a widespread licensing structure, which made him wealthy and remade northern England in his image. He was ennobled and honored. He left an estate valued in millions of pounds.

As Arkwright typified the entrepreneur, so did Henry Cort the relatively unknown genius. Early in the 1780s, Cort took out two patents for puddling and rolling iron. We have little information about Cort except that he went bankrupt, but we know a great deal about the results of his discoveries. Iron of a better quality could now be produced at less than half its previous price. Everywhere iron replaced wood or stone as a more flexible and durable material. It was a transformation similar to that in the textile industry. Small backyard smelters, closely tied to dwindling forest sources, gave way to large

[2]Rowland E. Prothero, Lord, Ernle, *English Farming Past and Present*, 3rd ed. (London and New York: Longmans, Green, 1922); George E. Fussell, " 'High Farming' in East Midlands and East Anglia, 1840-1880," *Economic Geography*, 27 (January 1951), 72-89.

integrated establishments, close to the sources of raw materials. Today no one can envisage society's functioning without cheap supplies of iron and steel. Thus did Cort play a significant role in shaping industrial society.

Closely related to Cort's innovations was the development of the steam engine. James Watt's discovery illustrates how social climate influences the process of invention and innovation. In the eighteenth century, education in Scotland was far more advanced and rigorous than anything south of the Tweed. Watt was a product of this educational structure. He came from a family already distinguished in mathematics. At Glasgow University, there were famous professors lecturing on what we call physics today. Adam Smith himself was sympathetic to Watt's ambition and aided him with university support. Lacking in Scotland, however, were the practical technical skills necessary to transform Watt's drawings into reality. For this, Watt had to cross the border. Fortunately, his English supporter, Matthew Boulton, was a businessman of broad vision and daring. Well known for his buckles and frying pans, Boulton introduced Watt to John Wilkinson, England's best known weapons manufacturer, whose skill in the boring of cannon had made him rich. Wilkinson produced easily the precision cylinders that had been for so long the obstacle to Watt's invention. Boulton's craftsmen did the rest, and by the 1780s Watt's engine was an operating machine. The first steam engine was sold to Wilkinson to work the massive equipment of his iron plant at Bradley, but by 1800 Boulton and Watt's stationary engine was a common sight in the industrial heart of England. Within a quarter century the railroad, made possible by this invention, would begin to transform all industries throughout the entire nineteenth century.

The clustering of innovations and inventions seemed so remarkable that observers saw in it a revolution. Each of these changes had a long history, and technical change alone could not account for the impact of these industrial alterations on English society. The social process had already prepared the ground for this gradual transformation. England had a more fluid society than the rest of Europe. Although the top rungs had been preempted by the aristocracy, there was considerable room for upward mobility throughout the society. The history of the firm of Walker and Sons is a good example. In 1741, when Sam Walker and his brother Aaron began making nails, they had no resources except their ability. By 1812, the holdings of the company were valued at over 1.5 million dollars.[3] Josiah Wedgwood provides another example. Within his lifetime he reorganized the manufacture of pottery, changed the taste and habits of Englishmen of every rank, introduced new methods of marketing, and became enormously wealthy.

In this society, there was no shortage of investment capital. Individuals might feel constrained by a temporary lack of liquid funds (some, like Arkwright, set up their own banks), but basically it was a rich society by nineteenth-century standards. Capital flowed into the new industrial undertakings from many sources, from the Duke of Bridgewater, the tobacco merchants of Glasgow, the moneyed interests of Bristol, the savings of London, and most of all from the plowed-back earnings of the manufacturers themselves. All segments of society contributed to the burgeoning industrial activity. The ideological atmosphere of the early nineteenth century was unusually sympathetic to the emerging capitalistic society. Mercantilism was totally crushed by Smithian thunderbolts, and the emerging doctrine of laissez faire was still full of youth and hope and promise. This momentum—technological, social, and ideological—did not weaken until after 1850. Instead of diminishing, capitalism spread in scope and magnitude. The force and technique of industrialization were widely copied in the Low Countries, France, Germany, Italy, and eventually in Czarist Russia by the end of the century. Outside of Europe, the United States and Japan developed as great industrial powers.

ON THE CONTINENT

The Industrial Revolution on the continent was intimately connected with the consequences of the French Revolution and Napoleon.[4] For more than two decades and a half, every aspect of traditional European life was subjected to the most extraordinary pressures, military and ideological. The Revolution itself, and the entire Napoleonic experience, moved a dramatic victory for state power. Religious establishments, Catholic and Protestant, never again were to wield the political power they had for centuries exercised. The new

---

[3]Ashton, *The Industrial Revolution,* pp. 95-97. Many similar examples could be cited.

[4]David Landes, *Unbound Prometheus; Technological Change and Industrial Development in Western Europe from 1750 to the Present* (Cambridge: Cambridge University Press, 1969).

state emerged as an unchallenged secular instrument. Nineteenth-century governments cannot be considered totalitarian in the modern sense, but they represented a qualitative and quantitative assumption of state power over society that had not existed in the eighteenth century.

Political upheaval accounts for the basic differences between the continental and English experiences. England had resolved the problem of political unification *two* centuries before, and her society, although class structured, did permit and in some ways encourage upward mobility. The destruction of the *ancien régime* made impossible a conservative return to the past and left a social vacuum of deep and lasting consequence. Social stress was more severe on the continent than in England. The concept of "class struggle" can be applied more easily to France and Germany than to England. The revolutionary forces that shattered the existing social order brought with them new concepts of power—and a new sense of the masses. To further "revolution," the masses had been exhorted to make physical and emotional commitments never imagined before. This sense of participation in society was to be a permanent legacy—a continuous problem, yet source of strength, for nineteenth-century Europe.

On the continent, economic needs ranked below many historical and political issues. Cavour used liberal economics as a means to popularize the cause of Italian unification much as List (whom we shall discuss more thoroughly in Chapter 5) used his economic program to aggrandize the strength of Prussia. One could point to many similar cases in almost every European state.

Other forces must be considered. Traditional agriculture was more significant as a rigidifying force than in England. Agricultural practices, except in isolated areas, were more backward. Tenures and obligations were more severe and restrictive. In Czarist Russia, the serfs did not achieve legal freedom until the 1860s and social-economic freedom until the decade before World War I. But even farther west, the peasantry still formed the very basis of society, and this social order would change only glacially in the next century. The peasant structure was subject to great stress. Society imposed on it a more effective and persuasive central government and new political demands, which it resented and only reluctantly accepted. Moreover, as population grew, the precariousness of rural life increased, and the strains of commercial agriculture made this tension almost unbearable. Rural Europe wrenched itself unwillingly into modern industrial urban society. Millions left the land and moved to cities or emigrated. Those who remained were frequently embittered by the incomprehensible changes, and they viewed the urban centers with unalloyed hostility. Urban centers were fewer and smaller proportionately on the continent than in England. There was less social mobility and less bourgeois leadership. There was less innovation and less capital for industrial undertaking. Overall there were fewer sympathetic bonds uniting social groups.

Marx wrote in England, but the atomization of society was a continental phenomenon. England possessed the residual strength needed to rebuild social ties, though not without difficulty and hardship. On the continent, social history was tragic. When Louis Blanc described working conditions in his L'Organisation du Travail, he pictured a piecework, preindustrial structure.[5] By 1848, France was still in the infancy of its Industrial Revolution. Only textiles in Alsace clearly foreshadowed the victory of industrialism. Elsewhere in Europe, one finds the same picture: Enclaves of advanced industrialization surrounded by seas of peasant agriculture. In 1848, revolution exploded across the continent, but where the explosion did not release pressures, the problems continued to build. By this tortuous course Europe was led into the incomplete capitalism of the early twentieth century (pre-1945), and to the tragedy of self-destruction in two world wars. Nationalism, socialism, militarism, imperialism, and industrialism— these were the mighty forces Europe was unable to bear. History had not prepared the masses for their role, and the pressures of events did not allow them to solve their problems. The successes of nineteenth-century Europe were immense, but two world wars destroyed the old Europe, and only since World War II can we have renewed hope of a European renascence on a healthier political and economic base.

RECONSTRUCTION OF ENGLISH SOCIETY

Among the major countries, England was most successful in the reconstruction of society. As noted previously, she did not have to cope with political problems of the magnitude of those that confronted continental countries. The English had no master plan for remaking society, but simply the long tradition of British empiricism.

---

[5]Louis Blanc, L'Organisation du Travail (Paris: Au bureau de la société de l'industrielle fraternelle, 1839).

Classical economists responded to the real stresses of English life by developing a rigorous body of thought that expressed the aspirations of the rising bourgeoisie and provided a firm basis for a laissez faire policy. The harsh implications of this theory were, however, softened in practice. What emerged was a viable structure of economic and social reforms. The negative aspects of classical thought have been overemphasized. Malthus emerges usually as an unfeeling and unsympathetic academician, and Ricardo as a one-sided Jeremiah. Malthus especially deserves reinterpretation. The blackest prophecies are drawn in this first edition of the *Essay on Population,* but these conclusions are modified by more mature judgment in his *Political Economy.*[6] The theorist immersed in the causes of population growth was also, we must remember, the same man who was equally concerned with increasing the effective demand of the poor during depression. Malthus was the first underconsumptionist, the first to recognize the problems of gluts under capitalism, that is, the inability of supply and demand to clear the market automatically.

The inherent optimism of Adam Smith was, however, in the long run more influential in shaping British policies than the pessimism of Ricardo and Malthus. For Smith and his followers laissez faire was a program of positive action not only for the bourgeoisie but also for the entire society. We see today the banner of laissez faire tattered and muddy, but it was gloriously new and exciting in the first half of the nineteenth century. Classical liberal ideology provided sufficient flexibility for certain social progress to take place; it did not, as some critics have suggested, prevent social improvement.

Britain had to develop effective techniques for dealing with social problems. The first change, the Reform Bill of 1832, enabled the newer propertied interests to enter a Parliament hitherto dominated by the landed establishment. The relative importance of this bill cannot be judged simply by comparing the composition of the House of Commons before and after its passage. Contemporary middle-class leadership rightfully regarded parliamentary reform as the first successful broadening of the constitution since the victory over Stuart absolutism in the seventeenth century.

Electoral reform in 1832 demonstrated that single-purpose organizations, carefully organized and led, could bring about significant

---

[6]Thomas R. Malthus, *Principles of political economy considered with a View to Their Practical Application* (London: W. Pickering, 1836).

change. The aristocratic leadership was not entirely unwilling to share power with responsible propertied classes. The country itself was willing to accept the participation of businessmen in political life. Gradually, social and economic reforms proceeded from the broadened legislatures. Almost all segments of societies except for the most extreme groups, abhorred the idea of the use of force. This modest extension of the franchise, however, was a demonstrable fact. The ruling class, contrary to Marx, divested itself of some power in 1832, 1866, and 1884, and on several occasions in the twentieth century, until complete political democracy was attained. The achievement of full suffrage for all citizens was one of the most striking and successful examples of social reconstruction; nowhere on the continent was it matched with the same commitment or sincerity.

Albert Dicey remarked in his *Lectures* that the flood of legislation was carrying England toward a social state, and that this depended during the nineteenth century "in the different currents of opinion bearing more or less directly on legislation. . . ."[7] No one can assess the effectivenes of the social legislation passed during this period. Not every act was well drawn or adequately suited to the problems it was meant to solve. Much legislation was framed within ideological limits, either classical or Benthamite, which today would not be acceptable. Mark Blaug's most revealing study of the old Poor Law tells much of the "reformers mentality." The Benthamites, for example, lacked statistical data for effective remedial legislation; furthermore, most of the available information on the old Poor Law system was totally inaccurate. Inhibited by their narrow ideology, the Benthamites groped unsuccessfully toward reforms that would provide "the greatest happiness to the greatest number."[8]

The Health and Morals of Apprentices Act, the first legislation to remedy specific social abuses in factories, was passed in 1802. No general social philosophy seems to have been involved. It was designed to improve working conditions for children, who were considered wards of the State. Beyond serving as a beginning, this bill achieved little, and real reform dates from the investigations of 1816 and the legislation of 1819. The 1819 bill was poorly administered, but from 1833 on, systematic efforts were made to establish an overall factory

[7]Albert Venn Dicey, *Lectures on the Relation Between Law and Public Opinion in England During the Nineteenth Century* (London: Macmillan, 1905). p. 61.

[8]Mark Blaug, "Myth of the Old Poor Law and the Making of the New," *Journal of Economic History,* 23 (June 1963), 151-184.

code. Industrial regulations were further elaborated in 1844, 1867, 1878, and many times subsequently.[9] Social legislation followed similar patterns in housing, public health, and social insurance.

The Benthamites. The reform movement stemmed primarily from brilliant eccentric Jeremy Bentham. We have that indelible picture of Bentham in his cottage, surrounded by cats and bric-a-brac and leading an almost eremitical existence.[10] However, Bentham's real genius was his ability to attract and hold in close communion with his ideas a small but extremely able group. What Bentham could never have achieved himself, his followers, the Philosophical Radicals, accomplished. In another environment, the Benthamites might well have been conservative, but in the England of the early nineteenth century, philosophical radicalism, or utilitarianism, became a powerful reform ideology and movement. As an ideology, it stood for a national quantitative measurement of all questions—political, economic, legal, social, even esthetic. The balance of right or wrong, good or bad, desirable or undesirable, was the outcome of a simple numeration. The conclusion that yielded the "greatest good for the greatest number" won the test and should be adopted. Utilitarianism was pseudo-scientific. On the one hand, it tried very hard to bring some rational, impersonal calculus into the wealth of archaic and anachronistic institutions and policies carried over into the first quarter of the nineteenth century. On the other hand, it suffered gravely from a naïve arrogance that all problems were of equal priority and that they could be summarized by simply counting. Once counted, the policies necessary to solve them could be easily implemented by legislative action.

Philosophical Radicalism was philosophically naïve, psychologically insensitive, statistically inadequate, and legislatively magnificent. The British could understand passing laws, and the beginnings of every reform movement from the franchise to education stemmed from Benthamite premises. It combined laissez faire in economics with

[9]Abbott P. Usher, *An Introduction to the Industrial History of England,* (Boston: Houghton Mifflin, 1920), chap. 16, pp. 387-431.
[10]Helen Bevington, *Nineteen Million Elephants and Other Poems* (Boston: Houghton Mifflin, 1950), p. 33f.
A Bomb for Jeremy Bentham (1940)
The teapot he named Dick
And Dapple was his stick
He cherished pigs and mice
A fact which will suffice
To hint, from all we hear,
He was a little queer.

universal suffrage. Legislation, for Bentham, was the only proper vehicle for reform, a tremendously important English view of social reconstruction. The dedicated elite who gathered around Jeremy were determined to help legislators make the proper decisions. This group is justly famous—the Mills, Edwin Chadwick, George Grote, Southwood Smith, John Bowring. Because of these individuals and others, Benthamism everywhere infiltrated the consciousness of British liberalism.[11] The law reformers—Samuel Romilly, James Mackintosh, Henry Brougham—were Benthamites in action. Robert Peel was the most prominent political convert to Benthamism; others such as Lord John Russell were sympathetic. At the other end of the political spectrum, Francis Place, a radical leader, may be included in the larger Benthamite circle. No intellectual group was untouched by Benthamite influence. The movement was so powerful because it filled the needs of the day. Benthamism provided Englishmen with a flexible ideology that could reform institutions in an orderly noncoercive fashion. Graham Wallas suggests that utilitarianism provided a body of "political expedients,"[12] and Dicey emphasizes again and again the harmony of philosophical radicalism, or "systematized individualism," as he calls it, "with the general tendencies of English thought."[13]

From this philosophy came the momentum for reform in local government, the civil service, and the administration of health and police service. From this source came the impetus for the reform of colonial self-government, brilliantly summarized by Lord Durham's report, and the beginning of changes in the administration of India. Most of all, however, Benthamism changed the law and politics of nineteenth-century England. The peaceful acceptance of franchise and political reform from 1832 on was the result of the widespread acceptance of utilitarian premises. Similarly, the movement to extend the social nature of the legal system gained in strength. The law became more conscious of individual liberty and more concerned with the adequate protection of civil rights. Lawyers and law reformers committed to Benthamite principles wrought these changes.

Finally, Benthamism stood for impartial social investigation as a

[11]Elie Halevy, *The Growth of Philosophical Radicalism,* trans. Mary Morris (New York: Macmillan, 1928).

[12]Graham Wallas, "Jeremy Bentham," *Encyclopaedia of the Social Sciences,* (New York: Macmillan, 1930) vol. 2, pp. 518-519.

[13]Dicey, *Lectures,* pp. 174-175.

preliminary to legislative action. Although this principle worked badly in the passage of the New Poor Law of 1834, still it clearly fore-shadowed the principle on which systematic and centralized bureau-cratic administration was to be based in the nineteenth century. The techniques needed much refinement, but the casual administrative structure of preindustrial society could not have carried the burden of a population of over 20 million by 1830. In the confused way by which ideas and ideologies influence society, Benthamism led from laissez faire individualism to Fabianism and welfare economics. For example, John Stuart Mill moved from orthodox utilitarianism to a position close to democratic socialism. Bentham partially failed, but he had more impact on the nature and content of British socialism than Marx. To see Bentham then as the strange recluse, a failure as a lawyer, the designer of star-shaped prisons, the mere summarizer of utilitarian thought—push-pin and poetry are equal—is to overlook one of the most powerful individuals in the social and intellectual climate of nineteenth-century Britain, a person who had great impact on classical and popular economic thought.[14]

James Mill, the father of John Stuart Mill, was one of the most important popularizers of philosophical radicalism. He transmitted the thought of Bentham to contemporary society and extended utilitarianism to economics. Bentham wrote little in the area of eco-nomic speculation, though in 1797 he did publish a pamphlet, *Obser-vations on the Poor Bill . . . [of] Mr. Pitt.* There are also scattered comments on monetary matters, and his brief *Manual of Political Economy* (1798), but he was largely interested in reform legisla-tion and ethics. It was through James Mill, a devoted and able dis-ciple, that the Benthamite and Ricardian views on classical doctrine were integrated, enlarged, and put forth as a cohesive and coherent economic doctrine. Mill published his *Elements of Economy* in 1821, a few years after he had achieved fame for his *History of British India.* His brief economic essay was no less widely acclaimed.[15]

We can easily see why *Elements of Political Economy* was so pop-ular in the 1830s. First, Mill had a charming style and the book itself is still sprightly. There was a deftness in his handling of problems, which

[14]Jeremy Bentham, *The Works of J. Bentham* (New York: Russell & Russell 1962).
[15]James Mill, *Elements of Political Economy,* 3d ed. (London: Bohn, 1844); *idem, The History of British India,* reprint of 5th ed., published 1858 (New York: Chelsea House, 1968).

undoubtedly appealed to his audience and still has a latent appeal more than a century later. His economics fitted nicely the conventional attitudes of his day; his handling of all the Ricardian rigor is done on a level that the intelligent middle class could well understand. Mill's book was the Samuelson of his generation, and by this we mean to compliment both authors. His ideology was obvious and clearly meant to please the bourgeoisie, which was growing in both political and economic power. Mill appealed neither to the very rich nor to the very poor, but to the middle group which contributed the most to society and who deservedly enjoyed the most from society.

. . . men with fortunes equal to all the purposes of independence, of physical enjoyment, even of taste and elegance, constituting the governing portion of society, and giving the tone to its sentiments and amusements, are not in the situation of men whose imaginations are apt to be dazzled by the glare of superior riches, and likely to pay to their owners any remarkable devotion. The laboring classes are cringing and servile, where the frown of the rich man is terrible, and his little favors important.[16]

Specifically, Mill dealt with production, distribution, exchange, and consumption. True, he was not very original in his treatment of any of these topics, but he did not start out to produce a rigorous essay. His analysis of production and distribution clearly followed Ricardian guidelines, which he accepted uncritically. Mill's Chapter 3, "Interchange" (exchange), clearly went back to Adam Smith and expressed the classical formulation of comparative advantage and laissez faire. His section on consumption is of interest to modern economists only because he disputed publicly with Malthus the question of market gluts. Mill, in what seems now to be tortured thinking, proved to his own satisfaction that no such thing was possible, but history and theory were to confirm Malthus' point of view. Keynes, a century later, would return to this troublesome fact of economic life, which Malthus first brought to the attention of the nineteenth century. To summarize then, *Elements of Political Economy* was an important work because it disseminated economic ideas and supported Whig liberal policies, not for its originality or contribution to theory.

John Stuart Mill. Mill's famous son, John Stuart Mill, would further develop economic theory and change the basis of nineteenth-century

---

[16]Mill, *Elements of Political Economy,* p. 54.

economic policy. If James Mill summarized the classical school as expressed by Smith, Malthus, and Ricardo, John Stuart Mill made the transition from the narrow perimeters of classical doctrine to the more flexible and humane standards of later Victorian thinking. In his life and in his intellectual growth, this genius moved from the rigid position he embraced as a youth toward a broader humanitarianism. In fact, this was the same process that the nineteenth-century English society itself was experiencing.

It is worth examining Mill's life.[17] The last of a large family, Mill was a product of his father's educational philosophy. In addition to learning Latin at age three and Greek at eight, he tells us of the long walks during which his father recited to him Ricardian economics and Benthamite ethics. It was his obligation to repeat, rephrase, and explain them. By his early teens, Mill was a young man whose mind had been cast in the most rigid pattern. The course of his life was slowly to transform these truths. We know of the first emotional crisis in his early twenties. We know of a second in 1826 and 1827, and a third on the death of his father in 1836. Each of these served to break down the inflexibilities of his earlier education and free him for the more mature thought that appears in his later writings. He himself relates that the most significant and lasting personal and intellectual experience of his life was his meeting with Mrs. Harriet Taylor in the winter of 1830, when he was twenty-three. Both Mill and Mrs. Taylor were ostracized by nineteenth-century society because of the awkward nature of their liaison. The relationship undoubtedly completed the transformation of Mill's life and thought.

Of greatest importance to Mill were philosophy, ethics, and economics, or, more precisely, the extension and completion of Benthamism. Mill rejected Bentham's abstract hedonism by subordinating utilitarianism to liberal ethics. This was a significant achievement for the nineteenth century, and probably as far as one could go without the insights of modern psychological and sociological theory. There may be no finer statement of liberalism's doctrines than Mill's brief and exciting essay *On Liberty,* which was published in the late 1850s. His other works on logic, value, and parliamentary reforms, extremely interesting in the history of nineteenth-century thought, reflected the changes in his approach to political economy.

[17]John Stuart Mill, *Autobiography of John Stuart Mill.* Published from the original manuscript in the Columbia University Library (New York: Columbia University Press 1924).

If the extension of Benthamism was one part of Mill's lifework, the extension of Ricardo's theories was the other. At first, Mill accepted fully the Ricardian position, as given to him by his father, and it was not until much later that he began to alter his position. Mill's *Essays on Some Unsettled Questions of Political Economy* were not published until 1844, fourteen years after their completion. These early writings do not indicate fully the significant changes that appear in his *Principles of Political Economy,* which was published after eighteen months' intensive work in the mid-1840s.[18] Mill intended initially to rewrite Adam Smith and only partially succeeded. Smith had spent more than two decades on his work. Mill spent no more than the same number of months. Thus, despite his real genius, he could not bring to bear the depth and thoughtfulness Smith invested in his subject matter. Moreover, Smith had no Ricardo to overcome, and Ricardo weighed heavily on Mill's *Principles.*

In Book I, on Production, there was very little that was new or radical. Not until Book II, on Distribution, did Mill indicate the direction he was taking. In a famous passage, Mill, attempting to distinguish between production and distribution, decided that the subject of production was bound by laws that were of a physical nature and could not be altered.

The laws and conditions of the production of wealth partake of the character of physical truths. There is nothing optional or arbitrary in them . . . . It is not so with the Distribution of Wealth. That is a matter of human institution solely. The things once there, mankind, individually or collectively, can do with them as they like. They can place them at the disposal of whomsoever they please and on whatever terms.[19]

This was the great divide for Mill. On one side of the rift he left production, the heritage of his upbringing and of the past. On the other side, he proceeded slowly and cautiously toward a new formulation of distribution. Book I restated Ricardo; Mill accepted at face value the terminology, definitions, and theoretical structures of the classical school. On the vital question of distribution, he tended more and more toward a review of received classical doctrine. His ideas of

social distribution made him draw late in life toward a broad defini-
tion of socialism, a socialism closer to the welfare state than to Marx.
The tradition of social reform that leads from Bentham to John Stuart
Mill to the Webbs and Fabianism can be found in the "harmonies" of
Alfred Marshall.

The entire economic process, both production and distribution as
Smith and others demonstrated, takes place within a social setting,
and each facet of economic life has broad physical and social components. Malthus, and particularly Ricardo, failed to appreciate
entirely the historical setting of economic life, and although both
contributed significantly to theory, their greatest error came from
their inability to understand the historical process. Mill then is an
advance over them. Courageously, he understood that his own society
and other societies would not accept the social inequities of the
classical structure.

In Book III, Mill examined in a traditional way the area of exchange
and the nature of value and cost. Book IV was concerned with the
influence of the society on production and distribution, and Book V
with the influence of government. In one of the important passages in
nineteenth-century economic thought, Mill envisaged the outcome of
economic development as a stationary state. The eighteenth-century
Enlightenment writers had a view of inevitable progress. During the
nineteenth century, the classical school perceived the inevitable
long-run decline of the economy. Mill believed that the physical laws
of production, modified by the social action of distribution, could
lead society to a position somewhere between hell and heaven.

I cannot, therefore, regard the stationary state of capital and wealth with
the unaffected aversion so generally manifested towards it by political economists of the old school. I am inclined to believe that it would be, on
the whole, a very considerable improvement on our present condition. I
confess I am not charmed with the ideal of life held out by those who
think that the normal state of human beings is that of struggling to get on;
that the trampling, crushing, elbowing, and treading on each other's heels,
which form the existing type of social life, are the most desirable lot of
human kind, or anything but the disagreeable symptoms of one of the phases
of industrial progress.[20]

[20]*Ibid.* vol. 2 pp. 261-262.

No passage better illustrates the overall dependence of Mill on middle-class rationality. In *On Liberty,* Mill pictured human nature as extensively moderate and rational, and he found the same tendencies in economic life.

Again, trade is a social act. Whoever undertakes to sell any description of goods to the public does what affects the interest of other persons, and of society in general; and thus his conduct, in principle, comes within the jurisdiction of society; accordingly, it was once held to be the duty of governments, in all cases which were considered of importance, to fix prices and regulate the processes of manufacture. But it is now recognized, though not till after a long struggle, that both the cheapness and the good quality of commodities are most effectually provided for by leaving the producers and sellers perfectly free, under the sole check of equal freedom to the buyers for supplying themselves elsewhere. This is the so-called doctrine of "free trade," which rests on grounds different from, though equally solid with, the principle of individual liberty asserted in this essay.[21]

We find in his analysis of government the same quality of rationality. Mill moved from a strong advocacy of laissez faire to a position that permitted far-reaching government actions.

But enough has been said to show that the admitted functions of government embrace a much wider field than can easily be included within the ring fence of any restrictive definition, and that it is hardly possible to find any ground of justification common to them all, except the comprehensive one of general expediency; nor to limit the interference of government by any universal rule, save the simple and vague one that it should never be admitted but when the case of expediency is strong.[22]

There are grave and serious omissions in Mill's *Political Economy.* Theoretically, it is not a strong work and does not match the rigor and power of the earlier classical writers. It was, nonetheless, a useful and necessary exposition of some of the highest tenets of British society. Somehow, the incubus of classical negative determinism had to be lessened. Marx did this explosively—Mill did it sympathetically. It may very well be that Mill's work, though less dramatic and less recognized, has had almost as great an impact as that of Marx.

[21]John Stuart Mill, *On Liberty* (New York: Bobbs-Merrill, 1956), p-115.
[22]John Stuart Mill, *Principles,* vol. 2, p. 305.

5

THE END
OF CLASSICAL
ECONOMICS

The Economic Setting

Classical economics—the economic thinking of Smith, Malthus, and Ricardo in particular—was as much the product of a revolt against the traditional mercantilistic ways of thinking as it was a product of the Industrial Revolution. The immense structural changes that we see were viewed by contemporaries only as gross images, masses of new forms and patterns whose total impact and texture could not be fully understood. The nineteenth century, even after 1830, was less a market economy ruled by impersonal economic laws than it was a conglomerate of past and present economic substructures. In fact, one could well argue, to use a different metaphor, that in most places industrial growth was viewed by society in much the same way that the body attempts—frequently successfully—to reject organ transplants. Hostility to industrialization was carried forward on every level—intellectual, institutional, personal, and psychological. In thought, theory, and action, every change in structure produced hostility and antagonism from interests threatened by these changes. Not only the intelligentsia but virtually all of the established order saw industrial changes as mischievous. By the end of the century, many elite groups had found ways to utilize these new strengths, and not only made their peace with the bourgeois-entrepreneurial interests, but also were ready to allow them into modest positions of power and social status. However, at the beginning of this generation—that is, 1830—hostility and opposition were more the rule than acceptance. Most opinion leaders did not agree that economics lay at the base of social values or that economic values should be given the highest priority. The accumulated social wisdom and experience of centuries did not give way easily; it yielded only to demonstrable strength. These new capitalistic forces spread only slowly during the course of the century. List, for example, had only a small following in his native Germany. Similar cases could be drawn from other countries.

AGRICULTURE

No area of life was more resistant to laissez faire economics than agriculture. Changes on the land encountered many sources of social opposition. Any alteration in agricultural techniques, market structure, or resource allocation upset established arrangements. Throughout the entire century, the aristocracy was based on land. This was true from England to Czarist Russia. Land, birth, and privilege were nowhere overwhelmed by grants of broadened franchise, constitutional reform, or legal change. The march toward a mass society was glacial in speed. Landed aristocracies in most places held their own, and they could ally themselves with the forces of the Church and clergy and the traditional conservatism of peasants and agricultural laborers. The heavy risk of agricultural change vis-à-vis crops, farming techniques, marketing arrangements, and leases provided further obstacles to rapid change. Furthermore, one should not overestimate legal changes such as the Stein reforms in Prussia or the freeing of the serfs in Russia, which altered only the legal status of the peasantry. In the main, the aristocracy was able to so channel these reforms that existing land patterns were not disrupted. Resiliency and adaptation are more accurate appraisals of nineteenth-century aristocratic maneuvers than rout and surrender.

English agriculture, as explained previously, more resembled the past than the future, though impartial observers would comment on the advance of English over continental methods. The Industrial Revolution only slowly affected the mass of the agricultural population.

Railroads were just beginning to touch the agricultural sector by midcentury.

The commercialization of English agriculture predated the eighteenth century, but the rhythm of agricultural life still had a different beat from industrial life throughout the nineteenth century; only at the peaks and troughs of business cycles did the two economic sectors come together clearly. Across the Channel and stretching over Europe, agriculture remained aloof and traditional.

Observers of the changes in European life have tended to give all of these occurrences an accelerated quality which contributes much to our distorted image of the nineteenth century. Everywhere in every country, from the Atlantic to the Urals, there were structural alterations, but the transformations came slowly and unevenly. In England, the elaboration of classical theory occupied a large segment of the intellectual environment. Opposition to classical economics, therefore, was never more than a minor chord, although it drew on some, though not all, of the romantic strands that attacked classical theory on the continent. By midcentury, the die had been cast in England; the worst social cruelties of the Industrial Revolution were over. Certain achievements could be recorded. Political control by the middle class under aristocratic leadership was assured. Between the late 1750s and late 1850s, the national standard of living had doubled and national product per capita had multiplied 2-1/2 times. The "British people enjoyed a richer and more varied standard of living."[1]

The English were probably the most affluent people in the world, measured statistically, though their *real* standard of life in overcrowded, unsanitary urban slums was lower than that enjoyed by many others—for example, North America and Australia, where money wages were lower. The British evolution into an industrial state was still a slow process, slower in rate of growth than in North America or Germany which industrialized later. The British rate of investment probably remained below 10 percent, and annual rate of population increase after 1830 was under 1-1/4 percent. By midcentury, "an increasing proportion of the new investments made out of the British national income were going abroad."[2] Moreover, almost a permanent reluctance to rapid change reasserted itself, and Britain found herself quickly bypassed by the end of the century. The British

[1]Phyllis Deane, *The First Industrial Revolution,* (Cambridge: Cambridge University Press, 1965), pp. 266-269.
[2]*Ibid.,* p. 272.

commitment to classical ideology, free trade, amateurish government, and lack of central economic policy, and the reluctance to use economic devices such as the tariff, probably further hampered her trading position. The future was not with the British doves, but with the German and American eagles.

In Germany and the United States, the groundwork for an industrial spurt was being generously laid. The development of specialized regional markets, the spread of machinery and innovations, the use of interchangeability of parts, a reasonably open, mobile, and motivated social philosophy —all gave impetus to working class and entrepreneurs alike. After the Civil War the United States emerged as the world's richest and most powerful manufacturing country.

By 1870, a unified Germany was approaching the "takeoff stage." An effective bureaucracy, a sizable railroad network, a strong educational orientation toward research and industrial applications, a risk-taking business group, and an overwhelming, aggressive national pride put Germany in a position of unquestioned strength. The remaining decades of the century were to see the emergence of industrial Germany. By 1900 industrial society had conquered the littoral areas of the world.

The Social Setting

By 1830, a small but dynamic new class of entrepreneurs had been firmly established in England and France, and beyond the Rhine this same industrial-commercial ferment was threatening the stability of the Germanies. The bourgeoisie armed with the new technologies and spurred by the promise of industrial revolution relentlessly undermined the traditional institutions. Europe changed; but not surprisingly, the old order opposed vigorously, and frequently successfully, both the rising bourgeoisie and its alien ideology, classical economics. In this long, uneven struggle, the established classes found unexpected supporters among many members of a rapidly growing intelligentsia of journalists, academicians, writers, and philosophers, even though the increase in the number, status, and role of the intellectual was itself very much a by-product of industrial revolution and the victory of middle-class mobility.

The anticapitalistic movement had many common elements: (1) the emergence of a dehumanized proletariat, (2) the visible growth of urban squalor, (3) the apparently widening poverty gap between rich and poor, (4) the emotional dissonance between the establishment and its subculture, (5) the contractual quantification of human values, (6) the sense of esthetic loss. All these racked the European consciousness. Some intellectuals found their metaphors in a landed romanticism. Was there a happy, innocent, nonmaterialistic past, an Eden governed by a noble and dedicated aristocracy and populated by a contented, self-reliant peasantry? This past may have existed, they thought, in feudal days when sturdy yeomen worked their fields alongside their squire, or it might have been the Marxist "Urkommunismus," when unspoiled by private property, noble savages lived peacefully together.

Early in the nineteenth century European intellectuals were caught up in a wave of a romanticism, an experience that affects to this day the character of intellectuals on both sides of the Atlantic, a revolt against the rationalism . . . of the preceding century, romanticism proved a potent generator of myth and symbols. Amid the social anxiety caused by the onset of industrialization, the quickening pace of change, and the fecundity of new institutions with new patterns of power, romanticism became a refuge—and a basis for the criticism of society. In general, it preferred emotional spontaneity to rationalized action, the farm to the factory, man alone to organization, and rebellion to established forms of power. Satan—Milton's proud and lonely fallen angel—became in Paris around 1830 a favorite figure, his picture hung in the rooms of romantic young intellectuals. A rebel foredoomed to be a loser, Satan was an appropriate symbol of that kind of passionate political activity and social criticism which does not really expect or seek to shoulder the responsibility of power.[3]

This romantic strain has underlain many of the anticapitalistic ideologies that emanated from disaffected intellectuals, bureaucrats, churchmen, and landowners. A great deal that is otherwise puzzling in the intellectual history of modern Europe becomes understandable once this common agreement of the anticapitalistic movements of the last century is understood. So deep a change indeed produced strange bedfellows. Of course, not every critic of classical economics was a romantic opponent of industrial capitalism, nor did every political opponent of the bourgeoisie bother to refute Smith and Ricardo.

[3]Max Ways, "Intellectuals and the Presidency," *Fortune* (April 1967), 211.

Much of the criticism of classical economics reflected the intense conflict of political and social as well as economic interests. Intellectuals, however, were the main spokesmen in this ideological battle, and a good many of them were aware that they had little to gain by a change in the prevailing power structure. But the 1830s were not unlike the 1930s or the 1970s, and Keynes's famous remarks apply to the nineteenth century as much as to the twentieth:

Practical men, who believe themselves to be quite exempt from any intellectual influence, are usually the slaves of some defunct economist. Madmen in authority, who hear voices in the air, are distilling their frenzy from some academic scribblers of a few years back.[4]

Criticism directed against classical economics is usually divided into three schools: The nationalistic, the socialistic, and the conservative. This division is, however, arbitrary. There is a good deal of overlapping among the groups, and several of the most articulate critics are not easily labeled. Perhaps it is better to regard European nationalism and conservatism as major sources of criticism of classical thought. From this criticism evolved not only many of the anticapitalistic ideologies and movements of the nineteenth and twentieth centuries, but also many of the forces that have led to the construction of welfare-capitalism over the past few decades.

The various anticapitalistic movements had much in common, and the difference between various viewpoints was rarely clear.[5] All serious critics of classical economics opposed the concept of natural harmony, the very foundation for the works of Smith and Say, the ultimate justification of laissez faire economics. The creation of a dehumanized proletariat and the economic crises that periodically shattered the early capitalist world were the consequences of excessive laissez faire and "wasteful competition" in the view of both conservative and socialist critics. These social evils could be alleviated. Poverty and depression were subject to state control. Above all, Smith's concept of the "economic man," the individual prompted by narrow, selfish utilitarian motives, was equally unacceptable to the critics of

[4]John Maynard Keynes, *The General Theory of Employment, Interest and Money* (London: Macmillan, 1946), p. 383.
[5]Recent research about the young Marx, for instance, has reemphasized the influence of the romantic, archconservative Adam Müller on both Marx and the "Jung-Hegelians" of the early nineteenth century.

the left and right. It was the reanalysis and reinterpretation of human nature that formed a broad common base for an unyielding attack on capitalistic ethics.[6] Again and again, this basic theme cuts across the pages of the intellectual controversy of the nineteenth century. The nature of man and the responsibility of society once more became key questions.

The Conservative Attack on the Classical School

One of the most interesting conservative opponents of classical thought was the obscure German economist Adam Müller (1779-1834). Müller would be of little interest except that his ideas reappear in virtually every twentieth-century anticapitalistic movement. Not only Fascism and Nazism reflected Müller's complaints, but also much of the rhetoric of Marxist and pseudo-Marxist intellectuals—especially among the developing nations—has been a distant, unpleasant echo of Müller's sentiments. Although Müller himself had no lasting influence outside Germany, he illustrates the common ideological bias shared by various critics of classical thought. His permanent influence in Germany was substantial. Othman Spann, the sociologist-economist who was responsible for much of the theoretical foundation of National Socialism had a considerable European intellectual reputation in the 1920s and 1930s, and drew heavily on Müller. The exaggerated rights of private property were strongly criticized by Müller, and the advocacy of state intervention to limit these excesses was used by him and by Spann in their attack on classical economic ideology. These arguments appealed to many liberal reformers in Germany and in other countries.

Müller built his imaginary, reactionary economics on a wide philosophical base. Although Burke's *Reflections* was probably the single major influence on his intellectual development, Müller also drew on Immanuel Kant, Johann Gottlieb Fichte, and Karl Schlegel. He attacked Smith's "cosmopolitanism," replacing it with a strong nationalistic economic program. Similarly, he rejected the individualistic axioms of liberalism. National rivalries, rather than individual competition, were the real incentives and forces toward economic activity

---

[6]The attitude of the Roman Catholic Church toward liberal capitalism has often expressed these basic anticapitalistic sentiments from Pope Leo's *Rerum Novarum* to Pope Paul's recent encyclical *Popularium Progressio.* Interestingly, *Rerum Novarum* formed the basis in the 1930s for both liberal Catholic workers' movements and clerico-Fascist parties.

and national economic development. Paper money, therefore, must replace cosmopolitan gold because a paper currency was clearly a better, more flexible tool for national economic policy. Moreover, paper currency avoided the creation of a national debt. Government borrowing per se was bad because it not only limited the freedom of action of the state, but also divided the people into creditors and debtors. Müller opposed any policy that, in his terms, undermined the organic nature of the state; any policy that strengthened the state, he supported. War was welcomed because it submerged individual greed and emphasized the commonwealth. Müller greatly admired the corporate life of the Middle Ages, and found it deeply superior to the emerging industrial capitalism. Worth more than any other form of economic activity, however, was the life of the peasant on the soil. Materialistic, hedonistic capitalism had destroyed the corporate body of the state; the position of the poor had deteriorated in consequence.

Müller expressed great admiration for Smith's contribution to economics in spite of his sharp and hostile criticism of the *Wealth of Nations*. Behind a good deal of pseudoromantic economic trivia, Müller had a thoroughly modern view of a number of economic issues. His concept of money, especially paper money as an active device of government policy, was thoroughly up-to-date and superior to the classical treatment of money. Similarly, he recognized the alienating tendencies inherent in a production process based on an ever-increasing division of labor. In his trenchant criticism of specialization and its psychological destructiveness, he sometimes anticipated such modern writers as Emile Durkheim, Elton Mayo, and Peter Drucker. Müller must be considered as one of the founders of modern German conservative thought; he was also a key figure in the emergence of an anticapitalism of the right. His work, however, quickly passed from the justified criticism of the one-sidedness of Adam Smith and the shortcomings of an unmonitored capitalism to irrational suggestions, which were far worse than the evils they were meant to cure. Nowhere do we find in Müller that concern for the rights of the individual that we find in Burke's thinking. Müller pointed the way to the emerging authoritarian cultural pattern that so distinguished German from British conservatism, and ultimately German from British socialism.

A far greater personality than Müller was the rebel politician and economist Friedrich List (1789-1849). Although he is commonly referred to as a "nationalist," List had very little in common with

Müller. List rejected completely Müller's regressive, dark, "back to medievalism" type romanticism. The future of Germany lay in the dynamic growth of progressive capitalism. It is easy to think of List as being very much at home among the supporters of the early New Deal, or with some stretch of the imagination, in the coterie of followers of President Johnson's Great Society. The major intellectual influence on List was Alexander Hamilton. Very much along Hamiltonian lines, List favored a strong interventionist government and a high tariff to protect infant industries from British competition. List, however, advocated much more than tariff protection; his criticism of classical thought and laissez faire capitalism went much deeper. List scorned the "school" (his term) as redefined by Ricardo and Say. He objected to its atomistic and cosmopolitan nature. He denied the existence of the natural harmony of laissez faire capitalism and rejected the premises of automatic adjustments in the capitalistic model. Thoroughly dissatisfied with the static nature of Ricardian thought, List concentrated above all on the dynamic aspects of the development of capitalistic society. He looked toward nationalism as the driving force to mobilize human endeavor, the major resource of "underdeveloped" countries. List's five-stage theory of economic development and growth was probably his major contribution to economic thought; it bridges the economic growth theory of Adam Smith with present-day formulations of Joseph Schumpeter and W. W. Rostow. First in List's model was the savage state where men hunt or fish; next followed the nomadic-pastoral stage, which merged into the agricultural stage of settled peasant societies; the agricultural stage, in turn, provided the opportunities, needs, and manpower for manufacture, thus creating the "agricultural and manufacturing" state; the last stage was one of world commerce, which combined international trade with manufacturing and large-scale commercial agriculture. Each stage represented an advance over the previous one. Therefore, the task of government was to create through proper legislation the environment that would make it possible for a country to reach the final stage as quickly as possible. Each stage of economic development required different kinds of government policies. Because at every time period, different countries fall in different stages, it was wrong, he believed, to develop general—that is, "cosmopolitan"—economic theories.

Political power and military strength depended, List argued, on a country's economic maturity. Fully developed countries found it in their interests to maintain the status quo and keep less developed countries in their dependent positions. In order for developing countries such as nineteenth-century Germany and the United States to reach full economic maturity, their industries must therefore be protected against the more efficient competition of the more advanced British manufacturers. Because the British interest was to maintain their national superiority, Britain could strangle the infant industries of other countries by selling below cost as long as necessary. Free trade was merely an effective mechanism to maintain a status quo favorable to the British, rather than an economic "law" of unquestioned validity.

If we substitute the term "nations" for "classes" and "England" for "bourgeoisie," List has the ingredients of a thoroughly Marxian criticism of classical theory. He replaced the general concept of harmony of interest with the thesis that the conflict and antagonism among nations was the source of economic as well as political activity. The Manchester theory of free trade merely masked the special interests of England behind a facade of harmony of interest and universality of application which did not exist. In the 1920s, when List became very popular in post-World War I Europe, his ideas were rewritten in Marxist terms.[7] List's attack on classical free-trade theory led him to deemphasize the concept of division of labor and to reject the entire classical emphasis on exchange value. List argued that "productive powers" were far more important than exchange values in measuring either a person's or a country's economic strength. Anticipating much of the current discussion in the field of economic development, he specifically emphasized that a Society's value structure was a significant force in its economic development, and that money spent on education and professional training could make a large contribution to economic progress. List recognized the "Protestant ethic" as a creative, productive force of great power.

The power of producing wealth is, therefore, infinitely more important than wealth itself; it insures not only the possession and the increase of what has been gained, but also the replacement of what has been lost.[8]

---

[7]Alfred Neusel, *List und Marx* (n.p., 1928).
   [8]Friedrich List, *National System of Political Economy*. G. A. Matile (Philadelphia: Lippincott, 1856) chap. 12, p. 3. (Our italics.)

Sismondi's Model

If we conceive of the development of economic theory as slowly converging toward a dynamic general equilibrium model that is able to account for the interaction of social and historical forces with economic variables, we have to consider a comparatively unknown Swiss economist. Simonde de Sismondi (1773-1842) combined the historical approach with a dynamic analysis of the "business crisis" and even postulated a necessary condition for a stable macroeconomic equilibrium. Sismondi, whose radical critique of capitalism concealed a basically conservative attitude, prepared, appropriately, the ground for both Marx and Keynes, and formed the natural transition from the nationalist to the socialist critics of classical economics. However, his concern with stability conditions for a general equilibrium, and his development of a rough "period analysis,"[9] represented Sismondi's major contribution to economic theory, though this significant intellectual achievement is rarely mentioned.[10]

NOUVEAUX PRINCIPES

In his major work, *Nouveaux Principes d'Economie Politique*

Figure **5.1** Systems Terminology

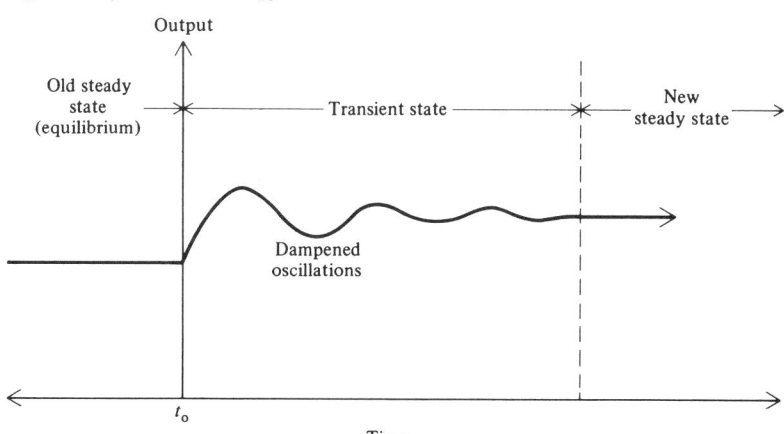

[9]Though Sismondi was obviously influenced by Quesnay's general equilibrium approach, we cannot claim that Sismondi had any direct impact on Walras.

[10]The only exception known to us is Schumpeter's evaluation of Sismondi [*History of Economic Analysis,* (New York: Oxford Univer. Press, 1954), pp. 484 ff]. Schumpeter, however, had only a very low opinion of Sismondi's theory of crisis, a view we do not share.

(1818),[11] Sismondi stressed the need to analyze economic problems in their historical context and severely criticized the Ricardians for restricting their analysis to what we would call today the "steady state."

Ricardo's procedure of first postulating an equilibrium, then disturbing the equilibrium by varying an input and, after the disturbances had disappeared, comparing the new equilibrium with the old (comparative statics), assumed implicitly that the new equilibrium is merely a function of the old equilibrium—that is, the system's structure and the initial perturbation.[12] Comparative statics is identical in assumption and methodology with the analysis of the structure of time invariant systems in engineering, except that the engineering analysis explicitly defines the dependence of the new steady state on the system's structure.[13] As a historian, Sismondi knew intuitively the importance of the transient stage and rejected the assumptions that the transient stage was unimportant and that the new equilibrium was exclusively determined by the initial steady state and its perturbations. Although Sismondi continued to assume that

[11] Simon de Sismondi, *Nouveaux Principes d'Economie Politique* (Paris: Chez Delaunan, 1819), 2 vol. Amonn's German translation (1949) of Sismondi's works served as our main source.

[12] The term "perturbation" is taken from Newton's astronomy; it referred originally to the slight discrepancies in the predicted orbits of planets due to the minor influence of the gravity of the other planets. "Perturbation" today means introducing a slight disturbance of a steady-state system in order to analyze its transient behavior and determine its stability characteristics.

[13] A "time invariant" system is described by a linear differential equation with constant coefficients. The variable time does not enter the equation explicitly. In "time variant" systems (i.e., truly dynamic systems), the coefficients are explicit functions of time. The analytic solution of higher order time variant systems is ordinarily impossible.

Example: Let $f(t)$ be some input function and y the system output, then the time invariant system is given by:

$$a_n \frac{d^n y}{dt^n} + a_{n-1} \frac{d^{n-1} y}{dt^{n-1}} + \ldots + a_0 y = f(t)$$

where a_i is a constant for $i = 0,1,2 \ldots n$; the time variant system is given by:

$$a_n(t) \frac{d^n y}{dt^n} + \cdots + a_0(t)y = f(t)$$

A specific example of a differential equation defining a time variant system might be:

$$4t^2 \frac{d^2 y}{dt^2} + y = f(t).$$

In this equation the term $a_1 = 4t^2$ depends explicitly on t.

the capitalistic system was stable (i.e., the disturbed output would ultimately converge to a new equilibrium), he stated that the new equilibrium would be determined by the nature and sequence of the various phases of the transient stage and the lags inherent in the economic system. Furthermore, the length of the adjustment process was alone of sufficient importance not to neglect the transient stage. Therefore, Sismondi divided the transient stage into time periods in order to show how the behavior of one period determined the next. He took it for granted that the effects of the initial disturbance would gradually diminish from period to period until a new equilibrium resulted.[14] The new equilibrium, however, would be the result of "transient stage" behavior.

The period analysis of the transition phase between equilibria provided Sismondi the necessary conceptual tools for developing his theory of crisis. The poverty of the laboring classes—a fact he assumed as obvious— weakened their bargaining power and resulted, thus, in wages that provided an inadequate living standard. (Note that the wages in his model are the indeterminate result of bargaining power rather than of demand and supply!) In the following periods, labor's inadequate buying power resulted in a decline of sales and profit, and subsequently, in unemployment and economic crises. Though the overall effective demand is insufficient for full employment, some industries experience a sharper decline in demand than others. The immobility of labor and capital, however, prevents a quick readjustment and further delays economic recovery.

Sismondi never explained fully how the economy would ultimately begin its recovery and reach a new equilibrium. He developed a rough conceptual theory of crises rather than of business cycles, and he even failed to account for the surplus the capitalist would gain from paying labor an inadequate wage. Malthus had recognized the role of saving in reducing effective demand, but Sismondi believed that the capitalists would merely spend the consequences of their superior bargaining power on luxury goods, without realizing that luxury goods also require labor for production (as a matter of fact, luxury goods have a higher labor content than cheap consumer goods). If his theory of crises was hence crude and incomplete, he did per-

---

[14]It is, of course, not at all obvious that a new equilibrium would ultimately emerge after the initial perturbation. The entire question of the capitalistic system was not considered explicitly until Marx and Walras.

ceive that periodic crises would primarily eliminate the small firm and would, therefore, lead to a concentration of economic power.

The rapid rate of what we call today technological change increased the production capacity of capitalism, without developing an offsetting capacity to consume. The necessary *equilibrium* between production and consumption, which was closely conserved in the medieval society, had to be reestablished if the devastating crises of capitalism were to be eliminated.[15] He recommended that the state intervene to reduce competition and technological change. Labor's purchasing power had to be raised by employer-guaranteed social insurance and a compensation arrangement that came close to a guaranteed annual wage.

This condensed representation of Sismondi's model may give the reader an impression of a rigor that his crude theories, in fact, lacked. Certainly his strength lay more in his intuitive insight and imagination than in his analytical reasoning. The development of the methodological tool of period analysis, together with a theory of crisis and exploitation was, however, a significant achievement. If we add to this an intuitive bargaining power theory of wages, a recognition of the immobility of capital and labor, a theory of economic concentration, and an elaborate social reform program, we must be impressed by Sismondi's contribution to economic theory and policy.

From Utopian Socialism to Marxism

Every history of economic thought must include a discussion of nineteenth-century socialism—both the so-called utopian socialism that arose as a response to the industrialization of European life and the "scientific" socialism that Marx authored. If Marxism became one of the most powerful of all intellectual forces in the second half of the century, left-wing protest had well prepared the terrain.

Socialist thought has long been a part of the intellectual framework of Western culture. Indeed, many aspects of socialism predate the capitalistic organization of modern economic society. Within Roman Catholic Christianity as well as many of the Protestant groups, there were strong sentiments in favor of economic equalitarianism and opposition to individual affluence and private property. Nineteenth-century socialism, however, had a sharper edge to it. The harshness

[15]Sismondi's view had been very much affected by the post-Napoleonic crises of 1815 to 1818.

of industrial and social change not only revived old quarrels but also brought new tools and new arguments to the controversy. Three individuals stand out as leading contributors in this period, though there were scores of others who popularized one argument or another of the indictment against laissez faire capitalism. Robert Owen, born a Welshman but linked to Scotland, England, and America, offered a living example of the workability of socialism. Two Frenchmen, Charles Fourier and Henri, Comte, de Saint-Simon, further revealed social and economic problems that classical economics had pushed aside.

THE UTOPIANS

The ideas of Owen, Fourier, and Saint-Simon may be considered a very early version of today's New Left revolution. All three opposed capitalism as it then existed: Its structure, its operation, its uneven pattern of wealth distribution, but mostly its values. Capitalism, as they examined it, was by far too harsh and too unfeeling. Men were corrupted both by capitalism's strengths, which placed so much emphasis on material goods, and by its weaknesses, the lack of concern for the individual's full development. They inevitably concluded that human nature could not be altered without a total and irreversible change in the industrial means of production. (Marx, of course, felt the same way emotionally, though he clothed his thinking in a much more intellectual and pseudoscientific model.) Owen knew at first hand the immense productive capacity of capitalist organization. His business success at New Lanark in Scotland in dramatically increasing productivity led him to the social and psychological metaphors that made him a revolutionary in middle-class England. Saint-Simon is recognized as one of the first technocrats. Brilliantly and intuitively, he sensed the new order that capitalist technology was developing. Engineers, as we shall point out, were the guiding individuals of the new society. They will appear again in Veblen and Galbraith. Fourier had the least practical experience. Nevertheless, even his absurd hypotheses and schemes demonstrated great imaginative strength.

All three advocated the communal organization of society in some form. The atomization of social structure that laissez faire capitalism produced was unacceptable to them. They desperately attempted to formulate schemes for group behavior not tainted by the tenets of capitalism. It was no accident that these three men rather quickly fathered quasireligious movements.

Today in the United States there exist thousands of communal experiments of one kind or another. They range from well-organized, well-financed, well-run agricultural operations to the most disorganized, poverty-stricken, chaotic, self-supporting *cum* handicraft groups. Most communes fall into this latter category. They cannot survive. Those that might not succumb to an invariably hostile environment are still bound to fail on even more fundamental grounds. In the twentieth century, the two best examples of successful communal organization are the Russian and the Israeli. The Russian system is tightly organized and controlled by the massive use of force; their communes "work" because the peasants have no choice. In Israel, the kibbutzim also work, but only for 4 percent of the total population. Here the operative forces are survival and idealism, though even under these conditions the kibbutzim are able to draw fewer and fewer new recruits.

Communal life, whether patterned after Owen's New Harmony, Fourier's "phalanxes" *(phalanstères),* or contemporary American versions of the flight from capitalist society, shipwreck on unsolved social and human dilemmas: Property, production, sex, and human nature. The assumption of most communalists is that individual property ownership is somehow an unnatural cultural growth which must be abolished before a healthy psyche can arise. The history of capitalism since the nineteenth century does show us that property rights need not be as broadly or liberally defined as Western countries originally permitted. The cost of industrial growth need not be universal pollution. However, the total abolition of ownership seems to fly in the face of a large body of fact and experience. Social anthropologists and social psychologists are trying to tell us that their data indicate that the possession of goods is important to human beings, and that these feelings develop very early in the process of personality growth. The modification of property rights through broadening social controls has had a more successful life cycle than any of the communal experiments.

From Robert Owen's writings to the contemporary press, communal supporters have consistently missed the thrust of technological innovation and the organization of production under this continuing revolutionary force. (Marx clearly recognized this.) Owen's New Harmony failed because he neglected the real industrial experience he had accumulated in New Lanark. Similarly, the potters and sandal-makers are economically incongruous with processes such as the continuous casting of steel, the Pilkington flotation method of glass-making, or the automated chemical plant. The future of capitalistic production does not lie with the idealistic. By every measurement, the force of technological innovation increases in every decade. Because of our scientific knowledge, we stand today at the edge of a massive technological leap forward rather than at the end of the age of industrial innovation.

Sex. What to do about sex? Freud once commented: "So perhaps we must make up our minds to the idea that altogether it is not possible for the claims of the sexual instinct to be reconciled with the demands of the culture."[16] On the kibbutzim and the Soviet com-munal farms, sexual norms similar to standard patterns in Western society have been established. The lesson from nineteenth-century Utopian experiments is the same as that learned by contemporary communalists: Inability to define permissible sexual parameters cre-ates a kind of chaos that destroys communal organization. The expe-rience of Owen, Fourier, and Saint-Simon is not so terribly different— minus drugs—from the hippie subculture of San Mateo county. Com-munal idealism and sexual freedom form an unstable combination.

All the utopians, nineteenth century and contemporary, believe that human nature (however they define it) can easily be changed by making some structural changes within their societies. Unlike suc-cessful entrepreneurs, they lack a realistic time sense. They envisage change as short run. And they inevitably fail. New Harmony, Queen-wood, Icaria, and today's many variations fall under the same deter-minism: Man changes only over long, long periods of time. Com-munal schemes have never demonstrated this level of frustration tolerance.

Robert Owen. In many ways, Owen was the most gifted and the most productive representative of utopianism.[17] Born in 1771, Owen received and reflected the major currents of both the eighteenth and nineteenth centuries. When he died at the age of eighty-seven, his ex-

[16]Sigmund Freud, "The Most Prevalent Form of Degradation in Erotic Life," in Steven Marcus, *The Other Victorians* (New York: Basic Books, 1964).
[17]G. D. H. Cole, *The Life of Robert Owen,* 3d ed. (Hamden, Conn.: Archon Books, 1966).

citing career had taken him through a range of social and economic experiences broader than that available to any of his contemporaries. Let us forget the spiritualism and mental breakdown of his final years; they neither add to nor detract from the richness of his contribution. Before 1815, Owen's career was meteoric. More than any other British figure, his life before thirty was linked with business success and public acclaim. Horatio Alger and Samuel Smiles would have loved him. With £100 borrowed from his artisan father, Owen at eighteen became an entrepreneur. Within a decade he had married the boss's daughter and was himself a co-proprietor and director of the New Lanark mills. Here he became an international figure. Kings and aristocratic notables came to see and marvel at the changes he had made in this grubby mill town. His recognition and popularity were relatively short-lived. First, he disagreed with his partners over the operation of the mills and the distribution of profits and was finally forced to leave the partnership. Some time after the depression of 1815, Owen moved intellectually toward a complete break with established institutions. Over the remaining four decades of his career, he managed to frighten and antagonize almost all the influential segments of British society. Unlike Bentham, whose impact spread throughout the century, Owen's ideas evaporated. The concept and development of cooperatives alone survived and preserve his fame, although he had little regard for them. Owen became part of the "underworld" of economic thought. Belligerent, militant, anticlerical, and antiintellectual, Owen estranged most of his supporters and reduced socialism in the 1830s to an epithet among the English middle class. It has taken more than a century of new economic crises and new insights into personal and industrial psychology to rehabilitate this strange genius.

Untrained and uncritical in his economic analysis, Owen made frightful errors such as his juvenile attacks on money and profit. More than the classical economists, however, he saw society as an organic whole, and more than Marx, he saw society as capable of change without violence and hatred. Although Owen's psychology was primitive, it drew on the richness of the great intellectual movements of the eighteenth century. Individuals rather than classes were his primary building blocks, and history may yet side with him against the arbitrary fictions of homogeneous classes based solely on economic criteria.

At New Lanark, Owen was a practical reformer. He was an efficient, enlightened manufacturer who recognized that his labor force required the same care as his machinery if it was to operate properly and efficiently.

> Experience has also shown you the difference of the results between mechanism which is neat, clean, well-arranged, and always in a high state of repair; and that which is allowed to be dirty, in disorder, without the means of preventing unnecessary friction, and which therefore becomes, and works, much out of repair.
>
> In the first case the whole economy and management are good; every operation proceeds with ease, order and success. In the last, the reverse must follow, and a scene be presented of counteraction, confusion, and dissatisfaction among all the agents and instruments interested or occupied in the general process, which cannot fail to create great loss.
>
> If, then, due care as to the state of your inanimate machines can produce such beneficial results, what may not be expected if you devote equal attention to your vital machines, which are far more wonderfully constructed?[18]

To these ends, Owen logically reduced the hours of labor, abolished fines, fostered education for employees, limited the age of employment of children to ten and improved the housing and care of the workers. New Lanark could have looked like Hershey, Pennsylvania, had he remained contented with this microcosmos. The Owenite reconstruction of New Lanark not only had the wholesome qualities— rediscovered by Elton Mayo and Fritz Roethlisberger in the twentieth century—of involving workers personally in their job structures, but also, unfortunately, contained a great deal of arbitrary and offensive paternalism.

Owenism never was and never became a systematic set of beliefs. Owen was unable to create a unified, rigorous analytical body of thought; Marx paid no attention to him and dismissed his ideas as "utopian." If Owen's ideas, however, lacked coherence and organization, they did not lack unity. Man was made by his social environment, the total community experience in which he lived and worked. Economic activity was part of this process, but not solely deterministic, as Marx insisted. The dynamic thrust of Owen's ideas followed this

---

[18]Robert Owen, "Essays on the formation of Character," in *A New View of Society and Other Writings* (London: Dent, 1927), p. 8.

thread: When the social milieu was remade, man would be reborn socially. Nineteenth-century society enhanced the sick elements in human life: It stressed competition instead of mutual aid; it glorified profit instead of a just price; it worshipped money instead of labor value; and its religion preached a debilitating doctrine of "responsibility" instead of a broad charity. Owen attempted in various ways throughout his life to rechannel these elements into new patterns and structures. At New Lanark in Scotland, in New Harmony in the United States, and at Harmony Hall or Queenwood in England, he built communal structures that *would* create the social environment of cooperation and communism. Each one of these colonizing efforts failed; the experiments cost Owen his personal fortune.

Owen's thinking never reached a very complex level. Nowhere is this better illustrated than in his confused and polemical attack on profit and money. Owen's argument had great force but no comprehension of economics. Profit was an evil force, and money was the instrument of that evil. He never defined profit in any but moral terms. "The secret of profit is to buy cheap and to sell dear in the name of an artificial conception of wealth which neither expands as wealth grows nor contracts as it diminishes."[19] Even the most limited definition of profit as an interest charge and hence an element in the total cost of production was not acceptable to him. Only labor was the source of value, and, therefore, goods must be sold for what they cost in labor units. Owen traced all the evils of the capitalistic system to this source, and his emphasis on a socialist organization of production was to annihilate this monster of profit competitiveness. Money too destroyed life. "Metallic money is the cause of a great deal of crime, injustice, and want, and it is one of the contributory causes which tend to destroy character and to make life into a pandemonium."[20] After his failures in New Harmony, Owen set up the National Equitable Labor Exchange. Here workers were to deposit their goods and receive "labor notes" with which they could buy other goods. The Labor Exchange did not work. Speculators milked the gullible. The most honest laborers became the prey of the most unscrupulous. Money as the instrument of value and of exchange was too useful to be disregarded. No verbiage and no idealism could replace its func-

[19]Owen, quoted in Charles Gide and Charles Rist, *A History of Economic Doctrine,* trans. R. Richards (Boston: Heath, n.d.), p. 240, note 2.
[20]*Ibid.,* p. 240, note 2.

tions. Although the Labor Exchange appealed to many craftsmen, it lasted only a short time. The experiment underlines three facts: The richness of imagination in nineteenth-century economic thought; the resistance of the handworker against the drive of industrialization; and the victory of economic science over amateurism. Although Owen rejected the cooperative movement and believed it unworthy of his ideals, the movement bears his name. Cooperatives flourished, not as a means to replace the capitalistic system but to abolish the middleman and his excessive charges. The Rochdale Pioneers were not forging a new social or economic order; they were accommodating themselves to an industrial society with its impersonal markets. Owen thought of them as "philanthropic institutions," and in a way they were organizations of self-help. Here toward the end of his life, one of his intuitive economic schemes had come alive and would thrive.

During the 1830s, Owen, who was really one of the founders of the model city concept, published several works around the concept of a New Moral World. He attacked traditional Christianity and with it the theme of "responsibility": "The idea of responsibility is one of the absurdest, and has done a great deal of harm."[21] Owen did not really mean this. What he really wanted was to free human beings from a socially imposed guilt that was not of their making. His formulation, however, was so deterministic as to be ludicrous, but again his perception was magnificent. In an anonymous industrial society, the individual is only partly master of his fate. The Protestant Ethic bore too heavily and too harshly on the wage earner. Historically, these quasireligious values impeded social legislation for many, many decades, and still form much of the folklore of the conservative doctrine of "character." No man is entirely a failure. Robert Owen, entrepreneur, socialist, deist, millionaire, visionary, polemicist, anticlerical prophet, served a worthwhile purpose. Through a life of example and a mass of written protest, he illuminated the sins of his society. He contributed to an awareness of the social and economic environment in which men are living. His emphasis on universal education preceded his time. Many of his social criticisms Marx welded into an organized, articulate, and embittered doctrine, but Owen expressed them earlier in a more esthetic form.

[21]*Ibid.,* p. 238, note 2. ("Catechism of the New Moral World," 1838).

Saint-Simon and Fourier. Two additional writers of most extraordinary talents and entirely different personalities and temperaments illustrate the range of imagination that industrialization brought to early
socialist thought: Henri de Saint-Simon, descendant of Charlemagne,
and Charles Fourier, traveling salesman and shop clerk. John Bell
discusses Saint-Simonianism as a "sort of comic opera," and Fourier
as someone who "would surely be put in the lunatic fringe."[22] Such
judgments are not surprising! Saint-Simon and Fourier filled their
pages with unbelievable naïveté. Yet sanity and reality are slippery
terms today, and more can be gained by looking at what these
reformers had in mind than by demonstrating how unhinged they
really were.

Both writers were stimulated by the mighty forces of modernization that the French Revolution and Napoleon brought to the continent. Saint-Simon had a fascinating early life as a participant in this
drama. He fought briefly with the French in the American Revolution, and was a colonel by the age of twenty-three. He retired, however, from military life to enter upon a scientific career useful to
humanity. Just as his life spanned both the eighteenth and nineteenth
centuries, so there is much in his writings that attempts to reconcile
the nationalism and individualism of the eighteenth century with the
new collectivistic forces of the nineteenth. Unquestionably, he was a
person of great ability. He quickly amassed a fortune by speculating
in confiscated church lands, but died in poverty after two decades of
intense activity to establish a system that would replace the outmoded
preindustrialism of the old regime. Saint-Simon summarized his new
philosophy thus: "Everything by industry; everything for industry."
The motto symbolized what was important in the doctrine. Let us
disregard all those elements of confused fantasy, which discredited
Saint-Simonianism and made it both a quasireligious cult and a laugh-
ingstock in nineteenth-century France. With the ideas he put forth so
strangely in books such as the *New Christianity,* Saint-Simon was the
first to recognize the role that could be played by the professional
technologist and engineer. Thus Saint-Simonianism—"technocracy,"
as it is called today—was a deliberate attempt to come to grips with
the realities of modern society. The future lay with the engineers, the
railroad builders, the canal designers—those who would shape society

---

[22]John F. Bell, *A History of Economic Thought* (New York: Ronald, 1953), pp.
364-365.

in a more rational and scientific manner, as dictated by the revolutionary forms of production coming into being with ever-increasing velocity. Saint-Simon rejected the classical economic doctrine of harmony of interests. Spontaneous unregimented economic forces were cruel, chaotic, and humanly destructive. These forces could be administered professionally by scientists, technicians, businessmen, bankers, and industrialists. He would preserve the system but administer it from above. Economic laws and social organization could yield to a trained paternal professionalism. The nineteenth century rejected Saint-Simonianism as gross nonsense, though individual ideas continued to affect the growing self-esteem of the professionals who *were* building railroads, canals, and managing enterprises. The twentieth century has had to wrestle with many of the problems anticipated by the Saint-Simonians; therefore, we think more highly of them. The future of industrial society lies with the professionals, with elitist categories (under democratic controls, one hopes), and with a great deal of planning, which was implicit in Saint-Simon, rather than in class conflict or a return to preindustrial rural Edens. Engels referred to the "genial perspicacity" of Saint-Simon which enabled him to anticipate all the doctrine of subsequent socialists other than those of a specifically economic character—that is, surplus value. This judgment would not have pleased Saint-Simon, but it is not far from the mark.

Let us suppose that France suddenly loses fifty of her first-class doctors, fifty first-class chemists, fifty first-class physiologists, fifty first-class bankers, two hundred of her best merchants, six hundred of her foremost agriculturists, five hundred of her most capable ironmasters, etc. [enumerating the principal industries]. Seeing that these men are its most indispensable producers, making its most important products, the minute that it loses these the nation will degenerate into a mere soulless body and fall into a state of despicable weakness in the eyes of rival nations, and will remain in this subordinate position so long as the loss remains and their places vacant. Let us take another supposition. Imagine that France retains all her men of genius, whether in the arts and sciences or in the crafts and industries, but has the misfortune to lose on the same day the king's brother, the Duke of Angouleme, and all the other members of the royal family; all the great officers of the Crown; all ministers of State, whether at the head of a department or not; all the Privy Councillors; all the masters of requests, all the marshals, cardinals, archbishops, bishops, grand vicars and canons; all prefects and subprefects; all Government employees; all the judges; and on top of that a hundred thousand proprietors—the cream of her nobility. Such an overwhelming catastrophe would certainly aggrieve the French, for they are a kindly-disposed nation. But the loss of a hundred and thirty thousand of the best-reputed individuals in the State would give rise to sorrow of a purely sentimental kind. It would not cause the community the least inconvenience.[23]

Charles Fourier believed that society had to be reorganized on the basis of small integrated collectivist units of 1620 people—the phalanxes. Nothing is easier than to make fun of poor old Fourier, waiting for the millionaire to underwrite his model communal Utopia. We can dismiss out of hand the novel idea of young children between three and five doing the menial work in the community such as garbage collecting, slaughtering animals, and general "K.P." arrangements. But one cannot dismiss Fourier's perception of the nature of work. He argued that routine economic activity had a dehumanizing effect, which could only be alleviated by his new organizational structure, the phalanx, and by a new programming of the working situation. Instead of a routine, hostility-producing, repetitive work process, each person would perform seven or eight different jobs! Spread over a ten-hour day, this work program would prevent boredom and permit the full realization of the individual. Fourier's impossible structure was to integrate work and living. These few suggestions were about all we may take from the confused mass of his writings.

He had no great insight into human personality and its complexities. He never comprehended the range of conflict and antagonism, which Marx perceived. Economic theory was virtually unknown to him. Industrialization and modernization could be contained, he concluded, within this interlocking mechanism of working-apartment enclaves. Urban industrial society remained outside the phalanstery. Neither Saint-Simon nor Fourier contributed to the "dismal science," but they both anticipated the concern of economists with social problems.

The Central Position of Marx

On the afternoon of the 14th of March at a quarter to three, the greatest

---

[23]Henri, Comte de Saint-Simon (1760-1825), *Selected Writings,* ed. and trans. F. M. H. Markham, "First Extract from the Organizer" (Oxford: Blackwell, 1952), p. 72.

living thinker ceased to think. Left alone for less than two minutes, when we entered we found him sleeping peacefully in his chair—but forever.[24]

In his funeral eulogy, Engels went on to describe the dimensions of the life that had just ended. First there was the loss "impossible to measure" that the fighting European and American proletariat had suffered. The loss to historical science was just as great.

As Darwin discovered the law of evolution in organic nature, so Marx discovered the law of evolution in human history: simple fact, previously hidden under ideological growths, that human beings must first of all eat, drink, shelter and clothe themselves before they can turn their attention to politics, science, art and religion; that therefore the production of the immediate material means of life and thereby the given stage of economic development of a people or of a period forms the basis on which the State institutions, the legal principles, the art and even the religious ideas of the people in question have developed and out of which they must be explained.[25]

But not only this:

Marx discovered the special law of development of the present-day capitalist mode of production and of the bourgeois system of society which it has produced. With the discovery of surplus value, light was suddenly shed on the darkness in which all other economists, both bourgeois and socialist, had lost themselves.[26]

Engels continued with even less justification to praise Marx's work in mathematics and interest in electricity. These middle paragraphs of the graveside speech disappeared into the empty air. But Engels returned to a greater and more substantial theme:

For Marx was above all a revolutionary, and his great aim in life was to cooperate in this or that fashion in the overthrow of capitalist society and the State institutions which it has created, to cooperate in the emancipation of the modern proletariat, to whom he was the first to give a consciousness of its

[24]Franz Mehring, *Karl Marx, the Story of His Life,* trans. Edward Fitzgerald (New York: Covici, Friede, 1935), pp. 554-556.
[25]*Ibid.,* p. 555.
[26]*Ibid.,* p. 555.

class needs, a knowledge of the conditions necessary for its emancipation. In this struggle he was in his element, and he fought with a passion, tenacity and success granted to few."[27]

Little else remained to be said.

And therefore Marx was the best-hated and most-slandered man of his age. Governments, both absolutist and republican, expelled him from their territories, whilst the bourgeois, both conservative and extreme-democratic, vied with each other in a campaign of vilification against him. He brushed it all to one side like cobwebs, ignored them and answered only when compelled to do so. And he died respected, loved and mourned by millions of revolutionary workers. . . .[28]

"His name," Engels concluded, "will live through the centuries and so also will his work."[29]

Marx's life has usually been portrayed within the ideological and political framework of nineteenth-century European intellectual movements. It may be of some use to add a brief description of Marx's career as it paralleled significant economic changes during this century. The span of Marx's life (1818-1883) takes in the establishment of industrial society in the West. The pace, however, of this momentous change was everywhere uneven. The city of Trier of May 1818, where Marx was born, had not yet recovered from the Napoleonic Wars. The London of 1883, where Marx died, was in the grips of a cyclical depression; England herself was now bypassed in growth by Germany, Japan, and the United States. We cannot merge completely the career of both the man and the European economic development, but the parallel development of Marx's thinking and Europe's economy partially explains the forces that shaped Marx's ideology and, in turn, influenced European political and socioeconomic development. Marx was, in fact, the central ideological force on the continent after 1850. Engels, in the funeral oration, stated that Marx made two seminal discoveries—first, "the special law of development of the present day capitalist mode of production and of the bourgeois system of society

[27]*Ibid.*, pp. 554-556.
[28]*Ibid.*, p. 556.
[29]*Ibid.*, p. 556.

which it has produced," and second, the "discovery of surplus value."[30] If these are the two great Marxist theoretical contributions, they derive a great deal of their force from the economic development of those decades through which Marx lived. However, they were not significant theoretical additions to the body of economic theory.

The first portion of Marx's life ends with the death of his father in 1838, when Karl Marx was twenty. Most accounts of Marx's origins mention a comfortable, placid, happy childhood. This account has been exaggerated. Behind the outward facade of middle-class professional success that Heinrich, Marx's father, achieved, lay a background of stress. The Marxes came from a long rabbinical tradition. Karl's grandfather was rabbi of Trier, his (Karl's) uncle Samuel succeeded to that position. The old grandmother Eva Marx, nee Mases, was still alive in 1825. Marx's mother Henrietta came also from a very long rabbinical background. Hirschel, or Heinrich, adopted Christianity in 1824 at the age of thirty-two (Marx was six at the time); undoubtedly, this conversion was an intense emotional wrench within the Marx family. Marx's biographer Franz Mehring associates the move to Christianity with the agricultural crisis of the 1820s and the consequent wave of anti-Semitism that swept the Rhineland, and the personal consideration that Karl Marx came of school age that year—education would be much easier for the son of a Christian than that of a Jew. However, conversions are personal experiences first, and economic rationalizations only second.

The family picture of a devoted, unintellectual housewife-mother, and a sentimental, old-fashioned, romantic-type father does not seem sufficient. Hirschel feared the "demon" in his son, not knowing whether it was "heavenly" or "Faustian." And Marx's own comments in a juvenile essay that "We cannot always take up the profession for which we feel ourselves suited; our relations in society have begun to crystallize more or less before we are in a position to determine them"[31] shows more inner stress and intensity than the romantic portrayal of growing up in Trier.

At eighteen, Karl became engaged to Jenny von Westphalen, a close friend of his elder sister Sophie. Jenny was four years Marx's senior, much courted, unusually beautiful. In many ways, the match

[30]*Ibid.*, p. 555.
[31]*Ibid.*, p. 33.

made no sense. Privy Councillor Ludwig von Westphalen, Jenny's father, came from a brilliant but erratic background (Philip Westphalen was the real chief-of-staff of the Duke of Brunswick during the Seven Years War). Ludwig von Westphalen occupied a position of high social prestige in Trier; the Marxes did not. Marx was to wait almost seven years and had to overcome considerable personal prejudice and opposition before he could marry.

These seven years laid the basis for Marx's later career. In 1836, when Heinrich Marx gave his permission for his son's engagement, he coupled it with his wish that the young swain continue his studies in jurisprudence at Berlin. The story of Marx's university career is well known. Berlin was the exciting center for the new Hegelianism. Into this intellectual ferment Marx threw himself with the energy and unrestraint that so characterized him. It is difficult to evaluate what he learned at the university—the intoxication with ideas, the spell of words, the hatred for Prussian authoritarianism, the disappointment and disillusionment of a blasted career. By the early spring of 1842, there was no chance for Marx to have an academic career in Germany. His doctorate in philosophy led nowhere, and he turned to radical journalism. It took just over a year for the Prussian government to close down the *Rheinische Zeitung* which Marx edited. By the end of October 1843, Marx, newly married, was in Paris. Two years later the Marxes took up their residence in Brussels, and finally, in 1849, Marx reached London, a permanent exile. As a journalist he had achieved no more success than as a philosopher, but these years of stress and trial had introduced him into the current radical social and economic milieu of western Europe. We see a growing maturity in Marx as he travels from Berlin to Cologne, Paris, Brussels, and London. At least some of his romantic intellectual baggage was thrown away and a trimmer, leaner thinker prepared for his life's work in the British Museum.

Marx lived in London some thirty-four years. He knew, however, little of England. No one was less attuned to the rhythms of English society or politics. How absolutely strange it seems to compare the life experience of someone like Disraeli, Gladstone, or Palmerston with Marx. Even in the nineteenth century would anyone be able to analyze an economic environment from reading about it? The base of Marx's perception was inward looking, which accounts for much of its genius and its limitations. Marx lived in various mean residences, underwent many humiliations and indignities, came in contact with a handful of German refugees, and made an even smaller number of friends. One need not draw the picture too darkly. The family was held together by a great deal of love and warmth from Jenny and their faithful servant "Lehnchen." The children suffered, and two died. Marx experienced evictions and penury, and was almost totally reliant on Engels for financial support. Marx, a man of genius, continued to work toward some kind of creative fulfillment. What a fantastic arrogance, exuberance, and ability this sturdy, heavy man must have contained within him to believe that he could alter the very nature of Western society.

The core of Marxist thought is not economic but moral. As Durkheim pointed out in his criticism of *Capital:*

The truth is that the facts and observations gathered in it . . . figure there as little more than arguments. The research . . . was undertaken to establish the doctrine . . . , far from the doctrine resulting from research. . . . It was passion that inspired all these systems; what gave birth to them and constitutes their strength is the thirst for a more perfect justice . . . . Socialism is not a science, a sociology in miniature; it is a cry of pain . . . .[32]

Although Marx read prodigiously and was closely familiar with the English Blue Book reports of economic conditions, his personal knowledge of industrial affairs was entirely academic. Engels, his long friend and collaborator, had a more direct knowledge of English reality and managed his family's textile firm in Manchester. Engels' monograph *The Condition of the Working Classes* (1844) is still a distinguished work of empirical research.[33] Marx did not have this abrasive experience of reality. Durkheim's evaluation is correct, despite Marx's vehement desire to be both realistic and pragmatic. We will discuss at considerable length the fundamental contributions of Marxist economics, but Marx's ultimate contribution lay not in theory but in historical perception and social comment.

[32]Emile Durkheim, *Le Socialisme: sa définition, ses debut, la doctrine saintsimonienne* (Paris: Alcan, 1928), p. 6; H. Stuart Hughes, *Consciousness and Society* (New York: Knopf, 1958), chap. 3, part 1, pp. 75-78.
[33]Friedrich Engels, *The Condition of the Working Class in England,* trans. and ed. W.O. Henderson and W. H. Chaloner (New York: Macmillan, 1958).

MARX AS HISTORIAN AND SOCIOLOGIST

Marx examined the Industrial Revolution and pointed to six important areas in which it had altered the framework of modern life. First, Marx exposed the visible character of nineteenth-century industrial change as a direct and often brutal exploitation of human beings. Industrial revolution was a human disaster to people wherever it appeared. To the participants without resources of protection, it was a disease that killed and crippled. No matter what the liberals said or promised, life for many was destroyed as industrialization became established in western Europe in the decades after 1850. Every picture book of the period graphically depicts the horror of urban industrial life. What was good and wholesome in the process of modernization *seemed* miniscule compared to the crushing atomization of human life. Marx dramatically brought to bear on this process the whole weight of his tremendous power. No one could ever disregard what he illuminated. Marx was not the first social reformer, but social reforms have the imprint of "before or after" the *Manifesto.*

Second, Marx dramatized the permanent revolutionizing aspects of technology. If anything, he was cautious and moderate in this regard. The revolutionizing nature of the ever-changing instruments of production was the underpinning of his sociological system. He clearly saw that industrialization could not remain static, that it had its own built-in dynamic. With this dynamic would come continuing changes not merely in production but also in personal and class relationships within society. Marx as a sociologist is not profound; his formulations were far too simplistic. Here, as elsewhere, his contribution was pyrotechnic: He set off sparks that would illuminate new avenues for investigation. Marx almost completely failed to perceive and understand the deep and real complexities of social structure. The vagueness and imprecision of the "class" as the building-block of social analysis has not been especially helpful in understanding the social order of the late nineteenth and twentieth centuries. Marx thought he had discovered a scientific law in the bifurcation of society into two hostile and competing classes; he never could envisage more than a two-class social structure. So many writers have praised Marx's deep reading that it may seem presumptuous to say that he still knew too little history rather than too much. Historical scholarship in his day gave little help to anyone interested in the structure of society, but this shortcoming of the historical discipline still does not make

Marx less vulnerable. In fact, there is throughout a great deal of Marx's analysis a kind of naïveté, a combination of childish simplicity and a self-imposed, overwhelming burden of Teutonic complexity. Side by side one finds gold and pyrite.

Marx could not bring himself to understand that history was more than economic relationships, that social relations were more intimate, more varied, and more nonrational than a cash-nexus. The modernizing onslaught of industrialization would make life more variegated, not only occupationally but also socially and psychologically. But Marx's contribution is still worthwhile. Ricardo's was an abstract social analysis; Marx did try to bring economic analysis back to its concrete social and political moorings. That he did not accomplish this does not detract greatly from the measure of his attempt.

Third, Marx recognized that the world was emerging as, and would become, a single economic unit. Some of the ideas that dominate our twentieth-century concern with economic development are foreshadowed by Marx. He was clearly one of the first economists to see the full implications of the Industrial Revolution. Marx today would be sympathetic to the thesis of "industrialize or perish." The future, he felt, was in the harnessing of these new powerful forces, which overarched all boundaries and encompassed all mankind.

Fourth, no one else saw as clearly as did he the real contribution of the bourgeoisie. He wrote: ". . . during its rule of scarce one hundred years, it [the bourgeoisie] has created more massive and more colossal productive forces than have all preceding generations together."[34] Bourgeois society not only had created these new productive forces but also it had altered by a quantum jump the levels of productivity. Inherent in this new capability was the promise of wider distribution, which would raise the real standard of living. This promise has been fulfilled dramatically in western Europe, North America, Japan, and in several other places. Marx as a revolutionary could not consider this development as a real alternative. The basis for social change was increasing hardship and social antagonism; making the pie bigger so that there would be enough for both the capitalist and the laborer would destroy the revolutionary basis of Marxist thought. If, in place of conflict, one could show that a complementarity of interest existed, one would not need to blow up the entire

---

[34]Karl Marx, *The Communist Manifesto,* in E. Burns, *A Handbook of Marxism* (New York: International Publishers, 1935), p. 28.

social-political structure. This reformist modification of revolutionary ideology has marked the course of nineteenth- and twentieth-century political history. From the Fabians to the Social Democrats, New Dealers, and Catholic Action groups, political leaders and social reformers found it to their interest to adopt and adapt capitalism. The reformers came to believe that they could have their cake and eat it too. Capitalism could provide sinews of power undreamed of, and social improvements unheard of. Capitalism could promise and almost deliver all things to all people.

If we are to give Marx his due, we might acknowledge his contribution to a number of disciplines—for example, economic history, social history, social theory, and sociology. In all of these, Marx opened new vistas of research and exploration. Marx made many mistakes, prodigious errors, but he did lay the groundwork for research and investigation into social phenomena hitherto neglected and unexplored. Marx's accusations and indictments against existing institutions and arrangements could not be dismissed out of hand. The importance of economic factors, the structure of society, the lines of authority, the nature of elites, the causes of protest—all these questions and many, many more come from the critical nature of Marx's writing.

Finally, and most significantly, Marx accepted industrial society. The thrust of Marxism was toward the future. He heaped abuse on the so-called Utopians. The clock of history could not be turned back. Human personality could be reshaped in this future state where the means of production and its control were utilized in significantly different ways. The full enthusiasm of the eighteenth century re-emerged through Marx's writing in his confidence that all this could be achieved. Marx made a prodigious mark on his society, and no history of economic thought can neglect him. The forces of production, the nature of distribution, the organization of technology, the shape of future societies, all of these he drew into a unified system. Captive of his own logical apparatus, Marx could not reach the freedom of intellect that would have allowed him to see that men were not dominated by economics, but that economics was only a secondary drive in man's overall personality makeup. Had Marx but looked in a mirror, he might have seen the limitations of a psychological theory based on economic determinism.

The Marxian System

Marx had been a philosopher and sociologist long before he became an economist by reading virtually every significant economics book in the possession of the British Museum. Upon the Ricardian foundation he built an imposing system that had to satisfy the sometimes conflicting demands of his already well-established ideological position and his intellectual integrity. The difficulty of satisfying both constraints forced him into tortuous obfuscations of an essentially simple system. Like Ricardo, he found it extremely difficult to maintain the labor theory of value in the face of empirical evidence to the contrary; very much like Ricardo, he kept modifying the value components of his model until in Volume 3 of his *Capital,* the labor theory of value had been so weakened that he finally had to admit "Je ne suis pas un Marxist." The Marx we shall discuss, however, is primarily the Marx of the *Manifesto* and Volume 1 of *Capital*—the essence of contemporary Marxism.

Marx did not need the labor theory of value for analytical purposes. Without it, his model could have exposed equally well the weaknesses of the capitalistic system, and could have withstood critical attacks with much greater success. But Marx knew, at least instinctively, that the labor theory was the ideological heart of his model. Indeed, without the labor theory and its offspring, exploitation and surplus value theory, Marx would have been merely another Sismondi.

In spite of the fact that comparatively few mortals have managed to fight their way through the obscure, convoluted *Capital,* the epitome of Teutonic philosophizing, Marx had an enormous impact on his and subsequent generations. There are millions, from cocktail party Socialists to hard-nosed union leaders, who claim a knowledge of Marx. This "vulgar" Marxism is based upon a few essential components of the Marxian model; it is this kernel that has prompted the rise of Socialist parties. Stripped of all accessories, this basic Marxian model is quite a sturdy structure. Interestingly enough, the "basic model" appears nowhere in Marx's writings as a unified whole, but parts can be found scattered throughout his works.

The primary cause of Marx's attack on contemporary society was the misery of the working class, a misery that became unbearable during the periodic crises that capitalism produced. Marx caught the imagination of all the disaffected and alienated by declaring that the misery of the working class was caused by capitalist exploitation and that both exploitation and crises were inherent in the capitalistic system. Only if the system was changed, therefore, could these evils

be banned. Reformers who believed that the twin evils of underconsumption and unemployment could be banished by social reform or
government intervention have been the target of the most vituperative
attacks of the Marxists. Certainly, if the business cycle can be controlled by government policy, then very significant tenets of the
Marxian system have been shattered. Since 1940, severe crises such
as Marx had predicted have disappeared in the Western world, and
unemployment has also become a serious problem in several communist countries. These facts have had a profound impact on Marxist
movements, and as a consequence most European Democratic Socialist movements have abandoned much of their Marxian rhetoric and
convictions. The true believers among the radical left, however, have
simply refused to admit that significant changes in the capitalist structure have taken place during the last twenty-five years.

The central problem of capitalism is caused by two factors inherent in capitalism: *underconsumption* and *structural division of the
economy into consumer-goods and producer-goods industries.* Marx,
very much like Sismondi, saw in the limited purchasing power of the
working class the cause for unemployment; unlike Sismondi, however, he made underconsumption an organic aspect of capitalism that
could not be removed by an enlightened public wage policy. It is the
crucial fact of capitalism, Marx wrote, that the worker sells his daily
labor (labor power) for less than the value of the goods he produces.
The worker produces this surplus value in all societies, but only
under capitalism does the worker no longer own the tools of production and, therefore, must suffer that the capitalist appropriates the
labor-produced surplus value. Labor, and only labor, produces a surplus value, but because labor, the chief consumer, does not receive a
wage sufficient to purchase all that it produces, there must be a
continuous gap between purchasing power and the total quantity of
all goods produced. This gap can be bridged only temporarily, even if
the capitalist reinvests the appropriated surplus value. The structural
division of the economy into producer-goods and consumer-goods
industries allows this gap to be closed only periodically because of
time lags in the investment cycle.

While Marx's underconsumption theory was merely an elaboration of
Sismondi's, his view of the structural division of the economy showed
deep insight and originality. Marx also acknowledged his debt to
Quesnay's macroeconomic, two-sector analysis. Of course, Marxian

Figure **5.2** The Basic Marxian Model

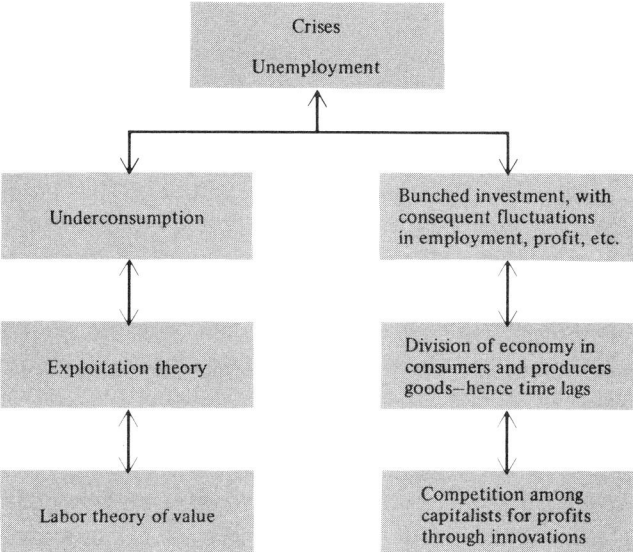

structural analysis was far more sophisticated, and his approach has greatly influenced all subsequent business-cycle analyses.

Like Quesnay, Marx saw in the relationship between consumer-goods and producer-goods industries one of the two major inherent contradictions of capitalism (the other "inherent contradiction" was the underconsumption propensity of capitalism, treated above). In an attempt to increase profits, capitalists will invest (innovate) in new equipment, but capitalist competition will force all entrepreneurs to adopt immediately the new methods. This will lead to a bunching of investments and, concomitantly, high demand for labor, rising wages, and consequent lowering of profits. At the very time when overall capital investment declines because of falling profits, a sharp increase in the output of consumer goods will occur as a result of the already completed earlier investments. The glut in consumer goods leads to a further decline in profits and further unemployment and wage reduction. This decline in wages, profits, prices, and employment is only ended with the disappearance of gluts and the reappearance of the profitability of new investments. Hence, periodic increases and decreases of investments cause fluctuations in profits, wages, and employment. Because small businesses are eliminated during every business-cycle recession, the periodic crises will lead to an increasing monopolization of society, and ultimately, the downfall of capitalism via the expropriation of monopolies.

Marx's recognition of a periodic business-cycle behavior—caused by periodic investments and the time lag between capital-goods and consumer-goods production—represents his most penetrating economic analysis. Virtually all modern business-cycle theory has taken the capital-goods-consumer-goods relationship as its starting point. In addition we know today from modern systems engineering analysis that random inputs applied to a delayed feedback mechanism will result in a sinusoidal output, which may either continue to oscillate, reach a steady state, or explode.[35] The market system is, of course, the feedback system par excellence, and Marx's two-sector model provides the time lag that must result in a sinusoidal output, very much like the business-cycle fluctuations recognized by Marx more than one hundred years ago.

This major contribution to economic analysis is rarely mentioned, either in modern texts or in scholarly discussion.[36] This may be, perhaps, because Marx himself did not present his business-cycle analysis as a coherent whole; nor did he tie it clearly to his dynamic theory of economic development, for expository reasons. Rather than refining his two-sector, dynamic business-cycle model, Marx slaved on making his notions of capitalistic crises compatible with his labor value theory. The careful reader will have noticed that these two aspects of Marxian theory contradict each other. If the capitalist invests in order to increase the productivity of labor and to increase his profit, then capital must be productive, and labor can no longer be the only source of value. Again and again, Marx is faced with the same difficulty that had already stumped Smith and Ricardo. Throughout Volume 3 Marx worked to reconcile the labor theory of value

[35]A. Tustin, *The Mechanism of Economic Systems* (London: Heineman, 1957).

[36]Three noteworthy exceptions are Joan Robinson, *Essay on Marxian Economics* (London: Macmillan, 1952), Paul Samuelson, "Wages and Interest: A Dissection of Marxian Economic Models," *American Economic Review* (December 1957), 884-912; Mark Blaug, "Marxian Economics," *Economic Theory in Retrospect* (Homewood, Ill.: Irwin, 1962), esp. pp. 211-221 . However, especially in Blaug's case, Marx, who was a poor mathematician even for his time, is altered fundamentally by being forced into Blaug's mathematical version of Marx; as a matter of fact, if Marx had been able to formulate a tight, interdependent economic model, he would have been a better economist, but of far less social or political influence. To wit: How many disciples of Professor Samuelson have been storming barricades recently?

with both empirical evidence and components of his own theory. Some of his more tortured reasonings are discussed below.

The logical pitfalls, however, must not overshadow the appeal of the Marxian model. The labor theory merely told the proletariat what it already knew: Somebody was exploiting them. The business-cycle theory merely explained the behavior of the economy and prophesied an ultimate end to the present system.

A CLOSER LOOK AT THE MARXIAN MODEL

Without in any way deprecating Marx's originality, it must be understood that Marx combined three distinctive theories into an imaginative, original, but inconsistent whole. Quesnay's macroeconomic concept of the circulation of money and production provided the analytical framework wherein the classical theory of the exchange of equal labor values, as well as the "laws" of subsistence wages and capital accumulation could be pushed far enough to make the results fit both the third pillar, Sismondi's underconsumption theory, and empirical observations. The whole, in this case, is greater than the sum of its parts, but the ingenious combination of Ricardo, Quesnay, and Sismondi represents the framework of the Marxian system. Marx's inflammatory language, coupled with his Old Testament scorn for the imperfections and for the rulers of the world, have turned this framework into revolutionary dynamite.[37]

In our brief overview of the essence of Marxism, we started with his theory of crises and the three supplementary doctrines of the accumulation and deepening of capital,[38] underconsumption, and the consumption-production disproportionality. A thoroughly dynamic, rigorous, and modern model could be built on these concepts without any resort to the labor theory of value, which could easily accommodate most of the Marxian axioms such as instability, periodic crises,

---

[37]Keynes did not think that Marx's *Capital* was either well written or particularly brilliant. How a book, as tedious and as poorly written, Keynes mused, could have such an impact, would always remain one of the marvels of this world.

[38]The wide acceptance of the term "deepening of capital" is probably due to Evsey Domar, who refers to an increase in the ratio of capital goods to labor as a "deepening" of capital. Marx's "change in the composition of capital" is less precise because it refers to the ratio of constant to variable capital. Marx, however, included raw material and "goods in process" inventories in his "constant capital." "By constant capital . . . we always mean . . . the value of the means of production actually consumed in the [production] process." Karl Marx, *Das Kapital, Kritik der politischen oekonomie*, Hrsg. von Friedrich Engels (Hamburg: Meissner, 1880-1894), 3 vols., vol. 1, part 3, chap. 9, section 1. (Our translation.)

and unemployment. The contemporary models by Evsey Domar, Michio Morishima, and Joan Robinson are, for instance, compatible with the basic tenets of Marxian dynamics (economic development), but carry no emotional or revolutionary fervor and are known only to professional economists.[39] Marx without his labor theory of value and the concomitant doctrines of surplus value and exploitation is no longer Marx. A careful analysis of the Marxian system must, therefore, begin with his treatment of the labor theory and his constant battle, throughout the three volumes of *Capital* and his correspondence with Engels, to fit the metaphysical aspects of his system into an empirically verifiable frame.

In Volume I of *Capital,* Marx deals primarily with the nature of profit in a capitalistic society. Profit, as we have already mentioned, is a surplus created by labor but appropriated by the owner of the tools of production, the capitalist. It is important to note that, especially in Volume I, Marx operates very much within the framework of classical economics, implicitly as well as explicitly. Nowhere does he reject the assumption of *homo economicus,* and he explicitly assumes competition and an *identical capital-labor ratio throughout the economy.* Once this last very important assumption is made, it follows from the classical labor theory of value that prices vary according to the amount of labor (and, incidentally, capital!) employed; the statement that the value of goods is, in the long run, proportional to the amount of labor embodied in them specifically equates price and value over the long run and is still very much in the classical tradition. Marx carries classical, and especially Ricardian, analysis further by analyzing the nature of profit in a capitalist society. We remember that Smith could not reconcile the existence of profit with the labor theory and finally came to the conclusion that labor determines value in a primitive society only; in a capital-using society, however, the value of a commodity is in the long run determined by its cost of production, which includes interest as a payment for capital, one of the factors of production. Ricardo, after a much harder struggle, came to a very similar conclusion and finally admitted his

---

[39]Significantly, Mrs. Robinson believed that the analysis of the circulation of capital and money, as well as the accumulation of capital, was Marx's major contribution. Cf. her *Essay on Marxian Economics* (London: Macmillan 1942), and her *Accumulation of Capital* (London: Macmillan 1958). Similarly, Schumpeter saw in Marx's adherence to the labor theory the unfortunate inheritance of Ricardian thinking which kept Marx from breaking the intellectual limits of his time.

inability to show that labor was the only source of value. Marx, however, carried Ricardo's analysis further by introducing the concept of labor power as a commodity. The worker sells his ability to work, his labor power, and receives as compensation the amount necessary to produce "labor power"—that is, a subsistence wage. Because the worker can produce in a day's time more than he needs to live, the value of his labor power is less than the labor value of the goods produced by him during his working day. In a capital-using society, labor is the only instrument that can thus create a surplus value. This surplus value is appropriated by the capitalist, who exploits labor by not paying a wage equal to the value of the commodities produced by labor. The capitalist's profit is therefore an amount equal to the total surplus value created by labor; however, the rate of profit and the rate of surplus are *not* identical.

Even at this early stage, one encounters the logical difficulties that kept torturing Marx, just as they did Ricardo, throughout his work. The capitalist can exploit labor because he owns the tools of production; similarly, however, labor becomes a tool of exploitation because the existing tools have increased his productivity to the extent that he can now produce a surplus; thus, quite clearly, capital goods produce more value than the amount of labor embodied in them, and labor is no longer the only source of value. We shall return to this point.

Marx's analysis, throughout his work, is unnecessarily complicated by his repeated failure to distinguish between stocks (levels), flows, ratios, and rates, as well as by his tendency to make significant assumptions implicitly rather than explicitly. In order to clarify several sticky points, we shall give algebraic definitions to Marx's concepts. Using capital letters for stocks, lower case letters for flows, Greek letters for ratios, and prime letters for rates, we have the following significant Marxian definitions:

c = "constant capital" = sum of depreciation charges and raw materials input per time unit.

v = "variable capital" = wages per time unit (of production workers). (Note: *Only* production workers can generate a surplus.)

C = stock of durable equipment + raw material inventory (and goods in process inventory at beginning of year).

V = working capital necessary to pay wages per time unit (in many cases this becomes very similar to a "wages fund").

$C + V = K$ = Total stock of capital invested at point in time (or average amount of capital invested during time period).

s = surplus value = total revenue − total outlays, per time period. In modern terminology, as applied, for instance, to Russian national income accounting, one could define s = Net National Product − industrial wage bill (service industries, etc., excluded).

s' = rate of surplus value per unit time = s/v = rate of exploitation.

p' = rate of profit per unit time = $s/(c + v)$.

π = profit ratio at a point in time = s/K (although p' and π are different concepts, Marx used these terms interchangeably; also note that K is a stock, while c, v are flows).

o = organic composition of capital = $c/(c + v)$. (Marx was not consistent in using this, his most sophisticated concept. Not only does he refer to the organic composition of capital as the ratio between $c/(c + v)$ at one time and as $v/(c + v)$ at other times, but also he defines a flow concept and uses it as if it were a stock $O = C/V$, the ratio of fixed capital to wage capital.)

It is necessary furthermore to assume explicitly *(as Marx did not)* that constant and variable capital turn over completely once per time unit; otherwise p' cannot be defined as the rate of profit on invested capital.

Capital in the Marxian model, of course, is not productive, but merely a necessary tool of exploitation. The entire apparatus of labor theory, surplus value, and exploitation rate is developed to prove the point that interest (profit) is an unearned payment that flows into the pockets of the capitailst *only* because he owns the tools of production. As the capitalist accumulates his profit, he is forced by competition to reinvest it in his business. An increase in a firm's capital equipment increases the worker's productivity; the capitalist who innovates will increase his profit because "his" workers are now more productive than the rest. All other capitalists are forced by competition to follow suit and adopt the most efficient production methods.

Here again Marx emphasizes explicitly the "productive" nature of capital; he also admits the capitalist's innovating function, and he even, implicitly, seems to recognize the existence of a reward for innovation, namely short-run profits, which obviously are not due to labor's efforts.

The Schumpeterian concept of profit as a short-run reward for innovation does not affect Marx's labor theory because he was, like all classical economists, primarily interested in long-run behavior. Especially in Volumes 2 and 3, Marx emphasizes the short-run fluctuations of prices and wages around the long-run values, intrinsic labor costs and surplus. It would have been very easy for Marx, therefore, to admit explicitly the capitalist's innovating function and recognize short-run profits as the wages (rewards) of innovations. Marx failed to concede this point and thus makes it even more difficult to defend labor as the only source of value.

It is impossible to justify Marx's view of the "unproductive nature" of capital in view of his repeated references to the increased productivity of a labor force equipped with the latest capital equipment. Marx referred to machines as "constant capital" because the (labor) value inherent in the machines is merely passed on to the commodities it produced. Only the capitalists, who produced machines as a commodity, derived profit from machines by appropriating the surplus value generated by the labor force in the capital-goods industry; the machine-using capitalist, Marx said, did not derive a profit from the machine itself, although an innovating capitalist obtained additional rewards from pioneering in the introduction of new capital equipment. Even this "extra profit," Marx claimed, merely represented the expropriation of an "extra" surplus value. This extra surplus value was produced by the innovating capitalist's work force, which could produce a larger surplus value in the ordinary working day because its productivity was enhanced by the new capital equipment; as soon as the other capitalists were forced by competition to adopt the new production processes, the productivity of their workers would similarly rise, or conversely, the (labor) cost of production would fall. Because it was the "socially necessary labor time" that determined the value of a commodity, the initial extra profit from the introduction of new methods of production disappeared quickly.

It was, however, precisely the successful, innovating capitalist who, according to Marxian dialectic, undermined capitalism. He quickly accumulates capital out of his profits, and forces a "deepening of capital"—that is, an increase in the amount of capital per worker—on the economy. This deepening of capital had three consequences:[40] First, it enabled labor, as mentioned above, to produce more efficiently and to lower the cost of production and price. Second, the accumulation of capital produced a change in the composition of capital. Third, the deepening of capital would lead to large-scale

---

[40]Quite typically, Marx did not treat these three consequences together. Especially the change in the composition of capital is only treated in Volumes 2 and 3.

production, the destruction of artisans and small independent entrepreneurs, and the consequent proletarization of society.

The first consequence sets the stage for the other two and is therefore crucial. The statement that increased capital enables labor to operate more productively and thereby lowers the cost of production leaves Marx, however, wide open to the the obvious objection (of Eugen von Böhm-Bawerk and others) that capital must *eo ipso* be productive. Furthermore, Marx had to show that increased capital investment led to lower cost, hence lower prices as well as lower profits, if the dynamic self-destructive process of capitalism was to take place. Although Marx never managed to deny the long-run productivity of capital successfully, he could rely on empirical evidence to reinforce his contention that lower costs and prices followed large-scale capital investment.

The stage for the second consequence of capital accumulation, the change in the composition of capital, is now set. Because technology and competition require a larger and larger share of "constant capital" per worker the ratio of constant capital to variable capital increases; however, as an increasing amount of capital is required to employ the same amount of labor, the rate of profit $[p^1 = s/(c+v)]$ decreases. Because capitalist development is characterized by increasing constant capital requirements, the capitalist is faced with a falling rate of profit. The more the capitalist, as an individual, will try to escape the falling profit rate by innovating, the more he will hasten the further deepening of capital throughout society, the quicker the rate of profit will continue to fall, and the better the capitalist will prepare the objective conditions for the establishment of socialism. One cannot but marvel at the inexorable nature of the dialectical process from which there is no escape; the more the capitalist struggles, the more he will be caught in the net of history.

The only escape for the capitalist, in the short run, is the intensified exploitation of labor. By increasing the work day, or by a speedup, the capitalist can temporarily increase the employment capacity of "constant capital" and thereby increase the surplus value. Increased exploitation, and with it the "miserization" of the working class, is therefore a direct consequence of the falling rate of profit. The capitalist does not intensify the exploitation of labor because he is necessarily evil, but because he is driven to it by the nature of the capitalist system; again he is but a tool of history. The increased exploitation and the miserization of the working class will merely fan their revolutionary ire and thus bring nearer the dawn of socialism.

A dialectical-process theory is a beautiful intellectual creation in which each component prepares the condition for the laws of history to take effect. It is also a very difficult system to defend. If one phase does not materialize, the entire structure collapses. Only if this fact is recognized can one understand the Herculean effort of contemporary Marxists to show that the miserization of the working class has actually occurred. This senseless exercise, in the face of all evidence to the contrary, is necessitated by the consequences that hang on this prediction. If, over the last hundred years, the lot of the working class has not deteriorated, in spite of the fact that the amount of capital per worker has vastly increased, then a change in the organic composition of capital does not necessarily lead to a reduction in surplus value, which, in Marxian terms, can only be explained if labor is not the only source of profit or value. With one stroke, the entire Marxian building is weakened, especially the labor theory of value and its consequences are greatly impaired. However, because the labor theory of value "must" be true, there "must" have been a falling rate of profit, an increasing rate of exploitation, and a miserization of the working class, whatever the "objective" facts in this matter indicate.

. Still more important for Marxian—and Ricardian—economics is the "law" of the falling rate of profit, one of the keystones of Marxian dynamics. Ricardo and Smith derived this law from the predicted increases in capital and the consequent diminishing returns. Marx, who rejected the law of diminishing returns, derived the falling rate of profit from his basic notions of surplus, profit, and the changing nature of the composition of capital. The declining secular profit rate was merely the other side of the coin of the predicted increase in the rate of exploitation. Marx was here on somewhat stronger ground than in his defense of the labor theory. Although no one has been able to collect clear-cut evidence to support the theory of the declining profit rate, neither do we have overwhelming evidence to the contrary as in the case of the miserization. Furthermore, not only was Marx here in the good company of the classical economists Smith, Ricardo, and Mill, but also all "underconsumptionists" from Malthus to Keynes have considered a secular decline in the rate of profit as one of the characteristics of capitalistic development. The difference between Marx and Keynes rests on the fact that the Keynesian model is not the least bit affected by the fate of the long-run profit rate; as a matter of fact, Keynes's short-run policy recommendations are much more effective if the profit rate should merely randomly fluctuate over a stable long-run level, which actually seems to be the case according to the most recent studies.[41]

The third consequence of capital accumulation, as deduced by Marx, is his most perceptive observation—the one corroborated by empirical evidence.[42] Capital accumulation leads to the establishment of ever larger production units and consequent change in the structure of society. The class of independent artisans and entrepreneurs is eliminated, and with them, according to Schumpeter, the "foreman class," which had a personal loyalty to the owner. In a world dominated by monopolies, virtually everyone becomes proletarianized, and once more the objective conditions for socialism are prepared. Large-scale production, Marx continued, has already introduced planning, and the new class that can take over from the capitalist has arrived. Schumpeter, one of the most sophisticated of contemporary economists, came to the very same conclusion almost one hundred years later.[43] In spite of his admiration for the achievements of capitalism, Schumpeter believed that the increasing size of the production units would ultimately undermine the political and social posture of the capitalist. Socialism would be the result, a consequence of capitalism's success, not its failure.

While Schumpeter foresaw a gradual transition to a state that could readily be called "socialist," Marx expected a more violent, revolutionary change. The large-scale nature of production would produce an increasing alienation of the working class that together with the miserization should create the revolutionary fervor that would lead to the downfall of capitalism. Large-scale production, however, would create an ever-growing uniformity of economic functions, which would

[41]If the profit rate fluctuates randomly over a basic stationary level, Keynesian policy would require a government deficit during periods of low profits and a government surplus during periods of high profit. The government budget, however, would be balanced over a given time period.

[42]The reader will recall that the first consequence of capital accumulation was the increased productivity of labor with the concomitant decline in cost of production, prices, and profits. The second consequence was the change in the composition of capital.

[43]Cf. Schumpeter's *Capitalism, Socialism and Democracy* (New York and London: Harper & Row, 1941 and 1942), and his *Theory of Economic Development* (Leipzig: Duncker & Humbolt, 1912, and Cambridge, Mass: Harvard University Press, 1934).

enable the disciplined, unified proletariat to acquire quickly the "simple" skills of management.

This is a grandiose concept of structural and social change as a consequence of capitalism's inherent tendency toward large-scale production. As Joan Robinson (see note 39) and others recognized, however, this theory does not need to be supported by a labor theory of value. This theory has been amply supported, at least superficially, by the facts of life of large-scale production, concentration, alienation, drive for profit, and periodic crises. Marx recognized these aspects of capitalism long before anyone else.

Without detracting from Marx's intuition, we do find flaws in his vision, flaws that became apparent only during the last four decades. The major flaw, which already has had far-reaching political significance, has been the relative decline in the number of blue collar production workers—Marx's proletariat—since the end of World War I. Increasing capital accumulation and large-scale production have brought with them the decline of the old middle class of independent entrepreneurs and artisans; but rather than creating a greater uniformity of production and management methods, they have brought about the development of myriads of technical and bureaucratic skills. The extremely complex, "roundabout" method of large-scale production has created a new middle class of technicians, engineers, clerks, and professional managers, which has rapidly become the dominant class in all advanced capitalistic countries.[44] Although this new middle class is primarily a class of employees rather than property owners, it has all the sociological aspects of a separate class, very much differentiated from the proletariat. Furthermore, during the last twenty-five years, even Marx's proletariat has rapidly accepted middle-class values, aspirations, and goals. As a consequence of this economic-social development, the Socialist parties of Europe have changed from "workers' parties" to broad "people's parties," and have abandoned at the same time much of the Marxian dogma along with most of the class struggle rhetoric.

The second flaw in Marx's vision was his inability to foresee that the state could play an increasingly interventionist role in society, both in economic and social affairs. Social and welfare legislation, along with countercyclical economic policy precluded not only the

[44]See C. Wright Mills, *White Collar* (New York: Oxford University Press, 1951), for an excellent discussion of this phenomenon.

predicted miserization of the working class, but also significantly decreased the innate instability of capitalism and produced contemporary welfare capitalism.

MARX'S THEORY OF CRISES AND ECONOMIC OSCILLATION

Many aspects of the Marxian system have been deduced as direct consequences of his labor value-surplus theory. Business-cycle fluctuations and crises appear at times as consequences of the search for surplus, profits, the concomitant deepening of capital, and the drive toward large-scale production. In other parts of *Capital,* however, Marx based his theory of crises and economic oscillation much more thoroughly on his analysis of the circulation of capital and money. It is here, where Marx carried further Quesnay's dynamic macroeconomic analysis, that he made his major contributions as an economist. Marx recognized what we would call today the "systems nature" of the economic process, and adopted Quesnay's "general equilibrium" approach to the analysis of the circulation of money, credit and goods.[45] Quesnay distinguished in his self-regulatory macroeconomic model between productive (agriculture) and nonproductive (industry, trade) sectors in the economy. Although Quesnay recognized the possibilities of disturbances for this self-regulatory (negative feedback) system, the disturbances did not necessarily emerge from within the system, but rather were the pathological results of outside influences (e.g., hoarding and exploitation of the lower classes that would lead to underconsumption and, in Keynesian terms, bring about a deflationary gap). Marx, however, recognized the much more significant distinctions between consumers and capital goods industries, and made this distinction the basis of his two-sector macroeconomic model. The two sectors are interdependent but structurally different, because the consumer-goods industry operates on a reasonably continuous basis but adjusts its output in accordance with anticipated demand fluctuations. The output of the capital-goods sector varies more drastically in response to the "bunched investment" that is caused by technological investment opportunities. "Disproportionality" in consumption and capital expenditures, however, must produce booms and crises—that is, sinusoidal departures from the equilibrium. The

---

[45]Marx praised Quesnay's *Tableau Economique* as the most brilliant idea in economics. Schumpeter used very similar words in praising the intellectual achievements of Walras, another heir of Quesnay's tradition.

Figure **5.3** Possible Developments of an Initial Oscillation

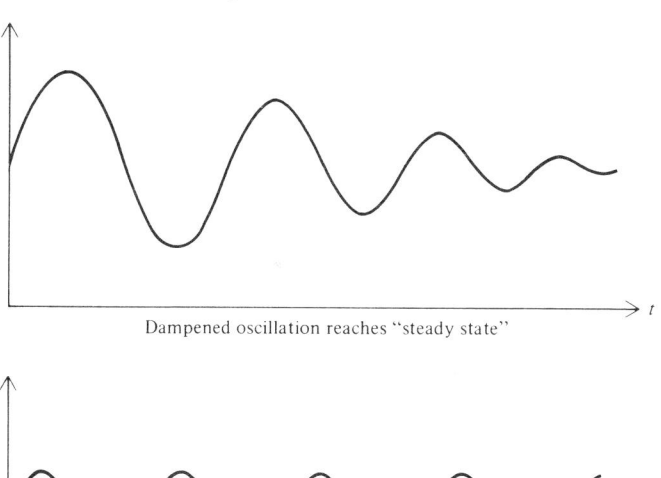

Dampened oscillation reaches "steady state"

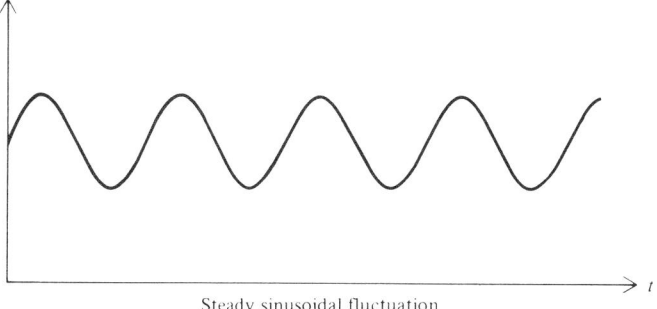

Steady sinusoidal fluctuation

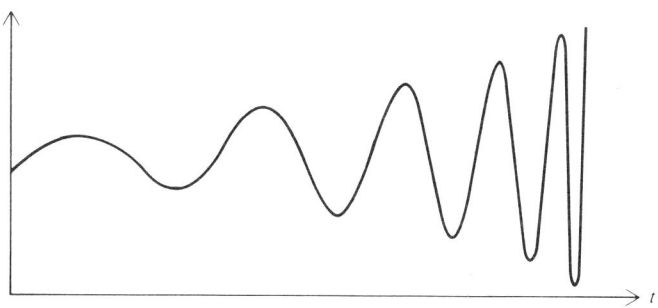

Explosive oscillation; note increase in amplitude and frequency

Marxian two-sector model is easily reconciled with the insight provided today by systems analysis. We know that delays will cause oscillations in the output of a negative feedback system. These oscillations may either be dampened, steadily fluctuating, or explosive. (See Fig. 5.3.) The steadily fluctuating output looks very much like business-cycle fluctuations from which the growth trend has been removed.

The explosive fluctuations, in which both amplitude and frequency of fluctuation increase over time, conform to Marx's prediction about the future of business cycles in a capitalistic economy. It is, however, virtually impossible to predict in advance whether a delayed feedback system will have an explosive output or one that will quickly return to its equilibrium position after some dampened oscillation. Only the value of the parameters within a feedback model, the length of the delays, the speed of the responses, the magnitude of the multipliers—that is, only the quantitative systems parameters—determine the oscillations of its output.

In Marx's two-sector model, the capital-goods sector produces machines for the consumer-goods sector, while the latter produces consumer goods for former workers employed in the capital-goods sector. Assuming a static system—Marx's "simple reproduction," where no growth takes place—we shall have an equilibrium if the total value of the goods produced during a period in sector I, the capital goods sector, equals the value of the capital goods used up in sector II, the consumer-goods sector, during the same time period.

Because, according to Marx, the total value produced must consist of wages and surplus value, he arrives at the following condition for equilibrium:

$$W_1 + SV_1 = TV_1 = Dep_{II}$$

where

W_1 = total wages of sector I
SV_1 = surplus value of sector I
TV_1 = total value produced in sector I
Dep_{II} = capital used during the given period in sector II

$TV_1 = Dep_{II}$ states that the total value of capital goods produced in sector I equals the value of fixed capital used up in the process of producing consumer goods in sector II, during the same time period; no net capital investment has taken place. The formulation $TV_1 = Dep_{II}$ is, however, valid as a condition for equilibrium only if the capital goods used up in sector I (Dep_I) equal the consumer goods (C_{II}) in sector II. Thus, $TV_1 = Dep_{II}$ is an equilibrium condition if, and only if, $Dep_I = C_{II}$. Marx never considered this second "necessary" condition for an equilibrium in his simple reproduction model.

Because it is highly unlikely that *both* conditions will be satisfied, we find that even Marx's stationary model is highly unstable. It was, however, Marx's purpose to show that the capitalistic process of capital accumulation produces instability—crises and depressions, which were to be typical for capitalistic economies only.

Returning to Marx's simple reproduction model, we note once more that he believed the system was in equilibrium if $TV_1 = Dep_{II}$; under these conditions a perfectly circular flow existed and the static simple reproduction system could go on reproducing itself. In a dynamic capitalist economy, however, the entrepreneur accumulates capital (i.e., saves) and reinvests part of his profit. His failure to consume his surplus value and his simultaneous investment decision reduce the demand for consumer goods in both sectors and increase the demand for capital goods. This causes a shift in resources between sector I and sector II. Marx conceived of this shift as a more rapid capital growth of sector I compared with sector II, although, in fact, various other combinations are possible. In order to maintain an equilibrium position, the accumulation (savings) ratio of sector I and II must be equal to the size and structure of the capital *already* invested in the two sectors. Because it is unlikely that such a proportionality will necessarily exist merely due to chance, another structural deficiency of capitalism has been discovered. The periodic crises are, therefore, no longer entirely the result of underconsumption alone, but are reinforced by the structural discrepancies between savings and consumption. As a matter of fact, the time delay between the savings action and the ultimate investment decision is the truly disequilibrating factor, both in the simple reproduction system and in the dynamic reproduction model. Marx, although still holding on to the classical doctrine that capitalists save in order to invest, perceived here the important distinction between *ex ante* and *ex post* investment decisions: Due to the time delay, a dollar saved in order to be invested will actually not necessarily be invested in the same time period. Assuming, furthermore, that saving—through corporate amortization funds—is a smooth, continuous effort, the periodic (bunched) investment decisions are responsible for business fluctuations. Marx's insight into the impact of delays on the smooth circulation of capital anticipated Keynes, and represents a more analytical expression of the Sismondi-Malthus attempt to explain booms and crises. Marx's mathematical demonstration of the necessary (but actually not sufficient) equilibrium condition is clumsy—Marx, a poor mathematician even for his own time, required Engels' help for his elementary algebraic equations— but still it was the first time that an economist even considered a rigorous definition of equilibrium conditions.

Unfortunately for Marx and Marxian economics, his reproduction models conflicted with his tenacious efforts to hold on to his value theory. In order to preserve his value theory, Marx was forced to distinguish at great length in Volumes 2 and 3 between (short-run) price and value. In Marx's equilibrium equations, the market forces are represented as prices, but the numbers also represent values.[46] This discrepancy was pointed out by various critics, and perhaps as a result of this criticism, Marx's equilibrium model soon disappeared from most discussions of Marxian economics. Marx, of course, had never succeeded in weaving the various strands of his economic thinking into a consistent whole. In the only two successful attempts to present a rigorous and consistent Marxian model,[47] Marx's two-sector analysis finds its place, however, even if it holds only a secondary position. Modern non-Marxian economists from Robinson to Domar and Morishima have selected the Marxian two sector model as a starting point in exploring the dynamics of capitalistic economics, as previously mentioned.

It is sometimes difficult to account for the practical consequences of Marxism; hardly two writers arrive at the same conclusions. Marx had an immediate impact on the small number of European radicals who either criticized the social conditions in Western capitalistic democracies or who conspired against the authoritarian regimes in eastern Europe. Marxism provided a unifying ideology for these small bands of bourgeois and aristocratic radical intellectuals who fueled the fires of discontent in various European cities. From this initial foothold, Marxist influence penetrated the emerging labor unions, strengthened the class consciousness of the skilled sections of the working class, and helped greatly in the stimulation and development

[46]The Austrian economist, Ladislaus von Bortkiewitz, corrected most of the mathematical inconsistencies of Marx's model at the turn of the century, but ended up with a rather complicated set of exponential equations, which were far too formidable for most Marxists to merit further discussion.

[47]Paul M. Sweezey, *The Theory of Capitalist Development* (New York: Oxford University Press, 1942) and M. Dobb, *Political Economy and Capitalism* (Westport, Conn.: Greenwood, 1937).

of labor parties throughout western and central Europe. The strongest labor parties—the Social Democratic parties of Germany and Austria-Hungary and the French Socialists—were outright Marxist parties, although the British Labor party was a weak conglomerate of trade unions, middle-class reformers, Fabians, and quasi-Marxist intellectuals.

Middle-class intellectuals comprised overwhelmingly the leadership of the German, Austro-Hungarian, and French parties; in the British Labor party, the reform-oriented trade unions held the real power until the election of 1970. In spite of a great deal of revolutionary-Marxist rhetoric, the Socialist-Social Democratic parties of western and central Europe pursued essentially reformist goals. These parliamentary labor parties received strong support from bourgeois and aristocratic-agrarian groups. The supporting groups shifted from issue to issue, of course, but at no time can we find the bitter class conflicts the Marxist ideologues postulated. The Socialist parties quickly developed skilled parliamentarians who enhanced greatly their political effectiveness because of the varied and shifting nature of middle- and upper-class support for their reformist goals. Although these parties remained permanent minorities, they were immensely important. Marxism had become respectable politics in western Europe by the turn of the twentieth century.

By 1900, most of the "revolutionary" demands of the *Communist Manifesto* not only had been adopted by most of the western European countries, but also generally had been imposed from the "top," with often only minimal support from the labor parties.[48] The demands

[48]The reforms called for in 1848 were:
1. abolition of property in land and application of all rents of land to public purposes
2. a heavy progressive or graduated income tax
3. abolition of all right of inheritance
4. confiscation of the property of all emigrants and rebels
5. centralization of credit in the hands of the state, by means of a national bank with state capital and an exclusive monopoly
6. centralization of the means of communication and transport in the hands of the state
7. extension of factories and instruments of production owned by the state; the bringing into cultivation of waste lands, and the improvement of the soil generally in accordance with a common plan
8. equal obligation of all to work; establishment of industrial armies, especially for agriculture
9. combination of agriculture with manufacturing industries; gradual abolition of the distinction between town and country, by a more equable distribution of the population over the country

of the 1848 manifesto were being integrated by gradualistic parliamentary measures. Prince Bismarck and Emperor Franz Josef, for
instance, had instituted in their respective countries nationalized health
insurance, protective social legislation, and a mildly progressive
income tax well before the end of the century. Railroads had been
nationalized on a piecemeal basis in most of continental Europe over
a forty-year period—the process was completed substantially by
1914—and the postal systems (later on, telegraph and telephone, and
after World War I, even radio) had been nationailzed in most of
Europe since the days of Maria Theresa and Frederick II. In England,
the great Tory prime minister Disraeli in the 1860s introduced very
advanced factory-labor legislation against strong bourgeois opposition.[49] Generally speaking, the landed aristocracy combined with
labor and—in France, Germany, and Austria—with the Catholic
petty-bourgeois parties[50] to overcome the opposition of the bourgeois
parties to legislation legalizing unions, to protecting small business
from capitalistic competition, and nationalizing the railroad and telegraph systems. The bourgeois parties, in turn, combined on the
continent with the Social Democrats to reduce the influence of the
aristocracy, extend the power of parliament, and increase individual
civil liberties.

How many of these changes were due to Marxism per se, how
many of them were the result of the "inherent contradiction" of
nineteenth-century society is difficult to measure. Certainly, European conservatism always has had a strong anticapitalistic strain, and
most of the social legislation of the nineteenth century would have
been acceptable both to Adam Müller and Karl Marx. Similarly, the
libertarian efforts of the liberal-bourgeois parties had their roots in
Locke, Rousseau, and Mill, rather than in Marx.

---

10. free education for all children in public schools; abolition of child factory
    labor in its present form; combination of education with industrial produc-
    tion, etc.
The Communist Manifesto, ed. Samuel H. Beer (New York: Appleton-Century-
Crofts, 1955), pp. 31-32.

[49]Until this very day, we find a considerable bloc of conservative votes among various labor union enclaves in England and Scotland.

[50]These parties were the forerunners of the Christian Democratic parties that governed most of western Europe from 1945 to 1970. Often their German name *Christlich
Social* is incorrectly translated as Christian Socialists. These parties were neither socialist
nor liberal, though often anti-big business, anti-Semitic, and suspicious of international
finance. Their social composition and values resemble the old "middle class" that
supported Teddy Roosevelt's Progressive movement.

In the United States, Marxism as an ideology and as a political force had no impact in the nineteenth century and remained virtually unknown, except to a handful of intellectuals, until well after the turn of the century. Americans, preoccupied with the enormous conquest of their continent, economic growth, and the political turmoil of the Progressive movement, found little in the involuted arguments of *Das Kapital.* Eastern European immigrants who had socialist leanings were so overwhelmed by the difficulties of surviving in American society that they had little political impact. Herbert Spencer, as we shall show, seemed oddly enough more perceptive to the American estab-lishment than the sage of Highgate. Even in the Great Depression, 1929-1939, hardly a first-rate American economist became a Marxist. By 1936, American economists could learn from Keynes; before that date, they searched for pragmatic solutions to economic problems. At no time were they attracted to Marxist theory.

Marx himself had been influenced by both Müller and Rousseau; the authoritarian-liberal contradiction has always been a basic issue in Marxist thought. This contradiction has now reappeared as one of the most crucial and violent controversies of contemporary Marxism. American conservatives have often complained that the Western press keeps referring to Stalinists as "conservatives" and to the anti-Stalinist groups within the various Marxist parties as "liberals." Within the context of European political history, however, this nomenclature seems to be fully justified, certainly if applied to the Czechoslovakia of the 1968-1970 period. The Stalinists within the Czech and Slovak parties who cooperated with Soviet Russia to crush the reformist Dubcek government were the heirs of Adam Müller and the Kameral-ists as well as of Karl Marx; Dubcek and his group had their roots in western European egalitarian-liberal thought.[51]

The various Social Democratic labor parties of western Europe and post-New Deal Administrations succeeded only too well in im-proving the lot of the working class. However, as the working class received middle-class incomes, it also took on, increasingly, middle-

---

[51]This is not necessarily a commendatory statement because Dubcek and his col-leagues also share fully the Western liberal's naïveté and ability for self-delusion. A sympathetic journalist characterized Dubcek as "remarkable for his innocent honesty. . . . His ingenuousness is ridiculous, but astonishing and refreshing" [*The Economist* (August 1970), 43]. Dubcek's biographer, William Shawcross, similarly emphasized his capacity for self-delusion and pointed to Dubcek's naïveté as his fatal weakness in *Dubcek* (London: Weidenfeld & Nicolson, 1970).

class values and aspirations. The various democratic labor parties had to change into liberal middle-class "people's parties" in order to stay in business. By the mid-fifties Marxism had been explicitly or implicitly renounced by most European labor parties, which attracted appreciable segments of middle-class support. The very success of this transformation process alienated the radical middle-class intellectuals who had constituted the left wing of these Marxist parties. The left-wing romantic, essentially un-Marxian antiindustrialism was only thinly covered by half-understood Marxian rhetoric.[52]

Radical neo-Marxism in western Europe and North America today has its roots primarily in the universities, primarily in the social science faculties. The relatively small number of students and faculty members involved has tempted many observers to discount the long-run political significance of this essentially nihilistic movement. The upper middle-class background of its leaders, their values and "direct action" methods, have suggested to some a comparison with the highly ineffective and naïve Social Revolutionaries of Russia at the turn of the century.[53]

If historical comparisons, however, are made, the National Socialist movement in central Europe during the early 1930s is a much better model than the Social Revolutionaries with far-reaching and frightening parallels. Perhaps more important is the fact that the social climate in the West has been drastically changed during the last five years. No one can speak any longer of the "end of ideology." The very success and affluence of applied Keynesian economics on the economic front have contributed to the weakening of the social constraints of Western society. Little of this social change has been due to

---

[52]How little students know about Marx is well illustrated by a conversation between Marxist students and their professor at Berlin's Free University:

Instructor:	What really is "capital," since you fellows keep throwing the word around?
1st Student:	That |capital| are major shareholders and the state.
2nd Student:	Yeah, a little entrepreneur with about 200 working-stiffs, that isn't "capital."
3rd Student:	Capital, that are the shareholders and management, for instance Stoltenberg, the Krupp manager.
4th Student:	Capital is an everpresent octopus.

From *Der Spiegel* (July 13, 1970), 69. (Our translation. The terrible English is an attempt to duplicate the horrible German.)

[53]Few of the leaders of the Social Revolutionaries survived. Most were killed at an early age by the secret police forces of the czars and the commissars.

the socioeconomic theories of Karl Marx. Marxist rhetoric and ideology have become merely a convenient vehicle for existing resentments, alienation, and frustrations. For today's revolutionary, a simpler, less intellectual piece of work—Ché Guevara's diary, for example—achieves much more than Marx's prescriptions.[54]

[54]One of the authors has in his possession the letters written by a young man who fought with the German "Free-Corps" (volunteers) in the Baltic states during the early 1920s. The similarity with Guevara's Bolivian diary is overwhelming.

6
THE NEOCLASSICAL PERIOD (1870-1936)

The Setting

During the last quarter of the nineteenth century, the attack on classical economics had lost much of its sting. The very impressive growth in wealth throughout northwestern Europe had removed some of the fervor from Socialist and nationalist dissent. At the same time, the landed aristocracy had begun to accept the Industrial Revolution and, especially in England and Germany, had set out to develop strong financial, political, and family ties with leading representatives of the "grand bourgeoisie." The time had come to reassess classical economics in the light of Marxian and institutional criticism.

It was quite obvious that the labor theory of value would have to bear the brunt of any reexamination. This theory was most vulnerable on analytical grounds. Neither Smith nor Ricardo nor Marx had been able to reconcile the labor theory with the obvious physical productivity of capital. At the same time, however, this theory provided both an emotional and a mythological justification for the aspirations of revolutionary radicals as well as reform-minded trade union leaders. The development of a new value theory that would be both analytically sound and ideologically neutral was, therefore, the first requirement in the reconstruction of classical economics.

Very much in line with the philosophical tradition of Western man, philosophers and economists had always looked for a single explanation of value. Though we can trace the beginnings of the labor theory to Aristotle and Thomas Aquinas, we can also find in their writings the beginning of the utility theory of value. Smith himself, as we know, was puzzled by the paradox of value. How could water, the very essence of life, be so cheap while useless diamonds were so dear? In one form or another this paradox has appeared throughout the literature, and was finally solved only in the nineteenth century with the full development of a new theory, which saw the value of a commodity determined by its utility and scarcity.

A legion of philosophers and economists have dealt at one time or another with scarcity and utility as the determinant of the market value (price) of a commodity.[1] A rough utility-scarcity theory had gained wide acceptance throughout Europe before Smith changed the course of economic thought by accepting labor as the determinant of exchange value. Just as Smith and his successors assumed demand as given at a particular point of time, and therefore concentrated on the factors that determined supply, so the utility-scarcity proponents emphasized demand and assumed supply as given or, at least, as determined by demand. In order to reconcile these two viewpoints, the notion of a schedule—that is, the willingness of consumers and producers to supply various quantities at different prices at a point in time—had to be developed. Although Lauderdale, Galiani, Gossen, Cournot, and several other early pioneers had come quite close to developing the concept of a schedule in order to express graphically the interaction of supply and demand, it was left for Alfred Marshall to perform this last step, which not only expressed clearly the interaction of supply and demand, but at the same time produced a synthesis of classical and subjective value theory.

[1] Among those who anticipated modern value theory were the British writers Barbon (1690), Locke (1691), John Law (1720), Lauderdale (1804), W. F. Lloyd (1834), Longfield (1834), and Jennings (1855); the Italian Galiani (1750), who developed a thoroughly modern utility-scarcity theory of value too early; the Frenchmen Condillac (1776), who restated Galiani's value theory, Turgot (1766), J. B. Say (1803), Dupuit (1844), and the Germans von Thunen (1826) and Gossen (1854), the latter two brilliant economists who had the misfortune of being ahead of their time.

Before Marshall's synthesis, the critics of classical value theory emphasized, above all, the role of demand in the determination of price. Because the demand for a commodity played a far too insignificant role in the classical economists' labor or cost of production theories, a revision of the then existing value theory had to stress the demand for goods. It was not surprising that "revisionists" such as Jevons should overemphasize demand and almost completely neglect supply in their theory of value. (Galiani and Condillac, who wrote before the labor theory of value held sway, were much less dogmatic in their treatment of demand.)

The attack on classical value theory—which had in Marx, whose formal logical and mathematical equipment was poor, a vigorous defender[2]—had to start with its logical inadequacy. It was no accident, therefore, that this challenge should attract analytically oriented economists who were, in most cases, first-rate mathematicians. J. B. Say led the way in substituting an analytical "science" of economics for Adam Smith's descriptive political economy. He urged economists to apply Bacon's scientific methods in order to find the underlying laws that govern all economic phenomena, and to cease concerning themselves with practical problems. Rather than advising statesmen, economists should imitate the physical scientists and discover cause and effect relationships through observation, and if it were possible, experiments.[3] Ever since Say, most economic theorists have looked to the scientist, particularly the physicist, for guidance,[4]

---

[2]It has been observed that Jevons, Menger, Walras and others probably had never heard of Marx in their formative years because the first volume of *Capital* did not appear until 1867. This view neglects the fact that a "Socialist" theory of surplus and labor value had existed long before Marx, who unified and adapted the theories of his French, English, and German predecessors. W. Thompson's *An Inquiry into the Principles of the Distribution of Wealth Most Conducive to Human Happiness,* which appeared in London, for instance, obtained considerable publicity and contained an excellent preview of Marx's example of surplus value. The Anglo-American J. F. Bray, whom Marx quotes approvingly, presented similar views already during the 1830s, and personifies the transition from Ricardian socialism to Marxism. For an excellent discussion of pre-Marxian theories of surplus value, see A. Menger, *The Right to the Whole Produce of Labor* (New York and London: Macmillan, 1899), especially Foxwell's introduction.

[3]J. B. Say, *A Treatise on Political Economy,* trans. from the 4th ed. of the French (Philadelphia: Grigg & Elliot, 1836).

[4]Quite recently the electrical engineer has replaced the physicist as a model. Because the electrical engineer is less concerned with discovering the ultimate truth and more with the pragmatic application of observed phenomena, he probably is a much better model for economists, though the economist does not necessarily need any physical model.

and thus have concentrated on the discovery of "true" physical relationships. Frequently this has lessened their interest in applying theory
to public policy.[5]

This change in the nature of economics is one of the most important aspects of neoclassical revisionism. In diverting its attention from
policy to abstract theory, economics became at the same time more
professional, more mathematical, and increasingly esoteric. Gone
were the Ricardian days when governesses were supposed to teach
their charges "political economy" along with French, literature, and
music. By the end of the nineteenth century, the public, and especially the businessman, could no longer understand economists.
Though Marshall and a few others took great pride in writing specifically for the businessman, it is very doubtful that many businessmen
in England or America ever read Marshall. The gulf between economists and the general public was not bridged until the late 1930s,
when Keynes' concern with policy transformed "economics" once
more into political economy. The "barrier" between economists and
businessmen finally began to disappear in the 1960s, when "managerial economics" and "cost-benefit analysis" turned much of economics
into a special case of general decision theory. However, the marginal
analysis of neoclassical economics laid the foundation for the current
development in mathematical economics, operations research, and
decisions theory.

WILLIAM S. JEVONS

William S. Jevons, the founder of Anglo-Saxon "marginal economics"[6] was the sort of economist the discipline required. Jevons
(1835-1882) studied mathematics and science at the University of
London, interrupted his studies to work as a surveyor in Australia,
and traveled widely in North and South America before returning to
England in 1859.

However, at the age of twenty-one, he came to the conclusion—although he
had never been intimate with anyone in his life—that the only things really

---

[5]Walras, one of the greatest pure theorists, maintained his interest in public policy
and wrote prolifically in this field. In general, however, Anglo-American neoclassical
economists emphasized pure theory and neglected policy issues.

[6]The English-speaking predecessors of Jevons are discussed carefully by E. R. A.
Seligman, "On Some Neglected British Economists," *Economic Journal,* 13 (1903),
46-54, reprinted in his *Essays in Economics* (New York: Macmillan, 1925).

worth having were love and friendship (those are his words): sometimes he inclined to think intellectual insight to be of a little use. At the age of twenty-two, he came to himself and realized how eminent he was; it became quite clear that his brain was full of original thoughts. He threw up his past and all his cash and came back to England for further education; it was not long before he boomed: but he suffered from sleeplessness and depression, and was drowned while bathing at the age of forty odd. . . .[7]

A brilliant man of great originality Jevons was largely self-trained in economics and learned about his many predecessors only after he had published his major works. He made up for this oversight by praising them, especially Gossen, extensively on all subsequent occasions. Although economists were slow in giving Jevons the proper recognition, he was widely acclaimed and honored for his work in the fields of logic, probability, statistics, Boolean algebra, and applied mathematics—the fields that underlie contemporary economics.[8]

The application of mathematics to marginal analysis was, of course, a natural step because marginal analysis is merely a specific form of applying the basic concepts of differential calculus to economics. (One could also, *pari passu,* develop the elementary concepts of limits, slopes, and derivatives by developing verbally the marginal argument.)

. . . believing that the quantities with which we deal must be subject to continuous variation, I do not hesitate to use the appropriate branch of mathematical science [calculus] involving . . . infinitely small quantities. The [marginal] theory consists in applying the differential calculus to the familiar notions of wealth, utility, value, demand, supply, capital, interest, labor, and all quantitative notions belonging to the daily operations of industry.[9]

If we recognize Jevons' quantitative approach to economics as his major contribution, and consider his work from this point of view we gain a more insightful appreciation of his total contribution. Most

---

[7]John Maynard Keynes to G. L. Strachey, July 8, 1905. (In R. F. Harrod, *The Life of John Maynard Keynes* [New York: Harcourt Brace Jovanovich, 1951], pp. 106-107.)

[8]Jevons was made a member of the Royal Society in 1872 for his contribution to both logic and economics. Sir William Petty, the only other economist accepted into the Royal Society prior to Jevons, had also considered economics a quantitative science. Both Petty and Jevons were early econometricians.

[9]W. S. Jevons, *Theory of Political Economy* (New York: Macmillan, 1871), pp. 3-4.

traditional reviewers of Jevons' work have overemphasized the unfinished aspects of his value and distribution theory, the superficial though sparkling analysis that almost, but never completely, led him to the threshold of presenting a modern, integrated value and distribution theory. Often, however, Jevons failed to develop certain concepts explicitly because he assumed they were implicitly obvious.

Given Jevons' mathematical training, which anteceded his interest in economics by many years, and his dislike of the objective (impersonal) materialistic nature of classical economics, his development of a subjective theory of value followed quite naturally. Jevons based his approach to economics upon the sensible assumption that man produces in order to consume and thus that consumption rather than production must be made the basis of economic analysis.[10] Once this departure from classical economics is made, the analysis of the demand for consumer goods must follow because wants and their satisfaction underlie all consumption. The analysis of consumption could have dealt with either individual or aggregate demand. Widespread intellectual dissatisfaction—both in England and on the continent—with the classical emphasis on material and objective considerations made it reasonable that a critique of classical economics would choose to study demand from the point of view of the individual.

Man's wants were infinitely varied, and the same commodity possessed different "utilities" for different persons at different points of time. Wants are practically infinite because "the satisfaction of every lower want in the scale creates a desire of higher character."[11] Jevons used the word "utility" to define the abstract quality of satisfying an individual want that each commodity possesses. The value of a commodity not only varies from person to person but also is affected by

---

[10]Economic historians with a strong liberal or Marxian bias (e.g., B. B. Seligman, E. Roll, R. Heilbronner, etc.) have attacked Jevons for separating economics from public policy. In many respects this charge was unjustified. Jevons could be considered the first welfare economist as well as the first econometrician. His *Theory of Political Economy* was written precisely in order to investigate methods to reduce the number of the poor and to optimize the (national) consumption of wealth. He did believe that once the "true" relationship between economic variables was discovered, policy makers would draw the "obvious" conclusions. In addition to seeking the fundamental verities of economics, Jevons published numerous tracts that dealt with specific topical issues—for example, *The Coal Question, The State in Relation to Labor, Methods of Social Reform,* and *Investigations in Currency and Finance.* He also served as a consultant to businessmen, and used correlation analyses of economic indicators as a forecasting tool.

[11]Jevons, *Theory of Political Economy,* 4th ed. (New York: Macmillan, 1911).

the scarcity of a particular commodity. Once a commodity has a utility—that is, the ability to satisfy a certain want—its "final value" will depend upon its scarcity. Thus subjective utility and scarcity determine value.

Repeated reflections and inquiry have led me to the somewhat novel opinion, that value depends entirely upon utility. Prevailing opinions made labor rather than utility the origin of value; and there are even those who distinctly assert that labor is the cause of value. . . . Labor is found often to determine value, but only in an indirect manner, by varying the degree of utility of the commodity through an increase or limitation of the supply.[12]

By making utility a function of scarcity, and applying the tools of differential calculus to the analysis of increments of utility, Jevons was able to develop the concept of diminishing utility and to distinguish between total and marginal (incremental) utility, and thus solve the value paradox of water and diamonds. The supply of water is so large that the value of the last increment of water a person uses is almost zero, though the total utility of water—that is, the area (integral) under the diminishing utility curve—is larger than the total utility of diamonds. Diamonds, however, are so scarce that an additional (or first) unit of diamonds possesses a high degree of utility.

The moment we associate total utility with the area under the marginal utility curve, we ought to make certain explicit assumptions about the measurability of utility. Jevons himself did not believe that utility was objectively measurable, but did, de facto, make "interpersonal" comparisons and normative welfare statements that were only valid if utility could be measured. The solution to this paradox lay in the reasonable assumption that the marginal utility of money is constant over a wide range for most people, and that, therefore, money could be used as a measure of utility.[13]

It is interesting to note that "scarcity" as a component of utility introduced a frequently overlooked objective component into Jevons' subjective value analysis. The total supply of diamonds or water in

---

[12]*Ibid.* p.1.

[13]We find the same assumption made in the related field of modern decision theory. Cf. R. Schlaifer, *Probability and Statistics for Business Decisions* (New York: McGraw-Hill, 1959), chap. 2. Very much like Alfred Marshall, we shall also employ a monetary measure of marginal utility; we shall define the marginal utility of commodity A as "the maximum amount of money a consumer is willing to pay for an additional unit of A."

existence in, say, England, will affect its value, as well as the amount of this commodity in the possession of the individual. Neither in Jevons' discussion of the water-diamond paradox nor, very often, in the general textbook discussion of diminishing utility is it entirely clear whether the scarcity of water is seen from the individual's or society's point of view. As far as society is concerned, however, the amount of water in existence at a given point of time is an objective fact.

The difficulty with subjective value analysis lies in the attempt to aggregate individual values to obtain a market value that can be related to price.[14] The objective fact of the existence of a limited number of resources affects both individual and market aggregation. Jevons implicitly recognized both the objective and the subjective component of scarcity by making scarcity the determinant of value: Cost of production determines supply. Supply (scarcity) determines final degree of utility; final degree of utility determines value.

It is commonly said that Jevons took production as given, just as Ricardo had taken supply as given, and that he failed to offer a theory of production. In fact, his production theory is rooted in his hedonistic view of man who will forever try to maximize his pleasure and minimize his "pain." The disutility of labor and saving is incurred in the production process and is presented by the negative values in man's utility function. Man's demand for goods and the supply of the factors of production (labor, savings) are determined by optimizing this utility function. Jevons was not able to present this view in sufficiently concise terms to develop the marginal productivity theory, though in our view he came closer to presenting implicitly a theory of production than George Stigler and other eminent critics concede.[15]

The marginal productivity theory does, of course, present a rigorous theory of production, which reconciles subjective and market demand with supply. Jevons did not develop fully a marginal produc-

[14]Note that, of course, the objective labor value theories of Ricardo and Marx could not reconcile price and value either; as mentioned above, the third volume of *Capital* was devoted—unsuccessfully—to a heroic attempt to solve this contradiction. Critics of Jevons' subjective value theory ought to add that by 1870 no other value theory had been able explicitly to reconcile the price with the "intrinsic" value of a commodity. Cf. Paul M. Sweezey, *Theory of Capitalist Development* (New York: Oxford University Press, 1942) p. 115, and Eugen von Bohm-Bawerk, *Karl Marx and the Close of His System* (New York: Kelley, 1949), pp. 28-32.

[15]George J. Stigler, *Production and Distribution Theories* New York: Macmillan, 1946), p. 35.

Figure **6.1** Jevon's Pleasure-Pain Calculus

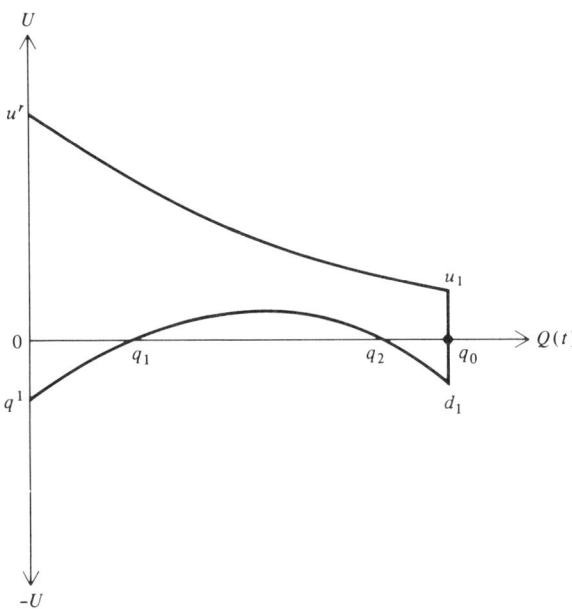

U = utility
$Q(t)$ = quantity of goods produced over time
For $q_1 < q < q_2$ the marginal utility of labor is positive.
At $q_0, \overline{u_1 q_0} = \overline{q_0 d_1}$

tivity theory, but he did relate both individual labor (supply) and demand for consumer goods to the same determinant factor—the pleasure-pain calculus. (See Fig. 6.1.)

Man will supply his labor, according to Jevons, until the satisfaction obtained from an increment in consumption is equalled by the pain incurred by an additional time unit of work. At the point q_0, the line segment $\overline{u_1 q_0}$ = the line segment $\overline{q_0 d_1}$, or the utility of the q_0's increment in consumption is offset by the q_0's negative increment (disutility) of labor. The maximizing individual will, therefore, not continue to work beyond q_0; if he had stopped working before the point q_0, or if he continued to work beyond this point, he would fail to maximize his total utility obtainable from consumption and work. We see clearly that at the point q_0 the maximum utility from consumption and work is obtained and an equilibrium between utility and *dis*utility exists. The amount of labor necessary to produce q_0 units of goods will be supplied and q_0 units of goods will be consumed.

Examination of Jevons' diagram clearly indicates that he did not consider that all labor has a negative utility. He merely argued that beyond a certain point in time man will not enjoy work and will only continue to work as long as the pecuniary benefits obtainable from labor exceed the disutilities of labor. Each individual, of course, will have different utility functions, but it is not difficult to imagine the aggregation of individual labor utility functions in order to obtain market supply curves of labor that will look very much like the traditional textbook supply curves.

Jevons relied heavily upon the pleasure-pain calculus developed by Jeremy Bentham to explain the psychological foundation of his subjective value analysis. Some time between 1787 and 1798, Bentham had originally expounded his theory that the sensation of pleasure is affected by intensity, duration, and certainty.[16] By 1850, the German physiologist E. H. Weber (1795-1878) supplied experimental evidence concerning the duration and intensity of sensations. His results were elaborated and extended by G. Fechner, another German psychologist. Thus the Weber-Fechner law: [17] In order for the intensity of a sensation to increase in an arithmetical progression, the stimulus must increase in geometrical progression, or conversely, the intensity of a sensation is diminished if the application of the stimulus remains constant over time.

The Weber-Fechner law provided a psychological basis for the law of diminishing utility, and within a few years value theories based upon a law of diminishing utility appeared virtually simultaneously in England, Austria, and France. We do not know whether Jevons himself had read Weber or Fechner, but it is certain that the experimental psychologists had made Bentham again intellectually respectable and, therefore, the concept of diminishing utility was "ready" to be adopted.[18]

---

[16]Much of modern decision theory could be considered to be an extension of Benthamite reasoning. Certainly risk, remoteness, and uncertainty are considered today in any attempt to maximize a decision function.

[17]G. T. Fechner, *Element der Psycho-Physik* (Leipzig: Breitkopf und Hartel, 1860).

[18]M. Blaug thought "neither Jevons nor Menger nor Walras . . . paid any attention to the Weber-Fechner law." This is a difficult statement to prove or disprove. Certainly there was no need for Menger to associate his nonhedonistic subjective value theory with Weber-Fechner. In Jevons' case, the remarkable thing is the fact that his utility theory is completely supported by the Weber-Fechner law, which in actuality is equivalent to the Bernoulli hypothesis (Bernoulli's solution to his St. Petersburg paradox). Jevons, of course, was well acquainted with the Bernoulli hypothesis.

We have already stated that Jevons applied the method of differential calculus, as well as the concepts of pleasure-pain optimization and diminishing utility, to production; he did not manage, however, to develop a rigorous marginal productivity theory though he came quite close to it intuitively, much closer than he is ordinarily given credit for. Virtually every economic historian at first condemns Jevons for neglecting production, but then finds that he made a major contribution to a particular field of production theory. Thus, for example, Seligman[19] and Stigler[20] approve of Jevons' interest theory, Roll[21] accepts his rent and capital theory as modern, and Mark Blaug holds that Jevons' theory of labor supply "is his most important contribution to the mainstream of neoclassical economics."[22] Adding all these comments we have here a fully developed theory of production. Jevons did not write one, of course, but he came close enough to permit the sophisticated reader to carry Jevons' reasoning just that one step further in order to reach a formulation acceptable to a contemporary critic. By choosing among Jevons' many references to interest, rent, labor, and capital, and combining these comments, one could come up with a fairly unified distribution theory. Such a theory, however, would represent the reader's hindsight rather than Jevons' thinking. One cannot, therefore, present a "Jevonian" model without a good deal of "editorial" revision. One can, however, present the flavor of his analysis, which is original and often quite modern.

Jevons treated distribution merely as another aspect of his general value theory. Scarcity, and hence the diminishing utility of incremental factors of production, determined the factor values at the margin of the last increment used. No single factor of production was a cause of value: "We must regard labor, land, knowledge, and capital as cojoint conditions of the whole produce, not as causes each of a certain portion of the product."[23] Each incremental production factor will be applied where it will receive the largest (incremental) pay. Opportunity cost as well as substitutability of the factors of production were

[19]B. B. Seligman, *Main Currents in Modern Economics* (New York: Free Press, 1962),p.265.
[20]George J. Stigler, *Production and Distribution Theories* (New York: Macmillan, 1941), p. 26.
[21]Erich Roll, *A History of Economic Thought,* 3rd ed. (Englewood Cliffs, N.J.: Prentice-Hall, 1956), p. 383.
[22]M. Blaug, *Economic Theory in Retrospect,* (Homewood, Ill.: Irwin, 1962), p. 288.
[23]Jevons, *Theory of Political Economy.*

implied, though not explicitly defined. The disutilities of labor and saving were the dominant constraints on production. Factors (labor) will be allocated among possible production alternatives until the ratios

$$\frac{\text{marginal utility of product}}{\text{marginal disutility of labor}}$$

are equal. The difficulties inherent in comparing and aggregating individual utility preferences prevented Jevons from arriving at a general definition of market equilibrium. It also made it difficult to show rigorously and explicitly the substitutability of factors of production, although Jevons used the concept of opportunity cost in defining the limits of factor application.

A man who can earn six shillings a day in one employment will not turn to another kind of work unless he expects to get six shillings a day or more from it.[24]

Ricardo, in developing his theory of rent, actually used the concepts of marginal analysis; as a matter of fact, Ricardo's "law of diminishing return" is not only conceptually and analytically very close to the modern concept of "diminishing utility," but quite compatible with the role of rent in the marginal productivity theory. Jevons was therefore able to accept the Ricardian rent theory and use it as an example for the principles that govern *all* factors of production. Jevons failed, however, to analyze carefully the various relationships between land, labor, capital, and their respective increments and ratios.[25] Still it must be emphasized that Jevons recognized the substitutability among the factors of production and restored the role of demand to its proper significance in a market economy.

[The worker] seeks the work in which his similar faculties are most productive of utility, as measured by what other people are willing to pay for their produce. Their wages are clearly the effect not the cause of the value of the produce.[26]

[24]*Ibid.*, p.437.
[25]Cf. Stigler, *Production and Distribution Theory,* pp. 21 ff.
[26]Jevons, *Theory of Political Economy,* p. 1.

Jevons' capital theory is an excellent example of his original insight into the capitalistic system. After Ricardo's and Marx's exhaustive but unsatisfactory attempts to reconcile the obvious productivity of capital with the labor theory of value, Jevons perceived clearly the inherent productivity of the capital-using system as a whole. Capital— tools, machines, preparation of work places, and advances of labor— lengthens the work process but increases the productivity of labor; an increase in the capital investment period is the same as an increase in the amount of capital in use. Interest is actually defined by Jevons as the increment of the products due to a time increment in the production process, divided by the entire product.[27] The time element (the roundabout method of production) makes the capital-using process productive!

The amount of investment of capital will evidently be determined by multiplying each portion of capital, invested at any moment, by the length of time for which it remains invested.[28]

It is this recognition of the productivity of the dynamic roundabout nature of capitalistic production that distinguishes Jevons and represented a major contribution to the state of the art.

Much that is unfinished in Jevons can be explained by his sudden death through drowning at the age of forty-six; had he lived longer, he might very well have unified his distribution theories. His contributions are very significant, however, without further refinements.

The Subjective-Marginalist Model

We have discussed Jevons' contribution in considerable detail in order to show the technical and intellectual difficulties that had to be met in the development of a subjective-marginalist value and distribution theory. The time was evidently ripe for it, and, almost simultaneously with Jevons' attacks on J. S. Mill and classical economics, similar revisions of classical doctrines were enunciated in France, Austria, and America. Carl Menger's *Grundsätze der Volkswirtschaftslehre* was published in 1871, the year Jevons' *Theory of Political Economy* appeared;[29] Leon Walras' *Elements d'economie politique pure*, in 1874;

[27]The rate of interest is "the rate of increase of the produce |occasioned by lengthening the period of production| divided by the whole produce."

[28]Jevons *Theory of Political Economy*, p. 229.

[29]Jevons can claim precedent over Menger, however, because he had finished his paper *Brief Account of a General Mathematical Theory of Political Economy* in 1862.

and J. M. Clark's *Philosophy of Value,* in 1881. Walras, Clark, and especially Menger were blessed with able and devoted disciples who spread and refined their "master's" theories, and thereby changed the nature and purpose of economic analysis for the next seventy years.[30] There were, of course, significant differences between Menger, Walras, and their followers; still one can construct a marginal model that epitomizes the views held in common by the Austrians and Walras and Jevons.

THE FOUNDATION OF THE MODEL

Utility theory and marginal analysis provided the unifying basis for the new "subjective" economics. The utility of a commodity—that is, its ability to satisfy individual wants—attained theoretical significance only by associating the degree of utility with the units of a commodity already in the individual's possession. The utility of "butter" per se was indeterminate, devoid of all meaning, but the utility of a pound of butter to a man who possessed no butter at all had a specific value, a value determined by the "intensity of need." Every additional pound of butter would have an ever-decreasing value for that man, until the point of "satiety," or zero marginal utility, was reached; beyond this point, additional pounds of butter would possess a negative utility (i.e., a man might pay money in order to avoid further acquisition of butter).[31]

In order for a particular unit of a commodity to have utility, it must therefore be scarce (scarcity, of course, is a necessary but not sufficient condition for utility). Only by making utility a function of the quantity possessed—that is, only by discovering the principle of diminishing utility—does the utility concept become an operational tool. Once marginal utility becomes operational, however, it becomes the predominant and unifying factor among the various strands of subjective economics.

METHODOLOGY

Classical economics had been concerned primarily with economic

[30]Carl Menger's best-known students were Fredrick von Wieser and Eugen von Bohm-Bawerk. Both, as well as Menger, were members of typical Austrian civil service—army families and had distinguished civil service-university careers. Their social milieu was very similar to that of Marshall and Keynes though they had even less social or business ties with entrepreneurs than their British colleagues.

[31]The fact that too much butter may have a negative utility is readily understood by American or Common Market taxpayers whose taxes have to pay for the storage of mounting butter surpluses.

development and had devoted itself to the analysis of long-run trends and their relationship to economic growth. It assumed distribution as given and looked toward an increase in total output as a means of improving the welfare of society. Subjective economics, however, began its analysis with the individual's demand for consumer goods. Assuming the supply of productive factors as given, it soon concentrated on the optimum allocation of resources in order to maximize output at a particular point of time. The concepts of marginal analysis permitted the application of differential calculus to the solution of this straightforward maximization problem.[32] Over the last forty years, contemporary economics texts have reflected the marginalists' viewpoint by defining economics as the science that analyzes the allocation of existing scarce resources among a given number of competing claimants. Only within the last decade have chapters on economic development been added, reflecting a slow return to the classical viewpoint. The marginalist concept of static equilibrium analysis, however, dominates until this very day the undergraduate economics departments in both western European and Anglo-Saxon countries.

The maximization of utility or profit functions, subject to various constraints, constituted the dominant methodological tool of marginal economics. Though the maximization process that was supposed to characterize the impulses of "homo economicus" could be traced verbally, as in the Austrian school, it was quite natural for everyone even faintly familiar with elementary calculus to apply mathematical methods to define and analyze the process. If a fixed quantity is divided among different claimants, an equilibrium (optimum) position is reached when no further transfer of small units of this quantity can occur without the incurrence of a loss in efficiency (or utility or production). This principle dominates all of marginal economics and permits the description and analysis of consumption and production processes *by the same means.* Whether a household allocates its budget among different goods, or an entrepreneur allocates his capital among various factors of production, the same principle of equalizing marginal values applies; a household will have reached its

---

[32] The differences between classical and neoclassical methodologies are brilliantly reviewed by G. C. Harcourt, "Some Cambridge Controversies in the Theory of Capital," *The Journal of Economic Literature,* Vol. 7 (June 1969), pp. 369 ff. Also see P. Sraffa, *Production of Commodities by Means of Commodities, Prelude to a Critique of Economic Theory* (Cambridge: Cambridge University Press, 1960).

optimum allocation when the last (marginal) units of *n* different consumer goods have the same (marginal) monetary utility; similarly, an
enterprise will operate at optimum efficiency if the last units of the
various factors of production produce *n* marginal physical products
of equal monetary values. The "law of diminishing return" and the
"law of diminishing marginal productivity" are merely names for the
behavior of the first derivatives of smooth consumption and production functions. As we shall see, this application of the substitution
and maximization principles of the marginal model became the
foundation of neoclassical and welfare economics. The marginal
substitution and maximization principles, however, only applied to
the allocation of resources at a point in time. Thus the marginalists
could show quite easily that, within their assumptions, (pure) competition would optimize the allocation of resources. However, because
capitalism, as Schumpeter emphasized, is essentially a dynamic process, static optimization techniques will merely find logically correct
answers to wrong questions. Both the mathematical difficulties of
optimizing multivariable dynamic models and the overriding concern
of the subjective-marginal school with the optimization of an individual's utility function at a point in time imposed upon economics a
static deterministic methodology with which to analyze a dynamic
stochastic process.

THEORY OF EXCHANGE

In order to develop a theory of price and exchange, the marginalists
had to overcome several apparent paradoxes that followed from their
individualistic, immeasurable definition of value.[33] If individual values
were incomparable, how could two traders arrive at a common price,
or how could a market price be determined?

The answer to the first question was surprisingly undetermined.
Two traders exchanging furs and tobacco would want to continue to
exchange until the last unit of the products exchanged were of equal
value. For example, for trader A who owns tobacco, the eighth unit
of tobacco and the sixth unit of fur might have the same final utility,
and therefore he would not be interested in continuing to exchange
his tobacco for furs once he has acquired the sixth unit of fur. But for

---

[33]Though Jevons denied the measurability of individual utility preferences, he did, in
fact, order and compare preferences by expressing the value of a commodity in terms
of its marginal utility of money.

trader B, who owns furs, ten units of tobacco and seven units of fur have the same final utility; he would like to continue to trade fur for tobacco until he has acquired the tenth unit of tobacco. As a result, there are two "separate points" where the "final utilities" of units of fur and tobacco would be equal.[34] Therefore the final price—that is, exchange ratio between the last two units to be exchanged—must lie between these two points, or "double limit," as the Austrians called it. Bargaining power, as well as bargaining skill, would determine the final price ratio (see Fig. 6.2).

This extraordinary explanation fits much better a bargaining theory of prices (and wages), and might have led easily to a study of imperfect market structures. By assuming competition, however, the Austrians were able to keep the final price at least within their double limit. There is no a priori reason why under conditions of monopoly or monopsony the final price might not lie outside the double limit. Walras, though linking utility to demand, glossed over the determination of an exchange equilibrium between two traders, and assumed given demand curves and market prices. The inability of the subjective-marginal school to give a unique price for the exchange between two traders led later followers (e.g., Casell, and Machlup) to reject the entire attempt to explain the cause of price as a form of "scholastic inquiry"; they preferred to take market price as given and continue their analysis from this point.

Though the price ratio of a single exchange was undetermined, the marginal school was able to determine a single market price by making the implicit "common-sense" assumptions that individual utility functions were additive,[35] and by assuming market demand curves, validated by experience as given.[36] Then it easily could be shown how the aggregate demand and supply curves would establish a market equilibrium price.[37] However, because the "utility of a commodity" con-

---

[34]The Austrians used the term "final utility" instead of marginal utility, and thought of it as the employment derived from the last enjoyable unit |of a commodity|.

[35]The entire controversy over the mathematical properties of utility curves did not develop until the late 1890s. For an excellent discussion of the issues involved, see Jacob Viner, "The Utility Concept in Value Theory and Its Critics," *Journal of Political Economy* Vol. 33, pp. 369-387, 638-659 (1925).

[36]Walras was able to derive demand curves heuristically from utility functions, but even Walras started his analysis with a given equilibrium price and price-determined demand and supply; only later in his analysis did he link his equilibrium model with his value theory by analyzing the relationship between utility and demand.

[37]Once the assumption is made that the demand curve for a commodity represents the aggregate utility of individuals, the intersection of (Marshallian) demand and

Figure **6.2** Double Limits in Bargaining Situation

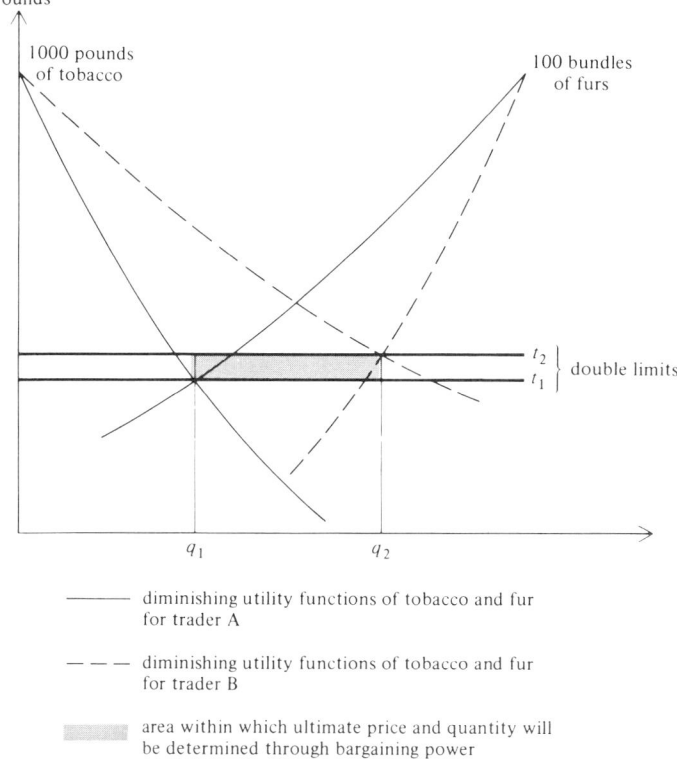

- diminishing utility functions of tobacco and fur
  for trader A

- — — diminishing utility functions of tobacco and fur
  for trader B

- area within which ultimate price and quantity will
  be determined through bargaining power

sisted for each single individual of the "incremental" utility of each separate unit, the marginalists had to show how a single market price for each commodity could exist in the face of those myriads of separate utilities. They managed to reconcile varying individual utilities with a unique market price by developing the concepts of "indifference" and "substitution," which make possible the allocation process described by marginal analysis. Reasoning somewhat in a *post hoc ergo proper hoc* manner, the marginalists held that identical and interchangeable goods had to have the same market price (exchange value). Hence, if a man possessed ten pairs of shoes (or hired one hundred laborers), none of these pairs would have a greater value to him than

---

supply curves gives the unique market price for that commodity. Cf. Alfred Marshall 8th ed. (New York: Macmillan, 1953) book 3, chap. 6. For an excellent thorough discussion of this topic, see George J. Stigler, "The Development of Utility Theory," *Journal of Political Economy* (1950) Vol. 58, pp. 307-327, 373-396.

the last one because any one of them could be substituted for the other; furthermore, because the individual supplier would be in the same bargaining position whether ten individuals wanted one pair of shoes each or one individual demanded ten pairs of shoes, the last pair of shoes demanded still determined the price since it could be substituted for any one of the previously demanded shoes. Therefore, the price (exchange value) of every commodity is determined by the value of the last unit purchased. Those who would have been willing to pay more than the market price for it will receive a "surplus."

The market prices of individual commodities and production factors were linked to related goods by the "law" of substitution: Whenever an exchange takes place whereby one commodity or production factor is substituted for another one in order to satisfy the same need or achieve the same purpose, the values of the two commodities (factors) can differ only very little because an *exchange* between two items of markedly different value is impossible, especially in a competitive market.[38] (The converse assumption would immediately lead to exploitation and imperfect competifion theories.) Hence the law of substitution is the basis for an interdependent market system. Substitution not only links the prices of individual commodities and factors to each other, but also transmits the consequences of changes in the demand and supply of individual commodities (factors) throughout the market.

THE THEORY OF DISTRIBUTION

We have already demonstrated how the marginalist theories of exchange and subjective value can be applied just as easily to the determination of factor prices as to the determination of market prices. The incremental methodology and the nature of the allocation process were so similar for the analysis of both commodity and factor markets that neither Jevons nor Menger nor Walras developed an explicit theory of distribution.[39] This occurred, we believe, *because* rather than in spite of the "obvious implications of the theory of subjective value" for distribution. Jevons, Menger, and Walras (ini-

[38]Note how this "substitution" concept resembles the notion of "continuity" in mathematics, and how easy it was, therefore, to express the marginal model in mathematical terms.

[39]Cf. Stigler, *Production and Distribution Theories*, pp. 2-4, 35, 147 ff., 246-260; Walras, however, came close to developing a marginal productivity theory in 1896, in the third edition of his *Elements*.

tially) were too occupied presenting a new economic theory *and* methodology to devote the necessary time to make explicit what was obviously implicit to them: the universal applicability of the basic methodology to exchange *and* distribution. The development of marginal capital and distribution theory was left, therefore, for the "second wave" of marginalists such as J. B. Clark, Wicksell, and Wicksteed, who fully refined and presented the most elegant creation of marginalism—the marginal productivity theory. Although there were significant differences among their distribution theories, the basic components were similar and are still taught to contemporary students. As a matter of fact, the marginal productivity theory is more firmly entrenched in American economics texts today than it was twenty or thirty years ago.

The value of individual units of labor, capital, and land are, like all other values, determined by the utility of the last "useful" unit—that is, the last factor unit employed in the production process. The individual entrepreneur is, of course, the "consumer" of various units of factors of production, and he will substitute various factor units for each other until the optimum production point has been reached, given his resources (budget). At the optimum point, a further substitution of, say, $100 worth of capital for $100 worth of labor would reduce rather than increase total production. The substitution process takes place in the form of a continuous sequence of trial and error decisions, in which the market mechanism supplies relevant "feedback" information to the decision maker in the form of changes in factor and commodity prices. Pure competition was assumed, either explicitly or implicitly, to optimize the allocation of resources,[40] and although this could now be shown mathematically, the mechanics of this decision-making process were analyzed much less by the marginal productivity theorists than by Smith or Marx. Again, we see how the concern with optimum resource allocation at a point in time forced economic analysis into a static model and left the study of dynamic economic development either to the "economic underground" or banished its discussion into highly segregated fields of "economic problems." For both businessmen and politicians, economics became increasingly irrelevant.

---

[40]"Optimization" of resources meant only the physical process of "clearing the market." The market mechanism under capitalism was not intended to deal with human needs.

If substitution among the factors of production determines the optimum factor mix, the possible substitution of homogeneous units of production factors guarantees that the last factor unit used will determine the factor price. Given a demand for consumer goods and a supply of production factors, the derived demand for units of production factors determines the factor price; it will be the highest amount the entrepreneur is willing to pay to the last factor unit that will, in turn, produce an additional commodity unit equal in value to the factor price.

Applying the concepts of marginal productivity to labor, we see that the employer in the example of Table 6.1 will pay his workers up to $5 if he can sell and produce 113 lbs.; he will pay his workers up to $8, the amount equal to the marginal revenue product of the eleventh worker, when he can only produce and sell 108 lbs. If we assume that there exists a sufficient pool of labor, the employer in our example would maximize his profits by employing 13 workers at $1 per hour. We can see easily how the marginal productivity theory could lead academicians to postulate that mass unemployment was impossible. If workers would lower their wage demands they would find employment at a wage equal to their contribution to the economy; a clear example of how a static analysis of a dynamic process can lead to nonsensical conclusions. We shall discuss this issue in greater detail in Chapter 10 when we examine Keynesian economics.

The same marginalist concept was applied to the contribution of the other "homogeneous" factors of production—labor and capital. In each case, the "factor returns" were determined by the value of the marginal product contributed by the last factor increment employed

Table **6.1** EXAMPLE OF MARGINAL PRODUCTIVITY OF LABOR
(UNDER PURE COMPETITION)

Numbers of workers employed	Total product	Price of product	Total revenue	Marginal physical product	Marginal revenue product
10	100 lbs.	$1.00	$100		
				8 lbs.	$8
11	108	1.00	108		
				5 lbs.	5
12	113	1.00	113		
				1	1
13	114	1.00	114		
				0	0
14	114	1.00	114		

in "equilibrium"—that is, after the price and wage fluctuations caused by substitutions of factors had time to subside. Obviously, this equilibrium was never reached, just as the pure competition postulated by the marginal productivity theory rarely existed. Further, only vigorous competition among entrepreneurs could assure the productive factors a reward equal to the value of their marginal product, and only competition among the factors of production could remove the dangers of monopolistic returns to the factors of production.

The investigation of economic variables at or near their equilibrium point under conditions of pure competition was and is a device used to reduce the complexity of the problem. Marshall applied it effectively in his analysis of long-run trends inherent in the economy. J. B. Clark and other marginalists became so enamored of their beautiful and rigorous marginal productivity models that often they seemed to forget that the real world did not operate under the assumptions of their models. Provided that firms operated under pure competition, the marginal productivity theory could be used to show that labor unions were at best unnecessary because market forces already assured labor its proper wage—the value of its marginal product; at worst, if labor unions were able to obtain more through monopolistic union tactics, this excess wage would be obtained only at the expense of other factors of production.

The answer to this charge was not the liberal contention that labor unions were not monopolistic—they most certainly are—but rather that in a world of market imperfections and capital concentration, union monopolies may play, under certain conditions, a countervailing market force. This theory of "countervailing (bargaining) power," formulated first by Sidney and Beatrice Webb at the turn of the century, and reformulated by J. K. Galbraith in the 1950s, is the very opposite of the marginal productivity theory.[41] The bargaining power theory postulates an indeterminate shaky equilibrium, and draws on sociological and institutional material to prove its case. Both theories are thoroughly static and equally inadequate to analyze or predict the dynamic aspects of capitalistic economics.

In the long run, and for the future of economic analysis, the static aspects of the marginal productivity theory had a much greater impact

---

[41]Sidney and Beatrice Webb, *Problems of Modern Industry* (London: Longmans 1898); *History of Trade Unionism* (1894), rev. ed. (New York: Longmans, Green 1920). John K. Galbraith, *American Capitalism: The Concept of Countervailing Power* (Boston: Houghton Mifflin, 1952).

on economic analysis than the shortcomings of the institutional bargaining power theories. Even though the "ethical," normative interpretation of the marginal productivity theory advanced by J. B. Clark and others generated a good deal of hostility toward the theory among radicals and institutionalists, the theory's "rigor" and "beauty" made it the foundation of various neoclassical syntheses that have dominated Anglo-American economics.[42] The rigor and beauty rest on the mathematically demonstrable fact that, assuming homogeneous and linear production functions, the sum of the payments to the factors of production exhausts the total product, and hence each factor, in turn, receives a payment equal to its marginal product.

As we shall see, Euler's "theorem" expresses the marginal productivity theory accurately and supplies the proof that, assuming homogeneity, the total product is exhausted by factor payments. Mathematically, the term "homogeneity" means that if the independent variables of a function are multiplied by a quantity λ, the function is merely multiplied by a power of this quantity, or if

$$Y = f(x_1 x_2 \ldots x_n)$$

$$f(\lambda x_1, \lambda x_2, \ldots \lambda x_n) = \lambda^n f(x_1, x_2, \ldots x_n)$$

If $n = 1$, we speak of a linear, homogeneous function. Marginal productivity theory assumes, generally, the existence of a linear, homogeneous production function; if, therefore, we increased all factors of production by, say, 10 percent, the gross national product (GNP) would also be increased by 10 percent if a country's production functions were homogeneous and linear. Let $P(x,y,z)$ be a positively homogeneous, linear production function, where $x =$ capital, $y =$ labor, and $z =$ land; then, at any point where P is differentiable, Euler's theorem states that, for homogeneous functions of degree 1,[43]

---

[42]We can distinguish among three neoclassical syntheses in recent history. The first, under Marshall, synthesized Ricardian and marginal theory, and formed the basis for F. W. Taussig's famous textbook. The second, under Joan Robinson and Edward H. Chamberlin, incorporated imperfect competition theories into the first neoclassical model, and dominated the college texts between the wars. The third, under Samuelson's leadership and epitomized in his famous texts, synthesized Robinsonian neoclassicism with both Keynes and general equilibrium analysis.

[43]Cf. A. E. Taylor, *Advanced Calculus,* (Boston: Ginn, 1955), pp. 184 ff. Note also that if

$$x \frac{\partial P}{\partial x} + y \frac{\partial P}{\partial y} + z \frac{\partial P}{\partial z} = P(x, y, z)$$

then $P(x, y, z)$ is a homogeneous function. It can easily be shown that factor payments exhaust the total product if, and only if, the production function is homogeneous

$$x \frac{\partial P}{\partial x} + y \frac{\partial P}{\partial y} + z \frac{\partial P}{\partial z} = P(x, y, z)$$

where $\partial P/\partial x, \partial P/\partial y, \partial P/\partial z$ are the marginal products of capital, labor, and land respectively, and $(\partial P/\partial x)x, (\partial P/\partial y)y,$ and $(\partial P/\partial z)z$ represent the share of capital, labor, and land. The sum of these shares exhausts the total product $P(x,y,z)$.

The opponents of marginalism have emphasized the unrealistic assumptions upon which the marginal productivity theory is based. Their attack misses the major drawback of the marginal distribution model. A good economist, unfettered by ideological chains and completely aware of the heroic assumptions that underlie this theory, would use the marginal equipment effectively to investigate market relationships at a point in time:

The marginal |productivity| principle *per se* is a tool of analysis, the use of which imposes itself as soon as analysis comes of age. Marx would have used it as a matter of course if he had been born fifty years later.[44]

Marginal analysis, however, is *completely* static and must therefore lead to wrong or completely irrelevant conclusions if it is not supported by dynamic analysis.

The danger of the marginal productivity theory came not from its often unrealistic assumptions, but rather from the elegance and internal rigor of its results. Economists found marginalism so attractive that many of them were captured by it completely, and lost all interest in developing a methodology to explore with more sophisticated tools the dynamic question classical economists had raised. Schumpeter, Veblen, and, more recently, Galbraith have pointed out repeatedly that by neglecting the dynamic aspects of capitalism the competitive equilibrium of marginalism would misallocate resources in the long run.[45] A competitive steel industry consisting of hun-

---

and linear. While the homogeneous nature of production functions can be defended, there really exists no a priori reason for the assumption of linearity. For a thorough discussion of the mathematical implications of the marginal productivity theory, see Stigler, *Production and Distribution Theory,* chap. 12, and Blaug, *Economic Theory,* pp. 421 ff.

[44]Joseph Schumpeter, in discussing the marginal productivity theory of J. B. Clark, in his *History of Economic Analysis,* (New York: Oxford University Press, 1954) p. 869.

[45]See especially Schumpeter's *Capitalism, Socialism and Democracy,* (New York: Harper, & Row, 1941) pp. 87-88; Thorstein Veblen's *Theory of Business Enterprise* (New York: Scribner, 1904), *passim*; also John K. Galbraith, *The New Industrial State* (Boston: Houghton Mifflin, 1967), pp. 189-198.

dreds of small firms would equate marginal and average revenue at the equilibrium price. Their price, however, would be higher than the price charged by the oligopolistic steel industries whose oligopolistic profits encourage them to operate at a physical and technological level that generates economies of scale and innovation.

The First Neoclassical Synthesis

Classical economics, weakened already by "historical" and "Socialist" dissent, was almost completely destroyed by the marginalist revolution. The entire field of economics threatened to be divided into innumerable schools, each with a different vocabulary, different premises, and different time horizons. It was Alfred Marshall's genius to combine the marginal methodology with much of the historical-institutional approach to reconstruct classical economics and give it a second life in the form of his neoclassical synthesis. Marshall was, however, not merely a great synthesizer. He had developed on his own most of the marginalist contributions of Jevons, Menger, Walras, and Clark. Marshall's gift for hiding his originality, and for finding his major contributions to be already implicit in the works of Ricardo and others, has often disguised his considerable impact on economic analysis.[46]

Marshall's neoclassical synthesis retains the concern of classical economics for the long run, in which the impact of short run irregularities have disappeared and only the major economic forces will prevail. He added the marginalist's short-run analysis of subjective utility and demand to long-run classical analysis, and applied a refined marginal supply and demand analysis to both short-run and long-run considerations.

Although the first edition of Marshall's famous *Principles of Economics* appeared in 1890, the bulk of his analytical work had been completed during the 1860s. In his various prefaces, Marshall admitted that he had learned from Jevons, but cited Cournot, von Thunen, and Ricardo-Smith-Malthus as the major influences.[47] It is exactly because

----

[46]In discussing the development of Keynes' thinking (Chapter 9), we treat in detail his tribute to Marshall's contributions.

[47]It is interesting to note that the only marginalist on this list was von Thunen, whose early pioneermg work *Der isolierte Staat* appeared in 1826. Von Thunen developed his marginal analysis and the early version of a marginal productivity theory by expanding Ricardo's rent theory. Marshall, by acknowledging von Thunen as his major influence, could thereby emphasize the classical roots of marginal theory and find another innovation to be already "implicit in Ricardo's works."

Marshall put the analytical innovation of marginalism squarely within the traditions of classical economics that some critics could speak of a reconstruction of classical economics. However, because Marshall's *Principles* contained most of the analytical refinements of marginal analysis, most marginalists throughout the English-speaking countries acknowledged the definitive theoretical nature of the *Principles,* and as a consequence muted their criticism of classical thought. Similarly, the influence of Roscher, Knies, and the historical school in general prompted Marshall to see his theoretical model in historical context and to emphasize, very much like Adam Smith, the historical-institutional aspects of capitalism.[48] It was easy, therefore, for American economics professors who had received their training in Germany and had strong historical sympathies to accept Marshall, who so effectively hid his analytical powers behind a smooth style, and who banished his sophisticated analyses to footnotes or appendices. By disarming marginalists and historical-institutionalists, Marshall provided a synthesis of three major economic currents—a synthesis that dominated economics textbooks and curricula completely until Keynes, and still plays a significant role in contemporary economic theory.[49]

THE MARSHALLIAN MODEL

Basic Assumptions and Methodology. Adam Smith defined economics as a study of wealth, and basically it had remained a study of wealth throughout the classical period. For Marshall *Political Economy . . . is a study of mankind* in the ordinary business of life; it examines the part of individual and social action which is most closely connected with the attainment and with the use of the material requisites of well-being. Thus it is *on the one side a study of wealth and on the other, and more important side, a part of the study of man.*[50]

Though Marshallian economics was a study of mankind, it concerned itself chiefly with the motives that "affect most powerfully and

---

[48]Cf. for instance, Appendix A of his *Principles:* The Growth of Free Industry and Enterprise. (All references are to *Principles of Economics,* 8th ed. (New York: Macmillan, 1953).

[49]Marshall, of course, was not able to include socialism, the fourth major economic current of his time, in his neoclassical synthesis. Characteristically, he sympathized with their efforts and had kind things to say about them: ". . . the socialists were men who had felt intensely, and who knew something about the hidden springs of human action of which the economists took no account. Buried among their wild rhapsodies there were shrewd observations and pregnant suggestions from which philosophers and economists had much to learn" (*Principles,* p. 763).

[50]Ibid. p. 1 (italics supplied).

most steadily man's conduct in the business part of his life."[51] Man's conduct and motives, however, can be measured by the amount of money necessary to prompt individual action:

> If the desire to secure either of two pleasures will induce people in similar circumstances each to do just an hour's extra work, . . . we then may say that those pleasures are equal for our purposes, because the desires for them are equally strong incentives to action for persons under similar conditions.[52]

Marshall found, however, that the same amount of money would offer a different inducement to different people, either because they own different amounts of money or because "their sensibilities vary." Hence the value of money was subjective and, most importantly, money had a marginal utility. Though this position is not unlike Jevons' or Bentham's, Marshall tried to disassociate himself from both, and carefully limited the area where quantitative measurements of human actions and motives could be undertaken.[53]

Marshall, furthermore, took great pains to define his assumptions and emphasized that his economic laws, "like nearly all laws of science," were merely "statements of tendencies." His concept that "every cause has a tendency to produce some definite result if nothing occurs to hinder it" is the basis for his analysis of long-run trends in an economy and prepares the application of the *ceteris paribus* principle, the theoretical device that makes certain that nothing will hinder the long-run forces from manifesting themselves. The essential long-run nature of Marshallian economics has often been neglected by contemporary critics concerned with the amelioration of short-run crises. Greater attention to the Marshallian analysis of long-run consequences of certain economic reforms during the past thirty years might have averted contemporary crises.[54] At the same time, virtually the entire economics profession has accepted the *ceteris paribus* methodology of analyzing economic problems. Unfortunately the significant economic variables are highly interdependent; hence the *ceteris paribus* methodology is responsible for the inadequacy

---

[51]Ibid.
[52]*Ibid.* p. 16.
[53]Note Marshall's lengthy footnote on Bentham and Hedonism in *Principles,* p. 17.
[54]A good example is the U.S. agricultural price-support policy, which removed the marginal farmer from the country and dumped him into the cities.

of neoclassical theory in the development and analysis of dynamic models.

This general weakness of neoclassical analysis was less noticeable in Marshall's work because of its "historical" style. Virtually every topic in Marshall's *Principles* is presented in terms of its historical development, with great emphasis on evolutionary changes whenever they have occurred. This peculiar mixture of static theoretical and dynamic historical analysis gave the *Principles* a realism and a usefulness for policy makers other neoclassical writings lacked.[55]

Demand and Supply Analysis. Very much like Adam Smith, Marshall relied heavily upon the forces of supply and demand in order to analyze and explain economic relationships.[56] He refined greatly Smith's essentially descriptive treatment of supply and demand by adding a diagrammatical methodology and by defining precisely the notions of utility, elasticity, and substitution. Except for Marshall's treatment of utility, however, we can expect that Smith would have been fully at home with the general flavor of Marshallian demand and supply analysis.[57]

Marshall, however, derived his demand analysis from the existence of individual utility functions, and did not, as the classical econo-

Figure **6.3** Demand Function

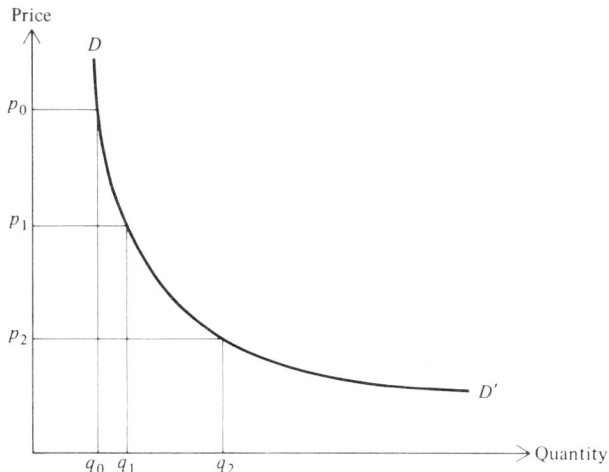

---

[55]For an opposite view, see Stigler, *Production and Distribution Theory,* pp. 62-63.
[56]See especially *Principles,* book 3.
[57]Although Marshall effectively used the diagrammatic treatment (*Principles,* book 3, chaps. 3 and 4), he was not the first to develop this method. The concept of

mists, assume that demand is given. Marshall defined clearly and explicitly demand as a schedule—that is, as a list of quantities, at a point in time, the buyer would buy at different prices. The demand price p_0 for the quantity q_0 reflects the existing *equilibrium* between the buyer's marginal utility of the commodity under consideration and the marginal utility of money, given a fixed income at point t_0 in time.

At price $p_1, p_2, \ldots p_n$, the buyer would be willing to buy quantities q_1, $q_2, \ldots q_n$, all preferences to exist at the same point in time t_0. The downward sloping demand curve is a result, of course, of the diminishing utility of all commodities (including money), and is referred to as the "law of demand" in contemporary texts.

Supply is determined in the long run by the cost of production. In the short run, "supply" means a supply schedule—the quantities the supplier is willing to sell at various prices—and the value of a product is determined by the intersection of the demand and supply curves. This is the equilibrium price toward which the actual (market) price would gravitate, *ceteris paribus*.

We have here one of the difficulties of neoclassical theories that

Figure **6.4** Equillibrium or Demand and Supply

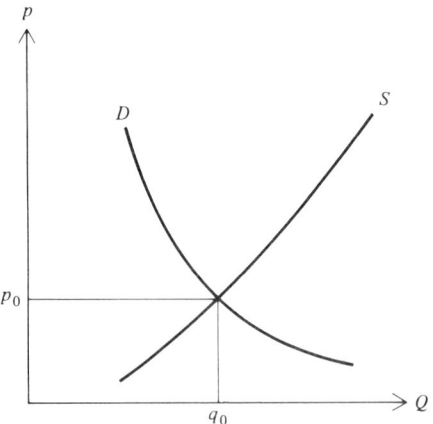

demand functions originated in their algebraic form with Cournot. The French engineer-economist Dupuit and the English economist-engineer F. Jenkins were the first to use the diagrammatical demand analysis known today. Jevons adopted this technique from Jenkins. Note the London School Reprint of Jenkins' economic essays: *The Graphic Representation of the Laws of Supply and Demand, and Other Essays on Political Economy, 1868-1884* (1931).

have plagued mathematically sophisticated students until this day. On
the one hand the demand and supply schedule is a graphical presentation of two functions at a point in time, t_0;

Figure **6.5** Development or an Equilibrium Between Demand and Supply

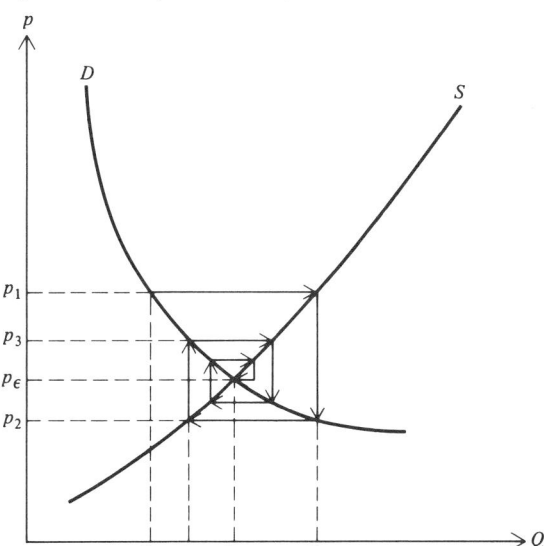

Equilibrium path: $(p_1 q_1) \longrightarrow (p_e q_e)$: at price p_1, quantities q_1
will be offered for sale and q_2 sold, $q_1 > q_2$; the price will then
drop to p_2 and q_3 amount will be forthcoming but q_1 amount
will be demanded, $q_1 > q_3$. The price will therefore rise to p_3,
and so on until p_e will be reached; at this point q_e will be
demanded and will be offered for sale.

their intersection (solution) gives the unique pair of points (p_e, q_e)
that satisfy this 2 x 2 equation. On the other hand, the demand and
supply curves can also be considered the paths that nonequilibrium
prices will follow until the equilibrium is reached, as shown in Figure
6.5. The dynamic process of price oscillations over time is reconciled
with the schedule concept by assuming that conditions prevailing at
t_0, will not change (the point in time t_0 becomes actually a period);
however, this disguises the fact that the demand-supply curves have
actually become the loci of the dampened oscillations of a feedback
system in which the equilibrium position signifies the system's steady
state. Marshall's diagrammatical analysis, supplemented by the hand-
waving and foot-stamping of the instructor in the classroom, turns out
to be a fairly clumsy tool for the analysis of dynamic behavior, even if

approached with the tools of comparative static analysis. Many decades elapsed before economists discovered that the intersection of
the demand and supply curve was not necessarily the equilibrium
point in a period analysis.[58]

Marshall made the tools of static analysis more useful by distinguishing between short-run and long-run equilibria. In the very short
run, the cost of production does not affect the equilibrium price and
supply can almost be assumed as given; the market price is determined by the marginal buyer whose purchase will clear the market.
The usual example for this situation is provided by the fish market, in
which the fisherman must sell his perishable goods. A series of low
price market days will, however, force the marginal fisherman out of
the industry; the supply offered will be reduced, and over the long
run the price must cover the fisherman's cost of production.

We see in this instance a true synthesis of marginal' and classical
value theory. In the short run the demand is the decisive factor; in the
long run it is supply—that is, the cost of production. In the short run
the marginalist's approach in which supply is assumed as given is
justified; in the long run the classical approach, emphasizing supply,
prevails. Marshall himself compared the interaction of demand and
supply with the two blades of a pair of scissors:

We might as reasonably dispute whether it is the upper or the under blade of
a pair of scissors that cuts a piece of paper, as whether value is governed

[58]Under certain conditions, it can easily be shown that the adjustments caused by a
nonequilibrium price will lead to an explosive oscillation away from the point where p_e
$= q_e$. See p. 55 above for further discussion.

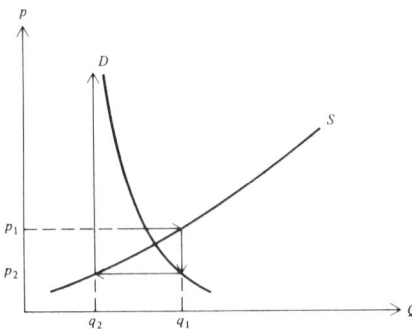

Cf. Henry Schultz, *Theory of Measurement of Demand* (Chicago: University of Chicago
Press, 1938), p. 80.

by utility or cost of production. It is true that when one blade is held still, and the cutting is effected by moving the other, we may say with careless brevity that the cutting is done by the second; but the statement is not strictly accurate, and is to be excused only so long as it claims to be merely a popular and not a strictly scientific account of what happens.

On the other hand we find some commodities which conform . . . to the law of constant return . . . . In such a case the *normal* level about which the market price fluctuates will be this definite and fixed money cost of production . . . . Thus we may conclude that, as a general rule, the shorter the period we are considering, the greater must be the share of our attention which is given to the influence of demand on value; and the longer the period, the more important will be the influence of cost of production on value.[59]

Neoclassical value theory rests on this synthesis of classical and marginalist value and price theory. However, the many qualifications and refinements must not hide the essential fact that Marshall merely restates Smith: The "higgling of the market" determines market price while the long-run "normal price" (Marx's value) is determined by the cost of production. Marshall's treatment is more sophisticated and the forces determining demand are explored, but the result is very much the same, except that Marshall defines the determinants of the cost of production to include the "exertions of labor" and the "abstinence" of savers.

Marshall, like Smith, applied his demand and supply analysis to the problem of distribution, but was able to use all the refinements of marginal analysis.[60] Consumer goods and the factors of production are essentially alike; there exists a market for both, and the process of substitution determines the value at the margin. This process, however, generates surpluses received by the buyer who had been willing to pay more for his goods than the price established at the margin, or the seller who had been willing to settle for less.

The concept of (consumer's) producer's surplus carried with it the connotation of unearned income. Marshall equated unearned income with the classical concept of rent, but extended it to all advantageous positions enjoyed in the competitive field of production. Monopolistic market positions, held by labor or capital, or

[59]Marshall, *Principles*, op. cit. , pp. 348-349.

[60]The similarity in the overall approach between Smith and Marshall is rarely emphasized. Schumpeter, however, points out Say's influence on Marshall, and Say, of course, followed Smith very closely.

Figure **6.6** Consumer's Surplus

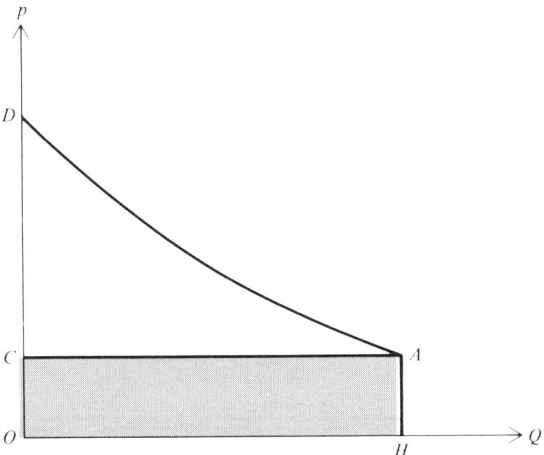

area *DCA* – consumer surplus
area *COAH* – price paid for
                quantity *OH*
(Compare *Principles*, p. 128)

Figure **6.7** Consumer's and Producer's Surplus

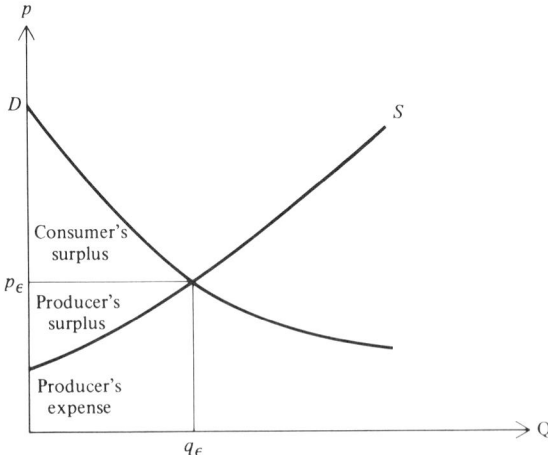

Compare *Principles*, p. 811.

merely the availability of especially skilled scientists or managers, would confer upon the firm the enjoyment of (quasi) rent.

The "national dividend," similar in concept to GNP, is therefore divided among wages for labor, interest on capital, and rent payments to the owners of land and the holders of monopolistic or quasimonopolistic production positions. The Marxian notions of surplus value and exploitation had lost their importance with the abandonment of the labor theory. The discovery of quasirent made possible the return on a more sophisticated basis of the concepts of surplus value and exploitation. Marxian economics cannot adequately explain the excess profits gained by monopolistic firms, nor can it analyze the rewards of powerful unions, or the rewards obtained from politically powerful vested interests such as farm blocs or oil lobbies. Marshall's concept of quasirents could supply the tools for the analysis of these phenomena. Marshall did not use the concept of quasirents in a derogatory manner. He assigned great importance to the entrepreneur but, unlike Say, who considered the entrepreneur as one of the factors of production, he did not consider the wages of management as a separate item of distribution. The above average wage going to the above average manager was a quasirent; the average managerial wage, a part of labor's wages.

The exact division of the national dividend was determined in the short run by the marginal product of each factor at the margin of its use. In the long run the quantity of each factor available was determined by its cost of production. This aspect of Marshall's distribution theory was essentially a restatement of classical theory. Land has no cost of production, but is a gift of nature; labor's cost of production is its ability to reproduce itself and its living standard in the long run. Capital's cost of production rests upon man's preference for immediate enjoyment of goods over future pleasures.

Marshall's distribution theory is again a synthesis of classical and marginalist doctrines. Applying demand and supply analysis, Marshall's marginal productivity theory added demand as a determinator of distribution to the classical cost of production theory, which, in turn, explained the supply of the factors of production.

In sum, Marshall wedded subjective value theory and marginal analysis to the classical tradition of Smith, Ricardo, and Say, and gave this synthesis a highly refined and rigorous static methodology.

7

GENERAL EQUILIBRIUM THEORY

TABLEAU ECONOMIQUE

Quesnay prepared the intellectual foundation for both the general equilibrium economics of Walras, Pareto, and Leontief and the macroeconomics of Marx, Wicksell, and Keynes.[1] As a matter of fact, Quesnay can be considered the first economic model builder, the first modern economist, and most certainly the theorist who influenced Marx *qua* theorist more than anyone else.

In the Marxian model, labor is the sole producer of a "surplus value"; Marx's predecessor Quesnay saw land (agriculture) as the sole factor of production, the *produit net*. The behavior of this factor of production was analyzed in the *Tableau Economique*, the first dynamic economic model.

---

[1]Quesnay's *Tableau Economique* appeared first in 1758, but was not translated into English for several decades. Smith referred to the *Tableau Economique* briefly, but Marx was the first economist who recognized its theoretical implications and value. Marx, however, referred to Quesnay's revised version of the *Tableau Economique* that appeared in 1766.

Quesnay, Louis XV's court physician, applied his biological training to economics. He derived the first model of the economy as a dynamic, self-regulated feedback system from his recognition of a similarity between the circulation of blood and the circulation of goods and money. Until this day, few other economic models come so close to the methodological approach of systems analysts and control engineers.[2]

The *Tableau Economique* emphasized the self-perpetuating, self-regulatory nature of the economic process, which reproduces the annual output through well-defined production, exchange, and distribution efforts that involve the "productive," "distributive," and "sterile" classes. (The farmers, of course, constituted the productive

Figure 7.1 Tableau Economique

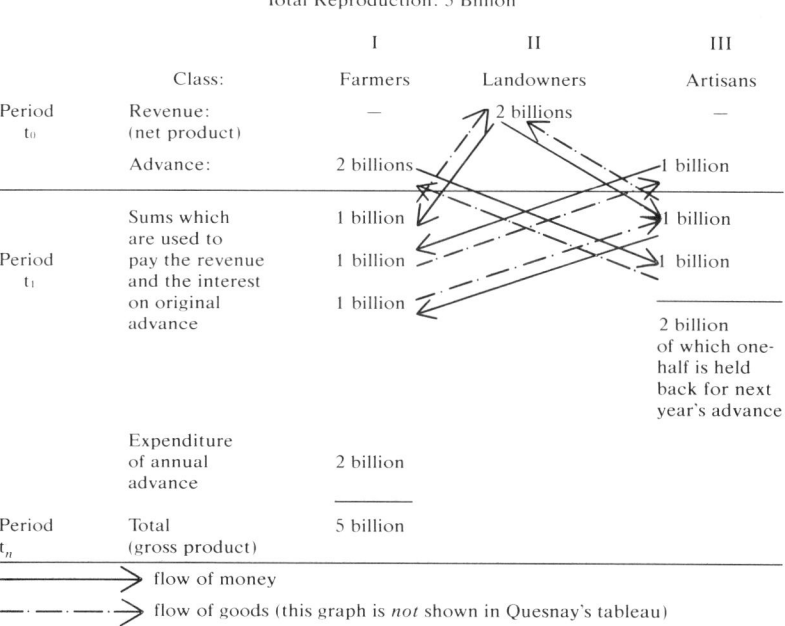

Total Reproduction: 5 Billion

	Class:	I Farmers	II Landowners	III Artisans
Period t_0	Revenue: (net product)	—	2 billions	—
	Advance:	2 billions		1 billion
Period t_1	Sums which are used to pay the revenue and the interest on original advance	1 billion 1 billion 1 billion		1 billion 1 billion 2 billion of which one- half is held back for next year's advance
	Expenditure of annual advance	2 billion		
Period t_n	Total (gross product)	5 billion		

————————> flow of money

—·—·—·—·—> flow of goods (this graph is *not* shown in Quesnay's tableau)

[2]For other models that apply dynamic feedback analysis to economics see Arnold Tustin, *The Mechanism of Economic Systems* (Cambridge: Harvard University Press, 1953); A. W. Phillips, "The Phillips Model" (Stabilization Policy in a Closed Economy)," *Economic Journal*, Vol. 64, (1964), 290-323; and the works of Kalecki and Goodwin. For a perceptive discussion of systems analysis and economics, see R.G.D. Allen, *Mathematical Economics* (London: Macmillan, 1957), chaps.5 and 9.

class, the landowners the distributive class, and the rest of society the
sterile class.) This simplified three-sector model enabled Quesnay to
demonstrate the interdependence of the economic factors and to
offer a structural analysis of the system.[3]

Quesnay's analysis assumes that all classes are equipped with the
necessary capital at point t_0, the beginning of the period. During the
ensuing period, this capital is (at least partly) used up and replaced so
that at the end of the period, at time t_n, the original position is
restored.

At point t_0 of period P, sector I (farming, mining, fishing) holds the
total output of the previous period, equal in value to $5 billion plus
$2 billion in cash, the total money in circulation. Sector II (land-
owners) holds $2 billion of rent and interest claims on sector I. From
the ouput $2 billion worth of food, seed, and so forth are immed-
iately allocated to sector I to provide (a) the "*avances annuelles*"—
that is, circulating capital (seed, fertilizer, tool maintenance, etc.) and
(b) the "*avances primitives*"—that is, the replacement of the depre-
ciated original investment. Sector I pays sector II $2 billion in cash
to satisfy rent and interest claims. Sector II buys $1 billion worth
of food from the farmers (sector I) and $1 billion worth of goods
and services from sector III. At this point, t_1 sector I and III now
hold $1 billion in cash and sector I still has left a stock of $2 billion
worth of food and raw material. Sectors I and III now exchange
$1 billion of food products and manufactured goods, and sector III,
in addition, pays $1 billion in cash for an equivalent amount of raw
material. The process is now completed. Sector I has again the economy's $2 billion in cash in its possession, and at the same time has
used the $2 billion input ("*avance annuelles*" and "*avance primi-
tives*") to produce an output (GNP) of $5 billion. The period ouput
exceeds input by $3 billion and this is the *produit net*, the surplus
value, which can be produced only in the agricultural sector.

For the modern reader it is probably easier if we present the tableau on the next page as a simple input-output model. Neither in its
traditional nor in its input-output format does the tableau show
explicitly the intrasectoral transactions, which have to take place
in order to make Quesnay's explanations fully understandable. The

[3]The historical implication of Quesnay's *Tableau Economique* was discussed in
Chapter 1.

Figure 7.2 The Tableau Economique in Input-Output Format (in billions)

Producing sectors (output)	Purchasing sectors (input) Farmers	Landowners	Artisans	Total Output
Farmers	2	1	2	5
Landowners	2	0	0	2
Artisans	1	1	0	2
Total Input	5	2	2	9

tableau, in input-output format, however, emphasizes the circular-flow aspect of Quesnay's analysis, one of the major achievements of the model. In addition, the input-output table shows as required productions inputs the two billion of agricultural products (the *avances annuelles*) the farmers retain. Furthermore, the agricultural input vector ($\frac{2}{2}$) presents the rent payment of two billion to the landowners (including state and church) as a necessary cost of production, analogous to contemporary "business taxes," since, according to Quesnay, agriculture alone is able to pay this differential rent. The ability of agriculture to create a "net product" is hence emphasized rather than concealed, by an input-output presentation. The input-output format furthermore makes Quesnay's 18th century period analysis explanation of how and when the various exchanges take place unnecessary. To the extent that Quesnay's period analysis primarily meant to elaborate the "zig-zag" transactions of a stationary economy, the input-output table gives a much clearer exposition of economic interdependence.

Our main interest in Quesnay's model lies in its theoretical approach. For the first time an abstract model is created that takes the system's output for granted, but tries to analyze its structure and behavior. As long as the input-output flow continues, this self-regulatory system will always reach the equilibrium (steady state) position at the end of the production period. System disturbances could either be induced by authoritarian interference with the self-regulatory (laissez faire) nature of the economy or by hoarding, the unwillingness of one sector to spend (consume) the amount of money necessary to absorb the entire output. Only rarely has Quesnay's role in anticipating the destabilizing effects of underconsumption been recognized. He pioneered too in endeavoring to obtain the statistical data necessary for deriving policy recommendations from his model, and he anticipated Leontief's contributions and thus can be considered the first input-output analyst, as well as the first general equilibrium analyst.

Economic Analysis and Mathematics

The general equilibrium tradition is closely linked with the mathematical tradition in economics, and both found their most imaginative and profound expression in Leon Walras (1834-1910), the son of the French economist and logician August Walras. The younger Walras spent his productive years at the University of Lausanne, where he founded the general equilibrium school which, after years of neglect by Anglo-American economists, has become one of the dominant intellectual influences of modern economics.[4]

It is important to emphasize the relationship between general equilibrium theory and mathematics. In partial equilibrium theory, the *ceteris paribus* methodology reduces the number of variables under consideration to one or two; hence a logical analysis of the variables' behavior does not necessarily demand mathematical tools, although the concepts of margin, maxima, minima, equilibria, and stability have precise mathematical meanings and were applied rigorously by economists with good mathematical training such as Jevons or Marshall. Yet, literary economists such as Menger or Böhm-Bawerk could arrive at substantially the same conclusions without mathematical tools. These writers may even have been less limited by the essentially static nature of the mathematical tools then available to economists.[5] Thus Böhm-Bawerk's capital theory, for instance, provided a dynamic, though literary, analysis of the capitalistic process, which was conceptually superior to anything contemporary mathematical economists had to offer.

---

[4]Walras' first edition of his *Elements of Pure Economics* appeared in 1874, but was not translated into English until 1954. The double barrier of French and mathematics created difficulties for many Anglo-American economists. Our references are taken from Leon Walras, *Elements of Pure Economics*, tr. William Jaffe (Homewood, Ill.: Irwin, 1954).

[5]The mathematics at the disposal of Cournot, Marshall, and Walras was quite rudimentary; it consisted of elementary calculus and matrix algebra, exactly the kind of material covered today in good high-school and freshman calculus courses. Though advanced work in mathematical economics requires today a considerable level of mathematical sophistication, the knowledge of "Walrasian mathematics" still is sufficient to understand 75 percent of the theoretical material published in current issues of, say, the *American Economic Review*.

Yet the real role of mathematics in economics is not, as Marshall perceived it, that of a handmaiden, which enables economists to express their concepts more concisely, trace through their model's logical consistency and state assumptions explicitly. The major contribution of mathematics is that it permits analysis of a much larger number of variables, over a longer period of time, than any literary economist can manage. With mathematics, more complex problems can be attacked and more sophisticated models can be built. There are, of course, limits to the model complexity even mathematical analysis can handle. It is difficult to find analytic solutions for most reasonably realistic, nonlinear, dynamic models with more than three variables. Fortunately, the mathematical economist now can explore the structure of highly complex models through the art of computer simulation. This entire process rests, however, on the ability to conceptualize the behavior of complex, multivariable models, and it was Walras' major contribution to show that economists can perform this feat when they are aided by mathematics.

THE WALRASIAN MODEL

Fundamental Conditions and Assumptions. We have already remarked that Walras was one of the co-founders of subjective utility and marginal analysis. The entire marginal equipment lies, therefore, at the base of his analysis. Whereas the Austrians attempted to connect utility, price, and cost through "causal" explanation, Walras, like Marshall, rejected this approach as an artificial and mathematically naive attempt to order interdependent variables. Marshall sidestepped the problem of causality vs. interdependence through his partial equilibrium analysis where all but one or two variables were treated as "given" (i.e., the variables became parameters), and it merely remained to be shown that a partial equilibrium existed. Implicit in Marshall's approach, however, was the assumption that the existence of n variables and n partial equilibria guaranteed the existence of a general equilibrium. This implicit assumption is made explicit in the beginning and closing paragraph of Marshall's Mathematical Note XXI:

We may now take a bird's-eye view of the problems of joint demand . . . with the object of making sure that our abstract theory has just as many equations as it has unknowns; . . . Thus, however complex the problem may become, we can see that it is theoretically determinate, because the number of unknowns is always exactly equal to the numbers of the equations which we obtain.[6]

We, of course, know today that the existence of n equations and n unknowns is at best a necessary but not sufficient condition for the existence of a unique equilibrium.[7]

More significantly, Marshall's partial equilibrium analysis abandoned the attempt to express the utility-cost-price or the producer-consumer relationships in terms of causal sequences without at the same time affirming explicitly their interdependence. Cournot, who laid the intellectual foundations for Marshall's analysis, also stated, in passing, that "for a complete and rigorous solution of the problems relative to some parts of the economic system, [it is] indispensable to take the entire system into consideration."[8] Cournot did not pursue this approach further because he considered the general equilibrium approach too difficult. It was Walras' genius to make this attempt, despite the intellectual difficulties it presented, despite the fact that he was mathematically not as well trained as Cournot (or Marshall), and despite the fact that no mathematical developments had occurred since the publication of Cournot's *Récherches* (1838) to facilitate this task.

We can reconstruct quite easily the intellectual puzzle that faced Walras by summarizing the propositions of marginal analysis and by drawing attention to the absence of any sequential order among those propositions:

Proposition (1). Each consumer will maximize his utility by allocating his income among n potential goods in such a way as to obtain the same marginal utility from each dollar spent. Algebraically:[9]

$$\frac{\text{MU good } i}{\text{price } i} = \frac{\text{MU good } j}{\text{price } j} = \cdots = \frac{\text{MU good } z}{\text{price } z}$$

---

[6]Mathematical Note XXI, *Principles of Economics,* 8th ed. (New York: Macmillan, 1953), pp. 855-856.

[7]In order to satisfy the mathematically trained reader, we shall admit immediately that n variables in an $n \times n$ system do not necessarily constitute a necessary condition for a unique solution. For our purposes, however, we can well assume that it does.

[8]A. A. Cournot (1801-1877), *Researches into the Mathematical Principles of the Theory of Wealth,* tr. N. T. Bacon, 2d ed. (New York: Kelley, 1927), p. 127.

[9]MU = marginal utility

Proposition (2). Each producer will maximize his utility by allocating his capital among the factors of production in identical manner:

$$\frac{\text{MU factor } i}{\text{price } i} = \frac{\text{MU factor } j}{\text{price } j} = \text{common marginal utility per dollar of capital}^{10}$$

Proposition (3). Pure competition (as defined by Cournot) is assumed.[11]

Proposition (4). The prevailing market (equilibrium) prices for goods are obtained by averaging individual consumer demand and individual producer supply prices, whereas in propositions (1) and (2) consumers and producers make their decisions in the face of already established market prices. Furthermore, the equilibrium prices in the factor market are the result of averaging producer demand prices and factor supply prices. The producer demand for factors, however, is a derived demand, and therefore dependent on both aggregate demand for consumer goods and the equilibrium prices in the consumer-goods markets. The consumer obtains his income from supplying the production factors for the producer. The aggregate income of the consumer sector determines aggregate demand for the production factors, which, in turn, determines consumer (household) income. Partial equilibrium analysis conceals the importance of this interdependence between consumers' and producers' efforts to optimize their respective utilities. Does the consumer (producer) look at the various prices and then spend his money, or do the market prices reflect consumer (producer) preferences?

No precise sequence can determine the complex interdependence between aggregate supply, aggregate demand, and market prices. It is however not at all obvious that there is a general equilibrium that satisfies all partial equilibria and the dual role of all households and firms as both buyers and sellers. Walras intuitively recognized the existence of a general equilibrium. The first mathematical proof of the existence of a unique solution (equilibrium) under certain restrictive assumptions was offered by A. Wald and John von Neumann in

---

[10]If "marginal product" is substituted for "marginal utility," we have the marginal productivity formulation of the optimum allocation of resources, as presented in contemporary texts.

[11]Cournot's definition is substantially identical with those offered in contemporary elementary texts.

the 1930s. In the early 1950s, McKenzie and Arrow-Debreu were able to offer solutions for a fully generalized Walrasian model.[12]

Theory of Simple Exchange. The theory of exchange, the basis of the Walrasian model, is developed from the "simple case" very much in the manner a teacher introduces the concepts of n-dimensional geometry by elaborating on the intuitive aspects of two-dimensional geometry. In the two-dimensional case, equilibrlum is reached in a competitive market when, at a given price, demand equals supply. If, at the existing price, demand does not equal supply, a new price is established (*prix crié*) until, through trial and error (*tatonements*), the supply and demand equating equilibrium price is found. Walras' analysis of the converging price oscillations around the (general) equilibrium is almost identical with Marshall's descriptions of the dampening price fluctuations around the (partial) equilibrium. In the two-dimensional case, the distinction between general and equilibrium analysis is, of course, primarily philosophical. Once the concept of a "partial equilibrium" is thus defined, it is possible to generalize this process mathematically and determine the n-dimensional general equilibrium.

General Theory of Exchange. In order to analyze the relationship among n goods, Walras relied on a common denominator, the *numéraire*, which is really money reduced to its role as a "standard of value."[13] The use of the *numéraire* implied the measurability of marginal utility, although in his discussion of utility theory Walras expressed the usual disclaimer about the measurability of subjective utility. However, the existence and fluctuations of market prices are objective facts, and for his major purpose, the establishment of the fact that the existence of n partial equilibria can be reconciled with the simultaneous existence of a general equilibrium, the question of measurability of individual utility was unimportant.

Walras' model consisted of three sets of structural equations, and a fourth set of auxiliary equations, to relate cost of production to price in equilibrium. The structural equations expressed:

---

[12]A. Wald "Über einige Gleichungssysteme der mathematischen Ökonomie," *Zeitschrif der Nationalokonomie* [(1936); a translation appeared in 1951 in volume 19 of *Econometrica*]. John von Neümann, "A Model of General Economic Equilibrium," *Review of Economic Studies* [(1945-1946); a modified translation of a previous article published in German in 1936].

[13]Classical economics, especially in Say's version, always considered money as "neutral." It only simplified exchange and was thus merely an accounting device. The *numéraire* plays, therefore, the role that classical theory had assigned to money.

1. the demand relationship among all goods produced and consumed
2. the allocation of productive factors (factor/supply relationship)
3. the determination of the optimum production function for each
   commodity.

Walras assumed, explicitly, the existence of a "given" level of consumer preferences, supply of productive factors, and technology. The
prices and quantities of consumer goods and the prices of the factors
of production were to be determined simultaneously in equilibrium
by the model. Implicitly, Walras held the usual classical assumptions:
pure competition and full employment.

1. The demand-supply equations: In the Marshallian model the
demand for butter may be expressed by the simple demand equation
$Q_b = F(P_b)$. The amount of butter demanded is a function of its
price; this functional two-dimensional relationship is then easily represented by the usual downward sloping demand curve. Clearly, however, the demand for butter is also affected by the price of bread
(P_{br}), margarine (P_m), national income (Y), the price of labor (π_a),
land (π_d), and cattle (π_c), and so forth, as well as the rate of change of
national income (Y') and the rate of change of the various prices.[14]

$$Q_b = F_i(P_b, P_{br}, P_m, \ldots; P_b', P_{br}', P_m', \ldots;$$
$$\pi_a, \pi_d, \pi_c, \ldots; \pi_a', \pi_d', \pi_c', \ldots; Y, Y')$$

The static partial equilibrium analysis disregards the rate of changes
of the variables and holds all prices except the price for butter constant at a given level of national income; in other words, these variables become parameters, and the term *ceteris paribus* really expressed
the relationship

$$Q_b = F(P_b, \hat{P}_{br}, \hat{P}_m, \ldots; \hat{\pi}_a, \hat{\pi}_d, \hat{\pi}_c, \ldots; \hat{Y})$$

where $\hat{P}_{br}, \hat{P}_m, \ldots, \hat{Y}$ are constants. The *static* Walrasian analysis also
disregarded the rate of change of the independent price variables and

---

[14]The relationship between demand and the rate of price changes is not mentioned
by Walras, but it has been established by various empirical studies since the 1930s.

failed to include national income explicitly.[15] The price parameters, however, become independent variables again, or

$$Q_n = F_j(P_b, P_{br}, P_m, \ldots; \pi_a, \pi_d, \pi_c, \ldots; \hat{Y})$$

In general, let there be m consumer goods, m consumer goods prices, and n factors of production and factor prices (costs); the quantity-price relationship among these m and $m + n$ variables is expressed by the demand-supply set of equations:

$$Q_1 = F_1(P_1, P_2, \ldots, P_m; \pi_1, \pi_2, \ldots, \pi_n)$$
$$Q_2 = F_2(P_1, P_2, \ldots P_m; \pi_1, \pi_2, \ldots, \pi_n) \qquad \text{(I)}$$
$$\text{- -}$$
$$Q_m = F_n(P_1, P_2, \ldots, P_m; \pi_1, \pi_2, \ldots, \pi_n)$$

This set of equations expresses mathematically the Walrasian concept that the quantities of all m goods produced and consumed in the economy are simultaneously determined by the prices of all the m goods and the n services in the economy.[16] The market demand equation for any consumer good is the sum of the individual demand functions.

2. Factor supply equations: Both partial and general equilibrium analysis assumes the existence of a given amount of labor and capital. In the partial equilibrium analysis the amount of dairy farm labor, for example, is merely a function of the wage offered at an instance of time; all other prices are again held constant. In complete analogy to the consumer-goods demand equations, the supply and allocation of the productive factors are simultaneously determined by all the consumer prices and wages in existence. We obtain the following system of n aggregate supply functions determined by $n + m$ prices.

$$S_1 = f_1(P_1 P_2, \ldots, P_m; \pi_1 \pi_2, \ldots, \pi_n)$$
$$S_2 = f_2(P_1 P_2, \ldots, P_m; \pi_1 \pi_2, \ldots, \pi_n) \qquad \text{(II)}$$
$$\text{- -}$$
$$S_n = f_3(P_1 P_2, \ldots, P_m; \pi_1 \pi_2, \ldots, \pi_n)$$

The assumption of constant returns, homogeneity, and constant variability of the factors of production permits the set of equations

[15]In his chapter on "The Continuous Market" in *Elements of Pure Economics* (pp. 377-381), Walras briefly considered variations in aggregate (i.e., national) income. Walras' law (budget equation), however, precludes variations in national income as a factor affecting the behavior of his general equilibrium model.

[16]There are actually only $(m - 1)$ independent prices in the Walrasian system because all prices are expressed in terms of one arbitrary commodity, the *numéraire*, or standard of accounts; hence there are only $m - 1$ independent final good-price relationships.

(II) to be expressed explicitly in the form

$$S_1 = s_{11} Q_1 + s_{12} Q_2 + \ldots + s_{1m} Q_m$$
$$S_2 = s_{21} Q_1 + s_{22} Q_2 + \ldots + s_{2m} Q_m$$
$$\text{-----------------------------}$$
$$S_n = s_{n1} Q_1 + s_{n2} Q_2 + \ldots + s_{nm} Q_m$$

where, of course, $Q_i = Q_i (P_1 P_2, \ldots, P_m; \pi_1 \pi_2, \ldots, \pi_n)$ and where S_i is the aggregate quantity of the ith production factor available in the economy (e.g., total number of agronomists), the production coefficient s_{ij} is the amount of productive factor i used to produce a unit of consumer (final) good j (e.g., the number of agronomists employed in the production of butter), Q_j is, again, the number of units of good j that are consumed (e.g., lbs. of butter produced and sold), and $s_{ij}Q_j$, therefore, is the total amount of factor i used in producing the total supply of good j. (In equilibrium, of course, the amounts produced will always equal the amounts consumed.)

3. Production function relationship: The first two sets of equations (sets I,II) express the market demand relationship for final goods and the factor supply equations. Walras recognized, of course, that each household entered the market as both consumer and supplier of productive factors. The full employment assumption required, therefore, an uninterrupted, constant flow between entrepreneur (firm) and household, very much in the manner first postulated by Quesnay, and usually described graphically in the form shown in Figure 7.3. In an economy where money is merely a commodity used arbitrarily as an accounting standard, the total value of all goods demanded must be

Figure 7.3 Simple Model of an Economy

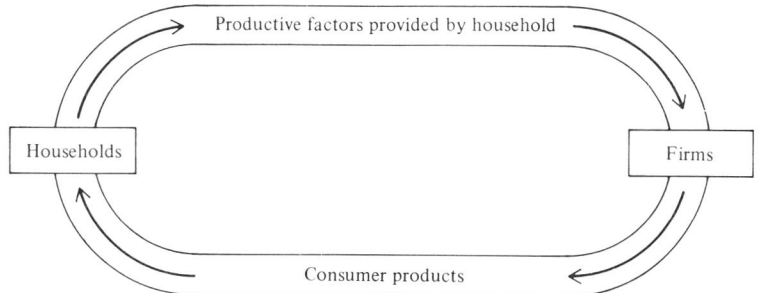

Productive factors provided by household

Households

Firms

Consumer products

identical to the total value of all goods supplied, or the total amount earned by the households in supplying the factors of production must equal the total demand for consumer goods.[17] The conditions are satisfied as already shown above (set III) by the $n + m$ set of equations that relate demand for final goods to the supply of factor services provided.

4. Auxiliary equations: Contemporary elementary texts still teach the Marshall-Walras lessons of neoclassical economics that, under pure competition, the price of a commodity equals its average cost in equilibrium.[18] The set of equations relating average cost and price of the final goods completes the Walrasian model:

$$C_1 = s_{11}\pi_1 + s_{21}\pi_2 + \ldots + s_n1\,\pi_n$$
$$C_2 = s_{12}\pi_1 + s_{22}\pi_2 + \ldots + s_n2\,\pi_n \qquad \text{(IV)}$$
$$- -$$
$$C_m = s_{1m}\pi_1 + s_{2m}\pi_2 + \ldots + s_{nm}\pi_n$$

and, therefore

$$C_1 = P_1$$
$$C_2 = P_2$$
$$- - - - - -$$
$$C_m = P_m$$

where C_i $(i = 1, 2, \ldots, m)$ is the unit cost of the ith product, and the coefficients and parameters are as defined above.

The four sets of equations have $2m + 2n$ independent equations,

[17]This relationship is generally referred to as "Walras' law," but is merely an extension of Say's law, which held that supply must create its own demand; unemployment was not feasible in either Say's or Walras' model.

[18]This relationship is always expressed by the familiar diagram:

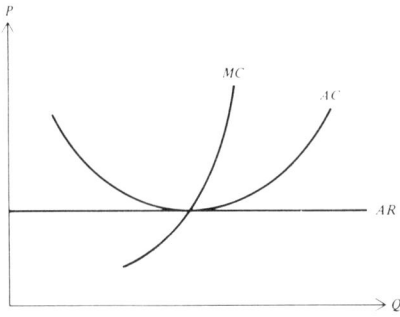

and the same number of variables.[19] (*m equations are supplied by set I, n* equations each by sets II and III, and *m* by set IV.) There are *n* productive factors, and hence *n* factor prices, *m* final goods with *m* prices. The number of equations and variables equal each other. This, as already mentioned on page 195, does not guarantee an equilibrium (solution) and Walras knew this very well, despite the often repeated, though completely unfounded, charge that he merely "counted equations."[20] First, Walras required that all equations be independent.[21] Furthermore, he recognized intuitively that an *n* x *n* set of simultaneous equations may have a unique solution, many solutions, or no solutions at all, a fact that was not generally known at his time, though it is taught to college freshmen today. What is more, he recognized the implications of these mathematical possibilities for economic theory. A system that has many equilibria or no solution is either indeterminate or carries inherent contradictions within itself that must bring about the system's breakdown.[22] (This was precisely what Marx tried to show!) Because the capitalistic system was not

---

[19]Actually, as pointed out above, the number of independent equations and variables are $2m + 2n - 1$, because Walras' law (budget equalities) eliminates one equation. For purposes of exposition we have not followed Walras completely.

[20]This charge is, surprisingly, repeated by Dorfman, Samuelson, and Solow in *Linear Programming and Economic Analysis* (New York: McGraw-Hill, 1958), p. 350.

[21]A system of equations is (linearly) independent if there is no single equation that can be expressed as a linear combination of at least two other equations. For instance

$$2x + 3y + z = 0$$
$$7x - y - 4z = 0$$
$$-x + 10y + 7z = 0$$

is a dependent set of equations because equation (3) can be obtained by multiplying equation (1) by 3, equation (2) by -1, and then adding the two—that is, $3(1) + -1(2) = (3)$. Dependence carries with it the connotation of redundancy, of over-determining a model by supplying more variables and equations than are necessary. The determinant of a dependent set of equations equals 0, which shows by Cramer's rule that a set of dependent equations has no unique solution. In our example the determinant

$$D = \begin{vmatrix} 2 & 3 & 1 \\ 7 & -1 & -4 \\ -1 & 10 & 7 \end{vmatrix} = 0$$

and the set of equations therefore has no nontrivial unique solution. It has either no solution or infinitely many.

[22]A system of equations in which $x + y = 0$, and $2x + 2y = 7$, has obviously no solution; the two statements are contradictory. Even in cases where a system of equations has a unique solution, this solution may be economically meaningless by demanding, for instance, negative inputs or outputs. *Admittedly*, Walras failed to take this possibility into account.

"chaotic" in Walras' view, he thought there was enough evidence to assume that a unique equilibrium solution would, normally, exist in an economy that had many consumers and many goods. As we know, the mathematicians Wald and von Neümann have proved that Walras' intuition was accurate.[23]

After considering the existence of an equilibrium, Walras turned to the analysis of the possible nature of this equilibrium. Was it stable or unstable? In high-school physics, the notion of stability is generally explained by the analogy of placing a ball either inside or on top of an inverted bowl. (See Figure 7.4.) In the first case, if the ball is displaced by a minor force, it will return to this equilibrium position, after a series of dampened oscillatory movements within the bowl; in the second case, however, even a minor force will displace the ball forever. Once this unstable equilibrium position is disturbed, it cannot be regained. The similarity between the behavior of the ball within the bowl, and the behavior of the price in the Marshallian partial equilibrium analysis, as represented in elementary economics texts, is quite striking. It is not at all obvious, however, that intuitively stable partial equilibria necessarily guarantee the existence of a stable general equilibrium. Walras looked at the price mechanism as the control (thermostat) of what would be called today a "negative feedback system." If prices exceed the equilibrium position, they generate excess supply which, in turn, generates prices below the equilibrium which will generate excess demand; these variations around the equilibrium are dampened, however, by the learning ability of the market, which manifests itself by a "groping" adjustment which moves toward the equilibrium position, analogous to the behavior of the partial equilibrium model.

Figure **7.4** Stable and Unstable Equilibrium

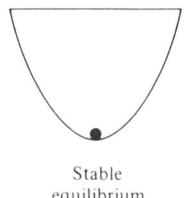

Stable
equilibrium

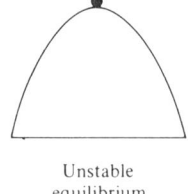

Unstable
equilibrium

[23]Both Wald and von Neümann developed modified Walrasian models. Von Neümann's model had no consumers and Wald's only one consumer.

The mathematical theory of stability is one of the most difficult parts of "hard analysis," and Walras did not and could not prove rigorously the existence and stability of the general equilibrium.[24] It was a testimony to his genius that he raised these very questions and provided intuitive answers which have been generally found to agree with more rigorous mathematical investigations.

We have discussed Walras' achievements in detail because they show so very clearly the important contribution mathematics can make to theoretical investigation. The questions of stability and equilibrium are vital to the design and performance of *any* economic system; they can be meaningfully approached only mathematically. The significance of these topics in modern economics is a lasting monument to Walras.

VILFREDO PARETO

The forty-five-year-old Italian economist Vilfredo Pareto (1848-1923) was chosen by Walras himself to fill his chair at the University of Lausanne when Walras retired in 1893. The aristocrat Pareto combined an excellent classical education with training in engineering and mathematics. Before accepting Walras' chair, he held high managerial positions in the railroad and steel industries, dabbled in politics, and worked actively in the fields of economic theory and policy. Pareto's major contribution to economic theory was his extension and refinement of Walras' general equilibrium model in his *Cours d'économie politique* (1896-1897).[25]

Pareto was a much better mathematician and writer than Walras, and the *Cours* is essentially a much more elegant, concise, and rigorous restatement of Walrasian general equilibrium theory. We find, however, that even in this work Pareto tried to avoid the interpersonal comparison of personal utility that is *implicit* in the Walrasian (and Marshallian) model. The indifference curve analysis of

[24]Interestingly, major recent contributions to stability theory have been made by Richard Bellmann, one of the few outstanding contemporary mathematicians who has been primarily concerned with the application of mathematics to economic theory, management science, and general dynamic systems analysis. For an elementary introduction to this topic, see W. Kaplan, *Ordinary Differential Equations* (Reading, Mass.: Addison-Wesley, 1962), chaps. 3 and 5.

[25]Pareto wrote in French and Italian; only some of his works have been translated into English. G. C. Homans and C. P. Curtis, *An Introduction to Pareto* (New York: Knopf, 1934), can easily be read by anyone interested in Pareto. Also note Umberto Ricci, "Pareto and Pure Economics," *Review of Economic Studies* Vol. 1, pp. 1-21 (October, 1933).

Edgeworth and Fisher avoided any necessity for interpersonal utility comparison. Pareto adopted this approach, together with modifications of other aspects of Walrasian theory, and presented this new synthesis in his *Manuale di economica politica* (1906). The real importance of the *Manuale* was, however, the attempt to introduce a dynamic viewpoint into the general equilibrium model. We find here an explicit insight into the general systems nature of economics, in which the market can be viewed as a closed-loop negative feedback system, subject to delays and input variations. Unfortunately, Pareto's increasing concern with sociology and politics kept him from developing a fully dynamic general equilibrium model.

As a consequence of his experience in Italian politics, Pareto adopted an extremely individualistic laissez faire position; he viewed any government action with deep distrust. In this respect he was very close intellectually to von Hayek and von Mises.[26] Unlike Hayek and Mises, however, he combined a strong elitist, antidemocratic view with his economic laissez faire attitude, which made him very popular with Fascist intellectuals. Fascist approval of his brilliant *Trattatto di sociologia generale* (1916) and *Les Systemes socialistes* (1903)[27] prevented a serious study and discussion of these two provocative works in the Western world.

Pareto's importance to contemporary Western economists is a result of his contribution to welfare economics, particularly his rejection of the cardinal measurability of individual utilities. If utility has a cardinal measure, then it can be added, and "optimum welfare" can be defined as the largest possible sum of all utilities. While few economists accepted explicitly the measurability of personal utilities, implicitly and de facto, such measurability provided the basis of Jevons', Walras', and even Marshall's utility theory. Pareto's development of indifference curve analysis gave him the opportunity to discuss the welfare implications of economic policy decisions without making interpersonal utility comparisons. It was sufficient, Pareto held, to express each person's preference in an ordinal manner, as represented by the indifference map. (See Figure 7.5.)

The various quantities of cheese and butter represented by points *a, b, c, d* in Figure 7.5 provide the same utility to a given indivi-

[26]Note F. von Hayek's celebrated *Road to Serfdom* (Chicago: University of Chicago Press, 1944), the best popular expression of this viewpoint.

[27]V. Pareto, *Trattato di sociologia generale* (Florence: Bera, 1916); *Les systemes socialistes* (Paris: Giard & Brière, 1903).

Figure 7.5 Indifference Curves

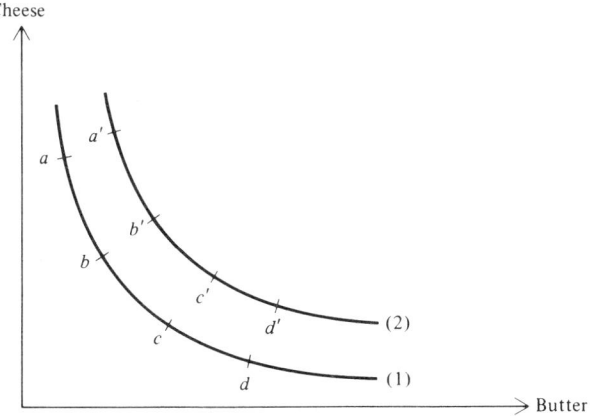

dual who, of course, would prefer any combination of goods expressed and a', b', c', and d', to all possible combinations on indifference curve (1). This indifference between two quantities on the same curve can then be extended conceptually first to three and then further n dimensions to give an n-dimensional indifference map of n goods and n persons, which can be expressed by a system of n differential equations. This system reaches an optimum, the so-called Pareto optimum, when any further exchange of goods will not improve total welfare.

The notion of a Pareto optimum, as we have mentioned, can be applied to policy decisions. Welfare is optimized in an economy if no further redistribution of goods and services would increase total welfare. Pareto, however, rejected the notion of a unique welfare optimum, lest interpersonal comparison be let in by the back door. Enrico Barone (1859-1924) succeeded in making Pareto's welfare optimality more practical by introducing the concept of compensating payments.[28] Very much like Marshall, Barone provided a monetary measure for the consequence of policy decisions that changed the welfare of individuals or groups. If, for instance, the elimination of steel tariffs will help the consumer but harm the steel industry, total welfare is improved if the steel industry accepted a sum of money as a compensatory payment from the steel consumers, and if the steel consumers,

[28]E. Barone, "The Ministry of Production in a Collectivistic State," in *Collectivist Economic Planning* F. von Hayek, ed., (London: Routledge & Kegan Paul, 1947).

having paid this sum, were still better off now that the tariffs have been eliminated.

The anticollectivist Pareto was not only the first non-Marxist to admit that a Socialist state could, solely on economic grounds, reach the same results as a free-enterprise economy, but he and Barone laid the theoretical foundations for an economic theory of planning, an impressive intellectual accomplishment.

WASSILY LEONTIEF

The Walras-Pareto general equilibrium model had generally little impact on Anglo-American economics until after World War II, not only because it seemed overly abstract and mathematical, but also because it seemed to have no practical value for applied economics. Though Walras himself had hoped that one day there would be enough data available to permit the actual numerical solution of his model, Pareto considered general equilibrium theory merely as a theoretical device to analyze the behavior of a market economy. Pareto stated that even if a small market of 100 individuals and 700 goods were considered, 70,000 equations would have to be solved, which was physically impossible in Pareto's day.[29] Even modern computing devices and national income statistics have not made the Walras-Pareto model operational, nor is there much likelihood that it ever would be.[30] There is little need for an operational Walras-Pareto model, however, because Wassily Leontief has reduced the dimensionality of their model sharply by aggregating firms and consumers into economic sectors. He is then in a position to analyze the interaction among the sectors (industries) in very much the same way Walras and Pareto examined the exchange of goods and services among consumers and producers. The interdependence of economic activity is now expressed by an input-output matrix that shows the flow of sector outputs to all segments of the economy.

Input-output analysis assumes consumption and investment as "given"—that is, as determined before the analysis is made; this re-

---

[29]Actually only 69,999 equations because 699 goods are expressed in terms of the 700th good, the *numéraire*.

[30]Another difficulty, correctly anticipated by Pareto, and discussed at length by Oscar Morgenstern on various occasions, is the truncating and round-off error, introduced by iterative numerical solution of large-scale equation systems. For a brief elementary discussion of round-off and truncating errors, see S. H. Fox, *Fundmentals of Numerical Analysis* (New York: Rowe Press, 1963), pp. 4-6.

duces the more ambitious Walrasian model to a simplified theory of production that is based upon three assumptions:

1. Each good is supplied by a single, distinct industry or production sector, which has only *one* primary output;
2. The inputs purchased by each industry (sector) are a direct function of that sector's output.
3. The productive efforts are "linear"—that is, additive and homogeneous; there are, therefore, no external economies or diseconomies of scale.

The basic input-output model is illustrated in Table 7.1 as a simplified four-sector model of the Italian economy.[31] We can easily see that the input-output table provides an accounting device that denotes the distribution of each sector's output throughout the economy. Agriculture, for example, has a total output of 250 units and uses up 25 units of its own output, supplies 40 units to the "Basic industry" sector, and 40 units to the "Finished goods" sector; the rest goes to the "Final user"—the "Consumer" of the Walras-Pareto model. The "Final user" sector includes the government, individual households, and exports.

Each sector appears twice in the input-output matrix. Reading down vertically in the "Agriculture" sector, we note that this sector uses up 25 units of inputs from the "Agriculture," "Services," and "Basic industry" sectors. The input-output model distinguishes between intermediate and final goods, and between primary and produced (value added) inputs. It shows how much of each sector's output is used by other sectors as an intermediate good, and how much is sold directly to the ultimate consumer (final demand). The input-output table provides, therefore, an immediate insight into the productive and distributive structure of the economy. The consumer sector provides, at the same time, the sole factor of production; the output of the consumer sector (labor) is exchanged against the sector inputs (goods and services). The basic input-output model is, therefore, a closed system, in which the unknown variables—final demand, employment, and wage rates—are determined simultaneously "in equilibrium." In solving the final demand and output requirements *simul-*

---

[31]This example is taken from H. B. Chenery and P. G. Clark, *Interindustry Economics* (New York: Wiley, 1959), p. 14.

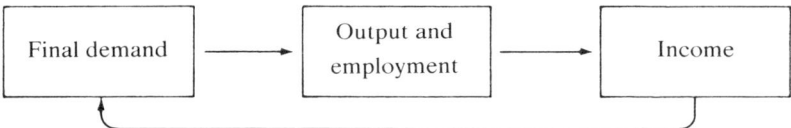

taneously, the feedback relationship between demand and supply are made instantaneous.

We have, in essence, a sharply reduced Walrasian model, in which the equilibrium prices and equilibrium quantities can be found by solving (inverting) the Leontief matrix.[32] General equilibrium analysis became operational with the emergence of input-output analysis and for the first time, economists had a tool to investigate the interdependence of the many variables that determine the stability and performance of the economy.

The original input-output analysis, however, was still a static tool that could, at best, find the new output equilibrium level after certain changes were introduced into the model (e.g., a 5 percent increase in steel production). The process of adjustment—the time required for reaching the new equilibrium and its stability—could not be analyzed by the methodology of comparative statics, which had characterized input-output analysis.

These theoretical questions have considerable practical significance. Can the equilibrium be maintained if the economy is expanded? Can a demand increase lead to a rapid increase in supply and hence a new equilibrium at a higher level of output without inflation, or is the economy's response so slow that the inflation generated will prevent any real growth? Can a significant growth in output over a given period stimulate disequilibrating capital formation? Static input-output analysis does not answer these questions. It neglects the role of net

[32] A concise mathematical formulation of the Leontief model can be found in G. Hadley's *Linear Algebra* (Reading, Mass.: Addison-Wesley, 1961, pp. 3-5), an excellent book written primarily with economics-statistics students in mind. A very good discussion of the relationship between input-output theory and marginal productivity theory can be found in C. Yan, *Introduction to Input-Output Economics* New York: Holt, Rinehart & Winston, 1969). Anyone seriously interested in input-output analysis, however, will have to read Leontief's *The Structure of the American Economy*, 1919-1939, (2d ed.; New York: Oxford University Press, 1951, esp., parts 1 and 2). For an analysis of the latest work in input-output theory, see Chenery and Clark, *Interindustry Economics, op. cit.;* Wassily Leontief et al., *Studies in the Structure of the American Economy* (New York: Oxford University Press, 1953); and M. Hatomaka's excellent *Testing the Workability of Input-Output Analysis* [Princeton, 1957 (mimeographed)].

Table **7.6** INPUT-OUTPUT (IN MILLIONS OF DOLLARS)

INPUT FROM	OUTPUT TO				INTERMEDIATE USE (W_i) +	FINAL USE (Y_i) =	TOTAL USE (Z_i)
	Services	Agriculture	Basic industry	Finished goods			
Services	20	25	15	80	140	60	200
Agriculture	0	25	0	120	145	105	250
Basic industry	0	25	45	40	110	40	150
Finished goods	0	0	0	80	80	320	400
Total purchases (U_j)	20	75	60	320	475		
Primary inputs (V_j)	180	175	90	80		525 (GNP)	
Total Output (X_j) $U_j + V_j = X_j$	200	250	150	400			1000

capital formation by making the production of current input proportional to the level of output in the same period. If a change is introduced into the model, input-output analysis assures the existence of a new equilibrium because the technical production coefficients are less than 1. For example, if we "disturbed" the equilibrium by increasing the production of steel by 5 percent and then determined new input-output tables every quarter for the next eight quarters, we would note that the indirect input requirements of the second quarter would be less than those of the first quarter, those of the third less than those of the second, and so on, and hence the indirect input requirements will converge, and the system must reach a new equilibrium. The disequilibrating consequences of delays, which play such a powerful role in Keynesian analysis, are thus ignored. Say's law still holds in input-output analysis.

In his mathematical investigations of Walras' model, von Neümann showed that a dynamic general equilibrium model could be developed. Furthermore, equilibrium could be maintained in such a model under certain conditions, if all sectors grew proportionally.[33] Von Neümann's work formed the basis for all recent attempts to develop a dynamic general equilibrium model.[34] A dynamic input-output model would have to add at least two factors to the static input-output model: technological change and capital formation. Crude dynamic input-output models have already been developed by Leontief and others, but the results are still tentative, and not yet fully operational.[35]

Of much greater importance has been Leontief's effort to develop an "open" input-output model by making the final demand independent of the supply of labor, thus breaking the rigid pattern of demand in the model, which formed a closed loop feedback relationship between aggregate demand and aggregate supply. The closed demand-supply loop was merely a mathematical expression for Say's law. As long as demand creates its own supply, unemployment cannot occur; once this assumption is dropped, however, the model can accommodate unemployment as a consequence of insufficient aggregate demand.

[33]Cf. Oscar Morgenstern, ed., *Economic Activity Analysis* (New York: Wiley, 1954), pp. 493 ff.

[34]Von Neümann's model did not use money nor, as we have already mentioned, did it provide for consumer choice; it led, however, toward the development of planning models. These ideas were greatly extended by other economists in the 1950s (see Chapter 11).

[35]Cf. Leontief et al., *Studies in the Structure of American Economy, op. cit.*, chaps. 3, 4.

Leontief's open input-output model can lend itself to Keynesian analysis and conclusions. As a matter of fact, the successful econometric forecasting model introduced by Daniel Suits presents such a blend of Keynesian and input-output analysis.[36]

One more promising elaboration of input-output analysis should be mentioned. The static assumption of a "given technology" finds its expression in the "fixed production coefficients" of the input-output analysis. This is quite logical because the major purpose—and accomplishment—of input-output analysis has been the analysis of the structure and interdependence of the economy. Classical and neoclassical economists have always held that under a given technology there is always a best way of combining factor inputs in the production process. Leontief's decision to continue this assumption was justified on both theoretical and empirical grounds. Empirical studies have shown that production coefficients are stable in the short run, and that, on a theoretical basis, the economy's de facto structure is more easily revealed if the complexity of variable production coefficients is disregarded. It is unnecessary, however, to assume that the existing, fixed production coefficients constitute the optimum input mix.

The development of mathematical programming permits the selection of different production coefficients in order to minimize either total cost of production or to maximize profits. The production coefficients become variables in the general linear programming models, and the input-output matrix becomes a special case of the more general problem of activity analysis. In the general case of mathematical programming, we consider all technically feasible production possibilities in order to find the input mix that will give us the most efficient production. In the special case of input-output analysis, we know that a unique solution exists—that is, there is only one production possibility mix (mathematically: only one point in solution space) that will satisfy all constraints, and therefore we do not have to ask whether this point will maximize a given welfare function. There is no other point, no other input mix, that will satisfy all input-output constraints.

Leontief developed his input-output analysis before the more general theory of "activity analysis" applied mathematical programming

---

[36]Cf. Daniel B. Suits, "Forecasting and Analysis with an Econometric Model," *American Economic Review* (March 1962) Vol. 52, pp. 104-132.

to economic analysis.[37] Leontief's assumptions are therefore more restricted but also more concrete; input-output analysis is more limited but also more operational and useful than activity analysis. The field of social accounting has been enriched considerably by adding input-output tables to the national income statistics, and our knowledge of the structure of inter-industry relations has greatly increased. At the same time, the future of general equilibrium analysis as a tool of applied economics lies in the further development of activity analysis.

[37]T. C. Koopman, ed., *Activity Analysis of Production and Allocation* (New York: Wiley, 1951), presents most of the early significant papers on the intellectual development of linear programming. Also note R. Dorfmann, P. Samuelson, and R. Solow, *Linear Programming and Economic Analysis* (New York: McGraw-Hill, 1958), an excellent book made unnecessarily difficult by the authors' attempt to simplify by not using matrix algebra. A brief but excellent discussion of input-output analysis and linear programming is found in Chenery and Clark, *Interindustry Economics*, New York: Wiley, 1959), chaps. IV and XIII. A brief, elementary survey of activity analysis appears in W. Baumol's *Economic Theory and Operations Analysis*, 2d ed. (Englewood Cliffs, N.J.: Prentice-Hall 1965), chap. XXI.

8

THE
WORLD OF
THORSTEIN VEBLEN

The Creative Environment

The most disturbing and one of the most creative American thinkers was born to immigrant parents on a small Wisconsin farm in 1857. Until his death in 1929, his strange ways and difficult language made him the *enfant terrible* of his time. Like all geniuses, he was a unique person. Like all human beings, he was a captive of his cultural environment. We shall examine several contemporaries who played an important part in his intellectual development and also look briefly at the growth and difficulties of the American economy in his lifetime. Finally, we shall sketch the major elements in Veblen's socioeconomic interpretation of economics.

We should start with Veblen's position in the tradition of economic thought. No writer is more controversial and difficult to place. Schumpeter, in his *History of Economic Analysis*, barely mentions Veblen, and did not regard him as an economist in the professional meaning of the word; others consider him an institutionalist. Veblen is not an easy person to categorize. We have included him as a very special case who has suddenly become relevant again, a profound writer who ought not to be neglected.

Most economists make little or no contribution to the theoretical advance of the field. They are content to repeat the established wisdom and to justify the existing economic institutions. They serve a useful, if conventional, purpose in establishing among the young some degree of familiarity with the means of production and distribution at any given time. A few do more—for example, a Cournot, a Gossen, a Jevons, discoverers of economic principles; an even smaller number are great synthesizers—for example, Smith, Ricardo, Walras, and Keynes. Veblen does not really fall into any category. His role was to dissect and destroy intellectually the fundamental premises of static neoclassical economic theory. For Veblen, Marshallian economics had far outlived any usefulness. Anything less than a dynamic model stood in the way of a clearer understanding of man and his economic environment. His writings, not always successful, combined economics with anthropology, sociology, and social ideology. In his time, despite occasional bursts of popularity, Veblen attacked every aspect of the capitalistic economic system, from the origins of property to the structure of higher education, in his search for an approach that would approximate the work of the biologist. Today he would have at hand a variety of patterns from dynamic mathematical economics to electrical engineering.

In the heyday of American economic growth, few people were interested in what appeared to be so negative and destructive a body of work. Today, however, Veblen has more than come into his own. His criticism of capitalistic processes is echoed by contemporary popular economists.[1] Herein lies his immense importance. We do not have to discover everything anew. We build on his suggestions; we can test his criticisms against our new dilemma.

To understand Veblen one must examine his social and intellectual environment. Three individuals illustrate the important influences that motivated him. Darwin represents the foundation on which Veblen built, though he was only two years old when the *Origin of Species* was published in 1859. Darwin represented science, especially the

---

[1] Galbraith, above all, is Veblen's intellectual heir. His *Affluent Society* (Boston: Houghton Mifflin, 1958) reminds us of Veblen's *Theory of the Leisure Class* (New York: Macmillan, 1899).

biological process, and for Veblen science stood for reality; he condemned economics for being merely a taxonomy—a static mono-chromatic representation. In order for economics to be useful, it had to become a theory of change, an "unfolding sequence." Economics had to become a dynamic science. If economists could not explain change, economics would remain useless.

The modern scientist is unwilling to depart from the test of causal relation or quantitative sequence. When he asks the question "Why?" he insists on an answer in terms of cause and effect. He wants to reduce his solution to all problems to terms of the conservation of energy or the persistence of quantity. This is his last recourse . . . . The great deserts of the evolutionist leaders . . . lie, on the one hand, in their refusal to go back of colorless sequence of phenomena and seek higher ground for their ultimate syntheses, and, on the other hand, in their having shown how this colorless impersonal sequence of cause and effect can be made use of for theory proper, by virtue of its cumulative character.[2]

Veblen starts his economics not with the Physiocrats or the classical economists but with the bearded eminence who broke the optimistic mold of an anachronistic eighteenth-century natural rights philosophy when he published the work started on a casual five-year voyage as scientific naturalist on *H.M.S. Beagle*. Darwin was not the greatest naturalist of his century, but he was clearly the most important. He enjoyed the typical upper-class advantages: His family's wealth and position provided him with ease, social acceptance, and a superficial education at Cambridge. He loved to hunt field mice. Before the eventful voyage around the world, there is every indication that Darwin would have joined that great and comfortable class, the English Gentlemen of the nineteenth century.

Slowly, as the *Beagle* made its way through the oceans, Darwin began to put together the million unassorted facts his head contained. Over many more years he continued his research and in 1859 published a revolutionary theory of life process. The Victorians were told unequivocally that life reflected a constant and complex natural process of reproduction, adaptation, struggle, survival, and growth. In nature, each species and each individual member of each species

[2]Thorstein Veblen, "Economics as an Evolutionary Science," *Quarterly Journal of Economics*, vol. 12 (July 1898), pp.373-397.

lives on the "tangled bank." Each species produces more of its kind than the environment can and will support. Hence there is constant struggle for survival; only those best able to adapt to the particular content of the environment will survive. From these relatively few will emerge the kinetics of the continuing drama. In 1871, in the *Descent of Man,* Darwin placed the human animal within the same life process. In unmistakable language, Darwin had the scientific courage to speculate that *all life* was descended from a few or even one basic form.

For the vast majority of the churchgoing middle class, Darwin laid open a world of terror; for a few, his method and conclusions opened a new scientific age. Veblen clearly belonged to the few. Decades before Darwin's books, intellectuals had begun to question beliefs based on natural rights, a crude, hedonistic-utilitarianism, and a literal interpretation of the Bible. Nineteenth-century economic wisdom was encapsulated in these beliefs. The emancipating force of the theory of biological evolution ramified all forms of intellectual thought.

We know today that Darwin was more influenced by Malthusian population theory than he admitted. Also, we know that life even on the "tangled bank" is more complex than Darwin's research recognized. Only men and rats fit the Darwinian model neatly.[3] For all other species in nature there is both competition and accommodation.

Veblen was no scientist. Although deeply influenced by this intellectual revolution, he had neither scientific education nor a quantitative mind; his training was in Kantian philosophy. His efforts at anthropology were juvenile, and, although he pointed the way toward quantification of economic data, it was left for his student, Wesley Clair Mitchell, to lay the foundations of the National Bureau of Economic Statistics. Though Veblen was primarily a great critic, he took from Darwin the great central principle of evolution, and made every other economist of his time intellectually conscious of economic change.

Darwin was a scientist. Veblen believed he was scientific. Herbert Spencer thought of himself as the father of social science. For much of the twentieth century, American liberals have been trying to mel-

---

[3]C. D. Darlington, "The Origin of Darwinism," *Scientific American,* vol. 200 (May 1959), 60-66. Contemporary research in social anthropology as well as in biology has softened the edges of the Darwinian model.

iorate the rigidities of laissez faire capitalism. The harshness of the American economic environment, and its sometimes brutal treatment of human beings, drew much of its ideological justification from the writings of Herbert Spencer, a rather obscure British engineer who perverted Darwin's biological theory of evolution into a crude theory of social evolution. Spencer's writings are terribly dated today; what he wrote seems impossibly passé. One finds it difficult to understand his great popularity in the United States at the end of the nineteenth century; in Britain and on the continent, he was generally neglected. We doubt that Spencer was really much read in the United States, but a small number of academic writers made popular a set of ideas that semiliterate business tycoons were working out pragmatically at a time of feverish business growth, competition, and amalgamation. Such is frequently the connection between ideas and action.

The most important American intellectual who "made" Spencer was William Graham Sumner; the most important business leader, Andrew Carnegie. Today neither intellectuals nor business leaders are interested in Spencer's confused social evolutionism. Only poor graduate students suffering for their comprehensive examinations skim Spencer's writings. Veblen, resident at Yale as a graduate student, was touched by the enthusiasm over Spencer. He was impressed with Spencer's particular emphasis on social evolution and "considered him a great contributor to intellectual advance." Spencer's *Study of Sociology* was much in vogue at Yale at that time, and Veblen's biographer notes that Veblen's Ph.D. thesis, the *Ethical Grounds of a Doctrine of Retribution*, shows a good deal of reading in Kant and Spencer.[4] Most writers on Veblen somewhat embarrassingly state that Spencer had no impact on Veblen's thinking. Unfortunately, that does not seem entirely accurate, though the direct connections are difficult to establish.

Herbert Spencer transformed Darwinism. The great scientific perceptions of biological evolution became rigid, meaningless sophistries under Spencer's hands. His sociology did not add to any critical awareness of either human or social institutions, but led eventually to an inflexible defense of the status quo. When Justice Oliver Wendell Holmes wrote in his dissent in the labor standards case *Lochner v. New York* that the Fourteenth Amendment did not enact Herbert

---

[4]Joseph Dorfman, *Thorstein Veblen and His America* (New York: Viking, 1935).

Spencer's *Social Statics*, he attacked the consequences of Spencerian influence.

In the universities the implications of these Spencerian ideas created great controversies. On the whole, most private American universities throughout the nineteenth and early twentieth centuries were controlled by religious denominations. American colleges not only were virtually ignorant of biological science, but also were bulwarks of religious and social conservatism. Theology, natural rights philosophy, and hedonistic psychology were the basic body of learning with which they worked. Darwin's ideas were revolutionary and confusing. Spencer's ideas were apparently easier to fit into the existing framework. But truly they had a tiger by the tail, for Spencer's philosophy had antireligious, anticonservative strands behind its usefulness for a crude Social Darwinism. Moreover, each season brought home bright young students trained at German universities who were dissatisfied with the lack of rigor in American higher education. They marked the beginning of a new era in American universities.

Andrew Carnegie persuaded Spencer to come to see the New World. Carnegie had in mind that when Spencer visited the great mills of Carnegie's Pittsburgh, the marriage of science and industry would be complete. Spencer turned out to be a dud. He could not stand the turmoil, atmosphere, or ugliness of Pittsburgh; somehow this was not what he had in mind. His visit ended, not with a bang, but with a whimper. In 1882, at his farewell dinner at Delmonico's in New York, Sumner lavished praise on the great guest, while Spencer actually trembled in the wings. Despite the compliment that Spencer's "philosophy of evolution" was a substitute for the worthless "traditional doctrines and explanations of human life," the leading businessmen were not impressed. Although the visit was unsuccessful, Spencer's amateurish psychology influenced many Americans, including Veblen. This influence is clearly reflected in Veblen's social model, which condemned the businessman, banker, teacher, and minister and praised so highly the engineer and the technocrat.

When Veblen taught at the University of Chicago, he gave a course on trusts. He was fascinated by the formation of U.S. Steel and its implications. We do not know what he thought of Andrew Carnegie, the man who made the merger necessary. In the folk history of American business capitalism, Carnegie is one of the *Vital Few*.[5] Only

---

[5]Jonathan R. Hughes, *The Vital Few* (Boston: Houghton Mifflin, 1965).

recently have we been given a brilliant and complete biography of him.[6] For most of this century, Carnegie's story has been a combination of myth, legend, and romanticism. How could one have less of a tale when a penniless immigrant made over $400 million and then gave his fortune to philanthropy? And it was no small achievement to emerge from the age of dinosaurs—Gould, Fiske, Drew, Rockefeller, Vanderbilt—with any kind of reputation at all. Carnegie achieved this; Veblen dispassionately must have admired his skill.

Many a young Scotch immigrant lad went to the mills at an early age. Carnegie's start as a bobbin boy makes a good story. Most immigrant boys stayed in the mills; Andrew Carnegie quickly moved on. By 1861, he was serving as a telegrapher along the routes of the Pennsylvania Railroad. Shortly thereafter, with a gambler's audacity, he borrowed his mother's entire savings (c. $10,000) and entered the steel industry, which was unable to meet the demand created by the frenzied competition among railroad magnates. Close at home, the Pennsylvania Railroad was an insatiable and friendly customer. Carnegie had the ability to seize the opportunity. Few companies had the managerial and leadership skills essential to transform the regional-local base of American industry to the national-international structure which was coming into being. The Age of the Robber Barons was, in part, a reflection of these tendencies throughout the economy. As new business frontiers opened, entrepreneurs surged forward, claim-jumping their rivals with the same moral standards that characterized every land rush from Kansas to Sutter's Mill. Only a few were successful; not one of them surpassed Carnegie's skill.

Veblen thought of Carnegie as a predator—one of his "captains of industry" as distinguished from his image of the small Norwegian freeholder-craftsman model who embodied the instinct of workmanship.[7] Schumpeter's entrepreneur comes closer to the facts of Carnegie's style and success. Veblen thought of Carnegie as the manipulator, the lineal heir of Palnatoki (a symbolic character Veblen discovered), who in the mid-tenth century organized the Vikings into an international trust which eventually failed through greed, overexpansion, and inept leadership. Veblen hoped that the same fate might befall these latter-day "Captains of the Strong Arm."

[6]J. F. Wall, *Andrew Carnegie* (New York & London: Oxford University Press, 1970).
[7]Veblen's "captain of industry" still retained some of the instinct of workmanship, but his "captain of finance" had no social usefulness whatsoever. Cf. his *Theory of Business Enterprise*, (New York: Scribner, 1904).

A Schumpeterian analysis of Carnegie would be more perceptive than Veblen's.[8] First Schumpeter warned against moral pseudohistoricism—that is, applying contemporary value judgments to the actions and activities of individuals from the past. Carnegie and many other nineteenth-century businessmen must be interpreted by their contribution to their times. Second, Schumpeter profoundly believed that economic progress in real terms stemmed from the actions of the very small number of particularly and specially endowed individuals. He called them *"Unternehmer"* (entrepreneur is a poor translation). The entrepreneur either (1) initiated a new good, (2) originated a new method of production, (3) captured a new market, (4) framed a new pattern of transportation, (5) contributed a new kind of leadership. Schumpeter's models of innovation might seem excessively romantic today, in a context of planned and team research; but the late nineteenth century had about it a built-in romantic structure, with its emphasis on expanding markets and new economic horizons. Andrew Carnegie, 5'2" tall, was such a romantic entrepreneur; he cut right across the Schumpeterian boundaries. Carnegie's greatest talent was his ability to see problems with incredible clarity—whether the particular problem lay in the method of production, the supply of new material, the organization of the industry. Carnegie knew the steel industry: His mills *were* the most modern and the most efficient; his profits were the highest; and his threat to move more vigorously into open competition with other steel companies was an ultimatum.

The "Relation of the State to Industrial Organization" was the title of the course Veblen developed to disembody the anthropology of corporate mergers. Veblen spent three days grilling a student on the capital structure and foundation of the steel trust put together by Morgan, who had bought the Carnegie interests for over $400 million. Morgan took $62 million for his services and organized the United States Steel Corporation, capitalized at over $1.4 billion. This new hybrid produced 50 percent of American steel. Despite its capitalized value, the physical assets of the company could be valued at no more than $680 million. Veblen thought the arrangement proved his argument. Particularly J. P. Morgan, the prototype of the captain of finance, represented waste, sabotage, and greed.

---

[8]Cf. Schumpeter's *Capitalism, Socialism & Democracy,* (New York: Harper & Row, 1942).

The Economic Environment

Veblen's life span, 1857-1929, covered a breadth of economic development and change in the United States that staggers the imagination. He saw the uncleared wilderness and the last risings of the Sioux Indians, and he died just before the Great Crash. These seven decades saw and completed the transformation of American economic life: Industrial maturity was achieved, the frontier was closed, the greatest surges of immigration took place, the continent was spanned and crisscrossed by a developed railroad system, and the oceans became mass economic thoroughfares with the perfection of iron ship construction and a revolution in world freight rates. The United States passed through the age of ruthless capitalism, experienced growth rates of 10 to 13 percent, fought a world war and chose to believe that it was not a world power. The country made very few structural changes in its governance of production and laid the basis for the most extreme economic depression in its history. Congress enacted virtually no social welfare legislation. On the whole the United States was badly governed, though most Americans were quite satisfied with these standards and feared most the rise of federal power. Political office was viewed with a certain amount of cynical aloofness, and local and state governments were up for grabs. Unlike many countries, the United States had no tradition of a public service as an honorable and desirable career; few of its educational institutions produced trained individuals for public careers. To look back on this world is to peer into an age that seems unbelievable.

The size, content, and wealth of this subcontinent permitted a level of liberty and license which would have been impossible in a country with fewer resources, a smaller population, less space, or more sensitive social values. Buttressed by a perverted Puritan ethic and by a corrupted Social Darwinism, the United States tolerated, accepted, and praised a wastage of human and natural resources impossible to measure. Not only the black and the immigrant paid heavy penalties, but the majority of all Americans consciously or otherwise paid dearly for the American drive to maturity. Few businessmen or politicians truly recognized the potential of technological capitalism or had the knowledge or will to mobilize or channel these forces in a social direction. No body of acceptable ideology proclaimed that unemployment, low wages, and waste not only were self-imposed and socially inflicted, but also were largely unnecessary. The country could have had as much or even more real economic growth with less economic and personal sacrifice. This is what Veblen saw—and what he condemned. It was good that he died before November 1929; no one as sensitive as he was could have tolerated being so accurate.

From the mid-1800s on, the United States became an international economy—a happening little contemplated or understood.

What an extraordinary episode in the economic progress of man that age was which came to an end in August, 1914 . . . . The inhabitant of London could order by telephone, sipping his morning tea in bed, the various products of the whole earth, in such quantity as he might see fit, and reasonably expect their early delivery upon his doorstep; he could at the same moment and by the same means adventure his wealth in the natural resources and new enterprises of any quarter of the world, and share, without exertion or even trouble, in their prospective fruits and advantages; or he could decide to couple the security of his fortunes with the good faith of the townspeople of any substantial municipality in any continent that fancy or information might recommend. He could secure forthwith, if he wished it, cheap and comfortable means of transit to any country or climate without passport or other formality, could dispatch his servant to the neighboring office of a bank for such supply of the precious metals as might seem convenient, and could then proceed abroad to foreign quarters without knowledge of their religion, language or customs, bearing coined wealth upon his person, and would consider himself greatly aggrieved and much surprised, at the least interference. But, most important of all, he regarded this state of affairs as normal, certain and permanent, except in the direction of further improvements, and any deviation from it as aberrant, scandalous and avoidable. The projects and politics of militarism and imperialism, of racial and cultural rivalries, of monopolies, restrictions and exclusion, which were to play the serpent to this paradise, were little more than the amusements in his daily paper and appeared to exercise almost no influence at all on the ordinary course of social and economic life, the internationalization of which was nearly complete in practice.[9]

Most American historians would not start with the international economy as the significant force in U.S. economic development during this period. Alfred Chandler has argued that the greatest economic

[9]John M. Keynes, *The Economic Consequences of the Peace* (New York: Harcourt Brace Jovanovich, 1920), p.10.

influences have been domestic—the rise of regional specialization and the growth and dominance of urban national markets by the end of the nineteenth century. For most companies the international market was—and until recently has always been—an incremental market, important but small in relation to their national objectives. Agricultural exports, however, dominated American international trade throughout the first half of the nineteenth century, and continued to be significant. "Agricultural commodities comprised between 73 and 83 percent of the exports in the period 1850 to the turn of the century, and the rapid increases in shipments of farm products were the major factors in the achievement of a steadily favorable balance of trade by the mid-1870s."[10] Each decade, however, would also show the increased importance of manufactured goods.

Perhaps even more fundamental than the statistical evidence is the fact that U.S. development took place in an economic climate that was determined by international forces. An integrated world economy emerged in the nineteenth century.[11] Great Britain, western Europe, the United States, the colonial lands of these powers, and their territorial enclaves in Latin America, and certain littoral areas subject to the developed countries made up this inner world. The organization of this world in economic terms followed more or less the general outlines of classical economics. Markets for goods and services, capital, and, to a limited extent, labor were integrated by private enterprise and individual risk. In response to economic opportunities, these factors of production moved in relative freedom throughout this extra-European world. In this interdependent world, so-called natural forces pressed toward economic harmony. The European countries exported the desired manufactured and semimanufactured goods, while the rest of this world produced the food and industrial raw materials. Both sides benefited. The demand for these raw and unfinished commodities grew rapidly in the nineteenth century and furnished the means whereby the underdeveloped world might enjoy the higher standard of living offered by European and United States imports. It was theoretically a superb opportunity for both sides; or

[10]Morton Rothstein, "The International Market for Agricultural Commodities, 1850-1873," in Alfred D. Chandler, Jr., Stuart Bruchey and Louis Galambos, eds., *The Changing Economic Order: Readings in American Business and Economic History* (New York: Harcourt Brace Jovanovich, 1968), p.313.

[11]W. Y. Elliott, *The Political Economy of American Foreign Policy* (New York: Holt, Rinehart & Winston, 1955), pp. 22-30.

faut de mieux this was the only arrangement possible because the great powers controlled the rules.

Three factors were crucial to the functioning—and to our understanding of the eventual demise—of this long-ago world. First, the operation of free trade was essential. To British capitalists, in particular, the classical doctrine of free trade was an article of faith, and because British manufacturers controlled the export world until the mid-1800s, principles of free trade dominated the environment of the trading world. Individual entrepreneurs bought the goods they needed and sold the products they made in markets largely unencumbered and unregulated by restrictions other than those imposed by cost-price (supply-demand) considerations. In many cases there were in this arrangement built-in advantages to the stronger, more knowledgeable Western traders. The most important thing, however, was that British leadership and commercial superiority made free trade effective despite the grumblings of German, French, or American business groups until the end of the century. Second, one could assume that "the condition of doing business throughout the trading world was reasonably calculable." Government economic policies, legal conditions, and monetary stability were permanently stabilized by the military superiority of the developed countries. In those few cases where local interruptions threatened institutional arrangements, European and U.S. forces could be moved in to reestablish order.

The most important factor, however, was that of the adjustment mechanism. Disequilibria in the trading world could be taken care of in two ways: either by adjusting the international arrangements or by allowing the factors that had gone awry to work themselves out domestically, no matter what the economic consequences in unemployment, production, and price might be. As we know, a hundred years ago the first alternative of manipulating international arrangements would have been considered a fundamental breach of economic principle. To our present-day dismay, this system operated by forcing domestic changes to move the economy back into its customary orbit. "Cyclical fluctuation in market demand, temporary surpluses or shortages, and foreign exchange difficulties were permitted rapidly—and often brutally—to correct themselves."[12]

This was the pre-World War I economy. We can easily understand why it no longer exists. Veblen hated it because, long before its actual

[12]Ibid., p. 25.

disintegration, he could see the impossible stresses within its structure. By 1850, the United States was a great industrial power. By 1900, she had been joined by Germany and Japan. Their world trading interests did not coincide with the British view of the free trade international harmony. One way or the other, they opted out. The United States was a leader in the race toward a new protectionism. With barely a single break, every tariff law from 1857 to 1930 raised rates to insulate American markets from foreign competition. French protectivism was very similar throughout this period. Several countries used devices other than the tariff to achieve the same ends. These selfish, nationalistic manipulations, often prompted by "vested interests," horrified Veblen, who insisted on a rational approach to economics.

British dominance, however, had not been restricted solely to free trade. The British Navy which "insured" Pax Britannica, had served as a comparatively inexpensive watchdog throughout the nineteenth century. This was quickly altered by the arms race that preceded World War I. From the great banks of the city, London finance ruled the world. International exchange was calculated in gold or pounds sterling. British banking, moreover, was oriented in its investment practices toward this outer world. World War I dealt the final blow to this financial structure. International finance, along with international monetary policy, became nationalized. This process was perceptively analyzed by Veblen in his *Imperial Germany*,[13] one of the very few critical *and* sophisticated studies of international finance. His interest in the international economy grew out of his study of corporate behavior that violated his cherished "production ethics."

Veblen's standards had been molded by his upbringing on a Scandinavian immigrant's farm. At the turn of the century American agriculture was going through a revolutionary process. When Thorstein Veblen's father settled in Wisconsin in 1848, he brought with him an idea of an agricultural way of life that had long dominated Europe: the subsistence farm with a small cash flow and a great deal of independence. Not only did the farm provide a livelihood, but also it was thought to mold unexceptionable character. All his life Veblen believed deeply in this rural mythology. He found in the Icelandic sagas the forbears of the free and noble peasantry of Scandinavia. For all his

[13]Thorstein Veblen, *Imperial Germany and the Industrial Revolution* (New York: Viking, 1939).

insight into conspicuous consumption and conspicuous waste, Veblen had no sense of the economics of esthetics. Veblen never recognized the fact that taste, beauty, design, pleasure, and sheer artistic delight all have economic value. They can be, and are, calculated by the market mechanism—neither very much less nor more accurately than for most other goods and services whose prices are determined by the intersection of demand and supply curves.

In popular imagination this small-farm myth has also dominated the American ethos. Free land, the frontier, the independence of a self-determined work schedule, the creativity of working with the land, the sense of ownership and pride were the essence of this agrarian mythology. Perhaps no one could see clearly in 1860 that America's future would lie in the mills and factories, in the industrial warrens and growing tenements, but the statistical data had already begun to point conclusively in this direction. It was not that agriculture was less important, but that manufacturing was becoming more dominant, and growing faster. John Black, a leading authority on agriculture, suggests that 1860 to 1910 marks "the great period of development of United States agriculture"; however, the decline in the percentage of the United States labor force engaged in agriculture had been continuous since 1820, and was broken only occasionally.[14]

During Veblen's lifetime, roughly from 1860 to 1930, the food producer experienced slow recovery (in the South) after the Civil War; expansion and intensive land improvement; a long agricultural period of economic stress and deflation in the 1880s and 1890s, which fueled the Populist and Easy-Money movements; a pre-World War I agricultural prosperity; then the precarious and inflated grain expansion of the war years; and finally the almost permanent depressed condition of American agriculture from 1920 on. Long before the Wall Street crash, gloom and doom had settled over the farm community. No less important than this economic picture was the evolution of distinct farming patterns which have altered permanently the structure of American agriculture.

Farmers either grew wheat, raised corn, fattened pigs, or trucked milk in regional zones determined by market considerations. Given the enormous risks in any agricultural undertaking, we must marvel

[14]John D. Black, "Agriculture," in Seymour Harris, ed., *American Economic History* (New York: McGraw-Hill, 1961), p.484. This trend has continued, and if we compare the period 1869-1878 with 1949-1959, we find that manufacturing output increased almost five times more in the twentieth century than that of agriculture.

at the range of agricultural innovation and adaptation. Major changes were developed largely by public bodies such as the Department of Agriculture and state agricultural colleges. Over the decades (1860-1930), the American farm became an integrated unit, combining the elements of large-scale, intensive mechanization and heavy capital investment into a single unit. With these elements, a skillful farmer had a good chance of making a profit and surviving the periodic crises. Agriculture, like industry, had entered the twentieth century. Millions of Americans—farmers and their political representatives— accepted this fact with great reluctance and great pain. Thorstein Veblen saw this transformation as a further deterioration of life under capitalism.

In this changing society, between the Civil War and the Great Depression, monetary, banking, and tariff policies were inefficient and unscientific. There was no coordination, no central monetary authority, and no definition of economic responsibility.

From 1900 on, prices rose steadily and substantially. Farmers in particular abandoned monetary inflation as their primary political objective. New discoveries of gold and new, more efficient technologies in the extraction of gold ushered in a brief pre-World War I period of quiescence in the long and passionate American monetary controversy over hard vs. soft currencies. The return to the gold standard after the Civil War did not grind down the poor and may even have contributed to the real growth that characterized the second half of the nineteenth century by helping to create an environment comfortable to business thinking. Although a good many of the inflationist arguments for both greenbacks and silver had little or no economic content, the instinct for a larger per capita amount of money in circulation is understandable. However, the American international position seemed to require the return to gold. Worldwide faith in gold persisted until the massive breakdown of the gold standard in the 1930s.

Veblen considered the debate over money as a specious argument which missed the real economic issues. "Business transactions, and computations in pecuniary terms, such as loans, discounts, and capitalisation, are without hesitation converted into terms of hedonistic utility, conversely." "Money is a medium for *controlling* exchange" was his overall summation.[15]

[15]Dorfman, *Veblen and His America*, pp. 293, 509.

We owe to the Panic of 1907 the modest reform of our banking system in the first half of the twentieth century. Practical men and hardheaded theorists had long agreed that our banking system operated in a perverse fashion. In times of crises and deflation, the unstructured arrangement of banks and banking habits led to the severe constriction of money supply and credit, and in times of expansion, the banks would overinflate the supply of funds. The Panic was a banking crisis of this genre, and the severe distress that followed had little to do with the country's economic health. Late in October the Knickerbocker Trust Company, the third largest trust in New York, with deposits of $62 million, began to run into clearing house difficulties. Within a few days the U.S. Treasury deposited $25 million with the major New York control reserve city banks. The panic, however, was not stilled until J. P. Morgan marched the leading bankers through his library and organized from their voluntary contributions a money pool of $25 million. By early January, 1908, the full reverberations of the panic subsided. Contemporaries believed that the banking system's rigidity and inflexibility had intensified what started out to be a very mild contraction. The latest interpretation of this crisis, however, suggests that the restriction of payments protected the banking system from further ruin until the panic wore off and provided the basis for a rapid recovery.[16]

Congress acted in 1908 by appointing a National Monetary Commission to study worldwide monetary and banking structures and experiences. From this mass of data came the stillborn Aldrich Bill which the Democrats killed in the Congress. Finally, in December, 1913, Congress enacted the bill "to provide for the establishment of Federal Reserve banks to furnish an elastic currency, to afford means of rediscounting commercial paper, to establish a more effective supervision of banking, and for other purposes." The Federal Reserve System had been created.

The new structure was a weak compromise. In place of one central bank with unified authority, Congress authorized a conglomerate of twelve regional banks, a Federal Reserve Board, and an Open Market Committee. Nevertheless, the Federal Reserve was an immense improvement over the past. It did more to regularize and rationalize monetary and banking practices than anything since the establish-

[16]Milton Friedman and Anna J. Schwarz, *A Monetary History of the United States*, 1867-1960 (Princeton: Princeton University Press, 1963), pp. 159-167.

ment of the First Bank of the United States, and it introduced public policy into the private banking system. Federal Reserve notes were more flexible and elastic than national bank notes. The combined resources of all twelve Reserve Banks strengthened the banking system's credit structure. Further, the Federal Reserve has rendered invaluable and incalculable services to the Treasury and to the funding operations of government securities.

In Veblen's lifetime, however, banking reforms failed in two major respects. Nothing was done to insure individual deposits. Nothing was done to prevent excessive credit fluctuations. Veblen's contemporary judgment condemning the operation of the banking system has been borne out by present-day monetary specialists:

Strong's death [Benjamin Strong, Governor of the Federal Reserve Bank of New York] left the System with no center of enterprising and acceptable leadership. The Federal Reserve Board was determined that the New York Bank should no longer play this role. But the Board itself could not play the role in an enterprising way. It was still weak and divided . . . . Moreover, most of the other Reserve Banks, as well as that in New York, were reluctant to follow the leadership of the Board, partly because of the Board's personnel, partly because they still thought of it as primarily a supervisory and review body. Thus it was easy for the System to slide into indecision and deadlock.[17]

Veblen died on August 3, 1929. Eighty-seven days later the market broke on Wall Street. It is now polite to refer to the 1930s as "The Great Contraction." Veblen would have enjoyed this phrase as much as any that he coined.

Veblen's life spanned the emergence of mature industrialization. Prior to the Civil War almost all the elements that were to emerge in the 1880s and 1890s were in existence. The United States knew and used the idea of interchangeability of parts, understood the rewards of mass production, had sketched out the shape and technology of a national transportation system, and had expanded the corporate idea and the legal conditions for an active competitive society. These conditions were further enhanced by a set of values, beliefs, and myths suitable for rapid economic expansion.

[17]*Ibid.*, p. 414.

Whereas the long-run severe recession of the 1870s put great stress on older business patterns, changes in the size of the market, the opportunities for large profits, and important shifts in the style of technologies offered undreamed-of potential.[18] This tension between need and opportunity led to the merger movement of the 1890s. Even more significantly, the strains led to the evolution of a style of big business: harsh, aggressive, punitive, anonymous, calculating, severe, ascetic, and even ruthless.

But the most important development of these years was the acceptance of the full implication of an industrial society. Even behind much of the Populist struggle lies the sense of industrial inevitability. Protest and opposition, however, played an important role in shaping these innovations. Pushed by needs and opportunities, entrepreneurs reshaped the American business system in something less than two decades.

JAMES HILL

A brief examination of several of these entrepreneurs, whose role Veblen failed to understand, will help illustrate the changes in the American economy. James Hill was born near Guelph, Ontario, Canada, on September 16, 1838, of Scotch-Irish background.[19] For eight years he attended Rockwood Academy, a Quaker school, which emphasized mathematics and Latin. Originally he had hoped to study medicine, but the death of his father put an end to his formal education at age fifteen. For the next several years, Hill worked in a country store, wandered over the country from Maine to Minnesota, and finally came to rest as a shipping clerk for the J. W. Bass & Co., agents for the Dubuque & St. Paul Packet Company. By the time he was thirty, he had become a recognized business specialist in river transportation and fuel distribution. For five years he pioneered and prospered in this limited area of small business, warehousing, coal merchandising, and general transportation services, which provided the financial resources for his later activities. From this mercantile base, Hill fantasized moving to India and building a canal system. He also dreamed of buying up the capital stock and defaulted bonds of the St. Paul and Pacific Railroad. In 1879, Hill acted on his second scheme. He reor-

---

[18]Alfred D. Chandler, Jr., "The Beginnings of 'Big Business' in American Industry," *Business History Review*, 33:1 (Spring 1959), pp. 1-31.
[19]J. P. Pyle, *The Life of James J. Hill*, 2 vols. (New York: Doubleday, 1917).

ganized this railroad scrapheap into the St. Paul, Minneapolis and Manitoba Railway Co., and took over its management. As soon as this line showed signs of economic vigor, Hill moved to expand the railroad. Between the lines of the Northern Pacific and the Canadian Pacific he saw a gap, which he began to fill by building the Great Northern System. Both the Northern Pacific and the Canadian Pacific had been built by public subsidy. Hill now enlarged the Great Northern at about the rate of a mile a day at a minimal cost of $30,000 per mile. In addition to this singular financial achievement, Hill was unique as a railroad president in his knowledge of the terrain, geography, and resources through which his railroad pushed. Unlike the more typical railroad president, Hill worked with mathematical precision and logical clarity. There is no question that he would be today a leading exponent of information systems analysis and computer technology.

In the spring of 1901, Hill and Morgan attempted a takeover of the Chicago, Burlington and Quincy Railroad, the key transportation link into the Midwest. They met head-on with the Harriman and Kuhn, Loeb & Company interests in the great and vulgar Wall Street struggle for control of Northern Pacific Common, which culminated in the Panic of May 1901, when the price soared to $1000 a share. Faced with potential disaster, both sides first retreated and then compromised by setting up the Northern Securities Company, with Hill as president. In 1904, the Supreme Court ordered this holding company dissolved, but Hill and Morgan retained control of the northern route. They, with the Vanderbilt interests in the Pennsylvania Railroad, now controlled 80,000 miles of track.

On the positive side, Hill's career is bound up with the opening to economic development of Minnesota, North Dakota, and Montana; he founded schools, built churches, opened banks, bred cattle, and encouraged large-scale immigration into the region. Above all, he operated an efficient transportation system which stretched from New York to the Far East. (He built ships to trade with Japan as an extension of the western outlet for his railroad.)

Like many "robber barons" (a most unfortunate description in this case), Hill was a self-made man with little formal education. But like Carnegie, Rockefeller, and Morgan, he combined unusual talents of preciseness and imagination. Every one of his major business decisions was preceded by the most careful investigation. Hill amazed his contemporaries with the amount and extent of his knowledge. Whether in the cost of selling a ton of coal or a bushel of wheat, or the flora and fauna of the area through which the tracks of the Great Northern ran, Hill did his homework. Despite Veblen's antipathy toward them, this unusual combination of personality characteristics repeats itself in many of his famous business contemporaries. Hill was perhaps the quintessential nineteenth-century railroad president. In what he believed and did he reflected much of the value structure of his time. He had no use for labor unions; their claims he considered an unreasonable attempt to limit his property rights. He was arrogant and superstitious. He collected art, endowed colleges, and regarded himself as a philanthropist. Unlike Carnegie, he seldom attempted either to justify or explain his business philosophy. He was content to leave a legacy of efficiency, organization, and rationalization in the Great Northern system that has rarely been matched.

ALFRED P. SLOAN

Veblen's distorted view of the businessman can be corrected by examining the career of a business leader like Alfred P. Sloan, Jr.

To tell how I came into General Motors it is necessary to begin with smaller matters . . . I was born in New Haven, Connecticut, on May 23, 1875 My father was in the wholesale tea, coffee, and sugar business . . . . My father's father was a school teacher. My mother's father was a Methodist minister. My parents had five children, of whom I am the oldest . . . . I think we have all had in common a capability for being dedicated to our respective interests.[20]

Sloan's autobiography, *My Years with General Motors*, is a fascinating story of the rise and transformation of the automobile industry. Sloan's important contribution consisted of developing the strategy of business organization. W. C. Durant had thrown "cats and dogs together and called them elephants"; Sloan made a company. The "Organization Study," which he wrote for General Motors in 1921, became a major landmark in corporate organization. When Sloan began to work on his management scheme, he found that in a corporate sense no real communications systems existed within the company. "The important thing," he said, "was that no one knew how much was being contributed—plus or minus—by each division to the

<hr>

[20]Alfred P. Sloan, Jr., *My Years with General Motors* (New York: Doubleday, 1964), p.17.

common good of the corporation. And since, therefore, no one knew, or could prove, where the efficiencies and inefficiencies lay, there was no objective basis for the allocation of new investment "[21] Sloan's pragmatic philosophy was clear: "It is not, therefore, a matter of the amount of profit but of the relation of that profit to the real worth of invested capital within the business. Unless that principle is fully recognized in any plan that may be adopted, illogical and unsound results and statistics are unavoidable. . . ."[22] What emerged was the multidivisional decentralized pattern of operation—the most widespread corporate managerial structure from 1920 to 1950.

Over the course of his career Sloan, like Hill, became a multimillionaire. Through his Alfred P. Sloan Foundation he followed the philanthropic role laid down in the early nineteenth century by American businessmen. He too was an empire builder like Hill and Carnegie. Although less of a dreamer, Sloan also was able to combine vision and exactness. Flexible enough to learn from his errors, calculating enough to make precise information the bedrock of corporate decisions, Sloan in some ways had a mind like a computer, plus the ability to think and command like a general. What happened to General Motors, in large measure due to his leadership, is a very impressive story. Durant's failing company became the world's largest manufacturer.

Many business leaders in the period between 1860 and 1929 fitted Veblen's description more closely. A few individuals like Hill, Carnegie, and Sloan, however, had the background and ability essential then to business success. They were dedicated to the "work ethic" and committed to the doctrine of material success. And they accepted and enjoyed the leadership role that followed from success and wealth. We have been given a picture of them as simple, primitive, ruthless types, but they made a distinct contribution to society and, by their own standards, they were socially minded. They do not seem to fit badly Max Weber's "Ideal Type," and Weber may have had them in mind when he talked about the American businessman who had so secularized his religious drives that he saw business as a "game." Much more significant than Veblen's harsh categories of "sabotage," "predation," and "conspicuous waste" was the sense of creative play these captains of industry enjoyed.

[21]*Ibid.*, p.49.
[22]*Ibid.* pp.48-49.

This discussion has commented on the economic environment in which Veblen wrote and thus has set the stage for analysis of the U.S. economy and economic theory during the twentieth century. Sven Svennilson's model of economic transformation best describes the alterations in the American economy to be considered in the balance of this chapter.

1. The change of production methods mainly in the direction of more advanced mechanization;
2. The change of input-output relations between raw materials and end products;
3. The development of new end products and shifts in the distribution of consumption between various products;
4. The changes in exports and imports in relation to the output of domestic industry;
5. The redistribution of manpower between different industries and occupations.[23]

The Breakdown and Reconstruction of American Capitalism

Six months after Veblen died in California, the American business system was shaken to its foundations. Veblen had predicted for more than thirty years that a "pecuniary society,"which was—in his analysis—opposed to human instincts and to the beneficent forces of technology, had to break down. However, he would have recoiled at the severity of the crisis. The Great Depression was a major economic catastrophe, which no economic theory could explain adequately. The neoclassical school was still handicapped by its implicit acceptance of Say's law. Both the Marxian and Veblenian explanations of depressions were simplistic. In Veblen's writings the continuing theme of sabotage, which began in *The Theory of Business Enterprise* (1904) and ended in *Absentee Ownership and Business Enterprise in Recent Times: the Case of America* (1923), provided an unsatisfactory framework for a theory of business cycles. To the Marxist the depression, which began with the stock market crash of November, was the result of contradictions within the capitalist system; the crash was both "predictable and inevitable." In fact, the structure of the American corporate system in the 1920s had little resemblance to the mid-

[23]Sven Svennilson, *Growth and Stagnation in the European Economy* (Geneva: United Nations Economic Commission for Europe, 1954), pp. 7, 20-40.

nineteenth-century Marxian model. The crash, though predictable, was surely not inevitable.

From the chaos of World War I, the United States had emerged as the world's premier economic power. While Europe struggled to rebuild, America entered the consumer revolution. In housing, automobiles, and electrical conveniences, the United States reached levels of consumption not attained elsewhere for three decades. It would have taken very little to curb the frenzy of the 1920s and without impairing the essential strengths and energies of capitalistic drive and innovation.

The decade of the 1920s was the harvest season; the economy had grown rich and irresponsible. Structural defects in the economic system had been allowed to develop in industrial organization, marketing, and finance. The American production system was now dominated by oligopolistic units and administered pricing. The most powerful corporations in the newest and fastest growing economic sectors shared those huge markets with a half-dozen or fewer real competitors; what was left of a particular market might then be fought over by a relatively large number of small units. For example, Du Pont, Union Carbide, and Allied Chemical might account for 35 percent of the chemical market; and, Hercules, Dow, and Monsanto another 15 percent; the remainder of the market might be composed of hundreds of small and middle-sized chemical companies which had carved out particular niches for themselves for one special reason or another. The steel, auto, rubber, electrical, and other industries followed this general description. In a few cases companies engaged in outright collusion. There is evidence that such practices in the electrical industry went back two or three decades before the government indictments of 1964. The testimony in the T.N.E.C. reports described similar cartel-like arrangements in the optical and chemical industries. Much more important, however, than these outright legal violations (for they were relatively few) was the essential demonstrable fact that American industry perceived itself in corner-candystore terms. This was self-deception of the highest order. Big business had come of age, which should have meant the orderly modification of laissez faire capitalism and neoclassical theory.

American enterprise could turn out a veritable flood of consumer goods. The market mechanism, it was assumed, would provide the means and the incentives to take up these goods. During the 1920s, the market was able, on the whole, to accomplish this, but on an increasingly precarious basis. Total personal consumption expenditures fell briefly in the short post-World War I depression to $56 billion, but then climbed to nearly $81 billion by 1929, while the GNP rose from $72 billion to $104 billion in the same period. These large increases, however, meant that employment, disposable income, and investments had to grow at ever-increasing rates if the economy were not to trip over its own success. No mechanism, either public or private, existed to coordinate these related factors. Economists in the 1920s were groping for the solution to less policy-oriented economic questions. Not until Keynes's publications in the mid-1930s did a comprehensive analysis appear that brought the disparate pieces of economic theory together.

In the seats of American banking and finance, the greatest anarchy reigned in the 1920s. Magic, mysticism, and myth dominated the operation of U.S. securities markets. There was much outright abuse. Managers of money, from the officers of great New York houses to the small banker in Babbittsville, carelessly violated their trust. The fault lay less in the integrity of bankers—most of whom maintained their integrity—than in the virulence of a securities speculation that reminds one of the tulip craze of the sixteenth-century, when hardheaded Dutchmen paid thousands of dollars for individual tulip bulbs. On every level the financial instruments of U.S. society were indescribably primitive. The Federal Reserve System did not operate as a system.[24] It neither functioned as a central bank nor used its powers to curb the financial excesses. Federal Reserve policies were a congeries of haphazard activities—frequently too little and too late. In Wall Street the impossible dominated. An average day in the New York Exchange saw anywhere from four to six million shares change hands. Virtually nothing existed to guarantee the honesty of these transactions. New issues without value were thrown to a frenzied public; old issues were inflated and reinflated by investment maneuvers. The insiders always won; sometimes the insiders permitted friends to win too. Several of the large investment houses had special lists of important public figures. These men would be allowed to buy shares at a lower price before the initial listing on the exchange. In the "permanent" bull market, insiders could gain twice—early and late. There

---

[24]Friedman and Schwartz, *Monetary History*, pp. 189-196.

was something in it for everybody. "If a man saves $15 a week, and invests in good common stocks, and allows the dividends and rights to accumulate, at the end of twenty years he will have at least $80,000 and an income from investments of around $400 a month. He will be rich. And because income can do that, I am firm in my belief that everyone not only can be rich, but ought to be rich."[25] Not everyone in the country was, however, in on the shell game. Though several other countries in the 1920s came perilously close to the American standard, no major country in modern times can demonstrate such a period of financial irresponsibility.

If the speculative boom could have gone on forever, there would have been no depression. In real terms, the decade of the 1920s had made impressive gains; GNP had risen nearly 50 percent and per capita income from $660 to $875. The worst excesses were bred in the financial canyons of lower Manhattan, and here the break occurred.

The big gong had hardly sounded in the great hall of the Exchange at ten o'clock Tuesday morning before the storm broke in full force. Huge blocks of stock were thrown upon the market for what they would bring. . . . Not only were innumerable small traders being sold out, but big ones too . . . again and again the specialist in a stock would find himself surrounded by brokers fighting to sell—and nobody at all even thinking of buying. . . . The scene on the floor was chaotic. . . . Within half an hour of the opening the volume of trading passed three million shares, by twelve o'clock it had passed eight million, by half past one it had passed twelve million, and when the closing gong brought the day's madness to an end the gigantic record of 16,410,030 shares had been set. . . . The average prices of fifty leading stocks as compiled by the *N. Y. Times* had fallen nearly forty points.[26]

By the first of the New Year, the U.S. economy was prostrate, and worse was to come.

Instead of a short panic, the 1930s featured a deflation and liquidation that became increasingly severe as time passed. National income dropped from $84.4 billion in 1929 to $68.9 billion in 1930 and $40.0 billion in 1932. The

[25]J. J. Raskob, with Samuel Crowther, "Everybody Ought To Be Rich," *Ladies Home Journal* (August 1929).

[26]F. L. Allen, *Only Yesterday* (New York and London: Harper & Row, 1931), pp. 333-334.

Federal Reserve index of industrial production fell from 110 in 1929 to 91 in 1930 and 58 in 1932. Unemployment was estimated at 3½ million in 1930 and 15 million in 1933. The wholesale price index declined from 95.3 in 1929 to 86.4 in 1930 and 64.8 in 1932.[27]

As the depression gained momentum, it pulled apart the mastic that held the economy together. Investment virtually ceased. Because prices were "sticky" and did not fall as rapidly as wages, unemployment soared. Foreign markets disappeared under a wave of autarchy aggravated by the Hawley-Smoot tariff. Good banks were destroyed as the abuses of bad banks were uncovered. Economic individualism in reverse gear turned out to be a new kind of disaster. As the federal government initially attempted to cut its budget, it increased the deflationary forces that were wreaking such damage. The retrenchment of states and municipalities had the same consequences. Individual businessmen adopted deflationary policies. To survive, they had to cut back as quickly and as completely as possible. In the midst of a hurricane, very few captains let out more sail. And John and Mary Doe, the traditional basic units of the laissez faire, self-regulating economic equilibrium, tried to survive by adopting the same kind of policies in their own little way. They too had a choice. In the face of rising unemployment and falling prices, common sense dictated the utmost financial prudence. The sum of individual efforts was the deepest, longest, and most destructive economic catastrophe in American history.

In his First Inaugural, F. D. R. showed courage and optimism.

The only thing we have to fear is fear itself. . . Values have shrunken to fantastic levels; taxes have risen; our ability to pay has fallen; government of all kinds is faced by serious curtailment of income; the means of exchange are frozen in the currents of trade; the withered leaves of industrial enterprise lie on every side; farmers find no markets for their produce; the savings of many years in thousands of families are gone. More important, a host of unemployed citizens face the grim problem of existence. . . . We must act and act quickly.[28]

[27]Paul Studenski and Herman Krooss, *Financial History of the United States* (New York: McGraw-Hill, 1962), p. 353.

[28]*The Public Papers and Addresses of Franklin D. Roosevelt* (New York: Random House, 1938), vol. 2, p. 4.

Despite the rhetoric, the United States had more to fear than fear. The country had to find out whether it could salvage its economic system. For almost a decade, in fits and starts, in bits and pieces, the economy struggled to break free from this immense deflation-depression psychology. On the one hand, there were the universal problems of unemployment and human sufferings; on the other, the need for legislation to modify the economic institutions which had broken down so overwhelmingly. The New Deal mounted no revolution; every major institution of the capitalist system was retained. But each institution emerged modified under some regulatory apparatus. Some New Deal initiatives were regressive and self-defeating, but still it is remarkable how lasting so many of these changes have proved. The key reforms of the 1930s are now part of the system, and both political parties fully accept their existence. The concepts of social security, federal deposit insurance, securities regulation, and others no longer are seriously challenged. Very few decades in U.S. history have marked so permanent a transformation in our national economic environment. Hardship and personal suffering between 1930 and 1940 made these changes necessary.

It may not be amiss to recall what some of these hardships were. In very rough terms, the economy was operating at between one-half and two-thirds of its capacity. Every industry suffered from unused capacity. Very few companies invested in new plants, new machinery, or innovations. Business leadership was totally broken. For long periods in the 1930s, businessmen suffered from severe ideological schizophrenia. They bewailed the growth of government involvement in and regulation of economic activity, but they became increasingly eager to depend on government aid and subsidies. Conservative businessmen hated Roosevelt passionately, but they could offer few alternatives. Between the deepest fear of Marxism in any form and Roosevelt's New Deal, they clung to the latter. Peace came to their tortured psyches only with the business prosperity of World War II.

Since 1945, a new generation of business entrepreneurs—leaner, tougher, abler, more secure, more highly professionally oriented—has found this new system of regulated or modified capitalism so productive, so creative, and so immensely profitable that they are wholly integrated into it. The modifications and regulations give them an economic security to expand and innovate that their forebears never had. The stated federal policy of permanent economic employment at high levels gives these business leaders opportunities for profit (after taxes) that have not previously existed. Only rarely at ceremonial functions does one hear the language and pale echoes of the struggle between government and business that marked the watershed of the 1930s.

Business organizations faced disaster during the Depression, and many individuals suffered cruelly. Perhaps as much as one-third of the working force was actually unemployed for very long periods. Even these figures conceal the real hardships. Lower-income groups depend on family income. To survive, multiple members of the family unit must bring home earnings. These supporting members of the family team were frequently less skilled and lower paid, but their marginal increment of income had been important to the family's well-being. Wives and older children who fell in this category either could no longer find jobs or replaced male heads of families as the primary wage earner. Men without work simply disintegrated psychologically in an industrial environment. Society had no use whatsoever for the skills of others. Engineers became taxi drivers; college graduates, real estate salesmen; young men destined for the foreign service, corset manufacturers. Life for many became focused on the small change of existence. Everything could be bought for pennies, nickels, dimes, and quarters. Everywhere there were queues and handouts and shabbiness. People looked ugly when they were only poor. Poverty was not genteel; it permanently scarred this generation and its children. The overindulgence of American children in the 1950s had only little to do with Dr. Spock's manual of child rearing, but a great deal to do with the trauma of the Depression era.

The New Deal provided temporary relief to millions on a subsistence level. New Deal policies attempted to stimulate and encourage economic recovery and remedy abuses that had contributed to the gross breakdown of economic life. In banking, finance, social welfare, and labor relations the New Deal made permanent contributions. In agriculture all New Deal policies were of a stopgap nature and provided no permanent resolution of endemic difficulties. In planning and in the reorganization of business activities, New Deal programs such as the National Recovery Administration (NRA) were actually either harmful or regressive.

Much more might be written about the Great Depression. In retrospect one ponders so many things: that so few Americans became

Marxists; that so many Americans retained their faith in the capitalist system through so much personal suffering; that the political system of democracy proved so resilient; that the social fabric did not come apart as it did in so many countries. Above all, the Great Depression ended the broad acceptance of neoclassical dogmas of automatic economic equilibria, of the beneficence of self-interest, and of the doctrine of government uninvolvement in economic growth and social welfare. The New Deal can be seen in the organic tradition of American development. Somehow it bridged the deepest fissure in our economic history. If the Depression and the New Deal form an epilogue to Veblen's writings, still the other side of the coin must be noted. Veblen could not have imagined the viability of contemporary American capitalism—stronger, more dynamic, more prosperous, more stable, and more responsible—an economic system capable of creating wealth undreamed of. For the first time in human history, a vast body of people, just over 200 million Americans, had broken the chains of scarcity.[29]

Veblen's System: The Economic Study of Institutions

Ultimately Veblen believed material circumstances determined the patterns of human life. He hoped that this might eventually redeem humanity from its melancholy position. But how did the human condition originate? In a curious way, it all began with women—a beginning not even as sophisticated as the Adam and Eve parable.[30] Veblen's tale is the same fall from grace, but told in property terms. For most of his timeless history man lived in a peaceful savage state. This noble savage exercised his creative bents and constructive instincts in simple but fulfilling agricultural pursuits—not unlike the small Scandinavian freeholder in ancient times. We do not know how or why this period came to an the end. One might assume that some major breakthrough in technology or some drastic alteration in the material conditions of life brought this period to a close. Veblen's theory of anthropology suggests, however, a more gradual alteration. In primitive communities men and women had appropriated some minor useful implements. They did not see themselves as owning these articles. The

[29]Seventy to eighty percent of the population of 240 million is statistically more accurate. But even the American poor fall into a different category than those in other countries.

[30]Veblen, *Theory of the Leisure Class*, in Max Lerner, ed., *The Portable Veblen* (New York: Viking, 1948), p. 73.

earliest form of ownership he posits is the ownership of women by able-bodied men. Men seize women as captives to display, as trophies. The male then sets up an arrangement of ownership-marriage which rests on coercions but simultaneously demonstrates to all his prowess and his ownership rights. Once this is done, the extension of property control to other persons and to things follows easily. "From the ownership of women the concept of ownership extends itself to include the products of their industry, and so there arises the ownership of things as well as of persons."[31] Just as final as the expulsion of Adam and Eve from the Garden of Eden is man's expulsion from the state of peaceful savagery. "Wherever the institution of private property is found, even in a slightly developed form, the economic process bears the character of a struggle between men for the possession of goods."[32] Veblen believed that we by this one act of human folly had left behind the age of peaceful savagery and moved across the boundary into the age of predatory barbarianism. Like the state of nature, the age of savagery was peaceful, serviceable, and creative. Neither war nor property had corrupted the human spirit; each man highly endowed with the instinct of workmanship sought to maximize his talents in ways that would benefit his community.

All of history since the "fall" postulated by Veblen falls into the single category of the predatory system with its subcultures of the premodern handicraft economy and the present-day machine technology. Life has become truly "nasty, brutish, and short." The four horsemen of Veblen's modern life are property, war, masculine barbarism, and the leisure class. Once man has entered this predatory culture, he puts aside "the unanalyzed and undifferentiated solidarity" between himself and the group. He begins to emerge as an individual dominated by aggressive and warlike design—a design to command, to excel, and to subjugate others. The instinct of workmanship becomes corrupted "into a straining to excel others in pecuniary achievement." The most powerful motive, save that of self-preservation, becomes that of individual emulation. This "is equivalent to saying that it expresses itself in some form of conspicuous waste." Although Veblen denies that "waste" has any moral or pejorative content, this is clearly not the case from the context in which it always appears in his writing. Throughout his entire life and certainly

[31]*Ibid.*, p. 74.
[32]*Ibid.*, p. 74.

in his domestic arrangements, Veblen had no appreciation of the esthetic or the artistic. A chair was something to sit on, shoes something to wear, food something to eat.[33] Veblen's analysis deliberately disregarded many aspects of human experience.

The Theory of the Leisure Class, which insured Veblen's popular intellectual reputation, contains his most seminal and creative ideas. If the leisure class developed as an outgrowth of war and invidious emulation, it became, with the technological advance of society, more and more refined and emasculated. Its primitive taboo against productive labor now became encased in symbolic forms of distinction and emulation, systems of ranks, titles, degrees, and insignia.

The criteria of a past performance of leisure therefore commonly take the form of "immaterial" goods. Such immaterial evidences of past leisure are quasi-scholarly or quasi-artistic accomplishments and a knowledge of processes and incidents which do not conduce directly to the furtherance of human life. So, for instance, in our time there is the knowledge of the dead languages and the occult sciences; of correct spelling, of syntax and prosody; of the various forms of domestic music and other household art; of the latest proprieties of dress, furniture, and equipage ; of games, sports, and fancy-bred animals, such as dogs and race-horses.[34]

Veblen's brilliance in excoriating this group of do-nothings is incomparably sharp. It is an early description of today's jet-set. Since leisure-class standards are standards of pecuniary decency, employment dealing immediately with large-scale ownership and finance is the most reputable and regrettable. Next come employment immediately subservient to ownership—for example, banking, which suggests large ownership, and law, to which "no taint of usefulness . . . attaches. The lawyer is exclusively occupied with the details of predatory fraud."[35] Veblen's outlook is so narrow that his comments sometimes lack basic perception of human motivation. For example, "the ideal pecuniary man [the modern captain of industry] is like the ideal delinquent in his unscrupulous conversion of goods and persons to his own ends, and a callous disregard of the feelings and wishes of others, and of the remoter effects of his actions."[36]

[33]Thorstein Veblen, *The Instinct of Workmanship* (New York: Huebsch, 1914).
[34]Veblen, *Theory of the Leisure Class*, in *The Portable Veblen*, pp. 91-92.
[35]*Ibid.*, p. 231.
[36]*Ibid.*, p. 237.

If we apply to Veblen some tests of modern scholarship, we find him sadly deficient. Where are the data to support these massive generalizations? Although Veblen could use statistics, he never liked them and avoided them whenever possible. Is it good enough for him to say that he used only those materials that were of common knowledge? Veblen did not use common knowledge—deliberately. Throughout his entire life he sought deeper and older anthropological data which he made the basis of current generalizations. Veblen avoided any personality theory that might upset his fragile structure based on a superficial observation, and even more superficial understanding of human needs, desires, and actions.[37] In many instances Veblen referred to man's need to excel, his propensity for purposeful activity, the desire for emulation, the instinct of workmanship, the need to create, and even the warped motive of pecuniary emulation, but he was unable to understand fully their significance. All his writing, all his satire and irony, all the massive pyramidal language structure conceals a terrible self-doubt, that awful barrier Veblen never surmounted. We have emphasized Veblen's Norwegian background and cultural isolation, his great catalogue of erudition, and his immense talents and energies; however, each essay is an effort to break out of his self-imposed prison; each essay ends on a destructive note. Man, present-day man, is found wanting. Only some noble savage in some primitive utopia can grasp life. This is the greatest irony, that Veblen came to be linked with the engineer and the technocrat. At heart he was a Luddite.

Men must labor to sustain themselves because of the scarcity of resources, but this is not the only motivation for human behavior. Economic institutions in all societies reflect the most basic and urgent psychological needs and drives of the individual and the community. Veblen made it all too simple: on the one hand, the instinct for workmanship; on the other, pecuniary emulation. Good against evil.

As early as 1897, Veblen began to criticize neoclassical theory. The essence of his attack was simply "that economics is helplessly behind the times, and unable to handle its subject-matter in a way to entitle it to standing as a modern science."[38] Economics was not an "evolu-

[37]David Riesman, *Thorstein Veblen: A Critical Interpretation* (New York: Scribner, 1953). Riesman's essay takes a view of Veblen that is stimulating and different from Dorfman's traditional biography.

[38]Thorstein Veblen, "Economics as an Evolutionary Science," in Max Lerner, ed., *The Portable Veblen*, p. 215.

tionary" science; it was not sufficiently concerned with process. Economics still showed too many reminiscences of the "natural" and the "normal," of "verities" and "tendencies," of "controlling principles," and "disturbing causes." The most positive thing that might be said of it was the history of economics, as a body of knowledge

. . . shows a long and devious course of disintegrating animism—from the days of the scholastic writers, who discussed usury from the point of view of its relation to the divine suzerainty, to the Physiocrats, who rested their case on an "ordre naturel" and a "loi naturelle." |Economists have used figurative terms for the formulation of theory, and kept alive an attenuated classical normality| . . . It is this facile recourse to inscrutable figures of speech as the ultimate terms of theory that has saved the economist from being dragooned into the ranks of modern science. . . . The outcome of the method, at its best, is a body of logically consistent propositions concerning the normal relations of things—a system of economic taxonomy. At its worst, it is a body of maxims for the conduct of business and a polemical discussion of disputed points of policy.[39]

What had to be substituted for Marshallian economics was a new way of looking at the whole of economic action.

It is in the human material that the continuity of development is to be looked for; and it is here, therefore, that the motor forces of the process of economic development must be studied if they are to be studied in action at all. Economic action must be the subject-matter of the science if the science is to fall into line as an evolutionary science.[40]

Veblen came close to the heart of the matter. "The psychological and anthropologic preconceptions of the economists have been those which were accepted by the psychologies and social sciences some generations ago."[41] The English classical and neoclassical economists, the Marxists, and even the Austrian school had made the same basic error—"a faulty conception of human nature." Classical economics had drawn the human material in hedonistic terms, "in terms of a passive and substantially inert and immutably given human nature

[39]*Ibid.*, 224-227.
[40]*Ibid.*, p. 231
[41]*Ibid.*, 232

. . . . The hedonistic conception of man is that of a lightning calcula-
tion of pleasures and pains, who oscillates like a homogeneous globule
of desire of happiness under the impulse of stimuli that shift him
about the area, but leave him intact. He has neither antecedent nor
consequent."[42] Veblen knew what was wrong, but he backed away
from developing a new theoretical system. Rather lamely he suggested
that until the present it may have been too difficult, or impossible, to
make economics a science. Now this could be done. Social and political sciences must follow the lead of the physical sciences toward a
"(substantially materialistic) habit of mind which seeks a comprehension of facts in terms of a cumulative sequence."[43] Veblen had discovered Darwin, but he never developed the biological metaphor
into a dynamic economic model.

From Smith to Marshall, Veblen found the same bias in economists, which he called animism.[44] Philosophically, economics assumed
either the moral presuppositions of Christianity incorporated in the
natural rights philosophy, or the values of a diluted Utilitarianism.
Value was defined in terms of a work ethic. The overall neoclassical
framework of economic life was conceived in static terms which
tended toward some self-adjusting equilibrium. Both normality and
competition were taken as the assumptions of economic reality rather
than as circumstances or conditions to be adjusted by society. The
conventional wisdom applied logical precision to these assumptions,
and arrived, therefore, at preordained conclusions which had little
relevance to the world of everyday economic life.

Veblen was not a Marxist, nor even a great admirer of Marx.[45] If
Smith and Marshall were dominated by an outworn animism, Marx
also was unscientific. No part of the Marxian assumptions could stand
Veblen's attack. The labor theory of value, the doctrine of surplus
value, the origins of the capitalistic hoard out of exploitation—all of
these were unproved assumptions. Even proletarian revolution was
only wishful thinking. Marx used history and philosophy as his analytical tools; Veblen turned to anthropology and biology. What did these
disciplines give him? Veblen's anthropology, we think, gave his inner

[42]*Ibid.*
[43]*Ibid.*, p. 240.
[44]Veblen considered Marx both in the mainstream of classical thought and yet outside it; he found Marx equally guilty of "animism."
[45]Thorstein Veblen, "The Socialist Economics of Karl Marx I,II, in *The Place of
Science in Modern Civilization* (New York: Huebsch, 1930), pp. 409-457.

life a sense of rootedness he desperately needed. Veblen was entirely self-taught, or more accurately, self-read in this field. Although he applied for a grant to study ancient Near Eastern finds, he did not get the grant, nor did he, as far as we know, have any direct anthropological experience at any time during his entire career. Furthermore, his entire anthropological system was constructed from romantic notions of primitive life. Just as his translation of *The Laxdaela Saga* embodied Veblen's personal view of the past, so his system reflected his search for the Eden that never was.

No single intellectual in the nineteenth century was more crucial than Darwin. Very few economists believed that what Darwin had to say touched their work. A handful used these scientific observations as reinforcements to classical laissez faire thinking—which was one of the reasons why Spencer's sociology was so popular in establishment circles. Veblen took the most important axioms of the Darwinian revolution and applied them to economics. He stripped economics of all values, and illuminated its superstructure. The most important fact of modern economic life, he discovered, was the ceaseless revolutionary change of technology. Like a great natural irrepressible force, like the building of great coral reefs over millions of years by hundreds of millions of tiny animals, new technological alterations moved forward against the habits, instincts, and institutions man had built up to secure himself against the pressures of change.

In 1904, Veblen published *The Theory of Business Enterprise*. It was, and is, his most important theoretical work.[46] So little was he still regarded in intellectual circles that Dorfman says Veblen paid for the plates and composition. Veblen's book is a deliberate, highly inflammatory attack on the capitalistic system, particularly as practiced in America at the turn of the century. Behind the screen of erudition and complicated language lay a hostility and aggression that had no equal, not even in Marx. Fundamentally Marx admired much in capitalism's achievements, if not in capitalism itself. It was through capitalism, Marx argued, that socialism would take over, and bring those structural changes that would create a new human personality. Veblen's indictment of the system was total. In this book the only measure of hope rested on his particular view of the machine process and the psychological changes it might produce. Later on, after World War I,

[46]Veblen's *Theory of Business Enterprise*, is also unusually bitter in its attack.

Veblen forced himself briefly to assume a more activist role, as editor of *Dial* and as a lukewarm supporter of the Soviet Union. But his heart was not in it. He really did not believe that much could be done in the short run, and even in the long run he remained pessimistic. Veblen blindly and savagely attacked the institutions of American middle-class life. In the *Innocents at Cedro* we are told that Veblen returned to the cabin he had built, and believed someone had taken it from him.[47] He took an axe. Slowly and dumbly, like some enraged and wounded animal, he destroyed the cabin. Neither reason, sympathy, nor humor could change his purpose: to destroy that which he felt had been wrongfully taken from him.

The Theory of Business Enterprise has three main themes: the shape of the latter-day predatory culture, what this culture does to human beings and the sacramental quality of the machine. The drive toward pecuniary emulation and invidious destruction creates not only a leisure class, but also a business society with its own built-in mechanism. American society best describes this self-imposed tragedy. Because he is blind, man substitutes pecuniary profit for wholesome labor; man strives to gain the intangibles of economic reality, rather than the reality itself. The end result is an economic monster. Yet the realities of modern economic life are best suggested by the machine, a clean, regular, methodical scientific process.

The nonrealities of modern economic life are best reflected by the drive for monetary profits and by those financial institutions which cater to this drive. Captains of business, captains of finance, are criminals, saboteurs of production. Their goal is to wreck the productive process because they may hope to gain more through the violent disruptions of the industrial process than through its healthy operation. The drive of the businessman is to wrest profits from the industrial process by any means. How does Veblen define profits? They are the results of the manipulation and acquisition of paper claims. Consequently, profits swing widely with every fluctuation—real or imaginary—of the business community. It is a vicious game in which the community always loses.

The modern captain does not create opportunities for increasing industrial efficiency, but only watches for opportunities to put his competitors in an

---

[47]R. L. Duffus, *The Innocents at Cedro: A Memoir of Thorstein Veblen and Some Others* (New York: Macmlllan, 1944).

uncomfortable position; cutthroat competition, rate wars, duplication, misdirection, wasted effort, and delay of improvements long after they are advisable are the price the community pays. When this game between competing business interests is played to a finish, in a coalition of the competitors under single management, then it may proceed more obviously as a conflict between the monopoly and the community.[48]

As these businessmen parasitically struggle for paper-money rewards, they sap the productive strength of the community because even minor vibrations become intensified throughout the delicate mechanism of the productive process. Veblen's entire discussion of credit, and indeed of the business cycle itself, derives from this exaggerated view of the behavioral drive of this socially irresponsible business leader. The modern capitalistic system is like a puppet on a string—jerked hither and thither, purposelessly and destructively. Helplessly the community watches this performance, but does nothing about it.

The shape of this latter-day predatory culture is nightmarish. A vast array of bankers, stock exchanges, manipulators, lawyers, public officials, and advertising specialists dance around the cauldron of the economic system which they keep in a continued state of agitation. Worst of all, not a single one of these individuals is productive, socially necessary, or indeed honorable. Our economic society has been turned over to criminal hands. Industry is manipulated by business. By the expansion of "loan credit," the rigging of stock prices, the jiggling of production, the businessman recoups higher and higher monetary rewards—his sole concern. The efficiencies of the machine process are deliberately wiped out by this intricate insidious mechanism. That which is sick becomes the "healthy" goal of confused society; depression becomes chronic and normal. This business culture erodes the very essence of man's drive to instinctual health—his instinct of workmanship. As businessmen push the expansion of loan credit, the rate of interest rises precipitously and consequently the capitalized value of enterprise falls.[49] In their greed, businessmen raise prices so high that demand falls sharply, raising costs and reducing profits. Vanishing profits, high interest rates, and tight credit generate a panic which topples the whole structure. Presumably the same drive toward pecu-

[48]Veblen's, *Theory of Business Enterprise*, chap. 3, pp. 20-65, elaborates this theme again and again.
[49]*Ibid.*, pp. 93-132.

niary emulation starts the cycle again, but unlike with Schumpeter, the configuration, dimensions, and trends of Veblen's business cycle are not clear.

For all who are marked by the predatory culture, who belong to the pecuniary class, Veblen offers little hope. Blindly they tread the maze of their own making. The group is a large one — businessmen and all who touch them, including religious mythmakers, educators, public officials, "people of small means," and all who feel themselves bound to and dependent on the institutions of property. Even some workers must be included in this group — those particularly who become seduced by these pecuniary standards and are caught up in conspicuous waste and conspicuous consumption.

There is however a sacramental quality about the machine process; it automatically imparts grace to the participant. How does this occur? For Veblen, the redemptive power of the machine is crucial. The machine takes on a life of its own — a life of process, continuous process without thought or feeling, impersonal material cause and effect. And this automatic process, Veblen hoped, might yet save all who fall under its sway. Though engineers and technical supervisors who understand the machine process are to be the largest beneficiaries, even the lowliest workman may instinctively come to be dominated by the discipline of the machine process. In this manner, both groups could free themselves from the thralldom of nonscientific thought, beliefs, and actions. Veblen recognized how deeply the drives of instinct and of the pecuniary culture were:

Which of the two antagonistic factors (regime of status or the machine technology) may prove the stronger in the long run is something of a blind guess; but the calculable future seems to belong to the one or the other.

The ubiquitous presence of the machine, with its spiritual concomitant — workday ideals and scepticism of what is only conventionally valid — is the unequivocal mark of the western culture of today as contrasted with the culture of other times and places. It pervades all classes and strata in a varying degree. . . . And as the concomitant differentiation and specialization of occupation goes on, a still more unmitigated discipline falls upon ever-widening classes of the population, resulting in an ever-weakening sense of conviction, allegiance, or piety toward the received institutions.[50]

[50]*Ibid.*, pp. 323-324.

How accurate a prediction was Veblen's analysis? In the way he constructed his system, singularly inaccurate in the long run. In a limited area, such as the instinct of workmanship, but shorn of the magical quality of machine life, remarkably perceptive. Why was he at once so wrong and so prophetic? All his life Veblen was beset by doubts. However complex his language, his conceptual and analytical framework was overwhelmingly simple. Because there was really no hope there must be some savior. Veblen could not accept formal religion of any kind; he turned, therefore, to the inanimate, to the machine. The machine, broadly defined, has played a central role in the industrial society that has been created over the past two hundred years in the Western world. Two centuries ago, the typical machine was a clumsy array of ill-fitting, slow-moving cranks and levers. Half a century ago, the machine was somewhat more sophisticated and increasingly driven by electric power, but still within the genetic tradition of the past. Today the machine is either computerized or about to be computerized. In every industry automation stands in the wings. From the accurate cutting and boring of generator shafts or engine blocks or the automatic baking of biscuits by numerical controls, the computer dominates the newest technologies. A man who works a simple lathe may form an attachment to it, though one should be very careful with this kind of romanticism. He may sense the rhythm of the machine, know its quirks, talk about it to fellow workmen in personal terms. He may take pride in it, and polish it like an adolescent with a new car. When the machine becomes part of a moving assembly line, these associations break down quickly. Production methods do not allow the development of any closeness to the machine as a separate implement. Production schedules do not permit the workers to have these quasipersonal feelings toward the machine. In fact, there seems to be a good deal of evidence that the mass-production process creates tremendous work hostility among the production workers. Against the metaphors of attachment to the lathe, shining it up and naming it, modern production methods frequently foster slowdown, work sabotage, and other forms of anger toward the work situation. Today the machine process is in another phase and pushes toward other emotions and social patterns. These new feelings are immensely complex—the computer (as a metaphor and symbol of the new machine situation) arouses admiration but also a great deal of fear.

Clearly the computer does not arouse identification. One can not talk about "my" computer, or when the day is done, one does not polish the computer and go home.

Veblen's entire emphasis is too subjective. Men, in fact, affect the machine by design, structure, and operation. Basic personality changes, those Veblen envisaged as necessary, do not come about as he suggested. The fundamental ways that man thinks and acts, as Veblen himself pointed out, lie deep within his biological-psychic mechanisms which in all probability are millenially old. Changes in such superficial arrangements as machine operation do not produce those personality alterations envisaged by Veblen or Marx. Both wanted a fundamental reordering of human change nature. Both had a strong Messianic drive; both believed that unless human change occurred, the basic economic life style would not change. Because Marx and Veblen knew, however, so little about the process of psychic change, they seized the most demonstrable metaphors current in their environment—the machine or technology—and turned it upside down. The machine system would produce the new men for a new world. Marx, therefore, became a revolutionary whereas Veblen withdrew into deep anger and pessimism. One became an activist, the other, pathologically passive. Men, however, do not change from outside in, they change from inside out.

There is some empirical evidence that the freeing of individual energy and its channeling largely toward material satisfaction can be economically stimulating as well as psychologically rewarding. The history of successful industrialized countries bears this out. Moreover, economic success, can help satisfy deeper needs such as aggression, power, and even esthetic pleasure.[51] Economic success may be the vehicle whereby lower socio-economic groups can quickly climb the ladder of social mobility and social esteem, particularly in societies where many upper-class roles of a noneconomic nature have been preempted by established older social groups. Examples of the use of economic mobility to gain social status are readily available from the history of the Jews to the Japanese in Peru, the Chinese in Indonesia, and the Indians in Africa.[52] Furthermore, the more we

---

[51]Talcott Parsons, "The Motivation of Economic Activities," *Canadian Journal of Economics and Political Science*, vol. 6 (1940), 187-202. Veblen's instinct of workmanship does not completely die.

[52]Bert F. Hoselitz, "A Sociological Approach to Economic Development," in David E. Novack and Robert Lekachman, eds., *Development and Society,* (New York: St.

know about economic development, the more impressed we are by Schumpeter's entrepreneur. One mistake has been to oppose entrepreneurs and socioeconomic planning as necessarily antagonistic forces. Clearly the last twenty years demonstrates that this need not be the case.

Finally, as we press deeper and deeper into the complexity of personality and motivation, we are less satisfied with the traditional description of businessmen. Veblen, for all his concern with the destructive nature of the "conventional wisdom," presents a conventional picture of the petty tradesman. If the term "robber baron" is a partially valid description in business history (and we would not question it), there is also set against this metaphor the long tradition of business-giving in American history, which dates back into the early nineteenth century. Opposed to the petty businessman who represented for Veblen the destroyer of the instinct of workmanship, there exists the business innovator and philanthropist. In part, public social services have developed slowly in the United States because of the role of private contribution. Much of the difficulty lies in the changing standards of economic life and human concern in a brief historical period of immense, rapid economic change.

What was wrong with Veblen's business society at the turn of the century was its overwhelming dominance of American life. Business came close to being a monolithic force controlling and affecting not only business decisions, but also economic, social, educational, humanitarian—in fact, all decisions. Thereby business corrupted the environment and distorted the multifunctional needs of the society. Slowly, however, this hard-core, self-reinforcing mass of business power has been fragmented. Business has become freer because some of those social burdens, which it was ill-equipped to handle, have been removed from its dominance. Modern industrial societies are heterogeneous and pluralistic in their needs and makeup, and business today must share power, prestige, rewards, and responsibilities with many other groups. Marx suggests that no ruling group voluntarily divests itself of power; Veblen thought the same way. Both were tied to the classical and neoclassical idea of an economy that would be either static or, in fact, diminishing in terms of real growth. During the crises of the late nineteenth and early twentieth centuries and, espe-

---

Martin, 1964), pp. 150-163. These minority groups are, however, frequently subjected to vicious persecution.

cially the first years of the Great Depression, there was some truth in this view. The lessons since 1940, however, demonstrate the immense potentials of modern economics, when it developed a more dynamic economic system. With the passing of the sense of psychological despair toward our economic future, much of the classical and neoclassical tradition, which includes not only Mill and Marshall, but also Marx and Veblen,[53] seems outdated, or in Veblen's own terms, an exercise in taxonomy. Veblen's contribution to economic thought was institutional: How do we create an environment satisfying "quality of life"? Modern economists such as Harrod in England and Galbraith in the United States believe that we have the essential economic knowledge to achieve this.

To reread Veblen is to savor a variety of intoxicating tastes. His language alone is an exercise of genius. His real contribution to economic thought, however, is not an exotic or esoteric one, but falls directly in the mainstream, of our analysis. Veblen's great learning led him to reject the neoclassical explanations of economic behavior and economic institutions. Veblen, neglected in his day, was the champion of a cause: To be meaningful economics must become an evolutionary science. Five decades before the computer, and the development of biological and engineering models to explain complex interdependent behavior, Veblen insisted that both fields—biology and engineering—were essential to economic theory. Few, of course, listened or understood, but his pioneering work provided the foundation for post-World War II efforts to construct dynamic general equilibrium models that combine theory, history, and social-political factors. Veblen would have greatly appreciated these new advances in economics.

---

[53]There is an Indian saying that one becomes that which one hates. Marx and Veblen, by their attack on classical and neoclassical theory, have become part of that very tradition.

9

THE TIMES OF JOHN MAYNARD KEYNES: FROM VICTORIAN ENGLAND TO THE GREAT DEPRESSION

The England of Intellect and Politics

Since 1930 one figure has been preeminent among contemporary synthesizers of economic theory: John Maynard Keynes. In this chapter we shall examine the intellectual, cultural, and economic climate in which he developed his ideas. Almost all of Keynes' mature life was clouded by the long post-World War I depression which between 1920 and 1940 paralyzed traditional export industries and was responsible for endemic unemployment. Keynes can be understood only in terms of the radical alterations in British society during his lifetime—a period that witnessed the decline from Victorian affluence to Baldwin's dole.

ALFRED MARSHALL

Keynes the economist begins with Marshall's inspiration: "Your son [to Dr. J. N. Keynes] is doing excellent work in Economics. I have told him that I should be greatly delighted if he should decide on the career of a professional economist. But, of course, I must not press him."[1] In his long obituary memoir, Keynes masterfully repaid the debt to his teacher who personified the intellectual integrity of economic inquiry. Economics will see no more giants of Marshall's stature, for the field can no longer be dominated by a single man. Today we have more than forty thousand practicing economists in the United States. Marshall would have liked this growth—and the emergence of a sharp and rigorous discipline. "Economics is not a body of concrete truth, but an engine for the discovery of concrete truth."[2] He had labored to free economics from the commonplace judgment and the empty phrase.

We have examined Marshall's theoretical contribution to neoclassical economics elsewhere. Here we shall focus on him as Keynes' mentor. Cambridge nurtured both; for Keynes it was his natural home, for Marshall, the place he came to love. The Borough of Clapham is far uglier today than it was in 1842 when Marshall was born there. William Marshall, his father, was a cashier with the Bank of England. He was strict, tough, bigoted, and as a father guaranteed to break the spirit of any son. It may not be entirely fair to attribute all of Marshall's personal difficulties to his father, but so stern an upbringing permanently damaged this gifted young man. His father patterned his role after James Mill, and proceeded to exploit his brilliant son. In place of Greek and Latin, Marshall studied Hebrew late into the night. This was his training for the Evangelical ministry for which his father had destined him. We know little of Marshall's mother. Was she the cause for Marshall's muddled tract *Man's Right and Woman's Duties?* Was she the ultimate reason for Marshall's own ambivalence toward women? In 1879, Marshall helped his wife complete a small book, the *Economics of Industry*, designed as a guide for extension lecturers in economics. In 1890, when he published the *Principles*, he deliberately suppressed this popular tract. Was the great man more threatened by his wife's modest contribution than he realized? Clearly, his opposition to the full acceptance of women at Cambridge in the 1890s was much more than an intellectual battle. Growing up in Clapham must have been hell.

At Cambridge, however, Marshall could study mathematics freely

[1]R. F. Harrod, *The Life of John Maynard Keynes* (New York: Harcourt Brace Jovanovich, 1951), p. 107.
[2]John Maynard Keynes, *Essays in Biography* (London: Hart-Davis, 1951), p. 174.

and without guilt. He had put his foot inside the door that would lead him to economics. Marshall's complex personal struggle, the quality of moral fastidiousness, which makes the *Principles* seem so dull today, the drive to preach, reform, and heal, which he could never fully submerge no matter how hard he concentrated, came from his early background. "If I had to live my life over again, I should have devoted it to psychology. Economics has too little to do with ideals. If I said much about them, I should not be read by business men."[3]

Marshall's coming of age at Cambridge reveals much of the emotional and intellectual conflicts of mid-nineteenth-century Victorian England. As a Cambridge student, he came into contact with the remarkably stimulating Henry Sedgwick. In one of the typical elite discussion groups, so characteristic a pattern of Cambridge society (a pattern Keynes himself was to repeat in the Apostles half a century later), Marshall's resolve to study molecular physics eroded quickly. The rarefied discussions in the Trumpington vicarage centered on fundamental religious and metaphysical questions. Marshall's intellectual pilgrimage took him from Evangelicalism to metaphysical agnosticism, to the shaky platform of Utilitarian ethics, and finally to political economy.

So I read Mill's Political Economy and got much excited about it. I had doubts as to the propriety of inequalities of opportunity, rather than of material comfort. Then, in my vacations, I visited the poorest quarter of several cities and walked through one street after another, looking at the faces of the poorest people. Next, I resolved to make as thorough a study as I could of Political Economy.[4]

Shortly before the end of his life Marshall described his conversion as follows:

About the year 1867 (while mainly occupied with teaching Mathematics at Cambridge), Mansel's *Bampton Lectures* came into my hands and caused me to think that man's own possibilities were the most important subject for his study. So I gave myself for a time to the study of Metaphisics; but soon passed to what seemed to be the more progressive study of Psychology. Its

---

[3]*Ibid.*, p. 176.
[4]*Ibid.*, p. 176.

fascinating enquiries into the possibilities of the higher and more rapid development of human faculties brought me into touch with the question: how far
do the conditions of the life of the British (and other) working classes generally suffice for fullness of life? Older and wiser men told me that the resources
of production do not suffice for affording to the great body of the people the
leisure and opportunity for study; and they told me that I needed to study
Political Economy. I followed their advice, and regarded myself as a wanderer
in the land of dry facts; looking forward to a speedy return to the luxuriance
of pure thought. But the more I studied economic science, the smaller
appeared the knowledge which I had of it in proportion to the knowledge
that I needed; and now, at the end of nearly half a century of almost exclusive
study of it, I am conscious of more ignorance of it than I was at the beginning
of the study.[5]

When Keynes, on his retirement from the editorship of the *Economic
Journal* in 1945, toasted the Society, he expressed Marshall's feelings:
"I give you the toast of the Royal Economic Society, of economics
and economists, who are the trustees not of civilization, but of the
possibility of civilization."[6]

To the possibility of civilization, Marshall with unflagging concentration and singleness of purpose dedicated his long life. He brought
to this task many qualifications, which Keynes so gently describes
(and which could equally be applied to Keynes)—great genius, scientific curiosity, mathematical talent, humaneness, intellectual incor-
ruptibility, and moral intensity.

By 1875, Marshall had "translated as many as possible of Ricardo's
principles into mathematics."[7] He had read widely, but had not been
impressed with the analytical ability of either the German historical
school or the Socialists, including Marx and Lassalle. He claimed to
have looked into "the broad features of the technique of every chief
industry; and on the other (hand) he sought the society of trade
unionists, co-operators and other working-class leaders."[8] This, of
course, is accurate only to a minor degree; there is little evidence in
Marshall's work to reflect any great understanding of the business
world save that of the city banker. Recognizing that "direct studies of

[5]*Ibid.*, p. 137.
[6]Harrod, *The Life of John Maynard Keynes*, p. 194.
[7]Keynes, *Essays in Biography*, p. 151.
[8]*Ibid.*

life and work would not yield much fruit for many years,"[9] Marshall turned to the study of foreign trade. This was to be to be "the first of a group of monographs on special economic problems; and he hoped ultimately to compress these monographs into a general treatise of a similar scope to Mill's."[10] He substantially achieved this grand goal over the next fifty years. (Mill wrote his *Principles* in twenty months, and Adam Smith the *Wealth of Nations* in twenty years.) No one has surpassed Marshall in constancy of purpose in the field of economics.

Marshall was not a great teacher. His growing fame as an economist of worldwide rank, particularly after 1890, drew substantial enrollments to his courses; his style and diffidence, however, drove many away. His wife tells us that his lectures were rarely written out, but were given from a few notes. In the classroom as in his writing, Marshall employed a deductive method of concentrated investigation. From four to seven, two afternoons a week, Marshall was at "home to give advice and assistance to any members of the University who may call on him, whether they are attending his lectures or not."[11] There, in Balliol Croft, on the Madingley Road, Marshall held forth, gently guiding a following of young men who would dominate economics in the first decades of the twentieth century. Keynes was the most gifted, but Pigou and scores of others made Cambridge the most significant economic school in the English-speaking world. As Foxwell wrote of Marshall, "Half of the economic chairs in the United Kingdom are occupied by his pupils, and the share taken by them in general economics instruction in England is even larger than this."[12] Marshall broke Mill's hold on Anglo-Saxon economic thought.

In his Marshall obituary Keynes described seven areas in which the *Principles* contributed to economics.[13] First, Marshall cut through and cleared up the "unnecessary controversy, caused by the obscurity of Ricardo and the rebound of Jevons, about the respective parts played by Demand and by Cost of Production in the determination of Value."[14] If Marshall rehabilitated the "forces of Supply above those of Demand," Keynes himself was to take the demand side and develop it into a powerful macroeconomic tool.

---

[9]*Ibid.*
[10]*Ibid.*, p. 152.
[11]*Ibid.*, p. 197.
[12]*Ibid.*, p. 208.
[13]*Ibid.* p. 182-189.
[14]*Ibid.*, p. 182.

Second, Marshall clarified the concept of "substitution at the margin." This idea, brilliantly but crudely presented by Jevons in 1862, Marshall elaborated into an analytical tool of great precision and utility (general equilibrium as conceived by Walras, was, according to Keynes, made articulate for both the factors of production and the substitution between alternative objects of consumption). The whole interrelatedness of wages, profits, and the various agents of production became a powerful new system of analysis.

On the one hand, they (the factors of production) are often rivals for employment; any one that is more efficient than another in proportion to its cost tending to be substituted for it, and thus limiting the demand price for the other. And on the other hand, they all constitute the field of employment for any one, except in so far as it is provided by the others; the national dividend which is the joint product of all, and which increases with the supply of each of them, is also the sole source of demand for each of them.[15]

Third, Marshall defined sharply "time" as an economic measurement. Keynes wrote: "The conception of the 'long' and 'short' period are his, and one of his objects was to trace 'a continuous thread running through and connecting the applications 'of the general theory of equilibrium of demand and supply to different periods of time.' "[16] Marshall recognized the difficulty and arbitrariness of the division between "long" and "short," but it enabled him and other economists to produce crude economic models, abstracted from reality, which could not otherwise be treated. His concepts of the "short and long run," like his notion of the "representative firm," permitted a sharper analysis.

Fourth, Marshall's definition of "consumers' rent or surplus," and fifth, his analysis of "monopoly and increasing returns to capital," were considered by Keynes two additional achievements which made the analysis of competition more realistic.

Sixth, Marshall introduced the concept of elasticity. "Mrs. Marshall tells me that he hit on the notion of elasticity as he sat on the roof at Palermo shaded by the bath cover in 1881, and was highly delighted in it."[17]

[15]*Ibid.*, pp. 183-184.
[16]*Ibid.*, p. 184.
[17]*Ibid.*, p. 187, footnote.

The algebraic concept of elasticity

$$e = \frac{dx/x}{-(dy/y)}$$

is typically Marshallian in its preciseness, and has been operationally one of the most useful tools of neoclassical economics.

Finally, Keynes spoke highly of Marshall's historical introduction to the *Principles*. Here perhaps Keynes was too generous, and Marshall's relegation of this section to Appendix A in later editions was undoubtedly appropriate. As history, this section fails in two ways: The generalizations are too broad to be accurate, and the prejudices too Victorian to be acceptable.

Marshall's *Principles* broke the dead hand of Mill's influence on economics, and routed the continental historical school. Marshall firmly established economics as an analytical science in the English-speaking world. When, during the great depression of the 1930s, the *Principles* ceased to dominate the teaching of economics, Keynes, his student, provided a new synthesis. "Economists," Keynes wrote of Marshall, "must leave to Adam Smith alone the glory of the Quarto, must pluck the day, fling pamphlets into the wind, write always *sub specie temporia*, and achieve immortality by accident, if at all."[18] Keynes was more than Marshall's most gifted protégé; essentially he complemented and extended fundamental Marshallian concepts. The similarities in their theories of interest and money are obvious. Marshall's view of a general macroeconomic equilibrium, especially as developed by Keynes, is easily recognizable as basic for Keynes' national income analysis. Similarly, Marshall's "national dividend" is not far removed from Keynes' "net national product," and Marshall's analysis of the "steady state" economy at full employment was fully accepted by Keynes.

G. E. MOORE

If Marshall was to provide Keynes with a methodology, a brilliant young Cambridge philosophy don was to furnish him with an idealistic philosophy which played a large role in Keynes' life.

[18]*Ibid.*, p. 174.

Oh! I have undergone conversion. I am with Moore absolutely and on all things—even secondary qualities. It happened while arguing with Ernst—who has read P. E. [Principia Ethica] seven times. . . . Something gave in my brain and I saw everything quite clearly in a flash. But as the whole thing depends on intuiting the Universe in a particular way—I see that now—there is no hope of converting the world except by Conversion, and that is pretty hopeless. It is not a question of argument; all depends upon a particular twist in the mind.[19]

This adolescent letter to Strachey from Keynes must be taken seriously. Keynes was then twenty-three, and his relation with Strachey was highly emotional. The *Principia* had swept through the Apostles, Keynes' club, and had had a profound effect on Cambridge: It marked in ethics the break with Mill, as Marshall's *Principles* marked the decline of Mill in economics.[20] We must be careful not to make Mill the villain of this era. There is a great distinction between Mill, the human being, and Mill, the intellectual tyrant. Personally, Mill finally achieved freedom and contentment; the intellectual Mill, to the last, was bound by the chains of Benthamite utilitarianism. Jevons hated Mill's *Principles*; Strachey hated Mill's *Ethics*. Strachey regarded Mill as "totalitarian, intolerant, and inquisitorial."

Moore's brilliance had been quickly recognized at Trinity, and he was given a prize fellowship unconditionally for a six-year term. At the age of twenty-nine, he was elected to the Apostles. Keynes knew him in two roles: from his lectures in philosophy, and from the Apostles, where Moore was renowned for his piano playing and singing. Moore was an impressive man, and his intellectual sincerity and commitment made many converts.

I am studying Ethics for my Civil Service. It is impossible to exaggerate the wonder and originality of Moore; people are already beginning to talk as if he were only a kind of logic-chopping eclectic. Oh why can't they see? How amazing to think that we and only we know the rudiments of a true theory of ethic; for nothing can be more certain than that the broad outline is true. What is the world doing? It does damned well to bring it home to read books written before P.E.[21]

[19]Harrod, p. 113.
[20]G. E. Moore, *Principia Ethica* (New York: Cambridge University Press, 1922).
[21]Harrod, *The Life of John Maynard Keynes*, p. 114.

We are primarily concerned at this point with what Moore meant to Keynes and to his intellectual development. In 1938, in a little memoir entitled *My Early Beliefs*, Keynes related Moore's impact on him:

Thus we were brought up with Plato's absorption in the good in itself, with a scholasticism which outdated St. Thomas, in calvinistic withdrawal from the pleasures and successes of Vanity Fair, and oppressed with all the sorrows of Werther . . . It seems to me looking back that this religion of ours was a very good one to grow up under. It remains nearer the truth than any other that I know, with less irrelevant extraneous matter and nothing to be ashamed of; though it is a comfort today to be able to discard with a good conscience the calculus and the mensuration and the duty to know exactly what one means and feels. It was a purer, sweeter air by far than Freud, cum Marx. It is still my religion under the surface.[22]

Keynes described how exciting and exhilarating he and his friends found Moore's work. They took from it what they needed. Keynes found in Moore a religion, "one's attitude toward oneself and the ultimate," a morality, and a freedom toward the outside world. This is the sense in which Keynes says he was an "Immoralist." Both of these avowals were important because they were freedom producing, creative in the larger sense. On the one hand, Keynes felt in contact with the loftiest of ideals; on the other, he felt free of all the conventions and constraints of English society. "The New Testament was a handbook for politicians compared with the unworldliness of Moore's chapter on 'The Ideal.' "[23] Perhaps even more important for Keynes' later career was the other side of the coin—"it follows that we were amongst the first of our generation, perhaps alone amongst our generation, to escape from the Benthamite tradition."[24] Later on, Keynes could see clearly how inadequate a guide Moore was to the life of a man of action, but in the mood of pre-World War I England "the right to judge every individual case on its merits, and the wisdom, experience and self-control to do so successfully"[25] nurtured the creative genius which was to produce such a rich harvest in Keynes' approach

[22]John Maynard Keynes, *Two Memoirs* (London and New York: Kelley, 1949), p. 92.
[23]*Ibid.*, p. 94.
[24]*Ibid.*, p. 98.
[25]*Ibid.*, p. 97.

to problems from the *Economic Consequences of the Peace* to the *General Theory*. Harrod suggests that Keynes' *Treatise on Probability* might have been a greater book if Keynes had not been trapped by Moore's concept of the undefinable. In any overall analysis, Keynes mightily benefited from this rich philosophical experience. "I can see us as water-spiders, gracefully skimming, as light and reasonable as air, the surface of the stream without any contact at all with the eddies and currents underneath."[26] Moore's rich personality, his great idealism, and the moral force that lay beneath, were the same personality traits that were to make Keynes more than a great economist. Moore's ideas never left him.

LYTTON STRACHEY

Keynes' closest personal friend at Cambridge and a symbol of the genteel, cultivated civilization, which Keynesian economics strove to preserve, was Lytton Strachey. Not many read *Eminent Victorians* these days, and those who do probably have some very special purpose.[27] Historians of the Victorian period have long since bypassed these "miniatures," and critics have challenged Strachey's cynicism and quickness to judge harshly.[28]

At the end of September 1899, Strachey went up to Trinity. His years at Cambridge opened a new stage in his life and brought him into intimate contact with Keynes. Cambridge was a beautiful, even idyllic place. Most undergraduates studied some, learned a few things, and "graduated" to their niche in English society. More significant than the formal classroom atmosphere, however, was the atmosphere of intimate, personal relations, the Cambridge of the small luncheons, afternoon teas, quiet dinners, and endless conversation between the dons and their adopted intellectual heirs. Keynes came to this environment naturally. Harvey Road, his parents' home, was part of this milieu, and it opened every door to him. Few accounts are more touching than the growing relationship between Marshall, the famous doyen of economists, and the youthful, undecided, but enthusiastic Keynes. Strachey, too, was admitted to the world of Cambridge, but

[26]*Ibid.* p. 103.

[27]Lytton Strachey, *Eminent Victorians: Cardinal Manning, Florence Nightingale, Dr. Arnold, General Gordon* (New York and London: Putnam, 1918).

[28]Michael Holroyd, *Lytton Strachey, A Critical Biography*, 2 vols. (New York: Holt, Rinehart & Winston, 1968). Holroyd's massive biography of Strachey may bring a brief revival of Strachey's literary essays.

not by virtue of birth. His brilliance as iconoclastic litterateur earned for Strachey his invitation to join one of the most famous discussion societies, the Apostles. Founded by F. D. Maurice, "The Society" boasted distinguished alumni: Tennyson, Hallam the historian, Clerk-Maxwell the scientist, Maitland the legal historian, Whitehead the philosopher, and many others.

For Keynes no less than Strachey, the Apostles embodied "his" idea of civilized men. Henry Sedgwick, another member, wrote:

But the spirit |of the Apostles| absorbed and dominated me. I can only describe it as the spirit of the pursuit of truth with absolute devotion and unreserve by a group of intimate friends, who were perfectly frank with each other, and indulged in any amount of humorous sarcasm and playful banter, and yet each respects the other, and when he discourses tries to learn from him and see what he sees. Absolute candor was the only duty that the tradition of the society enforced. No consistency was demanded with opinions previously held—truth as we saw it then and there was what we had to embrace and maintain, and there were no propositions so well established that an Apostle had not the right to deny or question, if he did so sincerely and not from mere love of paradox.[29]

The London equivalent of the Apostles was Bloomsbury, which was a place, a time, a movement. It was London, pre-World War I (after the war Bloomsbury became increasingly threatened and turned conservative politically), and it represented avant-garde values. Like the insulated elite of Cambridge, the Bloomsbury group "stood for" English civilization.

For both Keynes and Strachey, Bloomsbury marked a turning point. Keynes, as we shall see, would go on to a distinguished public and university career. Strachey's journey would be a harder one, with many years of inner suffering before his writing would bring him recognition and the means to live as he chose. In 1912, Strachey published his *Landmarks in French Literature*, a small volume in the Home University Library. Within two years, twelve thousand copies had been sold. Its author, previously unknown to any wide public, was hailed as a man of letters of great talent. Keynes, at this time a civil servant in the Treasury, had achieved no such distinction or recognition.

[29]Harrod, *The Life of John Maynard Keynes*, p. 71.

Until 1908, Keynes' closest friend was Strachey; by 1914, their worlds were beginning to divide; after the war, they had little in common. They remained friends; the bonds that drew them together at Cambridge were never fully cut.

Strachey moved from Bloomsbury to the Mill house in Tidmarsh, where he wrote *Eminent Victorians*. These skillfully wrought portraits were thought to illuminate not merely the age of the Victorians but the age of World War I, which had left England in shambles. The essays appealed equally to those who yearned for or rejected the past.

Over the next two decades, Strachey was to write other books— among them, *Queen Victoria,* and *Elizabeth and Essex,* —but his great work remains that slender volume, *Eminent Victorians*, published in 1918. Keynes's major work, *The General Theory*, was published only in 1936. Frail, sickly, neurotic, splendid, Strachey was a portrait from a *Spy* cartoon, with his awkward legs, strange clothes, and thin voice. He died in 1932 of stomach cancer.

DAVID LLOYD GEORGE

As different from Strachey as any man could be was the fiery Welshman David Lloyd George, Britain's wartime prime minister. Keynes' first major public role arose from his association with this superb politician. Lloyd George epitomized the qualities that linked Victorian and postwar worlds.[30] In Keynes' words:

How can I convey to the reader who does not know him, any just impression of this extraordinary figure of our time, this syren, this goat-footed bard, this half-human visitor to our age from the hag-ridden magic and enchanted woods of Celtic antiquity. . . . Lloyd George is rooted in nothing; he is void and without content, he lives and feeds on his immediate surroundings; he is an instrument and a player at the same time which plays on the company and is played on by them too; he is a prism, as I have heard him described, which collects light and distorts it and is most brilliant if the light comes from many quarters at once; a vampire and a medium in one.[31]

There was no Welshman more famous than this short, square-set, Bible-quoting politician of the World War I era. Lloyd George is best remembered for his role at Paris, in the middle, between the Tiger of

[30]Donald McCormick, *The Mask of Merlin* (New York: Holt, Rinehart & Winston, 1963).
[31]Keynes, *Essays in Biography*, pp. 35-36.

France, old Clemenceau, and the outwitted Presbyterian President of the United States, Wilson. His career, however, goes back decades before 1919, and it takes an effort to remember that he died as late as 1944, only two years before Keynes' fatal heart attack.

Lloyd George grew up as a radical in a period of revolution. In the late nineteenth century, Wales looked as if it might become a second Ireland. Many of the ingredients were the same: language, religion, poverty, English insensitivity. The difference was one of degree. In 1846, a Commission of Enquiry to Wales unanimously opposed the teaching of the Welsh language. If English were good enough for India, why not for Wales? The English prejudice continued late into the 1870s and beyond, long after the revival of Welsh made it clear that the rebirth of enthusiasm for the tongue was an expression of the deepest emotional feeling. Lloyd George rode the crest of this enthusiasm, and he mesmerized his audience with the passion with which Welsh preachers swept their congregations into religious revivals.

Socially the Anglican Church in Wales represented power and wealth. Politically, the church was the vehicle of Tory politics. Intellectually, it opposed the revival of Welsh language and literature. Emotionally, it was shocked by the sexual mores of the Welsh. For the Welsh miners and villagers, the English owners were hated rulers and interlopers. However, the English political system allowed bright young Welshmen to move upward into positions of power. This social mobility and the conservative nature of nonconformity prevented outright revolution. All these forces shaped Lloyd George's career, and brought him the political office where he and Keynes would meet.

In 1890, Lloyd George, then in his twenties, rode the Gladstone tide into the House of Commons. He stood for home rule for Wales and Ireland, disestablishment of the Church of England, land reform, abolition of plural voting, and renewal of restrictions on fisheries.

Westminster in 1890 was still the great political hall of the world. Lloyd George felt uneasily at home there. Ireland, and Welsh nationalism, took up most of his early years in Parliament. Occasionally he would change his diet and attack the church. "The Squire and the parson have broken into the poor box and divided its contents between them. The Tammany ring of landlords and parsons are dividing the last remnants of the money between them."[32] Although grossly exaggerated, it was great oratory.

[32]McCormick, *Mask of Merlin*, p. 47.

The war against the Boers in South Africa was in some respects similar to the war in Vietnam in the 1960s. The young, the fair, the liberals, the idealists, the good and the pure hated the war as a betrayal of honor and principle. Partly right and partly wrong, they stung the British conscience. Lloyd George was the angriest dissenter. He embarked on a one man crusade against the war throughout England and Wales. Never again was Lloyd George as sincere, as effective, and as courageous as he was in 1900. In Birmingham, he risked his life with a mob to speak out against the war. This image of resoluteness and strength brought him to 10 Downing Street in 1916 at the age of fifty-three.

Keynes went to Paris after the Armistice with Lloyd George as "Deputy for the Chancellor of the Exchequer on the Supreme Economic Council with full powers to make decisions; also |as| one of the two British Empire representatives on the Financial Committee of the Peace Conference; chairman of the Inter-Allied Financial Delegates in Armistice Negotiations with Germany; and principal Treasury Representative in Paris."[33] After four horrible years, no statesman attending the conferences was entirely rational. None of the leaders seemed capable of bold vision. Behind the small print of every settlement were the passions and emotions of war. For Clemenceau, all problems were reducible to French security, and for Wilson, a grand religious idealism was to impose permanent peace on errant nations. British goals and aims were uncertain. The essence of British policy was ambivalence, imperial and continental, partly in and partly out of European affairs. Was this the time for Britain to withdraw from Europe or to move closer? Lloyd George had no thoughtful answer. These difficult months of negotiations made Keynes' assignment impossible.

Keynes, the economist, could step back and see the chaotic nature of the economic decisions. Reparations would undermine peace. He believed that the decisions of Versailles would permanently poison the political environment and lead step by step to a new war.

By early June 1919 Keynes had given up. He wrote Lloyd George:

"I ought to let you know that on Saturday I am slipping away from this scene of nightmare. I can do no more good here. I've gone on hoping even through these last dreadful weeks that you'd find some way to make of the Treaty a

[33]Harrod, *The Life of John Maynard Keynes*, p. 235.

just and expedient document. But now, it's apparently too late. The battle is lost. I leave the twins to gloat over the devastation of Europe and to assess to taste what remains for the British taxpayer."[34]

Keynes was even more prophetic and accurate then he knew. He wrote *The Economic Consequences of the Peace* during August and September of 1919. This brilliant little book contained his indictment of the economic decisions.[35] Keynes' theme was clear: The reparations penalties were self-destructive. The full amounts could not be paid and insofar as they were paid, they would be economically catastrophic for both the Allies and the Central Powers. Britain's postwar economy could not tolerate this economic disequilibrium. After World War II, at the Bretton Woods conference, Keynes was to give his life for a saner approach.

The coalition government ended in 1922. In the general election, the Tories, led by Bonar Law, returned as the majority party; Labour was second; the Liberals, in two camps, third and fourth. Lloyd George never returned to a position of political importance, and the Liberal party sank lower and lower in political strength. Keynes' career also seemed over; many influential Englishmen never forgave him for the *Economic Consequences.*

LYDIA LOPOKOVA

Keynes was not considered a great economist before the 1930s but from the time of his marriage to his death, he matured both as a man and a thinker. Lydia Lopokova, his wife, deserves a brief comment.[36] She was not a great dancer, nor a great enough actress to merit much attention. Keynes met Lydia some time after she arrived in London, as a dancer with the Diaghilev company. In the fall of 1921, Keynes often watched her perform. He fell in love; thus commenced a four-year courtship. She became well known in Bloomsbury as Keynes' companion. At first, with his help, Lydia tried to join this closed fraternity. They admired her charm, her simplicity, her struggles with English, but Bloomsbury was not an accepting society. On August 4, 1925, Lydia Lopokova became Mrs. John Maynard Keynes in a simple ceremony in the St. Pancras registry office.

[34]*Ibid.*, p. 253.
[35]John Maynard Keynes, *The Economic Consequences of the Peace* (New York: Harcourt Brace Jovanovich, 1920).
[36]Harrod, *The Life of John Maynard Keynes*, pp. 364-370. Much of the material on Keynes' married life comes from this source.

After their marriage, Keynes largely withdrew from Bloomsbury, though he never entirely severed connections with these friends of his adolescence. More important for his academic career, Cambridge University had to accept his wife. With all its wisdom, Cambridge had difficulty differentiating between a ballerina like Lydia and a chorus girl. Mrs. Alfred Marshall won the battle for him. Cambridge came to love this exotic exile.

The act of marriage symbolized a dramatic shift for both. Keynes was forty-two, Lydia many years his junior. He was already widely known as an economist, though at this particular date his career was still largely academic. His criticism of the Versailles peace treaty had estranged him from large sections of British opinion, public and official. The role of *enfant terrible* was a costly one. Keynes had played that role successfully; now he was paying the price.

After his marriage, Keynes continued his very active career. His intellect deepened; he became more introverted as he groped toward a general theory of economics. Lydia lightened this burden by her charm, her gaiety, and her artistry. The culmination of all this intellectual ferment was the *General Theory of Income, Prices, and Employment.*

His marriage gave him that maturity and sense of balance which enabled him to produce the most important economic breakthrough of the first half of this century. Most of Keynes's earlier publications were the practical everyday work of a senior government economist. His previous major studies, the *Treatise on Probability* and the *Treatise on Money,* had serious limitations. The first work was too closely linked to G. E. Moore's philosophy and suffered badly from the limitations of this neo-Platonic idealism. The second, a *Treatise on Money,* was too catholic. Published in 1930, it embodied great knowledge and great competence, but it lacked daring. Keynes tried to substitute comprehensiveness for originality. Both books marked a stage on the way to the *General Theory.* Keynes was not yet ready to break with the conventional wisdom. All this is evident below the surface of these two volumes.

Keynes' married life changed drastically from the onset of serious illness in 1937. He was to live for nine more years, to make contributions of great magnitude both to Britain's war effort and to the founding of the major international economic institutions of the postwar world, the International Monetary Fund and the International Bank for

Reconstruction and Development. Each day, however, was lived under the shadow of heart disease. The attack that finally killed him at Tilton in the spring of 1946 was only the last in a long series. How had he been able to do so much with such a heavy burden? To be sure, Keynes had an immense zest for life and an appreciation of the importance of his work. But Lydia became for him in these years even more of a companion and help than Mary Paley had been for Marshall. Lady Keynes journeyed everywhere with him. She guarded and husbanded his strength. She saw to it that his energies were adequate to the jobs he had to do. She was a truly remarkable wife, especially during this final decade.

Keynes was more than an economist. He was an extremely rich, talented, and cosmopolitan human being. He was an ardent book collector, a skilled art purchaser, and a friend of the theater and the ballet. One of his most charming acts was the creation of the Cambridge Arts theater, which he and his wife made an exciting focus for university theater and dance. For many years, they took an active part in directing this "infant industry," and Keynes in his typical way left a trust permanently to endow it. On a national level, Keynes served as chairman of the Arts Council for Great Britain. Although the amounts various postwar governments have given to the Arts Council have been modest, Keynes believed that government has an obligation to support the arts, which capitalism under a profit calculus might otherwise overwhelm. Keynes and his wife greatly loved champagne; it was one of the loss-leaders at the Cambridge Arts theater. There was a champagne quality about their marriage—rich, strong, bubbly, and wonderfully lightly intoxicated. Mrs. Alfred Marshall confided to Roy Harrod that Keynes' marriage was "the best thing that Maynard ever did."

The Economy of Great Britain in Keynes' Lifetime

During the sixty-three years of Keynes' life, the British economy went from precarious world leadership to struggle for survival. Certain major developments in the British picture during this period illustrate the overall changes. The most obvious improvements were the rise in real wealth and population.[37] Marx was surely correct in observing

---

[37]Real wealth increased markedly measured in aggregate terms, although much of the population failed to share in this accomplishment, and unemployment after World War I became the greatest social problem.

that a modern capitalist economy could produce a flood of goods and services undreamed of by preindustrial systems. The aftermath of the initial Industrial Revolution was the continuing momentum of advances in technology plus the availability of even greater opportunity for those who could carry technology still further. But by the end of the nineteenth century, Britain had become an industrial and technological improver, not an innovator. Given her great lead in certain industries, particularly coal, textiles, and engineering, and her large capital investments in these areas, she could coast along on her success, at least in the short run. Britain's economy stagnated during the 1920s as a result of attitudes and policies which can be traced as far back as the 1880s.

Britain's population increased from 30 million in 1880 to 45 million in 1946, or by 50 percent. Three-quarters of a century earlier (1798) Malthus had been concerned with a population catastrophe, as masses of people exhausted the food supplies and in turn were pressed close to the margin of simple subsistence. Events did not follow the Malthusian prediction during the nineteenth and twentieth centuries, and in many ways life became more complicated than Malthus had anticipated. True a food shortage did not occur, but for millions life offered only poverty. Indeed, turn-of-the-century researchers established that 50 percent of the population of York and London lived in abject poverty. The aesthetics of small towns and countryside notwithstanding, everywhere hardship was the rule. Housing, medical care, and education were deficient; few had a real opportunity to move out of their class. Beneath the Victorian novelist's equipoise and the charm of upper-class life lay a world of the poor and helpless. Each time industrial conditions worsened, millions suffered cruelly. Unemployment in the collieries meant haggard faces and vacant stares. In the shadow of the beautiful Welsh valleys lay coal towns whose economic existence was more precarious than anything Malthus had envisioned. High up in Scotland, where the land was too thin even for grouse, the poor ate scantily amid some of the most beautiful scenery in the world. And elsewhere too, in the potteries of the West country, the textile towns of Lancashire, the weed-ridden overgrown holdings in East Anglia, economic security could quicky disappear, for the poor had no resources to fall back on and the state had no program to prevent a small deflation from becoming a major economic disaster. It is entirely accurate to conclude that no government policy had any impact on any depression between 1879 and World

War II. The Bank of England regulated its monetary activities with an eye on Britain's foreign accounts. Internal adjustments were supposed to be self-regulating and self-correcting, in accordance with neo-classical theory.

The increase in population had many other consequences. Britain became a crowded country, crowded not merely in numbers but in the more difficult problems that arose from the geometric increase in interrelationships. Think of an island that at the time of the Norman Conquest held one million people, ten million by 1801, and forty-five million by 1946, the year of Keynes' death, and the poor "consumed" even less space than the rich. They huddled together in ghettos, for the most part out of sight and conscience. Of course, not all closed their eyes to social problems. Sidney and Beatrice Webb, George Bernard Shaw, H. G. Wells, the Socialists, the new Labour leaders of the postindustrial era, researchers like the well-to-do Seebohn Rowntree, and many others did not devote their lives to gay Edwardian weekends.

Keynes certainly had little direct contact with the poor. In the world of Harvey Road, Cambridge, there were few hints of the misery of the urban masses. Keynes' mother, a remarkable woman, was mayor of Cambridge, but this university town had little in common with the awful slums of the large cities. The boy from Tilbury did not think, speak, dress, or act as did the son of a Cambridge intellectual. Birth, education, and association accentuated—perpetuated—these differences. Eton and Kings College were a far cry from the schools available to the poor, and Bloomsbury offered a milieu for companionship and conviviality vastly different from the local pub. There were no holidays in France, Italy, or Switzerland for the workingman. Keynes joined this upper-class world naturally. No Marxist sympathizer he. On personal grounds alone Keynes was revolted by Marx and Marxian analysis. He wished to enhance and preserve a social and political system he found to be basically good despite grievous problems. To achieve this the mass of people had to be pulled closer into the total society, the economic system had to work better and more evenly than it had previously functioned. Social conservation was the goal of Keynes' economics.

COAL

The traditional economy had broken down; British industry had stagnated. The coal industry was typical. An ancient industry, by the nineteenth century it provided Britain's light, heat, and force. Seams of coal stretched across Britain like an underground canal system. Production soared as industry learned to exploit it. Demand seemed insatiable, and supply virtually unlimited. There were no great break-throughs in coal mining. Men (no women or children after 1846) still clawed the chunks of black fossil from the seams, loaded them in carts, and dragged them upward. Rails, lamps, small engines for hauling and lifting, better tools and crushing equipment, and better pay for the miners when demand was high—these were the major gains during the nineteenth century. Many of the seams were thin and shallow. Much of the industry was undercapitalized and was operated on too small a scale and with little scientific knowledge.

Stanley Jevons, whom Keynes so well described, had sensed this approaching economic crisis in his book *The Coal Question*,[38] but no one had taken Jevons very seriously.

From the latter [*The Coal Question*] I have discovered someone whom I had not realized to be very good—namely Jevons. I am convinced that he was one of the minds of the century. He has the curiously exciting style of writing which one gets if one is good enough—particularly in the *Investigations into Currency and Finance*, a most thrilling volume. Moreover his letters and journal prove that he was probably apostolic. At the age of nineteen, he had to earn his living and was accordingly sent to Australia, where he earned a respectable and assured income. But he seems to have spoken to no one and to have devoted the whole of his spare time to the study of meteorology.[39]

Throughout Keynes' entire life, coal was vital to the British econ-omy. Not only the major source of domestic power, it also was one of Britain's major export industries. Further, until nationalization in 1947, it produced the worst record of crises in labor relations between workers, employers, and the government. In 1880, 147 million tons valued at £62.4 million were mined in the United Kingdom; in 1913, the coal industry reached its peak of 287.4 million tons valued at £145.5 million.

Before World War I the coal industry was, superficially, prosperous

---

[38]Stanley Jevons, *The Coal Question, An Inquiry Concerning ihe Progress of the Nation & the Probable Exhaustion of Our Coal-Mines* (London: Kelly, 1906)

[39]Harrod, *The Life of John Maynard Keynes* pp. 106-107. (J. M. Keynes, letter to G. L. Strachey, July 8, 1905.)

and successful. Except for the few years of major strikes and industrial depression, output increased steadily, and prices over the long
period were reasonably profitable. Wages too increased, though hours
were long and working conditions deplorable compared with other
industries. In 1880, almost 18 million tons of coal were exported; by
1913, this had quadrupled to 73.5 million tons. "Coal, iron and steel,
machinery and vehicles, ships and textiles between them accounted
for two-thirds of all exports in 1911-1913."[40] But coal's regal position
masked the real difficulties that were undermining the British economy. As William Ashworth has noted, many difficulties attributable
to World War I were, in fact, "plainly to be read in the prewar figures
of trade, production and national income and in the tensions within
British society."[41]

The signs of economic deterioration were widely evident. Output
per miner began to fall in the 1880s, and real costs increased in
Britain while they were declining in other countries. Far from being a
leader in the field, Britain became a high-cost, inefficient follower. At
the end of the century, world demand for coal was growing at 4
percent a year, but the British growth rate had declined to 2.5 percent
per year. As late as 1913, only 8 percent of the coal was cut me-
chanically and British pits were becoming backward.[42] Technically
the industry was falling behind its competition.

Until World War I, over a million men were still employed in mining. No labor shortage existed in the collieries, but epidemic strikes
during this period foreshadowed the violence that was to characterize relations between coal workers and employers. Labor, management, owners, and government remained oblivious to change.
While coal produced revenues and royalties, there was little concern
with the industry's basic dynamics. Profits, like those from other
staple industries, were not plowed back, but flowed to London and to
overseas investment opportunities.

With war came the complete government control of the industry.
Miners seized the opportunity to press their demands for better wages
and shorter hours. The government's strategy was to keep the domestic
price of coal low and allow the export price to soar and use most of

[40]Sidney Pollard, *The Development of the British Economy, 1914-1950* (London:
Arnold, 1962), p. 4

[41]William Ashworth, *An Economic History of England, 1870-1939* (London: Methuen,
1960), p. 301.

[42]Pollard, *The Development of the British Economy*, p. 5.

this monopoly gain to pay higher wages. Owners did not suffer because the excess profits were also used to guarantee their dividends. However, only minimal funds were allocated for capital equipment. The breakdown of the European economy at the end of the fighting gave the British coal industry some of its most lucrative years. The government alone gained £170 million in one year from this bonanza.[43] By 1920, however, the European market for coal had collapsed. Pledged to return the mines to their owners in August 1921, the government violated its promise and returned the mines precipitously that March.

In the short run, luck, simply luck, saved the situation from blowing wide open. A five-months' strike in the spring of 1921 created an artificial shortage and then a temporarily inflated demand. In 1922, American miners struck, which propped up the precarious market for British coal as did the French invasion of the Ruhr in 1923. But these were the last breaks for the coal industry. Domestic demand for coal ceased to grow. Even more serious, an industry that for more than two decades had been able to maintain its profitability because of exports now saw this market simply evaporate during the late 1920s and throughout the 1930s. While Holland increased its output 81 percent per man in the interwar period, the British could show a paltry increase of only 10 percent. Although by 1938 half the coal mined in Britain was cut by machine, and newer mines showed favorable cost figures, particularly in the areas where open mining could be carried out, the industry was plagued by too many high-cost, inefficient producers and inflexible union regulations.[44]

The government relied on amateurism and exhortation during interwar decades. Royal commission followed royal commission with halfhearted compromise suggestions for what was commonly referred to as a "sick industry." It was widely believed in Labour circles that only outright nationalization could remedy the situation. The polarization of attitudes toward resolving the coal question became even sharper after the ill-fated General Strike of 1926. Rightly or wrongly, the miners forced the issue—and were defeated. They felt that their backs were to the wall, that the owners were taking away little by little each of their wartime gains in hours, wages, welfare, and working conditions.

[43]*Ibid.*, p. 60.
[44]*Ibid.*, p. 111.

The strike destroyed the last chance for any rational reorganization of the industry. Some voluntary amalgamations were negotiated in the late 1920s and early 1930s, when cartel agreements were the style throughout the capitalistic world, but none achieved more than modest success, and then only for very brief periods. The short-lived Labour government of 1929-1931 attempted comprehensive legislation short of nationalization in the Coal Miners' Act of 1930. The miners' working day was reduced to 7.5 hours, but coal owners refused to give up their right to bargain district by district. In exchange the government fostered a widespread compulsory cartel scheme, which operated for a half-dozen years with mixed results. On the whole, the quota arrangements and the price maintenance scheme were never fully carried out. Part II of the act, which set up the Coal Mines Reorganization Commission "charged with the task of reorganizing the industry mainly by amalgamations and concentration of production," made no headway whatsoever. Under this legislation, coal royalties were finally nationalized, but the technical problems of high cost, inefficiency, small unit size, and technological backwardness remained unchanged.[45] Unemployment rates rose to 20 percent and more in coal mining areas after 1925. Today we cannot imagine the misery that was their lot. Almost a quarter million miners drifted out of the industry during the interwar period. Those who left were no less embittered than those who remained.

World War II temporarily broke the cycle of overproduction and unemployment. The government, which had little patience with this troublesome industry, was persuaded finally by a fuel crisis in 1942 to create a Ministry of Fuel and Power. Coal and miners were both in short supply, and wage increases and other benefits were quickly granted. "Yet unrest in the mines was not abated, and in 1943-1944 the bad industrial relations in the industry were the nearest approach to the rebellious spirit which was manifest in a wide range of industries in the later years of the 1914-1918 war."[46] Coal mining was the first industry to be nationalized at the end of World War II.

AGRICULTURE

If the decline of the coal industry dated from the 1880s, the preconditions for agricultural decline had been well established by mid-

[45]*Ibid.*, pp. 112-113.
[46]*Ibid.*, p. 319.

century. The acute crisis of English agriculture, however, predated Keynes's birth by little more than a decade. When the English government repealed the Corn Laws in 1846, it rewrote the ground rules under which agriculture would operate in the marketplace. The philosophy motivating this momentous change was clear and uncomplicated. Ideologically, it was justified by the claims of the free traders that this last bastion of protectionism had to go; until it went, the full benefits of laissez faire capitalism could not percolate down to the masses, and the working class could not fully benefit from industrial gains. Of all the tenets of the Manchester School, free trade was second in importance only to the idea of price determined by the forces of supply and demand. Free markets at home would be matched by free markets abroad. Thus the circle would be closed.

Politically, the achievement of free trade was the victory of the industrial capitalists—the leaders of the staple industries, coal, iron, and steel, textiles, and machinery. Perhaps 1846 was a more important date for these groups than the passage of the Great Reform Bill of 1832, for certainly the 1850s and not the 1840s signaled the shift to the political orientation of a capitalistic society. Free trade in 1846 did not break the economic power of the Tory aristocrats; it lowered their prestige only slightly. The political revolution of free trade caused the party chaos of the 1850s, the rise of the Liberal party to political dominance, and the reluctant willingness of the Tories to accept the Jew Disraeli. Many a back-country squire suffered severely in accepting so alien a leader.

Free trade had very broad social implications. It was sold to the industrial working classes, and sold very effectively, as the means whereby their real standard of living would rise because the cost of their food would markedly decline. On the whole, this promise was kept. England's competitive industrial position could be kept intact by letting the agricultural sector pay some of the costs of industrialization.

The passage of free trade marked the final phase in the commercialization of agriculture as an industry. Although the traditional relations of laborer-landlord-tenant remained intact until the agricultural depression of the 1870s, the swiftness of social change since then shows how ready for change the rural environment was. By the end of the century, laborers had set up rudimentary union organizations, farmers had created a trade association, and landowners had established the basis of an organization to watch over their interests. On both legal and organizational levels, the National Farmers' Union (NFU) rapidly established its leadership in the agricultural industry.

For many of the most important agricultural commodities, especially grain and meat, the legislation of 1846 was the final gesture in the acceptance of the laissez faire model, but it did not greatly change the economic situation until the "Great Depression" (1871-1900). Given the impressive efficiency of English agriculture (an efficiency that was to increase markedly during the period of so-called High-Farming in the 1850s and 1860s, when substantial amounts of capital were invested in draining land and improving stock), and given the high cost of transporting food, the English market was, in fact, for a brief period relatively tightly insulated. Between 1846 and 1870, English agriculture had enjoyed an "Indian summer"—of high prices, good weather conditions, satisfactory rents, rising land values, and docile labor. Domestic producers were spared the shock of worldwide competition. They took for granted a situation that would change swiftly once metal technology had advanced to building cheap freighters, which, in turn, would revolutionize international freight rates. By 1900, cheap ocean-freight rates, and a new technology developed to refrigerate meat products, destroyed the traditional pattern of English agricultural adjustment to economic crisis. For centuries, if grain prices sagged, English growers had been able to "up hoof, down corn." For the first time, British farmers succumbed to foreign competition.

By 1910, the acute crisis had largely subsided. Continuing adjustments over the previous four decades had fundamentally altered the structure of English farming; agriculture had reached a new equilibrium. Fifty-three percent of the land had been laid down as permanent pasture, and by 1914, less than one-fifth of the wheat was home grown. The agricultural work force had declined significantly. A new breed of farmers watched their costs and expected the government to protect their interests. Agricultural land ceased to have the romantic appeal for many an estate owner that it had had for his father. Only the richest and the most naive handled their acres as they had been used before 1870. Urban-industrial Britain, with a slowly rising living standard, no longer looked to the four-pound loaf for sustenance. Money could be made growing brussels sprouts or apples.

World War I forced the government to cope with agriculture. For the first two years, largely voluntary war agricultural committees, organized on a county basis, attempted to allocate such scarce resources as labor, fertilizer, and feed. By 1917, however, losses suffered through submarine attacks made central planning inevitable. Wartime policy reversed on a major scale the laying down of arable land to pasture, and guaranteed prices for a period long enough to protect farmers. In 1917, a million acres were dug up and planted to crops, the next year another two million acres were added to grain production. By harvest time 1918, England was growing 2.5 million tons of wheat, almost 4.5 million tons of oats, and over 9 million tons of potatoes.[47] This prodigious effort, successful despite shortages of agricultural labor, fertilizer, and feed grains, eased the burden on shipping and even enabled the British people to be better fed than their prewar dependence on food imports had permitted. But much had been done without careful regard to costs.

The Food Production Department mobilized and distributed prisoners of war, part-time workers, and a women's land army. As many as 350,000 workmen were spread across the land. A great deal of ploughed-up land was marginal for growing crops. Under the Corn Production Act of 1917, the basic legislation under which all these steps were taken, the government had guaranteed minimum prices for wheat, oats, and potatoes for six years. In 1920, this wartime commitment was reaffirmed and extended. The Agricultural Act of 1920 guaranteed not only minimum prices for the heavy grains, but also granted greater security to tenants and reinforced the machinery for fixing agricultural wages. It can be argued that both the wartime measure of 1917 and the act of 1920 promised more than was reasonable. Still, farmers and landowners had acted on these guarantees. Many had been persuaded that a new era for British agriculture had dawned—the orphan had finally found a foster home.

Such was not to be. Courage was not the banner of the postwar British governments. While Keynes castigated the world's diplomats in his *Economic Consequences of the Peace*, world grain prices collapsed, and the British government panicked, faced as it was, with potential claims of £20 million from farmers. The Repeal Act of 1921 threw British agriculture back on its own resources at the worst possible time. Wheat prices which had stood at 86s.4d. a quarter in 1920

[47]*Ibid.*, pp. 58-59.

were half that by 1922. Buildings, machinery, and the land itself had all run down during the war. Agriculture, as the coal industry, was betrayed. Throughout the 1920s and 1930s, it became "a declining, and generally depressed industry."[48]

During World War I, the British, U.S., and other allied governments had been forced to adopt programs for which they had no ideological or theoretical base. When the war ended, one by one these policies were jettisoned. Keynes witnessed the disastrous consequences of a precipitous return to laissez faire.[49] During the 1920s and 1930s, successive governments moved reluctantly toward piecemeal protectionism in industry as well as agriculture. These ad hoc measures, which lacked the justification of any general theory, were generally ineffective.

Britain entered World War II with an agricultural sector in worse condition than that of 1914.

These changes in agricultural conditions were reflected in many parts of the countryside. Less arable land was to be seen in the landscape; the number of derelict fields, rank with coarse matted grass, thistle, weeds, and brambles, multiplied; ditches became choked and no longer served as effective drains; hedges became overgrown and straggled over the edges of other fields; gates and fences fell into disrepair; farm roads were left unmade. Signs of decay were to be seen also in many of the buildings . . . the landscape of 1938 had, in many districts, assumed a neglected and unkempt appearance [50]

By the time of Keynes' death in 1946, agriculture had passed through its second wartime cycle, and had emerged with a structure heavily subsidized but little controlled by the state. Three agricultural organizations, the National Union of Agricultural Workers, the NFU, and the Country Landowners Association, battled annually with the treasury and the agriculture ministry for their subsidies. These price reviews became the means of guaranteeing that agriculture would not suffer a repetition of 1920. It is difficult to measure the success of this policy. British agriculture is more vigorous, more alert, and more progressive than at any time since the 1850s. This could not have been achieved by a laissez faire policy. The stimulation of market

[48]*Ibid.*, p. 135.
[49]John Maynard Keynes, *The End of Laissez-Faire* (London: Woolf, 1926).
[50]Pollard, *The Development of the British Economy*, p. 145.

competition is desirable, however, and the annual subsidy should be only one part of overall policy. Entry into the Common Market will serve as a dynamic stimulus for agriculture.

TEXTILES

To a considerable degree, the economic history of modern Britain is the history of the textile industry—its initial success and its subsequent failure. In the early days, from the mid-eighteenth century on, one textile innovation followed another in rapid succession, reinforcing previous changes and accelerating growth. Cotton, in particular, less dominated by vested interests than wool, silk, or linen, witnessed revolutionary developments in techniques of production and organization. It was here that entrepreneurs like Arkwright and Peel got their start and made their fortunes. But each invention, from the jenny to the power loom, was the work of a gifted amateur with little or no scientific training. Hence, the dimensions of continuing change were largely limited to the extension and elaboration of the original discoveries, which circumscribed the industry's competitive position and ensured its ultimate stagnation.

The core of the problem—and it permeated most sectors of the economy—was not only lack of basic knowledge of raw materials, technology, and organization; it resulted also from a system of education that considered scientific and managerial training unbefitting a gentleman. Businessmen knew little of basic science. Further, with few exceptions, their class background precluded their attaining the pinnacles of power, prestige, and social recognition. Even today, although the Queen's Honours List contains its percentage of business leaders, they are accorded less social recognition than, say, in the United States, Germany, or Japan. Signals received from the social aristocracy are apt to persuade the successful businessman to buy a country estate rather than build a new factory or laboratory. Keynes, for all his wide experience and great breadth, did not question these upper-class prejudices.

By the end of the nineteenth century, linen and silk were declining industries. Enterprising Scotsmen had already relocated jute close to its sources of supply in Pakistan. The woolen industry was still formidable, but it was almost everywhere dominated by the small producer —who wove a certain weight of cloth regardless of customer preference or need. As long as alternatives were lacking, British businessmen

ence or need. As long as alternatives were lacking, British businessmen sold textiles. But by the turn of the century alternatives were available and the downward spiral of British woolen sales became endemic. The British boasted neither marketing nor styling skills, and the foreign buyer could learn English or suffer the consequences. Nor was it imagined that there could be people who did not want to dress like the English; clothing suitable to Lancashire would surely be adequate for any other part of the world!

The gradual decline of the textile industry coincided with Keynes' life span. Britain's head start, particularly in cotton, could not be overcome quickly; her capital and certain skills and abilities insured that. But had the debacle occurred precipitously, dramatically, British businessmen might have mobilized their energies to change, in a radical fashion, their industry's structure and operation. Because the industrial cancer grew slowly, the individual producer could use old equipment and adhere to traditional methods and, in the short run, maintain his profit margins. The British manufacturer looked at his looms confident that they would run for an additional twenty-five years—the German or Japanese producer looked at his newly built factory and installed the latest looms.

In the decade of the 1920s, one out of five manufacturing workers, however, was employed in textiles, but the depression of the 1930s sounded the death knell of the industry. Keynes sharply attacked business leaders:

The mishandling of currency and credit by the Bank of England since the war, the stiff-neckedness of the coal owners, the apparently suicidal behavior of the leaders of Lancashire, raise the question of suitability and adaptability of our Business Men to the modern age of mingled progress and retrogression. What has happened to them—the class in which a generation or two generations ago we could take a just and worthy pride? Are they too old or too obstinate? Or what? Is it that too many of them have risen not on their own legs, but on the shoulders of their fathers and grandfathers? Of the coal owners all these suggestions may be true. But what of our Lancashire lads, England's pride for shrewdness? What have they to say for themselves?[51]

The scientific breakthroughs that led to the revolution in synthetics in the post-World War II era were mounted in the prewar period. In

---

[51]Harrod, *The Life of John Maynard Keynes*, pp. 379-380.

some of the fundamental work—for example, Terylene—British scientists played an important role. In no case, however, did the British textile industry capitalize on these opportunities. Initiative had passed to the industrial world outside the British Isles.

INTERNATIONAL TRADE

Britain's performance in international trade parallels its experience in coal, agriculture, and textiles. Between 1850 and 1875, Britain dominated world trade, at times capturing as much as 25 percent of all international trade, usually holding more than 20 percent. No country duplicated this feat in the next hundred years.[52] By 1870, these favorable conditions were changing, but both structure and momentum made it impossible for Britain to adjust her position. She could not, even if she had wanted to, return to a more insular posture. Already, of course, the United States had passed her as the greatest manufacturing country, but the absolute volume of exports and imports was so massive that it concealed the sharp cracks in the British trading structure. The emergence of Britain as the world's banker also veiled her declining position. Merchandise accounts per se were becoming less crucial than the total financial, shipping, and investments services she provided the international economy through a most delicate, sophisticated, and profitable mechanism centered in London.

Although in the late nineteenth century Britain was still selling more than she bought, the terms of trade were, in fact, more favorable to imports and, therefore, spurred the movement of her economic system toward the massive financial-investment service function that dominated her role in international trade in the decades prior to World War I. Great Britain had become both the world's bank and the world's monetary fund, and the world's leading source of funds for investment in undeveloped areas. In the last few years before the war, her merchandise export position improved considerably as prices and volumes rose throughout the trading world, though the structure of British trading and financial institutions did not change and her dominant role in the world's network of financial transactions increased. She was the world's clearing house for goods and accounts. In price terms, volume exports, including reexports, rose £283.20 million over the 1896-1900 figure, though the increase in volume in constant prices slipped almost 12 percent during this period (57.2 to 45.7 percent).[53]

[52]Ashworth, *An Economic History of England*, p. 138.
[53]*Ibid.*, p. 139.

It is clear that after 1875 exports were no longer increasing as fast as they had done. The annual value of exports for 1911-13 was almost exactly double that for 1871-75, while the volume in the later period was at least two and a third times what it was in the earlier. In other words, the proportionate increase in exports over the whole forty-year period was not greatly different from that achieved in the previous twenty-years.[54]

In a world steadily growing richer and more competitive, the failure of British exports to grow was damaging in the long run. To maintain her share of a rapidly expanding world market Britain had to do more. The largest opportunities lay in new scientific information then becoming available, and new technical innovations such as electrical motors. A massive redeployment of industrial assets at this stage might have overcome the crippling dependency on the old staple industries of textiles, coal, and shipbuilding. Even had the war not come, with its immense, almost total destruction of this prewar structure, Britain could not have continued to grow richer as the world's financial manager. The world had become smaller; better and shorter trade routes (e.g., the opening of the Suez Canal) lessened the dependency on British shipping. As Germany and the United States leaped into industrial leadership, British exports to the continent began to decline in the 1880s, and to North America in the 1890s. Proportionately, Britain increased her exports to the less developed world— Asia, Australia, and Africa. India became for a considerable time the most important single country in the entire British trading system. In China, Japan, Mesopotamia, and South Africa, Britain developed important commercial interests. Similarly, she gained in her trade with West Africa. Argentina was also an important enclave for British investment capital and for goods, and Britain had important economic beachheads in Uruguay and Chile.[55] However, most of these countries sought the products of Britain's staple industries and thus reinforced in the long run the British tendency to do nothing. By 1911-1913, Britain had doubled her exports of heavy capital goods compared to the 1850s. Machinery, railway rolling stock, ship hulls, motor vehicles, and electrical engineering equipment were important items, but even these shifts in exports were insufficient. Some of these products offset the loss of staples, but the overdependence on

[54]*Ibid.*, p. 140.
[55]*Ibid.*, p. 157.

coal exports was ominous; the period when most British textiles were going to non-European markets would last only until these customers could establish their own textile industries. The technology and skill needed to produce cheap cloth were easily imitated.

Further, Britain was becoming more dependent on some of her former major customers. Not only did food imports rise sharply after 1870, but also there was a rapid growth in the imports of manufactured goods and specialized industrial products. In 1860, these had been neglible; by 1900, they comprised more than 20 percent of the total. In the race toward more complex specialization, Britain was slipping behind. These new goods included products such as copper, rubber, and mineral oils, but also, and more sinister for the future, specialized chemicals and manufacturing equipment. For the latter goods, Britain now leaned heavily on Europe and North America at the very time, as we have noted, that these countries were becoming less and less dependent on Britain. Germany's best customer was Britain; Britain's best customer was not Germany. What was happening to Britain's share of world trade can best be illustrated by the following statistics.

1876-1880	19.65 percent of world trade
1891-1895	18.22
1911-1913	14.15

In the past few pages, we have mentioned many times Britain's role as purveyor of services—financial, investment, insurance, and shipping. Throughout this entire period these services produced large profits—and great dependency on their continuation. In 1871-1875, the estimated income from these accounts equalled no less than 63 percent of the f.o.b. value of home-produced exports. In 1891-1895, they reached the incredible level of 87 percent, and by 1911-1913, they still stood at the level of 75 percent.[56] These earnings provided the base for a rising standard of real income and governmental services for the British people and for heavy investments overseas. The largest single producer of these earnings was the prodigious British merchant marine. No less than one-third of the world's merchant shipping flew the British colors. British capital assets abroad also rose spectacularly:

[56]*Ibid.*, p. 147, 153.

1870	£ 700 million
1885	1500
1900	2400
1913	4000

In the early 1870s, Britain added to her foreign investments 16.7 percent of the income she earned abroad; by 1911-1913, she was investing 21.5 percent, primarily in colonial and imperial areas for the exploitation of national resources. By the early years of the twentieth century, about 50 percent of the proportion of British investment was in the empire, about 20 percent in the United States, another 20 percent in Latin America, heavily concentrated in Argentina. The annual return of these capital investments amounted in the early 1870s to £50 million a year in interest and dividends. By 1911-1913, this rebate had risen to no less than £188 million; almost 10 percent of the national income and more than 20 percent of all personal income came from these international transactions.[57] The strength and vitality of Britain's economic life rested precariously on the maintenance of these income flows. In 1907, one-fourth of the output of goods was exported, one-fifth to one-third of the goods consumed came from imports, and all the rest depended on investments abroad. For four decades, this system operated remarkably well, but over the period deep-seated changes had taken place. Before the 1870s most of the transactions were direct bilateral commitments; on the eve of World War I, the crisscross of multilateral patterns of trade and payments staggered man's imagination. Held together by London finance, a creaking gold standard and a precarious peace among the great powers, this system began to unravel. The war ended the reign of British finance.

Before the war, Britain was the major creditor of the international world; after the war, she was a major debtor nation. From 1850 on, her policies had been to fashion a framework of international arrangements based on free trade. Although goods always remained important, the vast range of services she provided became predominant. We have tried briefly to describe this interlocking multinational system. The breakup of this system was to be particularly unfortunate for British interests. North America emerged from the war greatly enhanced as an economic power. Many key commodities in world trade now bore the trademark "Made in U.S.A." For postwar Britain,

[57]*Ibid.*, pp. 158-159.

this new competition carried additional consequences. British exports now fell below prewar levels, but British imports from North America continued to rise. The trade balance with the dollar countries turned adverse, and the stage was set for the permanent disarrangement of Britain's international balance of payments. Of all the economic disruption wrought by the war, this change was the most profound and most permanent.

As Keynes had predicted, the war settlements undermined a world trading structure that had already become largely unbalanced. Over and beyond the anarchy caused by reparations and inter-Allied debts, many countries embarked on a protectionist course that virtually destroyed the prewar multilateral trading structure. Tariffs and artificial barriers of many kinds vied with each other in destructive effectiveness. All countries, but especially Britain, suffered in the long run from the return to neomercantilist policies.

In 1913, Britain's entrepôt trade stood at £100 million; by 1938, even at higher prices, it amounted only to £62 million.[58] Much of the 1920s was taken up with immediate postwar problems and war reparations; more basic trading-manufacturing adjustments were given only secondary priority in Whitehall. The return to the gold standard dominated the minds of politicians and civil servants.

By the end of the 1920s, the rise of imports and decline of exports had destroyed Britain's trade balance. Only a temporary, short-lived pattern of world prices that favored British goods cloaked the deteriorating, unfavorable trade gap. In real terms the standard of living briefly rose for the British—while the old staple export industries sank deeper and deeper into decline and permanent pools of unemployment. In 1929, unemployment caused by the decline in exports in six of these industries since 1913 amounted to 700,000 to 800,000 workers, almost the entire number of Britain's hard-core unemployed.

The strains on the system were too great to endure. Thus the depression of the 1930s. For the convinced Marxist, the ruin of this decade was the final chapter in the demise of the capitalist world. In the United States, France, Germany, and Great Britain, economies stood close to disaster, and millions of workers were permanently unemployed. Throughout the world of primary producers, mountainous surpluses of wheat, coffee, rubber, tin grew into huge, inde-

[58]Pollard, *The Development of the British Economy*, p. 183.

structible gluts. Sterling crumbled under these hammer blows. Dollars earned by Commonwealth countries and British colonies maintained a precarious balance in Britain's trading position. This prop went too, with the collapse of primary prices in 1930. Britain was left to her own resources. Although the adverse merchandise trade gap had grown to £200 to 400 million a year, offsetting this deficit were shipping revenues of £120 to 140 million, investment returns of £250 million, and £80 million in commissions of various kinds. However, by 1933, the economic situation had completely deteriorated; shipping revenues declined to £65 million, investment income to £150 million, and commissions to £40 million—a loss in "invisible revenues" between 1930 and 1933 of roughly 50 percent. "Throughout the 1930s," Pollard says, "repayments of capital slightly exceeded foreign lending for the first time since the Industrial Revolution."[59] Furthermore, almost all new lending in this decade went to countries within the Empire. The age of the Pax Britannica was over.

In 1931, Great Britain returned to a policy of tariff protection. The electoral mandate, however, was ambiguous, and politicians acted cautiously. Imports, particularly in agriculture, were subject to new regulations but so strongly did financial interests continue to dominate the British scene that protective duties on merchandise goods did not cover more than 2 to 3 percent of imports. In the half-dozen years before 1939, foreign policy became the major concern. Britain attempted to forge a network of imperial preferences to replace the shattered free trade structure. The neomercantilism of the 1930s was a shabby garment compared to the "coat of many colors" of the Victorian period.

[59]*Ibid.*, p. 191.

10
THE KEYNESIAN REVOLUTION

An age in the history of economics came to an end early in the 1920s. The British and continental economists who had forged the historical and neoclassical schools all had been born between 1850 and 1865 and all died within a similarly brief period after World War I. Keynes was part of the new generation which included Joan Robinson, Chamberlain, Hahn, Harrold, and many more. All contributed greatly to modern economics. Almost all of the new economic architects were mathematically oriented, and their analytical contributions would be framed in mathematical categories, not Marshallian niceties. They recognized that truth and reality could best be served by a language that freed economics from the constraints of the past. They sought to overcome conventional wisdom and to describe current economic reality. They had the courage to leave the security of established doctrines and embark on uncharted seas.

Economic growth came to a virtual halt in Europe during the post-

World War I period. Brief periods of hectic economic activity, particularly in England and Germany, alternated with lengthy periods of stagnation and unemployment. The primary concern of neoclassical theory at that time was the behavior of the price mechanism in long-run equilibrium under the condition of full employment of all factors of production. Established economic theory could neither explain the crisis nor suggest a remedy. It was not accidental, therefore, that economists, bankers, businessmen, and labor leaders launched an attack on the assumptions and theories of neoclassical analysis. The attack rested on underconsumptionist arguments, posed in the eighteenth and nineteenth centuries by Quesnay, Malthus, and Sismondi.[1]

In Germany the bankers Albert Hahn and Emil Lederer developed an oversaving theory in the 1920s that stressed effective demand and anticipated other Keynesian concepts.[2] In Sweden, Lindahl, Myrdal, and Ohlin developed Wicksell's monetary equilibrium theory into a highly sophisticated model that not only anticipated Keynes, but also was mathematically more rigorous.[3] In England, R. G. Hawtrey extended McLeod's theories and derived a purely monetary explanation of the business cycle. In all these theories, money had to be restored to the important role it had played in the writings of Steuart, Hume, Cantillon, and the mercantilists.[4] By reducing the role of money to a mere standard of exchange (*numèraire*), Smith and Ricardo had set the stage for the development of the "law of the market" that precluded unemployment because no one would produce without the intention to exchange his product for another commodity. Supply, hence, must create its own demand. This law was formulated most concisely by Say, and was fundamental to neoclassical equilibrium analysis. The attack on neoclassical theory in the 1920s and 1930s had to begin, therefore, with a reexamination of the role of money in the economy.

---

[1]Quite obviously, Marxist economists are not included in this group because Marxian theory had no difficulty in explaining the economic crises of the interwar period.

[2]Hahn himself returned to the classical fold in the 1940s and attacked Keynes' *General Theory* on the basis that (1) Hahn had long ago anticipated Keynes' theory and (2) the theories were wrong. Hahn himself had been heavily influenced by the truly original writing of the Scottish banker H. D. McLeod, whose *Elements of Political Economy* (1858) appeared eighty years too early.

[3]Cf. Gunnar Myrdal, *Monetary Equilibrium* (London: Hodge, 1923). (Translated from the German.)

[4]David Hume might be called the first Keynesian. He concluded that a slow but constant increase in the quantity of money will perpetually stimulate business.

MONETARY ECONOMICS

The technical complexities of monetary economics prevented any public understanding of the issues involved. In the 1930s intelligent laymen and civil servants had to choose between the "received wisdom" of orthodox economics and a "vulgar" version of popularized Marxism. The appearance of Keynes' *General Theory of Employment, Interest and Money* offered a third alternative.[5] The healthy controversy stimulated by the *General Theory* involved virtually every major Western economist, and contrasted sharply with the sterile debate between neoclassical and Marxist economists that had prevailed for the previous thirty years. Economic issues had not been discussed as passionately and as widely since the days of Smith, Ricardo, and Marx. Though Keynes' *General Theory* contained many sophisticated topics and was addressed to economists, its major issues and policy recommendations lent themselves to easy popularization. A simplified popularized Keynesianism, very much like the vulgar Marxism of the nineteenth century, quickly dominated the discussion and writings of the intelligent public on the fringe of the profession: civil servants, politicians, journalists, and intellectuals.

The "vulgar" version of the *General Theory* had already appeared in Keynes' previous writing, especially in his three great pamphleteering pieces, *Economic Consequences of the Peace* (1919), *A Tract for Monetary Reform* (1923) and *The End of Laissez-Faire* (1926). In each case, whether he dealt with the monumental blunders of the treaty of Versailles, or with specific monetary reforms, Keynes was concerned with the lack of effective demand and the consequent unemployment that had become an almost permanent feature of British life.[6] This concern with the effective demand necessary to

[5]John Maynard Keynes, *General Theory of Employment, Interest and Money* (London: Macmillan, 1936). References cited will be to the reprinted edition (London: Macmillan, 1946).

[6]The use of public works to fight unemployment was not an invention of Lloyd George or Franklin D. Roosevelt. It had been used extensively in Austria in the 1880s, in Prussia in the 1860s, and, of course, in Colbert's France.

[7]Keynes had formulated his macroeconomics concepts very early in his career.

For one of the extraordinary reasons why the world has enjoyed full employment since 1945 is that many of Keynes'. . . friends in 1916 were also pacifists. Keynes believed that conscription would "torture" his friends, and began to fulminate against it [conscription] both in internal Treasury memoranda and in . . . contributions to the press. It was during this debate . . . that he stumbled on the argument that, in a war economy which was approaching full employment, any transfer of more resources into the army

provide full employment in a mature, capitalistic society underlies most of Keynes' economic writing.[7] First, it led him into criticizing established policy, then into publishing numerous pamphlets for ad hoc reforms, and finally into developing the theoretical framework of his most important book, the *General Theory*.

The *General Theory* attacked the assumptions, techniques, and conclusions of neoclassical theory that dealt with effective demand, employment, money, and interest. By choosing to call these concepts "classical theory," he overemphasized the common tradition that united Ricardo, Say, Marshall, and Pigou. It was primarily Say's law of the market that bridged classical and neoclassical thought in these areas. Fundamentally, Keynes objected to the neoclassicists' narrow concern with "neutral" methodology and equilibrium analysis, and returned instead to the political economy of Smith, Ricardo, Malthus, and Marx. Very much like the classical economists, Keynes was concerned with economic aggregates, with economic policy, and with the distribution of national income. In the *General Theory* he was not interested in examining the capitalistic process per se, but rather attempted to provide a static short-run analysis that would assure economic equilibrium at a full-employment level.

An Overview of the Keynesian Model

Keynes' *General Theory* was addressed to trained economists, and was as inaccessible to the intelligent layman as Marx's *Capital*. Very much like Marx, however, he expressed the Zeitgeist; if, in Marx's time, the wretched state of labor *obviously* was due to the fact that *someone* must be exploiting it, the lack of purchasing power during the Great Depression was equally *obvious*. Thus, government intervention and the restoration of purchasing power had an intuitive appeal, and explain much of Keynes' success. The popularized version of Marx's works was often naive and hid the true intellectual achievement of *Capital*. However, the popularized version of Keynes, which we shall call the "employment model," has proved a solid structure, amenable to further improvement and research, whereas the sophisticated development of the *General Theory* has been much

---

must be a transfer away from other needs of the community . . . . Here was the first bud of what in our generation has become the Keynesian economic revolution.

"The infuriating genius," *The Economist* (April 24, 1971), pp. 55-56

more vulnerable to attack.[8] The basic building block of "vulgar" Marxism has been the labor theory of value, the emotional basis for the attack upon the exploiting capitalists; the major contributions to economic theory in *Capital* were quite independent of the labor theory, though totally ignored by the faithful. In Keynes' *General Theory* model, the interest rate plays a major role, which has been seriously questioned, on empirical and theoretical grounds, both by his critics and his disciples. In the popularized version of Keynes, however, the interest rate is of negligible significance, and the basic relationships among the other major Keynesian variables have been sturdy enough to survive criticism, refinement, and empirical verification.[9]

The Keynesian "employment model" rests on the observation, obvious in the 1930s, that persistent unemployment in a mature, capitalistic economy is possible and even likely. Keynes held that the autonomous self-adjusting market mechanism of classical equilibrium economics broke down because (1) wages and prices were too rigid to perform their allotted task of generating corrective economic processes and (2) the consumption and investment behavior of a mature economy makes the attainment of a full-employment economy difficult, even if the market mechanism performs reasonably well. Though consumption and investment behavior (propensities) are quite stable, in the short run, government intervention can affect the total amount consumed and invested. In the absence of a workable automatic control mechanism, the government must and can maintain full employment.

Effective demand—that is, ability to pay and willingness to buy—is the keystone of the Keynesian "theory of employment," the determinant of employment and income; unemployment is, therefore, merely a consequence of insufficient "aggregate" demand.[10] Effective demand viewed as a schedule is measured by the amount of money spent on goods and services during a given period. The money expended by

---

[8]By the "sophisticated development of the *General Theory*" we mean the entire model of employment, interest, and money presented in 1936 and extended by his elaboration of the role of expectations and uncertainties published in his important 1937 article, "The General Theory of Employment," *Quarterly Journal of Economics*, 51 (February 1937), pp. 209-223.

[9]Milton Friedman and his followers would disagree with this statement, though, for example, the works of J.S. Duesenberry and Simon Kuznets shows consumption and savings propensities that substantiate Keynes' generalization. (See also footnote 12.)

[10]This definition is somewhat redundant because Keynes measures the physical output of an economy by the amount of labor employed.

households is derived from wage and interest payments, but the entire amount earned is not spent; a part is saved. Because the percentage of earned income that is saved is stable at given levels of income the effective demand is, in turn, determined by the level of employment or income. Effective demand, employment, and income are therefore interdependent. If a given level of effective demand generates a level of output insufficient to employ fully the entire labor force, effective demand can be increased by either decreasing the percentage of income saved by the households or by increasing income through government action.

In the popularized and simplified Keynesian employment model, only households save. At this early stage of his theoretical development even Keynes himself ignored corporate savings, and was thereby able to sever the connection between saving and investment. In the classical model, people save in order to invest. In the Keynesian model, families save for a "rainy day," to send a child to college, or merely because they simply cannot spend all their income.

In the *General Theory*, Keynes employs two "behavioral functions" that express the consequences of psychological and institutional forces: the "propensity to consume" and the "propensity to invest." The propensity to consume, or consumption function, expresses at its simplest level the characteristic common to both individuals and nations: As income rises, a smaller and smaller percentage of each income increment is spent. The consumption function and its mirror image, the savings function, are clearly defined by the well-known diagrams given in Figure 10.1.

The 45° line in Figure 10.1a is the "equality line"—that is, tan (45°) = 1; hence from any point on the x axis, the vertical distance to the equality line equals the horizontal distance to the origin. If a person (or a society) spent his entire income, and only his income, the equality line would be identical with the consumption function, the measure of effective demand. The difference between the equality line and the consumption function is the amount saved (or "dis-saved"); it is shown in Figure 10.1a by the shaded area. An individual or a society can "dis-save" by drawing on previous savings (inventory) or by going into debt.[11] Savings is defined as the amount of income that is not spent.

----

[11]A country goes into debt if its "IOUs" are held by foreigners. Internally held debt represents merely a redistribution of income.

From these diagrams, we derive the first set of well-known equations that define the framework of the "employment model."

$$Y = C + S$$
$$C = f(Y)$$
$$S = 1 - f(Y)$$

The first equation is merely a definitional entity; the second and third equations, however, state that consumption and saving in a particular period are determined by the income earned during the *same* period.

Figure **10.1**

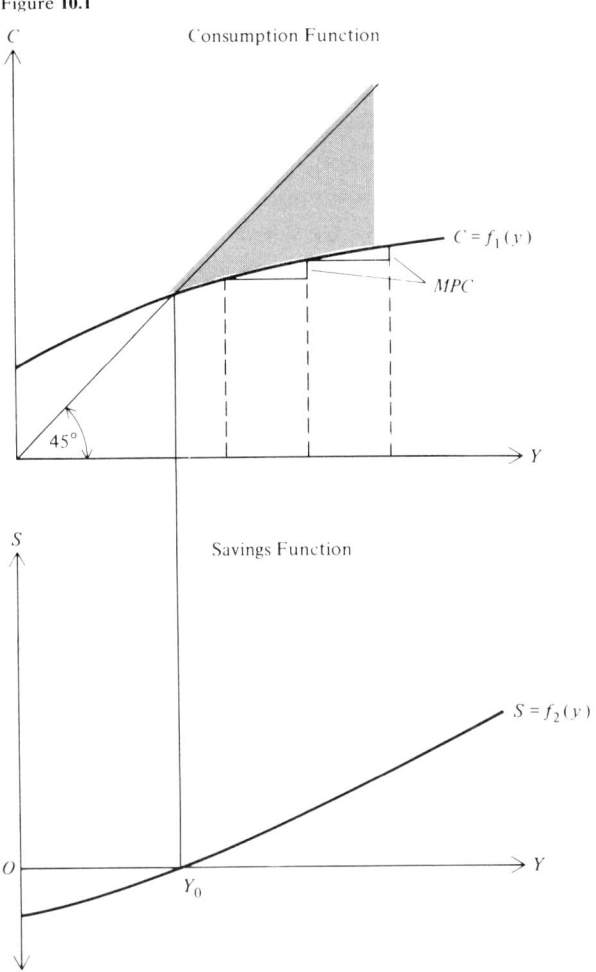

Moreover, the shape of the consumption-savings function—that is, the percentage consumed or saved at various levels of income—reflects behavior patterns that are stable and difficult to change.

The role of effective demand in the Keynesian model prompted an enormous amount of empirical and theoretical research on consumer behavior, which showed that the actual behavior of the individual spending unit was much more complex than Keynes postulated. Not only current income but, more importantly, changes in income, social class, and class mobility (Veblen's conspicuous consumption), as well as anticipation of future changes, determined individual savings habits. Still, Keynes' original definition turned out to be, in the aggregate at least, a rather "robust" assumption. Though everyone agrees now that individual consumption-savings patterns are much more complicated than Keynes assumed, the premise that a country's aggregate consumption depends on the level of its national income in the short run has proven to be an effective operational approach. In fact, more sophisticated statements about aggregate consumption have not added to the operational effectiveness of the Keynesian model.[12]

The *simplified* Keynesian employment model becomes complete with the introduction of the investment function. This function is made up of autonomous and induced investments, which are added together. The autonomous investment is an exogenous, noneconomic force that depends on the rate of technological change, population growth, the psychological attitude of the businessman, and so forth. The induced investment spending depends on the changes in the level of income during the period under consideration.[13] "Expectations," which play an important role in the complete Keynesian model,

[12]Quite arbitrarily, we cite merely two influential contributions: J. S. Duesenberry, *Income, Saving and the Theory of Consumer Behavior* (Cambridge, Mass.: Harvard University Press, 1949), and Milton Friedman, *A Theory of The Consumption Function* (Princeton, N. J.: Princeton University Press, 1957).

[13]It is very easy to make the simplified Keynesian model dynamic by letting the induced investment (and saving or consumption) depend on the income of the previous period. D. H. Robertson, *Essays in Monetary Theory* (London: King & Staples, 1940), was one of the first economists to attack the essentially static nature of the Keynesian model. His period-analysis approach was meant as a critique of Keynes, but actually he retained the essence of the *General Theory* but expressed it in terms of difference equations, with consequent changes in definitions. This point is easily verified by R. G. D. Allen's treatment of the Keynesian models in "period terms." The result is certainly Keynesian, but still not very different from Robertson. [Cf. R. G. D. Allen, *Mathematical Economics* (London: Macmillan, 1957, chap. 2).] The Keynes-Robertson controversy deserves mention today only because it was a major issue during the 1930s and 1940s.

and especially in its 1937 version, do not appear explicitly in the employment model which we will discuss more thoroughly later.

The diagrams in Figure 10.2 emphasize that all three Keynesian functions—consumption, saving, and investment—are schedules, *exactly like the demand and supply schedules.* At a particular point in time, one aggregate, the households, stands ready to spend or save various amounts of money, given different levels of income. Another aggregate, business, is equally willing to invest various sums at different levels of national income. Note that at this state we do not know how much consumption and investment will really take place.

Figure **10.2** Investment Function

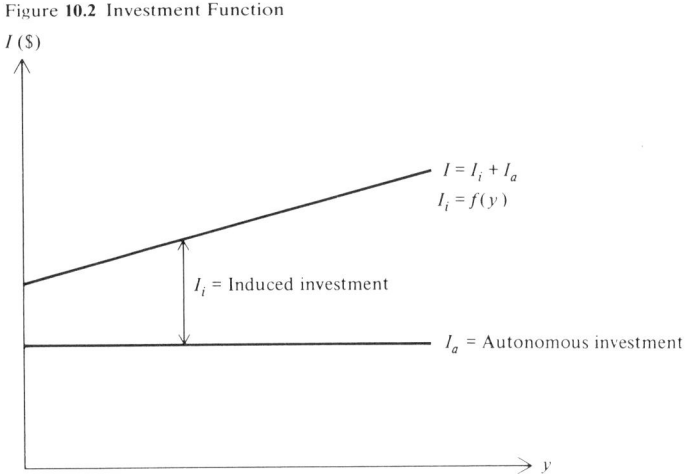

Keynes' behavioral equations thus far merely inform us of the shape of these functions before the actual action of saving (consuming) and investing takes place. Economists refer to this willingness to save or invest before the act as *ex ante* saving to distinguish it from *ex post* saving and investment that actually takes place. (See Figure 10.3.) The precise amount saved (consumed) and invested at a point in time is jointly determined by the intersection of the savings and investment schedules (or the consumption and investment schedules), just as the precise amount sold in a market is determined jointly by the demand and supply for a commodity.

Figure **10.3** *Ex post* Savings and Investment

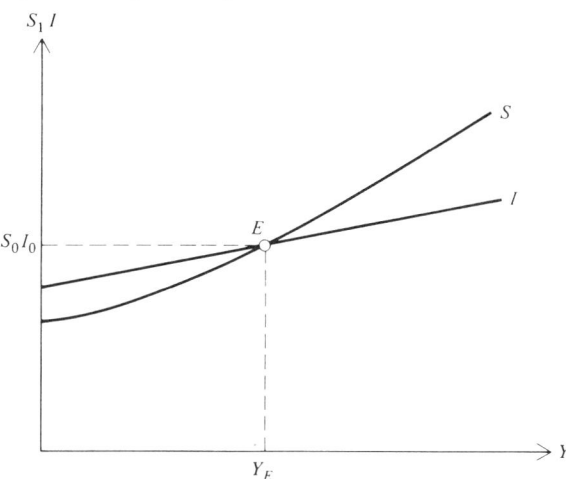

S_0, I_0 are the *ex post* amounts of savings and investments

The simplified Keynesian model is now completed. The equilibrium level of national income, Y_E, determined by the savings and investment schedules, may or may not be of a size sufficient to maintain full employment. As stated above, the level of the national income (output) determines the size of the work force, but there is no a priori reason to assume that Y_E will always be of a magnitude that will provide full employment. If Y_F is the full-employment national income, Y_E may equal, be larger, or be less than Y_F.

In Figure 10.4, I_1 intersects the savings function at E_1. In this instance, we have an underemployment equilibrium, and an unemployed work force equal to the number of workers necessary to produce output ($Y_{E_F} - Y_{E_1}$). If, perhaps through government action, the investment schedule suddenly moved up to I_2, we should have an overemployment equilibrium. At Y_{E_2}, there is full employment, but at an inflationary level. Because the output in goods and services at Y_F and Y_{E_2} are the same, the inflation is measured by the difference in the money national income, $Y_{E_2} - Y_F$.

Although Keynesian theory can handle under- and overemployment equilibria equally well, the demonstration of the possible existence of an *under*employment equilibrium was the major point of the employment model. Almost equally significant was the role assigned to sav-

Figure **10.4** The Simplified Keynesian Model

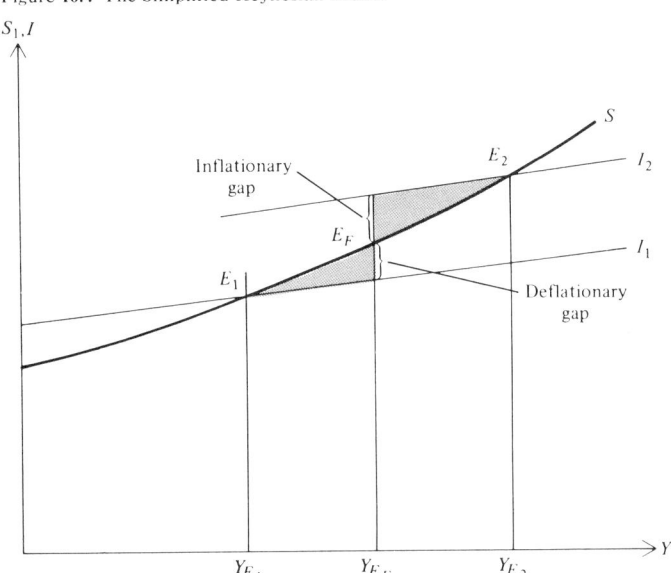

ing, which now became the enemy, not the foundation, of economic welfare. In the classical and neoclassical models, people saved only to invest. The circulation of goods and money in the classical model could easily be represented by a Quesnay-type diagram, as shown in Figure 10.5.

In the Keynesian model, the connection between savings and investment is severed. One group of people saves, another invests. The money saved may or may not be reintroduced into the economy. If it is not reintroduced, the circulatory flow is reduced, very much along the lines first sketched out by Quesnay, until *ex ante* savings and investment are equal.

The sudden emergence of savings as the culprit in the economic decline of the West provided additional arguments and intellectual respectability to the various egalitarian and radical movements of the 1930s. The purchasing power argument of the labor unions received for the first time the intellectual rationale Marxism could not provide; similarly, liberal forces in England and America, which had favored the redistribution of income for philosophical reasons, could now rely on economic arguments to strengthen their case. Keynes'

Figure **10.5** Economic Flow Models

Classical Model

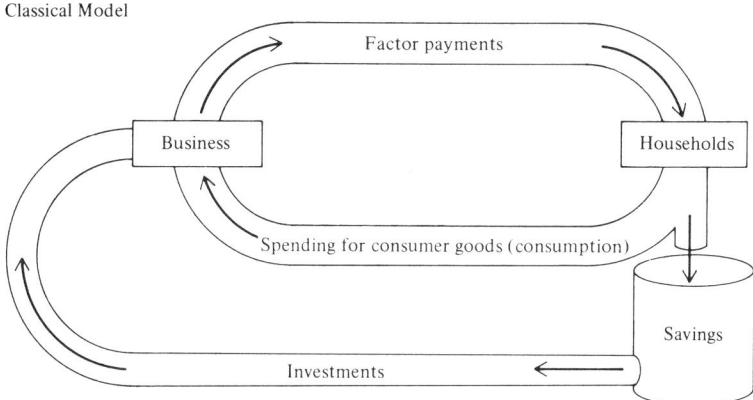

Keynesian Model

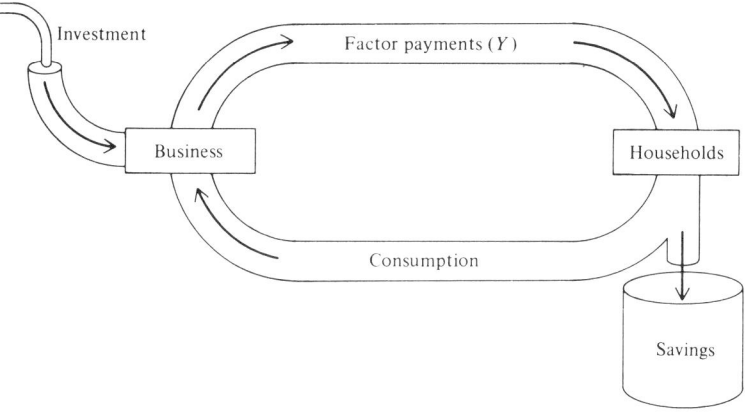

essentially conservative position was thrown into a radical light by liberal-radical groups in the United States and the United Kingdom who grasped the timeliness of the employment model. Keynes himself seemed less interested in achieving full employment by redistributing income and thus lowering the savings function than by increasing investment through government spending.

Keynes' advocacy of massive government spending received strong theoretical support from R. F Kahn, an "economists' economist," whose major contributions to the scholarly output of the post-Marshallian Cambridge school have been mostly hidden away in numerous footnotes.[14] Kahn had traced the effects of increases in investment on employment and concluded that the final net increase in employment would be a multiple of the employment produced by the original investment increment. Keynes merely expressed the multiplying effects of investment in terms of its impact on income rather than on employment. If the economy operates at an underemployment equilibrium, an increase in net investment of, say, $1,000,000 will employ an equivalent amount of unemployed labor and resources. This will be an extra $1,000,000 income added to the economy, and would appear immediately as a $1,000,000 increment in the national income statistics. The consequences of this initial increment have not ended yet, however. The recipients of this initial $1,000,000—workers, farmers, shopkeepers, and businessmen—would spend a certain amount and save the rest. If we assumed that the society's marginal propensity to consume is $4/5$—that is, at a given level of national income this society consumes $4/5$ and saves $1/5$ of each increment in national income—then the households of the income recipients will spend $800,000 (i.e., $4/5$ of $1,000,000) and save $200,000. The $800,000 spent, however, constitutes an additional income increment of which, again, the society will spend $4/5$ and save $1/5$. We have, therefore, a spending process in which continuously $4/5$ of each income increment will be spent. This process could be expressed mathematically as a geometric series:

$$1,000,000 + 4/5 \,(1,000,000) + (4/5)^2 \,(1,000,000)$$
$$+ \ldots + (4/5)^n \,(1,000,000) \ldots .$$

We know that the sum of an infinite geometrical series $1 + r + r^2 + \ldots + r^n + \ldots$ is $1/(1 - r)$ if r is less than one. In the present example, $r = MPC = 4/5$; hence the sum of this geometric series equals $1/(1 - 4/5) = 5$. Therefore an investment increment of $1,000,000 can set in motion a "chain reaction" that could theoretically lead to a fivefold increase in national income, provided the economy had a marginal propensity to consume of $4/5$.

[14]Aside from Keynes and Kahn, the most prominent members of the "Cambridge School" were N. Austin, C. W. Guilleband, N. Kaldor, D. H. Robertson, Joan Robinson, and P. Sraffa. The Cambridge group was an exceptionally tightly knit group where lengthy oral discussions preceded the written work of individual members. Schumpeter, for instance, believes that R. F. Kahn's contribution to Keynes' intellectual development made him a virtual co-author of the *General Theory.*

If the marginal propensity to consume (i.e., the slope of the consumption function) measures the amount consumed out of an additional income increment, the marginal propensity to save (*MPS*) is defined as 1 - *MPC*, and the "multiplier" becomes merely the inverse of the *MPS*, the marginal propensity to save. A high consumption economy will have a high "multiplier," and full employment can be obtained by a comparatively small increment in total investment spending. A high savings economy, within the framework of this analysis, is much more "insensitive" to changes in investment, and it is, therefore, much more difficult to move it from one equilibrium level to another. Expressed differently, a high savings economy is a much more stable economy, which is only undesirable if the economy operates at an underemployment equilibrium. In turn, the instability of a high consumption economy has dangerous implications if the economy, operating at or below a full employment equilibrium, is confronted with a decrease in net investment spending.

The two-sidedness of the income-employment multiplier attracted little attention during the 1930s. The Kahn-Keynes multiplier concept appeared above all as an impressive theoretical justification for increasing government spending to escape from the existing underemployment equilibrium. The immediate operational usefulness of the multiplier concept obscured its broader theoretical implications. Keynes himself, however, demonstrated the true nature of the multiplier concept in his little-noticed *How to Pay for the War.*[15]

An important recognition of the multiplier concept as a positive feedback appeared in Arnold Tustin's *The Mechanism of Economic Systems.*[16] In an economic system, just as in engineering or biological systems, the feedback occurs as a special form of sequential dependence among variables, as shown in Figure 10.6. The successive quantities Q_1, Q_2, Q_3, Q_4 measure a controlled variable at several stages in an economic or technical process; the k_{ij}s are the "factors of dependence" between successive Q_is and Q_js. In the absence of a feedback, for example, $Q_2 = k_{12}Q_1$, where Q_2 might be the level of spending at time t_2, if Q_1 is the spending level at time t_1, and k_{12} is

[15]John Maynard Keynes, *How to Pay for the War* (New York: Harcourt Brace Jovanovich, 1940). This work, together with the "General Theory of Employment," constitutes the mature, post-*General Theory* Keynes.

[16]Tustin, *The Mechanism of Economic Systems*, (Cambridge, Mass.: Harvard University Press, 1953).

a factor of proportionality. If we refer to the feedback circuit of Figure 10.6, we obtain the following results:

$$Q_2 = k_{12}Q_1 + k_{32}Q_3$$

but

$$Q_3 = k_{23}Q_2$$

therefore

$$\frac{Q_2}{Q_1} = k_{12} \times \frac{1}{1 - k_{23}k_{32}} = k_{12} \frac{1}{1 - \lambda}$$

where $\lambda = k_{23}k_{32}$ is the feedback coefficient for the complete closed loop. The Keynesian multiplier r is merely a special case of a feed-

Figure **10.6** The General Case of a Single Feedback System [17]

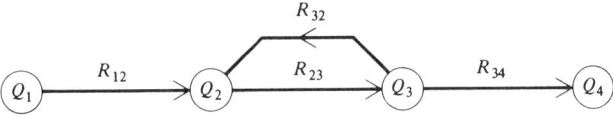

back coefficient. If ΔY is the net increment in national income and ΔI the increase in investment, $\Delta Y = \Delta I \,|1/(1 - r)|$ and $1/(1 - r)$ is identical with the general feedback notation $1/(1 - \lambda)$. As a matter of fact, Tustin pointed out that "an electric generator that is partly but not wholly self-exciting satisfied relationships identical in form with those in Keynes's model. . . . Perhaps in this electric age, the conventional metaphor of 'priming the pump' might be dropped in favor of 'exciting the dynamo.'"[17]

The Kahn-Keynes multiplier concept, therefore, is merely a special use of a dependence relationship that had already been thoroughly investigated and precisely formulated in biology and engineering. Even in economics, the multiplier concept was not entirely revolu-

[17]*Ibid.*, p. 7.

tionary. Wicksell, Myrdal, and especially Lundberg[18] recognized the "multiplier effect" of investment increments, and the popular notion of government spending as a pump-priming effort rested upon a intuitive awareness of the multiplier effect. It must again be emphasized, however, that most of the technical and all of the popular discussions during the 1930s dealt merely with the multiplying effects of additional government and private investment; those of reduced investment were neglected.

The multiplier concept became, therefore, powerful theoretical justification for direct government investment in public works. Because the effectiveness of governmment spending was increased if the country had a low propensity to save, saving was to be discouraged. The *General Theory* provided post facto justification for many New Deal reforms and strengthened the intellectual position of the anti-Communist left throughout the West. The enthusiastic response of the liberal left to the *General Theory* — especially the multiplier and propensity to consume concepts—hid the essentially neutral nature of the Keynesian methodology and delayed the recognition of the inherent conservative position of Keynes himself.

The political neutrality of the Keynesian policy recommendations was clearly exemplified by the success of Hjalmar Schacht's policies in Germany during the 1930s. Schacht, president of the Reichsbank and de facto director of the German economy, sprang from the same group of technocrat-bankers that had produced Lederer and Hahn; he managed to retain the confidence of German business and attained full employment by relying heavily on government spending and tax incentives to increase the total investment function.[19] Similarly, we find a ready acceptance of Keynesian concepts by European businessmen and postwar governments, regardless of their political convictions. In *How to Pay for the War*, Keynes urged governments to increase savings and reduce consumption by a deflationary fiscal

---

[18]Eric Lundberg's *Studies in the Theory of Economic Expansion*, 1937 (New York: Kelley & Millman, 1955) was a technically highly sophisticated study, in which the multiplier effect was integrated into a sequential analysis. Lundberg's work appeared a year after the *General Theory*, but presented the culmination of years of research.

[19]K. W. Rothschild, in "Some Recent Trends in the Literature of German Economics," *American Economic Review Supplement*, 54 (March 1964), emphasized the isolation of German economics during the years 1933-1945. This isolation applied much more to university teaching than to the work of established scholars and researchers. Banks and research institutes continued to receive Anglo-American journals throughout this period, routinely up to 1939, via Sweden and Switzerland during the war. Certainly, Schacht and the Reichsbank were not cut off from the Keynesian revolution.

policy.[20] In the United Kingdom, both Conservative and Labour governments have repeatedly used the new orthodoxy of Keynesian fiscal policies to inflate the economy and encourage growth.

The operational effect of the "employment model" has suffered from neglecting the role of business expectations in a capitalistic society. Just as in the 1930s the prevailing pessimism among businessmen retarded economic recovery, similarly the anticipation of continued inflation greatly hampered the effectiveness of deflationary fiscal policies in the United States and Great Britain in the late 1960s and early 1970s. The definition of the investment process given in the employment model disregarded time lags and grossly oversimplified the significant psychological role business expectations played in formulating investment policies. Business investment was not merely affected by changes in national income and technology, and Keynes himself developed in the *General Theory* a complex methodology to analyze business investment behavior. Most of his analysis of business expectations, treated below, never had any significant impact upon the broader public, nor has it proved to be operationally significant. One year after the publication of the *General Theory,* Keynes refined and emphasized the entire question of risk and profit expectations in a masterful article in the *Quarterly Journal of Economics.*[21] Keynes argued that it was impossible to form a scientific basis for long-run expectation. Businessmen and technocrats pretend to behave rationally by assuming (1) that the present is a "serviceable guide" to the future; (2) that the existing prices are based on "correct summing up of future prospects"; (3) that our own judgment is worthless, but that the rest of the world is better informed; hence we are guided by "conventional" judgment. Keynes stressed that all three assumptions were very weak and that opinions formed by conventional judgment are subject to sudden and violent changes."

The practice of calmness and immobility, of certainty and security, suddenly breaks down. New fears and hopes will, without warning, take charge of human conduct. The forces of disillusion may suddenly impose a new conventional basis of valuation. *All these pretty polite techniques, made for a*

---

[20]A deflationary fiscal policy would produce treasury surpluses, encourage savings, and discourage consumption. These recommendations were the complete opposite of those proposed in the *General Theory.*

[21]Keynes, "General Theory of Employment," *Quarterly Journal of Economics,* Vol. 51 (1936-1937), pp. 209-223.

well-paneled board room and a nicely regulated market, are liable to collapse. At all times, the vague and unreasoned hopes are not really lulled and lie but a little way below the surface.[22]

Keynes was skeptical of economists' attempts to analyze entrepreneurial anticipations. Because rational long-run expectations do not exist, and all but the shortest short-term expectations are too unstable to be of use to any rational calculus, the very simplified "employment model" takes on a new meaning. It is no longer merely a simplified, popularized version of the Keynesian model, but by its very short time horizon it becomes really the only operational aspect of his entire model. Keynes himself was not able to reconcile his criticism of economists' naive attempts to deal with business expectations and uncertainty with the significant role interest and profit anticipation played in his own *General Theory.* He was never able to resolve the inherent contradiction between the role he assigned to "expectations" in his *General Theory* and the indeterminateness of long-run business decision-making described in the 1937 *Journal* article. Keynes approached the ideological problem from a different point of view. From his work on probability, he moved slowly toward a crucial insight that uncertainty was the basic consideration underlying economics. It was the uncertainty of timing, decision making, consumption, and investment—and particularly the ambiguities, ambivalences, and irrationalities of human personality and behavior that made the neoclassical structure meaningless.[23] From this interpretation he developed the concepts of the marginal propensities of consumption and saving, the linkage of the multiplier and accelerator principles, the nature of private investment, the necessity for fiscal and monetary policies, and the dangers of bureaucratizing the economic system. Because of the overwhelming predominance of uncertainty, one could manage the economy only in macro terms. Rather than individual demand, we would have to consider aggregate demand; in place of individual consumption and investment, we would have to measure overall consumption and investment, and so on. The most accurate measurement could only be mathematical probability. Each step led Keynes further away from Marshall, his teacher.

[22]*Ibid.,* p. 215 (Italics ours.)
[23]Cf., especially, Keynes' "General Theory of Employment" for an emphatic discussion of the role of uncertainty in classical and Keynesian economics.

The Complete Keynesian Model: A Brief Summary

Basically, the *General Theory* postulates three determinants of national income: consumption, or more precisely the marginal propensity to consume, the marginal efficiency of capital, and the rate of interest. It is the role of the interest rate that makes the formal relationship between income and its determinants more complex than it is in the employment model.

Because the marginal efficiency of capital is determined by the interest rate i as well as by exogenous forces, we can describe the structure of the model by three equations:

(1) $$Y = f_1(C, i, I)$$

(2) $$I = f_2(i, Y)$$

(3) $$M = f_3(i, Y)$$

where Y = national income, C = consumption, i = rate of interest, I = investment (it is considered as "given" in our initial discussion), and M = the amount of money (currency and bank deposits) held by the public.

1. $Y = f_1(C, i)$: If we recall that Keynes defined total income as equal to total output, we recognize that income saved rather than consumed and production invested rather than consumed must equal. We therefore obtain the two equations for national income, which are already obvious from Figures 10.1a and 10.1b.

(1.1) $$Y = C + I$$

(1.2) $$Y = C + S$$

and therefore

(1.3) $$I = S$$

Does equation (1.3) contradict our previous discussion and diagrams, which showed merely that savings and investment were equal (intersect) at a unique point, and hence are unequal everywhere else? Not at all. Our diagrams of the saving and investment *schedules* showed the generally unequal amounts of saving and investment decisions people are willing to make at various levels of national income. Our national income accounting requires that the amounts actually saved must equal the amount actually invested. If *ex ante* saving is larger than *ex ante* investment, the national income will fall to the point where *ex ante* saving equals *ex ante* investing. During this process *ex post* saving and *ex post* investment will always remain equal because involuntary increases in inventory are defined as investment.

If we assume, for example, that the economy is in equilibrium, business will carry a certain amount of inventory necessary for the given level of transactions. A sudden change in psychological behavior may prompt a sufficient number of people to increase their *ex ante* saving by one billion dollars. This will immediately result in a one billion dollar increase in total inventory held by business; the increased saving (decreased consumption) is offset by an increase in involuntary investment. (See Figure 10.7.) The inventory increase will prompt businessmen to reduce production to bring inventory in line with the new spending level. The resulting layoffs will reduce both national and personal income, saving and investment, and will once more equate *ex ante* (intended) savings and *ex ante* investments.

The equality of *ex post* savings and *ex post* investments as "definitional equalities" hides the true meaning of the $S = I$ identity, which epitomizes the underconsumption aspect of the Keynesian model, because in a mature economy the ever-rising propensity to save presents the most serious danger to economic stability.

So far, this exposition has merely been a more detailed version of the income-consumption-saving relationship, discussed above as the simplified "employment model" and expressed in the equation

Figure **10.7** Inventory and Investment

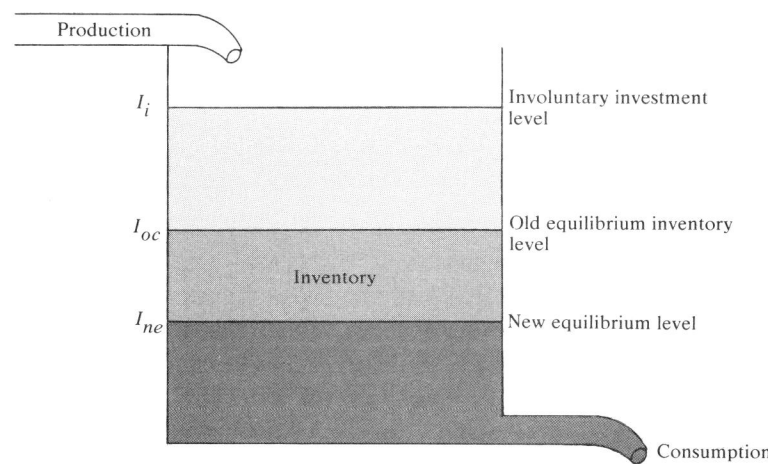

$Y = f_1(C)$. In the complete Keynesian model, however, the interest rate plays a significant role in determining income through its impact on investment; the mechanics of the relationship $Y = f_1(C, i)$ are discussed below.

2. Investment as a function of net profit: In the "employment model," we first assumed that investment was determined exogenously by the existence of technological investment opportunities and subsequently by changes in national income. In the complete *General Theory of Employment, Interest and Money* model, this relationship becomes more complicated. Defining net profit as the difference between gross profit and' interest payments, we can see that anything that will increase this difference will increase investment and, ultimately, national income.

Gross profit is a function of the marginal efficiency of capital, which, in turn, is affected by *new* technological innovations, *new* population, and *new* increases in national income. The interest rate, however, is determined by the liquidity preference and the amount of money generated by the banking system. [We are now looking more closely at the ramifications of equations (2) and (3) on p. 320, which express implicitly the relationships determining the marginal efficiency of capital and the interest rates.]

Because investment is affected by the exogenous and often random events of technological innovations, we can expect investment to fluctuate with business anticipation. The interest rate, however, is determined by the liquidity preference (L) and the amount of money held (M).

In classical theory, interest was a reward for saving, and the amounts actually saved rather than consumed rose and fell with the interest rate, which always equated saving and investment. In the Keynesian model, the interest rate is a payment for not holding cash for speculative and other reasons. Depending on the anticipated fluctuations of asset prices, savers will hold varying proportions of their wealth in liquid or asset form. A rise in the interest rate, *ceteris paribus*, will prompt the savers to transfer a part of their cash holding into stocks or bonds. The same rise in the interest rate will reduce both the marginal efficiency of capital and net profits.

In the discussion of the simplified theory of employment, we disregarded the interest rate as a determinant of investment, and drew one investment schedule (see Figure 10.2.) as the sum of autonomous and "induced" investment. In terms of the complete Keynesian model, we should have drawn a three-dimensional diagram with a family of investment surfaces plotted against investment, national income and interest rate.

If we return to equations (1), (2), and (3) on page 320, we note that the interest rate appears in each one. Keynes, who first attacked the enormous equilibrating role which the interest rate had to play in the neoclassical model, required in the end an almost equally demanding task from the interest rate in his own model. Though in the Keynesian model the interest rate merely equates the supply of money generated by the banking system with the amount the public is willing to hold, the interest rate affects, indirectly, net profits and hence investment and income. There is little empirical evidence, however, to substantiate the role Keynes assigned to the interest rate, especially if the Keynesian model is made more dynamic by making investment and consumption dependent on the income of the previous period. The operational difficulties in applying Keynesian policies, however, have their roots in the political complexities of mature capitalistic democracies. The significance of the interest rate pales by comparison, and the "employment model" becomes operationally more effective because of its very simplicity.

The New Economics: Criticism and Consequences

More than thirty years have passed since Keynes published his *General Theory of Employment, Interest and Money*.[24] To measure the vast changes in economics before and after the *General Theory* is to cross another of the great intellectual divides—from medieval economics to mercantilism, from mercantilism to classical economics, and from neoclassical economics to the New Economics. Like the other economic "revolutions," the Keynesian model was not a sharp break with the past. Some of Keynes' most ardent critics claimed that there was nothing at all original in his formulation. The reception of the *General Theory* provoked as much intellectual disdain as it did enthusiasm. Pigou, Hawtrey, D. H. Robertson, and even his close friend Roy Harrod, initially had grave misgiving over the manuscript; they feared that Keynes was merely pouring old wine into new bottles and labeling the bottles with clever-sounding names. Within a decade

[24]John Maynard Keynes, *The General Theory of Employment, Interest and Money* (London: Macmillan, 1946).

every major economist in the Western world had come to grips with the basic question Keynes had perceptively reformulated. The breadth and depth of the debate made the Keynesian analysis truly revolutionary. The *General Theory* marked the opening salvos rather than the *Treatise on Money*,[25] in which so much of Keynes' later thinking had already been embedded. The *General Theory* was difficult to read because it represented Keynes' struggle to free himself from neoclassical anachronisms. Keynes had to convince first himself, then his colleagues. Only later would the politicians, policy makers, businessmen, bankers, and the man in the street be able to follow across the narrow bridge he had built between a capitalist system that had been shaken to its economic foundations and a capitalist system that could free man from his age-old dependence on scarcity and insecurity.

I have called this book *The General Theory of Employment, Interest and Money*, placing the emphasis on the prefix general. The object of such a title is to contrast the character of my arguments and conclusions with those of the *classical* theory of the subject, upon which I was brought up and which dominates the economic thought, both practical and theoretical of the governing and academic classes of this generation, as it has for a hundred years past. I shall argue that the postulates of the classical theory are applicable to a special case only and not to the general case. . . . Moreover, the characteristics of the special case assumed by the classical theory happen not to be those of the economic society in which we actually live, with the result that its teaching is misleading and disastrous if we attempt to apply it to the facts of experience.[26]

No twentieth-century economist had a more orthodox and traditional intellectual upbringing than Keynes. Rooted in Cambridge but forced to grow in many directions, his genius flourished. It was a noble and generous mind that started off the *General Theory* with

This book is chiefly addressed to my fellow economists. I hope that it will be intelligible to others. But its main purpose is to deal with difficult questions of theory. . . . For if orthodox economics is at fault, the error is

---

[25] John Maynard Keynes, *A Treatise on Money*, 2 vols. (London and New York: Harcourt Brace Jovanovich, 1930).

[26] Keynes, *General Theory*, p. 3.

to be found not in the superstructure, which has been erected with great care for logical consistency, but in a lack of clearness and of generality in the premises. Thus I cannot achieve my object of persuading economists to reexamine critically certain of their basic assumptions except by a highly abstract argument and also by much controversy. I wish there could have been less of the latter. . . . Those who are strongly wedded to what I shall call "the Classical theory" will fluctuate, I expect, between a belief that I am quite wrong and a belief that I am saying nothing new. . . . I myself held with conviction for many years the theories which I now attack, and I am not, I think, ignorant of their strong points.

The matters at issue are of an importance which cannot he exaggerated. But, if my explanations are right, it is my fellow economists, not the general public, whom I must first convince. At this state of the argument the general public, though welcome at the debate, are only eavesdroppers at an attempt by an economist to bring to an issue the deep divergences of opinion between fellow economists which have for the time being almost destroyed the practical influence of economic theory, and will, until they are resolved, continue to do so.[27]

No writer has more clearly discussed the psychic turbulence in economic theory in the post-World War I period than Shackle in his brilliant *The Years of High Theory.* The finest minds in economics were deeply disturbed over the state of the art and were groping for new formulations.

The Great Theory constructed by Walras, Pareto, Jevons, Menger, Marshall, Wichsteed, Wicksell and John Bates Clark was in some sense a calculus of scarcity for the use of perfectly informed economic man, whose society, because of his perfect knowledge, had no need for storable general purchasing power, only for an accounting unit. The theory of employment and general output, which emerged from the work of Wicksell, Keynes, Kahn, Joan Robinson, Harrod, Hicks, Meade, Kalecki and Lerner, and from that of Myrdal, Lindahl and Lundberg, with aid and refinement from Ragnar Frisch, Alvin Hansen, Paul Samuelson, Nicholas Kaldor and others; was an account of the consequences of the natural and ultimately unavoidable lack of information suffered by human decision-makers.[28]

[27]*Ibid.,* p. 5.
[28]G. L. S. Shackle, *The Years of High Theory* (Cambridge: Cambridge University Press, 1967), pp. 290-291.

Though many economists, particularly the brilliant Swede Wicksell, were searching for explanations similar to those that ultimately appeared in the *General Theory,* none had an impact on public awareness and policy as great as Keynes. The measure of Keynes' significance lies everywhere about us—in the use of national income accounting by every government, every major industry, and every large financial institution; in the acceptance of national accounts terminology as part of our normal day-to-day language; in the conscious application of Keynesian theory over the past four decades. Although Keynes was the prophet of doom during the depression years of the 1920s and 1930s, in the long run, because of Keynesian policies, modified capitalistic economies have shown unbelievable strengths and flexibilities.

Alvin Hansen, professor of economics at Harvard, deserves the credit for being the first major American economist to recognize Keynes' contribution. Deeply distressed by the immensity of the depression of the 1930s, Hansen found the comforting explanation of the American past useless. The great stimulating forces of the frontier, of immigration, and of striking innovations like the railroads were past. We had entered, he feared, a "mature phase of capitalist development in which net saving at full employment tends to grow, whereas net investment at full employment tends to fall."[29] Indeed, if this were so, the danger of "secular stagnation" and chronic unemployment seemed almost an inevitable and permanent part of our future. We could not look forward to a gentle plateauing of economic life, which John Stuart Mill predicted, but to economic stagnation characterized by "sick recoveries which die in their infancy and depressions which feed on themselves and leave a hard and seemingly unmovable core of unemployment."[30] In his books and in his seminars, Hansen replaced neoclassical doctrines with Keynesian analysis and became a leading force in bringing the Keynesian revolution to the American graduate schools.

Keynes' admirers and critics agreed, however, that his model was essentially static. It was Roy Harrod, one of Keynes' closest friends, and ultimately his official biographer, and Evsey Domar, a fine Amer-

[29]Alvin H. Hansen, *Full Recovery or Stagnation?* (New York: Norton, 1938); *Fiscal Policy and Business Cycles* (New York: Norton, 1941); "Growth or Stagnation in the American Economy," *Review of Economics and Statistics,* 26; 54 (November 1954), 409-414.

[30]Hansen, *Fiscal Policy and Business Cycles,* p. 353.

ican mathematical economist, who provided the reformulation that made the Keynesian model dynamic. So close was their thinking that their work in this particular area is linked together and usually referred to as the Harrod-Domar model.[31] Like a great many other economists, these men asked the two crucial questions: (1) What were the requirements to maintain a steady growth of full-employment income without deflation or inflation? (2) Could national income grow at a rate sufficient to maintain full employment but without incurring inflation? At the center of the problem of steady growth is the level of investment. Investment generates income but at the same time inevitably increases the productive capacity of the economy. What will society do with this increment? Depending on the behavior of income (especially the propensity to consume), this increased capacity can result, positively, in greater output and a rise in real income or, negatively, in greater unemployment and a fall in real income. Left to itself, the economy may randomly choose either alternative, but most likely because of structural defects it will tend toward deflation and unemployment. However, we need not passively accept depressions. Statistically we can determine the conditions necessary for the behavior of income that will sustain a full-employment economy and fully utilize the increased capital productive capacity. By measuring and regulating the size of the multiplier and the productivity of the new investments, equilibrium at full-employment levels and at full utilization of capital stock can be achieved and sustained. The chronic ups and downs of the capitalist business cycle can be replaced by a steady advance whose only aberrations would be the failure of fiscal and monetary policies to reconcile the actual rate of growth, which the unrestrained forces of a free economy will generate, with the warranted rate of growth, which is essential for full employment and full utilization of capital stock.[32] Inflation and deflation are human errors. In place of either a romantic roller-coaster business cycle or a violent Marxist catastrophe, we have a model for a dynamic economy, though an economy that must be continuously kept in balance, hopefully by "bureaucrats [and economists] who hate their jobs."[33]

In 1948, Professor Paul Samuelson of the Massachusetts Institute

---

[31]For an excellent summary, see Gerald M. Meier and Robert E. Baldwin, *Economic Development: Theory, History, Policy* (New York: Wiley, 1957), pp. 101-112.

[32]Socialist economists have become increasingly aware that output fluctuations can also occur in Socialist economics.

[33]Even Keynes realized that this assumption might not be relevant.

of Technology published his first edition of *Principles of Economics.* This elementary text marked a crucial shift in the economics education of millions of Americans. Although later editions have added more traditional chapters, this book and its many imitations have made Americans thoroughly familiar with Keynesian economics. More than any other work, it transformed America's economic outlook.

1. Whatever the individual's motivation to save, it usually has little to do with society's investment opportunities. . . .

2. Unless proper policies are pursued, a laissez-faire economy cannot guarantee that there will be exactly the required amount of investment to ensure full employment, not too little so as to cause unemployment, nor too much so as to cause inflation. As far as total investment or money-spending power is concerned, the laissez-faire system is without a good thermostat. For decades, there might tend to be too little investment leading to deflation, losses, excess capacity, unemployment, and destitution. For other years or decades, there might tend to be too much investment leading to periods of chronic inflation—unless prudent and proper policies in the fiscal (i e., tax and expenditure) and monetary (i.e., Federal Reserve System central bank) fields are followed.[34]

No one has adequately studied the reception of Keynesian ideology into the American economic environment. Arthur Schlesinger Jr.'s comment that the second New Deal was largely Keynesian is grossly overstated. Because of the severity of the Great Depression, a large number of American economists were working out pragmatic solutions to problems of unemployment, government spending, and budget deficits, and at times were drawing close to the same conclusions Keynes had assembled in the *General Theory.*

Although college students were beginning to learn the New Economics, the older generation lagged behind. World War II delayed any real economic discussion. War mobilization erased unemployment, excess plant capacity, economic indecision, and ideological confusion. During the 1930s, businessmen had cowered in storm shelters, afraid in their inmost hearts that Marx indeed had been correct—that the capitalist system was shattering itself in one great *Götterdämmerung.* Arrogant government bureaucrats who swarmed over

[34]Paul Samuelson, *Economics, an Introductory Analysis,* 1st ed. (New York: McGraw-Hill, 1948), p. 213.

Washington in the 1930s, in turn, made businessmen feel that they had some horrible infectious disease. At the depth of the depression Keynes wrote President Roosevelt:

Businessmen have a different set of delusions from politicians; and need, therefore, different handling. . . . You could do anything you liked with them, if you would treat them (even the big ones) not as wolves and tigers, but as domestic animals by nature, even though they have been badly brought up and not trained as you would wish. It is a mistake to think that they are more immoral than the politicians. If you work them into the surly, obstinate, terrified mood of which domestic animals wrongly handled are so capable, the nation's burdens will not get carried to market; and in the end, public opinion will veer their way.[35]

During World War II, American businessmen could operate without external criticism or morbid introspection. Millions of planes, thousands of boats, almost legendary amounts of war goods rolled off assembly lines and out of factories. This was the kind of game that businessmen liked to play: a market that could not be oversupplied, where there was no chance of failure, and where the nation paid dutiful homage to their great achievements. The war brought back to businessmen their confidence, and restored American capitalism much more significantly than New Deal ambivalent policies. These war years demonstrated what businessmen could really do if the environment could provide the conditions under which they could function without fear of failure. Yet, there was a subtle but important change. For over a century, businessmen had assumed that prosperity was largely determined by the axioms of a laissez faire, free enterprise structure. World War II laid the basis for the acceptance of Keynesian thinking by important segments of the business community. Most would not fully grasp the shift in emphasis for another decade, but it became clear that Keynesian theory could easily explain the achievements of wartime American economic growth.

After World War II, businessmen operated in a strange intellectual and emotional environment. For many of them their hearts still lay in a pre-1929 romantic never-never land. In practical terms, they made their peace quickly. Whatever lip service they felt they owed

---

[35]Robert Lekachman, *The Age of Keynes* (New York: Random House, 1966), p. 122.

the past, they accepted as working principles the formulation of $Y = C + I + G$, in which G (government) would play the decisive role in determining the conditions under which economic activity would take place. Basically, the concern shifted from whether government had a role in the economy to the more realistic problem of determining the degree and kind of government participation. The questions of postwar America were not easier economic questions but they were more realistic. To a large degree, Americans marched slowly toward a healthier, less mythological economic literacy. The journey is not over, but the levels of both debate and action have moved forward significantly.

Since the war, there have been five recessions in the United States — 1948-1949, 1953-1954, 1957-1958, 1960-1961, 1969-1971. In each case, the government stepped in to play a decisive role. All of Eisenhower's instincts in 1958 made him sympathetic to the "conventional wisdom" of the 1920s, but his brilliant intuitive grasp of complex situations led him to adopt de facto Keynesian policies. Some critics at the time (particularly the Democratic opposition in Congress) argued that Eisenhower relied far too heavily on monetary policy during the recession (i.e., lower interest rates and easing of credit), and that he missed the opportunity to expand growth by increased government spending. Yet in 1959, after the recession, the federal government ran the largest peacetime budget deficit in American history.[36] By Keynesian standards, unemployment remained too high (over 5 percent) and the full potential for economic growth had not been advanced. Eisenhower was, however, more concerned with the problem of inflation.

The victory of Keynesian economics in the universities was translated into a "new orthodoxy" in Western economic policy, which contributed to the high employment and high growth rate of the west European and Anglo-American economies during the 1950s and early 1960s. By the early 1960s, full employment had become the "normal" state of affairs, and increasing attention was paid to the inflationary forces that accompanied the growing wealth of the democratic, Keynesian West. The destabilizing effects of inflationary price movements were aggravated by balance of payments difficulties, which were particularly severe in the United Kingdom and, later, in the United

---

[36]In 1971, the Nixon Administration exceeded the deficit of the Eisenhower Administration.

States. Keynesian economics prescribe antiinflationary measures which were merely the reversal of the antideflationary measures, and ought to have been equally effective.[37] However, the deflationary measures of the new orthodoxy—budget surpluses, higher taxes, especially sales taxes, and spending cuts—were politically unpopular and especially difficult to apply in American circumstances, where Congress has to face the voters every two years. The United States experienced, especially during the years 1967-1971, largely because of the war in Vietnam, grave difficulties in restraining inflation. First the unwillingness, and then the delay in applying the classical Keynesian prescriptions of tax increases and expenditure cuts strengthened the inflationary forces to such an extent that even a combination of severe fiscal *and* monetary measures could not halt price inflation, although they did increase unemployment. The successful application of an antiinflationary Keynesian policy required a sophisticated, quick acting, decision mechanism which the American political system could not provide, especially in the face of the unpopularity of "orthodox" Keynesian deflationary policy. In addition, the price rigidities that have prevailed in the American (and all other Western) economies as a result of corporate and union market power had not been sufficiently considered by Keynesian economists. Although it can be easily understood why Keynes did not pay more attention to questions of market structure and price policies during the 1930s, these price rigidities have impeded programs to cool the economy, especially because the full-employment policies of British and American governments have fostered an anticipation of continuous price increases by management and labor.

The inability of Anglo-American governments to provide steady growth without inflation produced a certain disenchantment with the new orthodoxy during the late 1960s, and Milton Friedman, the chief critic of Keynesian economics, seized the opportunity to present his views before a suddenly very attentive audience of economists, businessmen, and government officials.

Professor Friedman is a technically brilliant economist who has made significant contributions to mathematical economics, economic history, and monetary economics.[38] Until quite recently he had a

---

[37]See especially Keynes, *How to Pay for the War.*

[38]Milton Friedman and Anna F. Schwartz, *Monetary History of the U.S.* (Princeton: Princeton University Press, 1963); Friedman, *A Program for Monetary Stability* (New York: Fordham University Press, 1959).

difficult time in obtaining a hearing, and as a born debater and pamphleteer, he has frequently overstated his case. Briefly, Friedman holds that:

1. Monetary policy has been neglected as a countercyclical device in recent years.
2. Fiscal policy—that is, Keynesian policy—is much less effective than equivalent monetary measures, which would affect the quantity of money in circulation. Specifically, the reason for the post-World War II prosperity "is not because of the positive virtue of the fine tuning [i.e., countercyclical policy] that has been followed, but because we have avoided the major mistakes of the inter-war period. Those major mistakes were the *occasionally severe deflations* of the money stock."[39]
3. Monetary and fiscal policies are both unable to smooth minor business cycles (Friedman calls this "fine tuning"). Hence an automatic policy that would increase the quantity of money a certain percentage each year would be very much superior to the ineffective efforts of the Federal Reserve Bank and the Council of Economic Advisers, especially if this automatic policy were accompanied by major efforts to reduce price rigidities through reduction in the monopoly powers of labor unions and big corporations. A steady but small increase in the quantity of money would maintain the effective demand of a slowly growing population at full employment level, without serious inflation.

We can immediately concede to Friedman that monetary economics and monetary policy may not have received the proper attention recently, though we could add that the monetary-fiscal policy mix of the Nixon Administration did not restrain the inflationary forces but merely increased unemployment. In the United Kingdom, a heavy dose of classical monetary measures, supported by orthodox Keynesian fiscal measures, seemed to have stabilized the economy momentarily during the early 1970s, though at the heavy price of bringing growth to a standstill. The inherent structural defects of the British economy, however, make it virtually impossible to discern whether the current stability is a consequence of the monetary or fiscal measures taken.

[39]Milton Friedman, *Monetary vs. Fiscal Policy* (New York: Norton, 1969), p. 79. (Our italics.)

Friedman's criticism of the "fine tuning" efforts of Anglo-American policy makers may be valid, except that we ordinarily do not know whether, for instance, a significant cost-of-living increase over a three-month period is a short-term movement or the beginning of a significant inflationary trend. If it is the latter, the more rapid the countermeasure, the shorter the delay, and the quicker will the system's stability be restored. Friedman's attack on the "fine tuning" efforts only makes sense, therefore, if we really could assume that long-run economic stability and growth could be guaranteed by merely letting the quantity of money grow a fixed percentage each year. Most economists are not at all convinced, however, that the Friedman policy guarantees full employment and growth, though the influence of monetary economists has undoubtedly grown during the last five years.

Finally, it is undoubtedly true that the effectiveness of both monetary and fiscal policy would be enhanced by reducing the price rigidities in the economy. Virtually all economists would theoretically endorse this goal. De facto, however, it would take a real revolution, one more fundamental than the New Deal or the Keynesian revolution, to bring about a significant weakening of union-corporate power.

If Keynes was politically naive in disregarding the parliamentary-political aspects of his policy recommendations, Friedman is equally naive and visionary in disregarding the monumental obstacles that prevent a significant decline in price rigidity. Still, Friedman's criticism has pinpointed the timing and the political difficulties involved in economic decision making, and he has forced economists to give renewed attention to monetary economics, industrial organization, and market structure, topics that had been neglected by the Keynesians. Friedman's role as the *enfant terrible* of the economics profession ought to result in the long run in a more sophisticated approach to economic decision making, and will lead to more fundamental research in the structure of modern economic systems.

In the short run, the inability of purely economic measures to control inflation during the early 1970s prompted even such a soft-spoken economist as Arthur Burns, the head of the Federal Reserve System, to proclaim that, since 1967, the market forces have become sufficiently weakened to compel the recognition that an entirely new economic system has developed. Burns, who made major contributions to business cycle theory before becoming economic advisor to

Presidents Eisenhower and Nixon, is not given to making exaggerated statements. If anything, he has shown a persistent tendency to deflate excessive appraisals of fashionable slogans and theories.[40] If such a man now throws up his hands at the inability of both fiscal and monetary policies to cope with the inflationary pressures of the affluent economics of the 1970s, it is worthwhile to examine if there really is any evidence of a structural change in the corporate capitalism of the post-World War II era, and if any theory of capitalistic development exists that could provide an explanation of the current dilemma.

Perhaps the only economist who provided us with a model that could accommodate simultaneously the triumphs of postwar capitalistic affluence and the defeats of permanent inflation and social disintegration was Joseph Schumpeter. Profoundly independent as a thinker, Schumpeter's major economic contributions were in the fields of economic development and business cycle theory. He caught the imagination of the educated public, however, by his romantic formulation of the role of the capitalist entrepreneur and the latter's relation to the business cycle. Like Marx, Schumpeter saw economic development under capitalism as a violent, uneven, disharmonious process. Unlike Marx, he did not argue that these cyclical swings end in a frenzy of massive self-destruction; rather, he perceived them as the means by which capitalism reached higher levels of real income growth. Central to this entire process was the entrepreneur. ". . . the function of entrepreneurs is to reform or revolutionize the pattern of production by exploiting an invention or, more generally, an untried technological possibility for producing a new commodity or producing an old one in a *new* way, by opening up a new source of supply of materials or a new outlet for products, by reorganizing an industry and so on."[41] Who creates? The entrepreneur, the innovator whose leadership grasps the opportunity to exploit the creative situations offered by the environment. Why does the entrepreneur act this way? What must be the emotions that drive the entrepreneur to leap so far beyond his peers? Schumpeter is never very clear on this point. Surely there must be more than the pursuit of gain for the entrepreneur and his family.

How does the entrepreneur manipulate the economic environment?

---

[40]Arthur E. Burns, "Economic Research and the Keynesian Thinking of Our Times," National Bureau of Economic Research, *Annual Report,* 1946, vol. 26, pp. 1-38.

[41]Joseph Schumpeter, *Capitalism, Socialism and Democracy* (New York: Harper & Row, 1942), p. 132.

Here Schumpeter links him to a fascinating and ingenious explanation of the business cycle under capitalism.[42] Hypothetically at equilibrium, there is the plateau of full employment, the absence of
investment pressures or population growth. More important, however, there exists a stream of possible innovational opportunities with
great profit potential, which await only their parturition. Schumpeter's
entrepreneur seizes the opportunity. Unconcerned by the rate of interest, the entrepreneur borrows from credit-creating banks, because he
sees the interest rate solely as a fraction of his potential profits, which
are considerably larger than the bank cost of money. A few entrepreneurs spark the beginning of an innovational boom. Their example
and success are copied and followed by a "swarmlike" appearance of
much larger superficially imitative entrepreneurial activity.

As the business cycle mounts in economic intensity, the traditional
movement of economic factors occurs. Prices, wages, and money
incomes rise. Productive capabilities are shifted from consumer activities to the manufacture of increased productive capacity. Older firms
without any alteration of their processes, but encouraged by the heady
wine of a booming economy, expand their operations, and a broad
expansion of economic growth occurs under conventional production processes. The psychology of boom spreads quickly and speculators move in rapidly to take advantage of special situations. By this
time, however, this secondary economic expansion has overarched
the original innovational experience. The stage is set for Schumpeter's
famous process of "creative destruction." When the legitimate reasons for innovational expansion are over, productive facilities rapidly
begin to shift back to the output of consumer goods, but of course at
higher levels of capacity. Competition and price cutting are heightened
by the struggle between older firms trying to survive with firms that
have adopted newer products or newer techniques and can challenge
the market at lower prices. Thus begins the inevitable but painful
process of readjustment. The mechanism is well-known—bankruptcies,
unemployment, deflationary policies, and a frantic flight toward
liquidity. If the avalanche can be stopped early, we have a recession;
but if the collapse becomes overgeneralized, the downward movement may well carry us into a full-scale depression. When this occurs,
there must be further economic liquidation until the environment

---

[42]Joseph Schumpeter, *Business Cycle, a Theoretical, Historical, and Statistical Analysis of the Capitalist Process* (New York and London: McGraw-Hill, 1939).

provides a new stage attractive enough for the entrepreneur to reenact the new script of successful innovation. Although Schumpeter clearly recognized that this "creative destruction" was a heavy price to pay, he was convinced that it was necessary. He was certain that over the long run national income and per capita income in real terms rose via this process. If labor suffered more from the unemployment effects of these crises, it benefited, too, because the "major share of innovation under capitalism pertains to mass-produced consumer goods." This anarchic mechanism was the ladder for real income to climb under capitalism.

Schumpeter was convinced that the capitalist system could withstand these business cycle experiences. These cyclical drops would not cause capitalism's demise, but death from other causes was almost certain:

Its very success [the capitalist system's] undermines the social institutions which protect it, and "eventually" creates conditions in which it will not be able to live and which strongly point to socialism as the heir apparent. . . . we know nothing as yet about the precise way by which socialism may be expected to come except that there must be a great many possibilities ranging from a gradual bureaucratization to the most picturesque revolution.[43]

The Schumpeterian dialectic, a close parallel to Marx's dialectical materialism, recognized that capitalism carried the seeds of its destruction within its own system. In the Schumpeterian system, however, the downfall of the bourgeoisie is caused by capitalism's sucess, not by its failures. Schumpeter believed that the intellectuals, who had reached a stage of unprecedented affluence under capitalism, have been responsible for creating much of the anticapitalistic atmosphere that produced the short-run ameliorative reforms that in the long run, however, make the operation of a capitalistic market economy impossible. The conclusion, held by both Schumpeter and Marx, that capitalism cannot exist in the long run "half free and half regulated" seemed invalid during the period 1945-1965, when liberal Keynesian economic policies were apparently responsible for full employment, social stability, economic growth, and ever-widening affluence.

By 1971, when Burns admitted the ineffectiveness of economic theory, Schumpeter's analysis and prediction of the downfall of capi-

[43]Schumpeter, *Capitalism, Socialism and Democracy*, pp. 61, 162-163.

talism took on a new importance, and his *Capitalism, Socialism and Democracy* became an oracle for many college students, academicians, and intelligent observers.[44] The triple threat of price-wage rigidities, neomercantilistic government practices, and corrosive efforts of the anticapitalistic intelligentsia had become sufficiently noticeable to make Schumpeter's prediction of the downfall of capitalism quite conceivable.[45]

Schumpeter's brilliant analysis diagnosed the ills of a stagnant capitalism in overly dramatic terms. These postwar years have not only been marked by unprecedented economic growth, they have also witnessed the development of technological and analytical skills that now permit the development of rigorous dynamic models designed to integrate economic, social, and behavioral forces. In the history of economic thought, only a few giants such as Smith, Marx, and Schumpeter had heretofore developed dynamic models that combined economic theory with economic history and social-political analysis. Their models, however, were of necessity basically descriptive in nature. In the 1970s, the immense breakthroughs in computer technology and mathematics, coupled with insights from the fields of biological and engineering systems, have opened up new horizons. The maturing of dynamic economic theory can utilize these developments to fashion policies that recognize the interaction and interdependence of historical, economic, and social-political factors. Economic analysts can now develop necessary policies to solve problems of a dynamic nature. The gloomy predictions of economic chaos and collapse are not inevitable. In fact, never have economists been more powerfully armed for their tasks. The next chapter will examine some of the new methods and techniques that competent economists can now easily use.

[44]*Ibid.*, p. 131ff.

[45]The term "intellectuals" is intentionally avoided because in the 1970s it has become suspect in the Schumpeterian reexamination of their role. The acute English historian and journalist Crankshaw, for instance, sounds very much like Schumpeter himself when he asks:

Was the rise of the radical intelligentsia [during the nineteenth and twentieth centuries] desirable, was their unchecked progress necessary in order that mankind might be led to the broad uplands of democratic freedom? Or was the very concept of democratic freedom a blind alley, developed to make the world safe for an intelligentsia which is only happy when playing at politics, at no matter what cost in suffering to the multitude?

Edward Crankshaw, *The Fall of the House of Habsburg* (New York: Viking 1968), pp. 20-21.

11

THE NEW BEHAVIORAL ECONOMICS

Economists have forever attempted to describe the socioeconomic conditions of their time and to analyze the nature and consequences of technological change. Few, however, seem to have recognized that technology itself affects the very mode of economic thinking—of theorizing; furthermore, the operational significance of economic models is almost entirely dependent on the support of the prevailing technology.

The National Economy and Policy

The history of general equilibrium theory admirably illustrates this point. Social scientists are well aware today that Walras' general equilibrium model was a purely theoretical creation never intended to possess any operational value. During Walras' time, the absence of national income accounting made it impossible to find numerical values for the coefficients of his multiequation model.[1] The insufficient

---

[1] Even today we have insufficient information to supply numerical values for Walras' system of equation; however, by "aggregating" firms (producers) and consumers into

knowledge of linear algebra made it doubtful whether the system even had a stable, unique, and feasible solution, and the lack of mechanical computing equipment and numerical methods for the solution of large-scale systems made it impossible to find solutions for Walras' model, even if a theoretical solution had existed and even if the numerical values of the coefficients had been known.

All this changed in the years after World War I. The mathematical contributions of von Neumann and Wald and the subsequent generalization of their pioneering efforts by Arrow-Debreu and McKenzie,[2] not only proved that the Walrasian system possessed a stable equilibrium, but also laid a firm mathematical foundation for the primarily "operational" advances in economic theory that occurred in the decades following World War II. The demands of engineering and the military sciences in the 1930s encouraged intensive work in numerical analysis and the rapid development of efficient desk calculators. The depression of the 1930s and the scientific management movement of the 1920s and 1930s increased the businessman's interest in cost cutting and made sophisticated entrepreneurs receptive to a more theoretical approach to business decision making. Finally, the Keynesian revolution spurred the development of national income accounting, and the technical contributions to this art by the National Bureau of Economic Research made macroeconomic analysis respectable

---

a manageable number of sectors and by focusing on the interrelationship of firms rather than producers and consumers, Leontief provided us with an operational general equilibrium model for which our national income accounting is adequate.

[2]The first analysis of the Walrasian equilibrium conditions was undertaken by Wald during the period 1933-1935 and presented in the proceedings of Karl Menger's famous mathematical seminar [*Ergebnisse eines mathematischen Kolloquiums,* 6 (1933-1934), 12-20, and 7 (1934-1935), 1-6]. Subsequently Wald published a revised version, "Über einige Gleichungssysteme der mathematischen Ökonomie," *Zeitschrift fur Nationalökonomie,* 7 (1936) 637-670. The English translation appeared in *Econometrica,* 19 (1951), 368-403, fifteen years later. Wald made the mathematically simplifying assumptions that demand was a function of quantity $[p_i = f_i(x_1, x_2, \ldots, x_n)]$. In another early existence proof, von Neumann also made sharply limiting assumptions that led to a pure production model, with no final demand and no fixed factor, that laid the foundation for current "balanced growth models" ["Über ein ökonomisches Gleichungssystem . . . ," *Ergebnisse eines mathematischen Kolloquiums,* 8 (1937), 73-83; English translation, "A Model of General Equilibrium," *Review of Economic Studies,* 13: 33 (1945-1946), 1-9]. A truly general proof of the existence of a competitive equilibrium is due to Arrow and Debreu, who extended Wald's results [K. J. Arrow and Gerard Debreu, "Existence of an Equilibrium for a Competitive Economy," *Econometrica,* 22 (1954), 265-290]. A further and most elegant generalization is due to L. W. McKenzie, "On the Existence of a General Equilibrium for a Competitive Market," *Econometrica,* 27 (1959), 54-71, and "On Equilibrium in Graham's Model of World Trade," *Econometrica,* 22 (1954),147-161.

and effective even for those economists and business establishments that distrusted the policy implications of Keynesian economics.

By the beginning of World War II, we find that in a brief period of less than twenty years the technical environment of economic analysis had changed more profoundly than in the previous one hundred fifty years. The reluctance of economists to accept new analytical tools disguised at first the potential technological revolution that awaited the profession. During the early 1940s, most academic economists had been too preoccupied to digest the significant contributions to economic theory of the 1930s—monopolistic-competition theory and national income analysis—to equip themselves with an entirely new toolkit. Monopolistic-competition theory was, in fact, but an extension of neoclassical marginal analysis and did not require economists to master a new set of analytical theories. The Keynesian revolution did, however, produce an entirely new set of macro-economic tools; at least part of the hostility the Keynesian analysis engendered among well-established older economists can be explained by the age-old antagonism of master craftsmen to emerging techniques that endanger their intellectual capital.

The Keynesian model itself, however, did not affect in any way the marginal analysis approach to the theory of the firm. Furthermore, once an economist had mastered the new Keynesian concepts of national income, consumption function, investment multiplier, and so on, he could safely fall back upon his old cherished devices of merely altering one variable while keeping all others constant (*ceteris paribus*), of ascertaining the marginal substitution rates among the determinants of national income, and of avoiding the mathematical difficulties of dynamic analysis by relying upon the convenient and deceptively logical approach of comparative statics. Despite or even because of the Keynesian revolution, the technology of academic and business economists had changed very little by 1940, and the potentially tremendous change in the technological environment in which economists operated had not yet been reflected in the development of new analytical techniques. As far as the individual businessman or engineer was concerned, economic theory was still far from having much operational significance. On the macroeconomic level, the simplicity of the Keynesian employment model gave it enormous immediate usefulness for politicians and government officials alike, but Keynes' choice of "ultrashort" time periods for his analysis delayed, perhaps even set back, the emergence of a truly dynamic general equilibrium model, which we have considered to be the goal of economic analysis since the days of Cantillon and Quesnay.

Thus we can *sometimes* regard our *ultimate independent variables* as consisting of (1) the three fundamental psychological factors, namely the psychological propensity to consume, the psychological attitude to liquidity and the psychological expectation of future yield from capital assets, (2) the wage unit as determined by the bargains reached between employers and employed and (3) the quantity of money as determined by the action of the central bank; so that, if we *take as given* the factors specified above, these variables determine the national income, and the quantity of employment.[3]

Keynes' emphasis on the short run enabled him to consider as independent basic variables that are clearly mutually dependent even over a brief three to five year period. For instance, "the wage-unit as determined by bargaining" is clearly affected, after some delay, by another independent variable, namely "the quantity of money as determined by . . . the control bank"; similarly, the "psychological expectation of future yield" will certainly and almost instantaneously be affected by the changes in the "propensity to consume," which we know today is not as stable as Keynes postulated; still, the assumption of a stable propensity to consume has operational value over the *very short run*.[4]

Keynes quite clearly meant to restrict his theory to short-run analysis, and it is, therefore, highly questionable whether the Keynesian analysis could really provide the basis for a long-run dynamic model of the Harrod-Domar type, which was intended to examine the secular growth of capitalistic economies.[5] Because the Harrod-Domar model

---

[3]John Maynard Keynes, *General Theory of Employment, Interest and Money* (London: Macmillan, 1936), p. 65, our italics. Note that Keynes carefully pointed out that these variables can only "sometimes"—that is, in the short run—be taken as independent.

[4]*Ibid.,* p. 65.

[5]Haberler considered the application of Keynesian short-run theories by Harrod and Domar to the analysis of secular growth a "sin . . .flagrantly committed." Cf. Gottfried Haberler, "Sixteen Years Later," in *Keynes's General Theory: Reports of Three Decades,* Robert Leckachman, ed. (New York: St. Martin, 1964), p. 293. The fact that the authors of the only existing texts on growth models explicitly disregard demand-oriented, Keynesian-type dynamic models, and only deal with (essentially classical) long-run supply-oriented models supports Haberler's position [cf. E. Burmeister and A. R.

formed the starting point for further exploration in dynamic economics by Phillips, Samuelson, Hicks, and others, the operationally
unsatisfactory state of post-Keynesian dynamic economics can be
traced to the unsuitability of the explicitly short-run Keynesian model
for long-run analysis.[6]

The difficulty in the application of the static Keynesian model to
the development of dynamic growth models lies in the mathematical
and conceptual foundation of the Keynesian model. Mathematically,
the Keynesian assumption of the independence of key variables is
only relaxed for a few variables at a time. The multiplier and accelerator lend themselves readily to the exploration of the interdependence of consumption, investment, and national income and of the
consequences of delays, or time lags, in this dependency relationship
on the model output, without affecting the other variables which are
pertinent to a growth model of the economy. The simplifications of
the dynamic growth models have been justified by their use for illustrative purposes in examining basic concepts. But another reason
may have been that the simplifications enabled the theorist to represent his dynamic systems by second-order difference or differential
equation models, which can be analyzed easily by well-established
mathematical methods. The consequence of this simplification has
been the separation of growth and cyclical models, and hence the
necessity to make completely unrealistic assumptions.

Much—but not all—of current dynamic analysis is still a methodological continuation of partial equilibrium analysis. Starting with a
static model, a few variables are made dynamic, whereas for the
others the *ceteris paribus* assumption still prevails. The results are
neat, precise models which have little operational usefulness. Worse,
this methodology has cut off the economist from the biologist and
engineer who also deal with complex dynamic systems. Conceptually,
the specific explicit awareness of dependency, feedback, and delay as
the prime characteristics of dynamic systems that has been developed
by the systems engineer, ecologist, and biologist has until recently

Dobnell, *Mathematical Theories of Economic Growth* (New York: Macmillan, 1970),
p. 2|.
    [6]A brief but highly lucid discussion of the Harrod-Domar, Phillips, and Samuelson-
Hicks models can be found in R. G. D. Allen's *Mathematical Economics.* (London:
Macmillan, 1959), chap. 3. Phillips, incidentally, has gone substantially beyond the
Keynesian model in later works.

been lacking in economics. This has not only prevented cross-fertilization between economist and engineer, it has also delayed the emergence of a dynamic, time-variant general equilibrium model. Appreciable recent advances in optimal control theory and general systems analysis bring this goal within reach.[7] A brief treatment of a few basic concepts in systems analysis may be useful before further discussion of dynamic economics and recent growth theory.

General Systems Theory: A Tool for Social Analysis

The significant conceptual features of a self-regulatory system are delay, feedback, both positive and negative, and the concept of the "black box." A thermostat is an excellent example of such a self-regulatory negative feedback system. Set for a desirable temperature of, say, 72° Fahrenheit, the furnace—that is, the "black box"—is activated whenever the *difference* (error) between desired and actual room temperature exceeds say 2°. At 70° an impulse activates the furnace and it operates until the room temperature reaches 72°, when it shuts off. The input (oil) into the sytem is regulated by its output

Figure 11.1 Automatic Negative Feedback Control

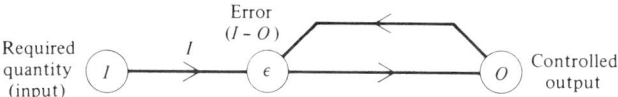

Figure 11.2 Performance Chart of Thermostatic Heating System

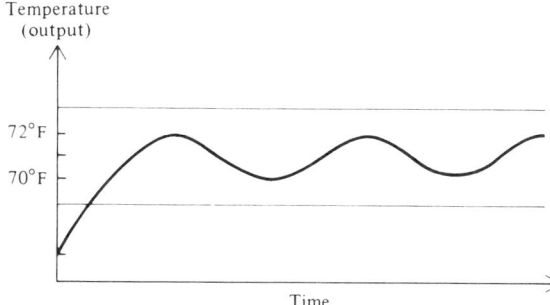

[7]The rather sudden importance of optimal control theory for economists has been reflected in recent texts on mathematical economics, which deal extensively with these topics, hitherto the exclusive domain of control engineers [cf. M. D. Intrilligator, *Mathematical Optimization and Economic Theory*, (Englewood Cliffs, N. J.: Prentice-Hall, 1970), chaps. 11-16, Kevin Lancaster, *Mathematical Economics* (New York: Macmillan, 1968), chaps. 10-12].

Figure 11.3 Performance Chart of "Man in Shower" System (No Delay)

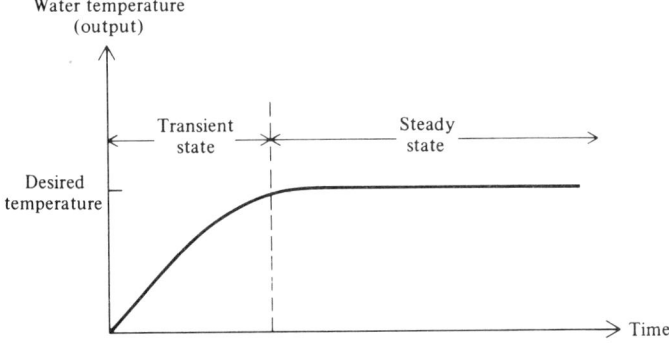

(heat). The technical characteristics of the furnance are, for control purposes, unimportant; hence the furnace is the "black box" of this system. Merely the fact that the input, oil, is transformed into heat in this "black box" is important. Delay plays no significant role in the above system.

A "man taking a shower" can be considered as an interesting man-machine feedback system, in which delay does play a considerable role. A man turns on a shower in his hotel room and receives a stream of ice cold water; quickly he will turn on the lever toward hot. If there is no delay—that is, the turning of the lever immediately produces warmer water—then there will be no fluctuations; the lever will merely be turned until the desired temperature is reached.

Unfortunately, however, there is ordinarily a considerable delay between the instant when the lever is moved toward "hot" and the time warmer water will pour from the shower. In such a case, our man will not notice an immediate effect from his initial action; because extremely cold water keeps pouring forth he will keep pushing the regulatory lever further and further toward hot. At last the warming effect of his *initial* regulatory step—the first movement of the lever—will make itself felt and the water will become pleasantly warm; shortly thereafter the delayed consequence of the subsequent manipulation of the lever will make the water burning hot. Quickly our man will turn the lever toward "warm". If, by temperament and intelligence, he possesses "learning ability," the fluctuation in the water temperature reaches a steady state. If no learning takes place, the lever may be pushed back and forth with increasing speed and vigor, and the

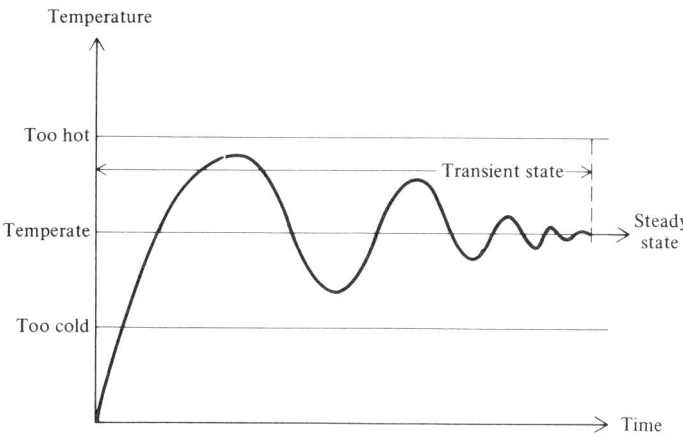

Figure **11.4** Performance of Water Temperature in "Man-Shower System" with Delay and Learning Ability (Damped Oscillation)

temperature will fluctuate with increasing frequency and amplitude.

The man-in-shower example has demonstrated that delay causes oscillation in a negative feedback system. It is, however, ordinarily impossible to predict in advance whether an even moderately complex system—a system that contains several delays and feedback circuits—will react with dampened or explosive oscillations to input variations. In the example, the outcome depended entirely on learning ability, a characteristic that would be buried inside the "black box" in every *first* approximation model. (In more realistic and sophisticated adaptive control models, learning ability would affect the control mechanism directly.)

The diagram of the explosive oscillatory output (Fig. 11.5) resembles greatly the business cycle fluctuations of a capitalistic economy as predicted in Marx's theory of crises.[8] Similarly, the dampened fluctuations of Figure 11.4 are compatible with a Keynesian compensatory spending model. The philosophical differences between Keynes and Marx are epitomized by their respective attitudes toward the learning ability of the capitalistic system. Marx was convinced that capitalism was inherently unable to "learn" from its performance—that

[8]Though Marx did, of course, not write a cohesive theory of crisis, Dobbs attempted to weave together into a consistent theory Marx's numerous discussions of crises found throughout his works. See Maurice Dobbs, *Political Economy and Capitalism* (Westport, Conn.: Greenwood, 1937).

Figure **11.5** Performance of Water Temperature in "Man-Shower System"
without Learning Ability (Explosive Oscillation)

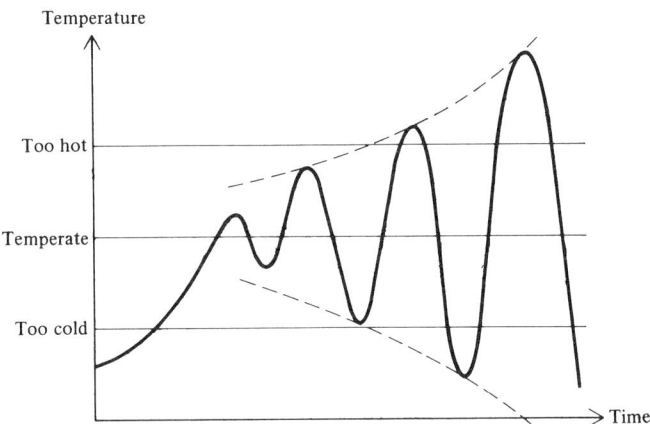

is, modify systems parameters— while Keynes' model is predicated
on the learning ability of democratic capitalism. The "compensatory"
Keynesian model is simpler and far less ambitious than Marx's. In its
simplest and most naive form, the government is the controlling thermostat in the Keynesian model. The difference between the actual
and the desired level of total spending (consumption plus investment)
will accentuate compensatory government policy (more spending if
aggregate spending is low; less spending, more taxes if aggregate
spending is too high). If there were no delays, either between the
decision, say, to increase government spending and its impact on
national income, or between the economic indicators and the actual
performance of the economy, the oscillation of economic activity
would resemble those pictured in Figure 11.3. With minor delays, and
with the absence of other groups that may suddenly and independently vary their spending, the output of a compensatory model would
resemble the dampened oscillation of Figure 11.4. Unfortunately,
however, the delays in the actual economic system are serious, and
autonomous changes in businessmen's investment decisions especially detract from the effectiveness of the government thermostat.
Although *skillful* compensatory policy may enable a government to
dampen the economic oscillations around the desirable reference
level, such a successful outcome cannot be predicted from the model,
but depends on behavioral characteristics—that is, the skill and ability
of government policy makers. Though in more complex, post-

Keynesian models elaborate conditions for the existence of an equilibrium (absence of explosive oscillations) are given, in practice it is still the "black-box" quality of government policy makers that decides the performance behavior.[9]

Marx was, of course, a much more ambitious system builder than Keynes. The very greatness of his design, as well as his philosophical predilections, made it virtually impossible to fit the various subsystems neatly together. Volumes 2 and 3 of his *Capital* are a testimony to his unceasing efforts to remedy the weaknesses in his "grand design," which his intellectual integrity could not disregard.

Significant components of the Marxian system can be deduced as direct consequences of his labor-value-surplus theory. Even business cycle fluctuations and crises appear at times as consequences of the search for surplus, profits, the concomitant deepening of capital, and the drive toward large-scale production. In other parts of his work, however, Marx based his theory of crises and economic oscillation on his analysis of the circulation of capital and money. It is here, where Marx carried further Quesnay's macroeconomic analysis, that he made his major contributions as an economist. Marx recognized the "systems nature" of the economic process, and adopted Quesnay's "general equilibrium" approach to the analysis of the circulation of money, credit, and goods.[10] In his self-regulatory macroeconomic model Quesnay distinguished between productive (agriculture) and nonproductive (industry, trade) sectors in the economy. Although Quesnay recognized the possibilities of disturbances in his "self-regulatory, negative feedback system," the disturbances did not necessarily emerge from within the system, but rather were the pathological results of outside influences (e.g., hoarding and exploitation of the lower classes that would lead to underconsumption). Marx, however, recognized the much more significant distinctions between consumer- and capital-goods industries and made this distinction the basis of his "two sector macroeconomic model," as it would be called today.[11] The differ-

[9]Cf. Evsey D. Domar, "Capital Expansion, Rate of Growth and Employment," *Econometrica,* 14 (1946), 137-147, and A. W. Phillips, "Stabilization Policy in a Closed Economy," *Economic Journal,* 64 (1954), 290-323. In the latter paper, Phillips, who had been trained as an electrical engineer, applied explicitly control engineering concepts to the economic stabilization concept.

[10]Marx praised Quesnay's *Tableau Economique* as the outstanding contribution to economic theory.

[11]Karl Marx, *Capital,* (Moscow: Foreign Languages Publishing House, 1954) vol. 3, part 1.

ences between capital and consumer goods produced "disproportion-alities" in the periodic capital expenditures of the two sectors. "Disproportionality" in consumption and capital expenditures, however, must produce booms and crises—that is, sinusoidal departures from the equilibrium.

The Marxian two-sector model is easily reconciled with the insight provided today by systems analysis. We know that delays will cause oscillations in the output of a negative feedback system. The market system is, of course, a massive, high-order feedback system. The Marxian two-sector model analyzed the specific dynamic feedback relationship between consumer- and capital-goods industries, and concluded that the inherent disproportionality in the system's structure must result in oscillations. He postulated then that this oscillation must be of the explosive type. We know today that a Marxian-type feedback system with several delays will have an oscillatory output. However, the fluctuations do not have to be explosive; they can just as well be steadily fluctuating or dampened—that is, leading to a new steady state (equilibrium). The nature of the output would be determined from the nature of the differential (difference) equations that describe a dynamic model. From Marx's algebraic formulation of his two-sector model no analytic conclusion about the nature of the oscillations can be made.

We must, of course, not criticize Marx for the fact that the formulation of his dynamic model does not meet the standards of the mathematical systems analysis of the 1970s. Precisely because Marx was one of the very few economists who thought in dynamic terms, his two-sector model has been a much sounder starting point for modern dynamic theory than the relatively static Keynesian analysis.[12]

Models

The demands of World War II and the experiences of the boom and the Cold War of the 1950s changed the intellectual climate in which economists operated. World War II required the utmost sophistication in the planning of production and in the allocation of resources. The existence of an excellent national income accounting system in the United States and Great Britain and the developments of high-

[12]Harrod claimed that "Keynes must be truly regarded as the father of dynamic theory" because the development of a static macroeconomic theory was the "indispensable foundation" of modern dynamic theory (cf. Harrod "Retrospect on Keynes," in *Keynes's General Theory,* p. 138).

speed electronic computing equipment made the Walrasian general equilibrium approach promising. Wassily Leontief's input-output analysis, first published in 1941, demonstrated persuasively that a modified general equilibrium model could be effectively used for operational purposes. The interdependence of American Industry and the inadequacy of Marshallian partial-equilibrium theory for planning purposes—purposes it was never intended to accomplish in the first place—required a new analytical approach sufficiently sophisticated to evaluate simultaneously the interacting variables of an entire system.

The operational effectiveness of input-output theory was continually enhanced by simultaneous advances in computer technology, national income statistics, and numerical computation methods of large-scale systems. Increasingly, the technology could provide better data and faster solutions for larger and larger systems. As the number of variables increased, the models became more realistic and supplied more reliable answers. By the 1960s, we find that the expansion of input-output tables enabled economists to build more realistic simultaneous equation models in which possible policy alternatives could be "fed" into the model and their consequences measured. The famous 35-variable "Michigan model," built over several years by Suits and his associates at the University of Michigan, is an excellent example of the advances in contemporary economics due to the changed technological environment.

The "Michigan model" started out, essentially, as a simple, short-run Keynesian model concerned only with the major macroeconomic parameters of savings, consumption, and investments. Increasing refinements of the model produced both a large number of industry parameters and a recognition of the interdependence of the model's variables. Today the Michigan Model presents a happy combination of general equilibrium and national income analysis; with each year, additional refinements (i.e., addition of more variables and inter-industry relations) increased the predictive ability of the model until in 1964, it predicted with great accuracy the consequences of the cut in income taxes enacted later on by Congress in the spring of 1965.

As the confidence in the predictive ability of short-run economic models increased among government officials, businessmen, and economists, the very nature of applied economics approached a profound qualitative change. Economics had been hampered in the past primarily by its inability to test and verify by experiments certain basic hypotheses. Hence every theory, every policy recommendation, had been confronted by two contentions: (1) "It" (i.e., the policy recommendation) is "unrealistic" and does not work; (2) even if "it" worked, the consequences would not be desirable. The second contention is a result of the different value structures that exist among men, and will, hopefully, remain forever a part of economic controversy. The "it won't work" contention, however, not only baffled and frustrated noneconomists for a long time—nothing is more discouraging for the laity than to watch the experts disagree on the very fundamentals—but also gave economics a definite "scholastic" quality, where nothing ever seemed to be resolved.

Simulation

Technological advances in the field of economics have for the first time equipped the practitioners with a tool that may be a reasonable substitute for physical experimentation, the basis for the success of the natural sciences. This substitute for experimentation is represented by the new concept of "simulation." Simulation per se is, of course, nothing new. It has been used successfully in engineering for centuries. Essentially simulation means merely to imitate nature, to construct a device that is exposed to the same forces present in the problem under consideration. Mechanical devices, or the scaled-down physical models of engineering structures, were the first significant examples of model building. Once these models were completed, they could be exposed to the various contingencies that awaited the real thing. The advantages of these physical models lay in four significant areas:

1. The models were cheaper to build than the originals; hence errors could be remedied easily.
2. The models could be exposed artificially to the most extreme contingencies possible, contingencies that in real life might occur only with a very small probability.
3. The model could be reduced to a dimension sufficiently small to enable the human mind to understand the totality of the problem under consideration. The problem itself might thereby become understandable to nontechnical personnel interested in this very problem.

4. The parameters of both the model and the forces acting upon it could be varied in an almost infinite number of ways in order to test all the permutations and combinations of the factors considered in the basic design. Such variations in the basic parameters could therefore give the model builder an insight he otherwise could gain only through years of costly experience.

In economics (and, of course, in the natural sciences) the physical models have now been replaced for the most part by systems of equations that can be fed into digital computers. These mathematical models add to the four properties of physical analogues the additional advantage of reducing to manageable proportion the time dimensions of design and of evaluation through use. Economic variables, though interdependent, are interdependent only "over time"; it takes a comparatively long time period before the perturbations transmitted to an economic system by a change in one of its parameters have run their course and the equilibrium is either reestablished or the unstable nature of the system becomes apparent. A computer, however, enables us to follow from one time period to the next the changes in the economy caused by, say, a cut in taxes, a change in the tax structure, or an increase in private investment.

Simulation not only enables economists to trace through the consequences of major economic decisions, but, most importantly, it makes it possible to test the behavior of the model as various, possibly contradictory, changes in the major parameters are introduced. Any number of feasible reactions can be considered and countermoves planned, long before the decisions are ever implemented in the real world. Moreover, once the economic decisions have been made, the actual results can be compared against the theoretical forecasts at the end of each quarter, and proper steps can be undertaken if discrepancies should occur. By continuously changing the simulation model, additional information is obtained, economists can generate a self-contained, closed feedback information system wherein actual and simulated results should converge.

It is no coincidence, therefore, that economists have appropriated many of the tools of the systems engineer, especially the Laplace transform and the Nyquist diagrams.[13] By emphasizing the mathemat-

---

[13]For an excellent discussion of the application of the above techniques to economics, see Allen, *Mathematical Economics*, chap. 9. A treatment of control systems

ically isomorphic nature of economic and electrical engineering models, economists may have relied too heavily upon linear models. As long as the prediction periods of each model were kept quite short, however, and as long as the additional information gained in each period was fed back into the model, the assumption of linearity apparently did not affect the validity of the model.

For the long run, the biologist's more conceptual and less mathematical systems approach may be of greater value than the precise control engineering methodology. Certainly the influence of W. Ross Ashby, Ludwig von Bertalanffy, and Anatol Rapoport on an economist like Boulding and a social scientist like Simon indicates the validity and power of the insight gained in the examination of biological, psychological, ecological, and physiological feedback systems.[14] Especially because a dynamic general equilibrium model that can accommodate changing social parameters must be an adaptive (learning) control system, the economists will quickly outgrow the tools of the control engineer, which are primarily applicable to linear, time-invariant systems.[15]

Decisions in the Firm

The exploding computer technology affected not only macroeconomics but also "business economists" and their operational models of the firm. As a matter of fact, the emergence of a new breed of economists as advisors to industry at various levels of decision making has been a novel development, due almost entirely to the new technology contemporary economists have at their disposal.

MARGINAL ANALYSIS

Prior to World War II, the neoclassical theory of the firm dominated macroeconomics; relying primarily upon Marshallian partial-

---

theory that is accessible to most economists can be found in O.I. Elgerd, *Control Systems Theory* (New York: McGraw Hill, 1967), esp. chap. 5, "Concepts of Controllability and Observability."

[14]Cf. Kenneth E. Boulding, "General Systems Theory," and W. R. Ashby, "Regulation and Control," in *Modern Systems Research for the Behavioral Scientist,* W. Buckley, ed., (Chicago: Aldine, 1968). For an earlier application of these concepts, see H. A. Simon, "Theories of Decision-Making in Economics and Behavioral Science," *American Economic Review*, 49 (June 1959). pp. 253-283.

[15]A time invariant system does not contain the independent variable time explicitly. Mathematically, this means that the difference or differential equation model has constant coefficients. Adaptive (learning) control systems are time variant, and the variable coefficients are explicit functions of time.

equilibrium theory, marginal neoclassical analysis did not intend to explain determination of output, prices, or employment by the firm but rather intended to explain the effects which certain changes in conditions may have upon actions of the firm.[16] Regardless of how successful marginal analysis might have been in explaining the consequences of a small change in a decision variable, the language as well as the explicit and implicit assumptions underlying marginalism seemed so completely foreign even to the sophisticated entrepreneur that neoclassical marginal analysis *qua* economic analysis never played a significant role in the decision-making process of pre-World War II management. The business unit in the marginal theory was a single plant, single product firm with a continuous, U-shaped average cost curve that represented the optimum allocation of production factors at each level of output. This hypothetical firm tended to operate near the minimum point of its cost function; hence increases in output beyond the point of optimum efficiency (lowest average cost) had to be accompanied by cost increases (average costs ordinarily would increase at a faster rate than output).

Conventional cost accounting procedure made it difficult even for a prewar single-plant, single-product firm to consider seriously the operational value of marginal analysis. The management of a multiplant, multiproduct firm had, at best, only a vague notion of the nature of its average cost curve, but knew very well that it produced most efficiently (i.e., with lowest unit costs) when it operated at or near full capacity. It is not surprising, therefore, that marginal analysis had absolutely no relevance for corporate management as an operational tool. To the extent that both the assumptions and the policy conclusions of marginal analysis supported generally the business ideology of the interwar period, we do find frequent policy pronouncements by sophisticated management spokesmen couched in the terminology of marginal analysis. Thus one of the nation's senior executives may have discussed publicly the position of his firm as if it were the small, family-owned, single-plant, single-product firm of Marshallian theory rather than a giant steel corporation. It is quite possible that most of corporate management accepted this idyllic picture as a reality at their ideological level of consciousness. In its everyday decision making, however, corporate management operated without the aid of marginal analysis.

---

[16]The sterile nature of this approach contributed to the lack of trust in the worth of economic theory to solve practical problems.

It is important to note that prior to World War II there did not exist the technological environment to give marginal analysis an operational value even if it had been possible to drop some of the most unrealistic assumptions. While some assumptions such as the U-shaped cost curve could have been relaxed without endangering the model, others, introduced originally merely for expository purposes, could not be removed without increasing the mathematical complexity of the model to such a degree as to make it of questionable value as a theoretical tool and completely useless as a pedagogical device.

By proposing the single-product, single-plant firm as the normative case and then building their model around it, the marginalists assumed away all the mathematical complexities of optimizing a multivariable function subject to nonlinear restraints. An analysis centered on the single-product firm could easily utilize the two-dimensional graphic analysis. In two-dimensional space, such an analysis could demonstrate clearly the existence of a unique equilibrium toward which a profit-maximizing firm could gravitate. If the objection arose that the typical twentieth-century firm can be analyzed in two dimensions, an n product firm could be considered to lie in $n + 1$ space and to have n independent variables in its profit could be as easily extended, they would claim, from a single-product to a multiproduct firm as two- and three-dimensional Euclidean geometry could be extended to n dimensions. If the behavior of a single-product firm can be analyzed in two dimensions, an n product-firm could be considered to lie in $n + 1$ space and to have n independent variables in its profit function. The mathematically sophisticated marginalist might even have referred to Weierstrass' well-known mathematical theorem that a continuous multivariable function "f" defined over a bounded set of points assumes a maximum and minimum value at least once over the set.[17]

The marginalists seemed to believe that such an existence theorem made it unnecessary to investigate the multidimensional case and concentrated, therefore, on the two-dimensional, single-product case (spiced occasionally by brief excursions into three dimensions). From an operational point of view, however, an existence theorem is not enough. We know that mathematical complexities increase sharply if we merely attempt to maximize a function of two independent varia-

[17]Cf. Taylor, *Advanced Calculus*, p. 496. The above theorem is generally referred to as the "extreme value theorem." For an exhaustive discussion of this subject see H. Hancock, *Theory of Maximum and Minimum* (Boston: Ginn, 1917).

bles subject to no restraints. The optimization of an n-dimensional nonlinear function subject to m nonlinear restraints may become virtually impossible even though we know that a solution exists, even if we had access both to an electronic computer and the most modern computational procedures.

Pre-World War II management had, of course, neither the accounting methods, the theoretical tools, nor the electronic computers to apply marginal economic analysis to business decision problems. Certain engineers and businessmen did apply successfully a certain procedure inherent in marginal analysis. This procedure, called "incremental analysis," had a certain amount of popularity, especially among industrial engineers and financial managers.

The "incremental" approach to decision making compares the savings or profits to be realized from various alternatives. Incremental analysis completely follows the partial equilibrium approach by keeping all but one variable constant; it ignores, however, most of the other theoretical assumptions of neoclassical economics. A manager utilizing incremental techniques will compare the savings that might result from, say, replacing an old machine by a new model, or he might investigate the profits to be realized from alternate investment possibilities. The comparatively recent development of direct costing provided post-World War II management with the necessary cost information to compare the relative profitability of various products and processes. For the first time a sophisticated manager could really discover the marginal cost or marginal profit of certain operations.

Unfortunately, incremental analysis failed to be a truly significant tool for top-level management decison making. The difficulties were, of course, that (1) incremental analysis, relying on the *ceteris paribus* approach, could not account for the interaction of important variables that refused to remain constant while one was changed; and (2) incremental analysis can find the most profitable answer at every single stage of a decision problem, but it cannot assure an optimum solution to multistage decision problems.

Point (1) can be illustrated by the company that decided to add a line of electromechanical relays instead of solid state relays because the first were more profitable. Incremental analysis could not show that the development of a solid state product would have added the expertise to the company to improve the profitability of its control equipment division; the latter product was one of those "variables" that remained constant while merely alternate relays were considered.

Point (2), the inability of the incremental method to maximize a multistage decision problem, can best be explained by comparing this method with a mountain climber who would like to reach the highest point of a mountain range. Although he may choose the steepest ascent (largest increment) in moving from one level of the range to the next, there is no assurance that he will ultimately reach the highest point. Similarly, the incremental method may possibly assure a company of the most profitable short-run solution every time it is faced with alternatives; it is not certain at all, however, that a sequence of decisions that produces the largest increment at each step will not bypass the truly important alternative that might have produced the largest profit over a series of decisions (this would be expressed mathematically by saying that maximizing single-stage decisions will not necessarily maximize a multistage decision process).

In spite of its shortcomings, for a considerable time incremental analysis presented the most logical approach to difficult business decisions. The most serious disadvantage of this method, its inability to handle a large number of interacting variables, was at the same time its greatest operational asset because it reduced the dimensionality of complex problems. The technological developments of the 1940s and 1950s, however, produced all of a sudden operational tools of much greater power and sophistication.

LINEAR PROGRAMMING

Linear programming ranks foremost among the analytical tools that were the product of this period. In its economic and mathematical development it resembles input-output theory, a direct descendant of Walrasian general equilibrium theory. Its operational significance, and hence its widespread acceptance by business economists and management alike, is entirely due to the successful development of large-scale computers. Linear programming is but an iterative method for maximizing a multivariable linear function subject to a number of linear restraints. This method is extremely cumbersome for any real-life problem without an electronic computer. With the aid of a computer and an appropriate computer program, extremely large-scale linear optimization problems can be solved in a very short time. Because linear equations are generally reasonable approximations, in the short run, to a firm's profit and allocation functions, economic theory for once supplied the businessman with a highly useful tool of great operational significance. The businessman could now decide what his optimum product mix and optimum production function were without neglecting the interaction of the significant variables.

The economic analysis of business behavior was, moreover, no longer restricted to the questionable assumption that a firm always strove to maximize profit. Linear programming could handle the optimization of any rational decision function, and it could even handle nonrational considerations by adding suitable restraints to the model. Mutually exclusive alternate assumptions could quickly be evaluated by letting the computer solve the problem for various sets of restraints (assumptions). Quite suddenly, technology had made certain aspects of economic theory extremely relevant to corporate management.

The practical value of linear programming for managers and engineers must not overshadow, however, its great theoretical importance for economics. The methodology of linear programming not only has made general equilibrium theory operational, but also has become the moving force in the new synthesis of Walrasian equilibrium theory, Marshallian analysis, and modern activity analysis.[18] As a matter of fact, linear programming was essentially developed to solve the economic problem of optimum resource allocation, and many of the early contributors to this field were either economists—for example, W. W. Cooper, T. Koopmans, Leontief, O. Morgenstern, and Stiegler —or mathematicians who have been primarily interested in the application of mathematics to economics and the social sciences—for example, A. Charnes, G. Dantzig, D. Gale, H. W. Kuhn, A. W. Tucker, and von Neumann.[19]

[18]For an excellent exposition of the theoretical implications of linear programming, see R. Dorfman, Paul Samuelson, and R. Solow, *Linear Programming and Economic Analysis* (New York: McGraw-Hill, 1958), esp. chaps. 9-14. This book is mathematically self-contained and can be read with benefit by anyone interested in modern economics. Some of the same material is covered in a more rigorous manner by David Gale, *The Theory of Linear Economic Models* (New York: McGraw-Hill, 1960). Daniel C. Vandermoulen's *Linear Economic Theory* (Englewood Cliffs, N. J.: Prentice-Hall, 1971) falls halfway between the above-mentioned two books. It is primarily a textbook for first-year graduate students who also might find it an invaluable aid for their comprehensive examinations.

[19]The origin and development of linear programming are ably presented in George D. Dantzig, *Linear Programming and Extensions* (Princeton, N. J.: Princeton University Press, 1963), chap. 2. Many of the most important early papers are presented in T. C. Koopman, ed., *Activity Analysis of Production and Allocations* (New York: Wiley, 1951).

Linear programming began as a mere extension of Leontief's work, but in the end was able to give new meaning and insight to input-output analysis. Similarily the second major methodological development of this period, the theory of games, turned out to be closely related to linear programming, and became suddenly a synthesizing force that unified many strands of "new" and neoclassical economics.[20]

One of the most striking events in connection with the emergence of modern linear economic model theory was the simultaneous but independent development of linear programming on the one hand and game theory on the other *and the eventual realization of the very close relationship* that exists between the two subjects.[21]

Mathematically, linear programming consists of optimizing a linear "objective" function—for example, profit or cost—subject to a set of linear restraints, which are generally expressed in terms of in-equalities. Interestingly, the simplex method, the most effective numerical solution of the linear programming problem, makes use of the marginal concept in searching, step by step, for an increased marginal profit due to a one-unit increase in the allocation of some factor. Moreover, the linear programming problem has the interesting property that maximizing profit will automatically solve its "dual" problem of minimizing cost. In general, linear programming solves simultaneously a "primal" and a "dual" problem—that is, the maximization of an objective function will simultaneously lead to the minimization of a related function. In solving the dual problem, accounting, or shadow prices are often created in a mathematical process that imitates the market mechanism, and follows again a stepwise marginal move toward the optimum position. The very fact that linear programming imitates the market mechanism should be of great help to planners, either in the large multinational corporations in the West or in the Socialist countries in the East. The actual results in the application of linear programming to large-scale planning have so far not quite satisfied the promise inherent in both linear programming and input-output analysis. In the solution of well-structured problems in

[20]John von Neumann and Oscar Morgenstern, *Theory of Games and Economic Behavior* (Princeton, N. J.: Princeton University Press, 1947).
[21]Gale, *The Theory of Linear Economic Models*, p. 216.

manufacturing and engineering, linear programming has been most successful. This very success of linear programming as an optimization tool must not hide, however, its theoretical importance for economics. Certainly, at the very least, linear programming has made the static general equilibrium model fully operational.

OPERATIONS RESEARCH

Linear programming is, of course, not the only operationally significant tool economists have developed during the last twenty-five years. It is merely the most glamorous and useful device among a whole new set of tools economists and mathematicians have put at the disposal of decision makers. This bag of problem solving devices, commonly referred to as "operations research techniques," is much more significant for its philosophical implications than for the elegance or effectiveness of its various devices.

During the 1950s and 1960s, the operations analyst, backed by the most modern electronic computers, information retrieval procedures, and social and business accounting systems, expressed an almost nineteenth-century-like faith in the rationality of men and the power of the scientific method. Under the influence of operations research, economists and economics became increasingly concerned with the operational values of microeconomic theories. The businessman, in turn, rediscovered his interest in economics together with a new-found willingness to listen to theoretical formulations of decision problems. This interest in theory had developed solely because of the apparent operational effectiveness of the New Economics which, in turn, was largely the product of the post-World War II computer revolution.

The Kennedy years saw the peak of arrogance of the technocrats in general, and the New Economics in particular. Today, less than a decade later, there is much less faith in the ability of the New Economics to manage the economy, and so far, even operations research techniques have not kept their promise to revitalize microeconomic theory. The common ground for the failure of micro- and macroeconomics (and their auxiliary operations research) to live up to their promises probably lies in their analytical methodology. The near-static Keynesian models and the static, mostly linear optimization techniques developed in the post-World War II period encouraged a short-run "problem-solving" philosophy that methodologically was essentially an extension of neoclassical partial equilibrium analysis. Micro- and macroeconomic problems were approached from a *ceteris paribus* basis, and their solutions had to satisfy the demands of the moment. Much of the apparently highly successful reform policies of the 1936-1966 period in Anglo-American countries was based upon the "ultra short period" analysis of Keynes and his followers.[22] By 1970, the long-run consequences of these short-run policies made themselves felt, quite suddenly, and led to a new appreciation of classical long-run analysis.

A sudden increase in the propensity to save, for instance, would generate unemployment in the Keynesian short-run analysis, whereas it would accelerate growth in any long-run economic development model. Quite similarly, business economists (re)discovered that short-run optimization of production and inventory schedules had little relevance for long-run corporate goals. Transportation economists began to realize that more parking lots do not solve urban parking problems, just as additional freeways will not solve the traffic problem, and so on.

The new emphasis on long-run dynamic models in both macro- and microeconomic theory (and in ancillary fields in the social sciences) brought about a rediscovery by economists of the calculus of variations,[23] and its offspring, dynamic programming and optimal control theory. For the last one hundred years, economists have used differential calculus to find the maximum or minimum of a function, and much of economics, especially neoclassical economics, can be considered as dealing with the constrained maxima-minima problems of differential calculus. The calculus of variations, however, can be used to find the function between two points that can best accomplish a specific task. A famous example is the so-called brachistochrone problem in which a curve joining two points is to be found from which "a particle starting from rest will slide under gravity from the first point to the second in the least possible time."[24] A somewhat similar problem

[22]Though the term "ultra-short period" is now quite widely used, the authors encountered it for the first time in Hans Brems, *Output, Employment and Growth*, (New York: Harper & Row, 1959), pp. 50 ff.

[23]R. G. D. Allen, the mathematics teacher of the economics profession, wrote a masterful introduction to the concepts of the calculus of variations in his *Mathematical Analysis for Economists* (London: Macmillan, 1938), chap. 20. An equally lucid introduction to optimal control theory is R. Dorfman's "An Economic Interpretation of Optimal Control Theory," *American Economic Review* 59:5 (December 1969), 817-831.

[24]W. E. Byerly, *Introduction to the Calculus of Variaton* (Cambridge, Mass.: Harvard University Press, 1917), p. 2.

Figure **11.6** Optima of a Function

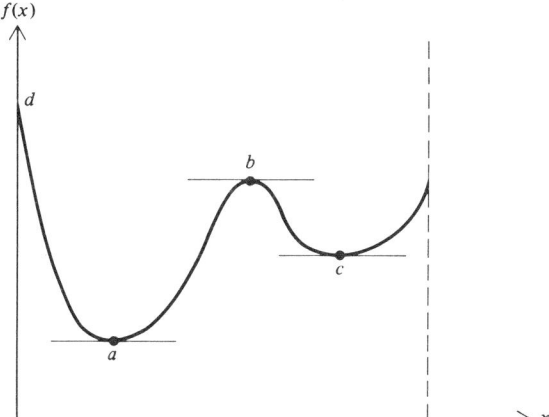

Relative optima exist at points *a, b, c,* where the necessary
condition $f'(x) = 0$ is satisfied. The *absolute* maximum in
this example is at point *d;* the absolute minimum is at point *a.*

Figure **11.7** Some Alternative Trajectories of Economic Growth

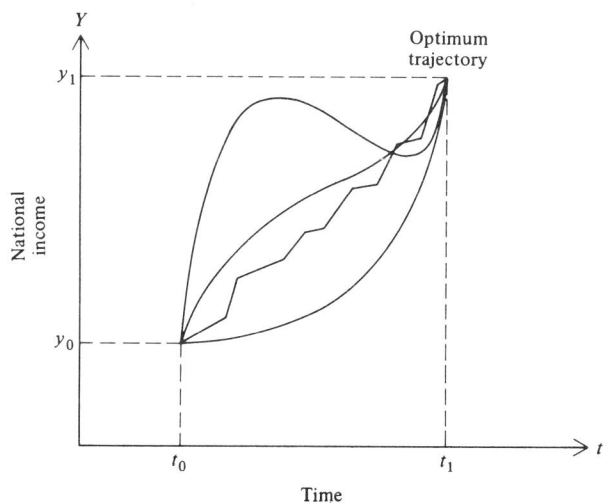

Y = national income
t = time

for the economist consists of finding the trajectory of optimum equilibrium growth of an economy between two points in time. A solution to the optimum trajectory problem in the calculus of variation is an admissible trajectory $y(t)$ which maximizes the value of an integral objective functional:

$$\max_{\{Y(t)\}} J = \int_{t_0}^{t_1} I[Y(t), \dot{Y}(t), t]\; dt$$

where

$$Y(t_0) = Y_0$$
$$Y(t_1) = Y_1$$

and

$$\dot{Y}(t) = \frac{dy}{dt}$$

The necessary condition for obtaining an optimum in the differential calculus is the existence of at least one point where the first derivative of the function will vanish (i.e., $f'(x) = 0$). The analogous condition in the calculus of variation is the existence of the Euler equation, a second-order differential equation, which is obtained by considering the *vertical* variations about the postulated solution trajectory. Unfortunately, for many functions, and especially for multivariable

Figure **11.8** Variation about the Solution Trajectory

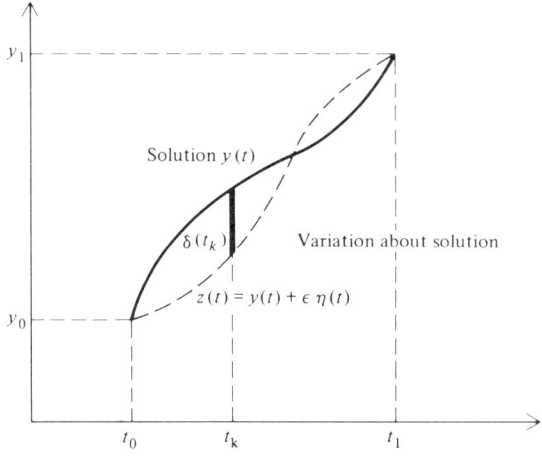

functions, the Euler equation either may not exist or may be extremely difficult to solve. Economists, however, have rarely been concerned with numerical solution; they are concerned rather with the conceptual aspects of the calculus of variations.

Optimum control theory may be considered to be a generalization of the calculus of variation. In its application to economics, the optimal control problem deals with the allocation of scarce resources among competing ends over a given time period. Mathematically, the problem becomes one of choosing time trajectories for certain variables (e.g., capital investment) called "control variables" from the set of all feasible trajectories. The variables defining the system are called the state variables. Though optimal control theory has been very successful in engineering—the most striking example is the success of the Apollo program—the large number of nonlinear variables in economic problems, and the unpredictability of human nature have, so far, deprived optimal control theory of any real operational value in economics, in spite of its current vogue in the growth literature.

Dynamic programming, a somewhat more practical approach to the development of dynamic growth models, has already proved itself very useful in solving *specific* dynamic inventory and capital re-

Figure 11.9 The Two-Dimensional Control Problem (One-State Variable)

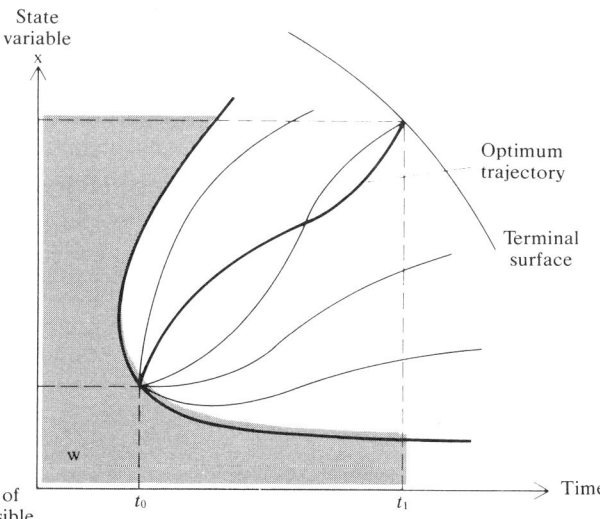

placement problems. Dynamic programming is a technique to break up a dynamic decision problem into sequential time periods, and then solve each step at a time by applying Bellman's "principle of optimality."

An optimal policy has the property that whatever the initial state and initial decision are, the remaining decisions must constitute an optimal policy with regard to the state resulting from the first decision.[25]

Unlike linear programining, dynamic programming does not provide a standard mathematical formulation for a "class" of dynamic decision problems, but is merely an "approach" to the solution of dynamic programs. Although a few computer programs have been developed for a few specific dynamic programming problems, in general the appropriate equations must be developed anew in each special case. A good deal of ingenuity and insight into both the structure of a decision problem and the nature of dynamic programming is required in order to formulate and solve dynamic programming problems. Although Bellman and several of his colleagues have been amazingly successful in solving a wide variety of problems,[26] economists as a rule have not been too successful in analyzing complex dynamic growth models with dynamic programming techniques. Aside from successful application to adaptive control problems in engineering, dynamic programming has provided practical solutions to specific well-defined problems in managerial economics and industrial engineering.[27]

In spite of the sophistication and technical brilliance of the modern extensions of the calculus of variation, the most significant foundation of modern dynamic economics has been von Neümann's work during the 1930s. Von Neümann's famous growth model[28] provided both the most promising direction for development of a dynamic general equilibrium model and the most solid basis for really promising work.[29]

---

[25]Bellman, *Dynamic Programming,* (Princeton, N.J.: Princeton University Press, 1962) p. 83.

[26]R. Bellman and S. Dreyfus, *Applied Dynamic Programming* (Princeton, N. J.: Princeton University Press, 1962).

[27]For a simple but penetrating exposition of typical dynamic programming problems, see Frederick Hillier and Gerald Lieberman, *Introduction to Operations Research* (San Francisco: Holden-Day, 1967), pp. 239-262.

[28]von Neumann, "A Model of General Economic Equilibrium."

[29]See above all M. Morishima, *Equilibrium, Stability of Growth* (London: Clarendon,

Almost equally important has been the return to essentially classical "supply-oriented" models, which are philosophically more closely attuned to Smith, Ricardo, Malthus, and Marx than to Keynes. Very much as in the days of Walras and Pareto, the economic data and the mathematical techniques are at present insufficient to make the current theory of economic process and growth operational.[30] The calculus of variation and its modern extensions cannot solve any realistic dynamic equilibrium problem, but merely present formal conceptual tools for a rigorous multivariable analysis.[31] The similarity to Walras' approach to his general equilibrium model should be apparent.

Lastly, the post-Keynesian models of Cassel-Harrod-Domar should be mentioned[32] though less ambitious than the work of the neoclassical synthesis group of Solow, Meade, Samuelson or the neo-Marxian Joan Robinson, their contribution is perhaps of more "intermediate" run interest, and of greater practical value. "Long-run" economic planning in both Socialist and democratic countries, rarely exceeds a three-to-five-year period, and seldom has practical validity for more than two years at a time. For these relatively short time periods, the post-Keynesian demand-oriented models of the Harrod-Domar type seem most appropriate. They might not assume an optimum growth path of the economy over the "long run," but they may help in solving current economic problems. Therefore, we can consider the post-Keynesian models as intermediate building blocks toward the emerging general dynamic equilibrium models that will combine the conceptual insight of classical economics with the analytical rigor of the present.

[30]For example, Dorfman, in "An Economic Interpretation of Optimal Control Theory," p. 824, states: "We have *only* to determine a set of starting values to find a time path that satisfies the necessary conditions for being optimal," and then adds in a wry footnote: "Only! Reputations have been made by solving this problem." (Our italics.)

[31]The Russian L. S. Pontryagin and the American R. Bellman, have laid the foundation for the modern extension of the calculus of variations. Bellman, very much like von Neumann before him, has been very much aware of the implications of his mathematical work for economic theory. Cf. Bellman, *Dynamic Programming,* and *Adaptive Control Processes—A Guided Tour* (Princeton: Princeton University Press, 1961); and L.S. Pontryagin et al., *The Mathematical Theory of Optimal Processes,* trans. K. L. Trirogoff (New York: Interscience, 1962).

[32]For an excellent discussion and extension of the Harrod-Domar model, see Brems, *Output, Employment and Growth,* part 4.

Economics and Economic Theories of the
Post-Keynesian Age: 1968-1980

Although the Keynesian tools were developed during the dismal 1930s, they seemed particularly well attuned to managing America's and Western Europe's economic growth during the 1950s and 1960s. The "hubris" of the liberal reformers during the Kennedy-Johnson period could be expressed most fittingly by the old American can-do slogan: "The difficult we shall do immediately, the impossible takes a little longer." The confidence in the manageability of all social and political problems ended with the Johnson administration in 1968. Since then supposedly "Keynesian" policies and liberal reforms have been unable to cope with stagflation, unemployment and social ills. A brief look at the economic issues of the troubled period, 1968-1980, will provide a setting for the examination of the economic theories this era produced in the United States.

ECONOMIC PERFORMANCE IN THE UNITED STATES, 1968-1980

Slow economic growth, declining business investment, the simultaneous occurrence of inflation and unemployment, falling productivity and pervasive trade and international payment deficits have plagued the United States over the past dozen years.[33] Some of these phenomena have been caused by uncontrollable exogenous forces, such as the OPEC oil embargo of 1973-74; some may have been due to secular factors, such as the decline in natural resources and the possible long-run investment cycles postulated by Schumpeter and Forrester.[34] There is little doubt, however, that some of the "quasi-Keynesian"[35] policies of the post-war years have carried the seeds of the economic problems of the century's last quarter.

[33]Most of these phenomena occurred also in the United Kingdom, Canada and most Western countries with the exception of Germany, Japan, Switzerland and the rapidly developing Asian countries of Hong Kong, Singapore, South Korea and Taiwan. For simplicity's sake our discussion will restrict itself to the United States.

[34]In the early 1900s the Russian economist Kondratieff perceived the existence of "long-run investment cycles," which imposed a thirty-year oscillation on business fluctuations. Schumpeter accepted Kondratieff's evidence and included the "long-run Kondratieff cycle" in his own business cycle explanation. MIT's Professor Jay Forrester and his associates have discerned an even longer hundred-year "life cycle" as the most fundamental trend underlying economic activity in a capital-using market society. The authors have found Professor Forrester's analysis most persuasive, though the mainstream of the economics profession has continued to ignore ostentatiously the findings of the MIT group. The attention given in the Forrester "national model" to Kondratieff has, however, triggered renewed interest in the Russian economist.

[35]The quotation marks are meant to indicate the authors' distinction between the economics theories and policies developed by Lord Keynes and the policies and social

The Keynesian short-run remedies of the great depression have had considerable impact upon the economies of the Anglo-American countries half a century later. Although, as Keynes exclaimed, "we are all dead in the long run," all of us also feel the cumulative impact of fifty years of short-run policies. The attempt to explain these "consequences of Mr. Keynes," or, more appropriately, the "consequences of the Keynesians," has generated several new approaches to economic policy. The new analytic developments of the '60s and '70s emerged in responses to the unanticipated consequences of Keynesian government policies, and can be understood only in the context of the unresolved economic questions of this period. A brief survey of the economic problems of the years from 1968 to 1980 is therefore necessary.

THE PERPETUAL DEFICIT

By the end of World War II most governments and economists accepted the necessity of deficit spending during the recessionary phase of the business cycle. Governor Dewey, the Republican presidential candidate of 1948, for instance, had drawn up a plan for replacing the annual budget with a 5-year compensatory budget, which was to be balanced over the business cycle. Although there are passages in chapter 12 of the *General Theory* that seem to accept long run deficits over periods of secular decline, Keynes never expected that governments would fail to run surpluses, or at least balance their budgets, during unprecedented periods of prosperity and growth. The Keynes who wrote *How to Pay for the War* and *A Treatise on Money* was very much aware of the dangers of inflation. What Keynes did not anticipate, however, was the attractiveness huge deficits and large government spending would acquire for politicians and bureaucrats; moreover, writing in the elitist Cambridge environment of the 1930s, Keynes could not and did not anticipate the political power that vested interests in government spending programs would acquire.[36]

---

reforms advocated by Anglo-American Keynesians during the sixties and seventies. The distinction between the views of Keynes and the Keynesians was first made by the Dutch economist Axel Leijonhufud in his *On Keynesian Economics and the Economics of Keynes* (London: Oxford University Press, 1966) in the mid-sixties.

[36]In the U.S., any attempt to reduce a specific government spending program is thwarted almost invariably by the "iron triangle," i.e., the unholy alliance of Congressional committees and their staffs which supervise a particular program—say shipbuiding subsidies, the government bureaucracies which exist to disburse the funds, and the powerful lobby which represents the recipients of a particular instance of governmental largesse.

In the United States every single budget during the 1970s ended up in deficit, although the presidents of this period, Nixon, Ford, and Carter, claimed to be fiscally conservative. The consistent deficits, financed by the Federal Reserve Bank's purchase of treasury bonds, the economic equivalent of printing money, generated an excessive national and international dollar liquidity, and laid the foundation of the two-digit inflation of the mid-seventies, late seventies, and early eighties.[37]

INFLATION AND TRADE DEFICITS

During the 1950s and much of the 1960s, inflation in the U.S. had been less pronounced than in most other Western countries. By 1970, however, deficits, price-wage rigidities and rapid salary increases for federal, state, and municipal workers, pushed costs and inflation indices up. The United States' trade and international payment deficits, a perennial problem since the early 1960s, became more severe and forced America's trading partners to help finance the U.S. deficits. Increasing reluctance among foreigners to hold dollar balances produced by January 1980 a 16 percent trade-weighted decline in the dollar from "pre-June, 1970 parities."[38]

The dollar devaluation further fueled inflation through rising import prices, without bringing the decisive export increases that orthodox theory and treasury officials had postulated. Toward the end of the '70s, structural weaknesses in the economy were further illuminated by a series of dismal performances: an inflation rate in the teens, a Dow Jones stock market index lower in December 1979 than in December 1965, a private sector productivity growth rate of less than 1 percent a year since 1973, a 1979 discretionary savings rate of less than 3.5 percent of disposable income, and a low capital investment rate.[39]

Inflation, trade deficits, falling productivity, and investments are, of course, only symptoms of an ineffective economic policy, based upon an unrealistic economic model inaccurately referred to as

[37]Insufficient attention has been paid to the successful deflationary policies of the Ford administration, which succeeded in reducing double-digit inflation to less than 5 percent (as measured by the CPI) by 1976, at the cost of a short and relatively mild recession. The CPI began to rise again sharply after Carter administration policies to reduce unemployment turned out to be much more inflationary than its advocates had anticipated.

[38]Cf. "Hobbled Giant," *The Economist* (January 5, 1980), p. 45.

[39]*Ibid.*

"Keynesian;" even the perennial deficit and the concomitant growth of the government bureaucracy have been consequences, rather than the determinants, of this economic philosophy. When Keynes confronted the pervasive unemployment of the 1930's, he was primarily concerned with the deficiency of effective demand that seemed to be caused by the perverse nature of the "propensity to consume." In the absence of strong investment opportunities, only a consistent effort to encourage consumption and discourage personal savings could lead, therefore, to full employment without continued heavy government intervention. The consumption deficiency aspect of the Keynesian model was further emphasized by Professor Domar in his important 1947 paper "Expansion and Employment."[40] It was this paper, and others like it, that prompted American Keynesians to advocate successfully a tax system which discouraged savings and encouraged consumption to an unparalleled extent.[41]

TAXES, SAVINGS AND CONSUMPTION

The major culprits in the tax system's discouragement of savings and investments are not the theoretically high marginal tax rates, as often assumed, but rather the system's peculiar reward for borrowing and spending, and its punishment of savings and investments. Interest charges, especially, mortgage interest charges, are tax deductible, while stock dividends and savings interest are taxed at the taxpayer's highest marginal rate.[42]

The tax system's bias toward consumption is further emphasized by its treatment of capital depreciation. The Treasury's insistence on long-term payback periods has sharply reduced the cash flow and the investment profitability necessary for capital expansion. As a consequence U.S. capital investment has been low; U.S. Steel, for instance, continued to use an open hearth steel plant in Youngstown, Ohio, which was built in the 1890s, while Germany and Japan have been scrapping ten-year-old foundries; the last major steel plant in the U.S.

[40]Evsey Domar, "Expansion and Employment," *American Economic Review* (March 1947), pp. 34-55.

[41]("The American) tax system . . . would be more appropriate to a country suffering persistently from too little household consumption and too much productive investment. That is not America's case." *The Economist, op. cit.*.pp. 45, 46.)

[42]A taxpayer, earning $35,000 in salaries and $1000 interest on bonds or savings acounts, would have to pay more than 50 percent of his interest income to federal and state tax collectors. If, on the other hand, he had to pay $1000 interest on an outstanding debt, the government would actually reimburse him for one-half his interest payment.

Figure **11.10** Washington in the Red

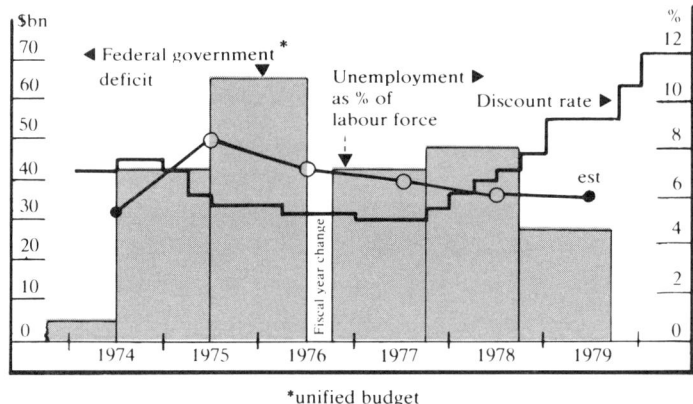

*unified budget

Sources: OECD; IMF; *The Economist*, Jan. 5, 1980, p. 46.

was built in the 1950s. The Treasury's unrealistic depreciation policy has contributed, undoubtedly, to the unsatisfactory investment performance of American industry.

The unsatisfactory performance of the American economy and the inability of orthodox Keynesian policies to halt inflation or maintain full employment has led to a broad reappraisal of both the economics of Lord Keynes and Keynesian economics. We shall take a brief look at the three most significant "post-Keynesian" developments.[43]

The Empirical Investigation of Keynesian Paradigms

During the post-World War II decades, economists expended considerable effort to test empirically Keynes' most significant intuitive assumptions. Keynes cited little or no data to support his contention that consumption was a stable and reversible function of national income (during the same time period), and that nonexogenous (induced) investment was chiefly a function of aggregate demand (in the

[43]The term "post-Keynesian" economics has acquired, unfortunately, two distinct meanings. In its narrower definition, it refers to the post-World War II investigation and elaboration of Keynesian paradigms by Keynesian economists; in its broader definition the term refers to economic theories of the last decades which emphasized economic factors not considered by Keynes in the '30s or Keynesians in the '50s and '60s. We shall use the term post-Keynesian in the broader sense. The new and exciting economic journal, *Post-Keynesian Economics,* represents primarily the narrower view.

same time period).[44] Similar statements can be made concerning the public's propensity to save and the "money illusion" that dominates wage and price behavior and, hence, the all important trade-off between inflation and unemployment.[45]

We shall deal here briefly with the analyses of consumption/saving behavior and the unemployment/inflation trade-offs. We have chosen these two topics for their significance for policy and their implications for post-Keynesian economics, especially during the 1970s.[46]

THE DETERMINANTS OF SAVINGS AND CONSUMPTION

A survey of empirical work in this field must begin with the two significant contributions by Arthur Smithies and James Duesenberry.[47] Both Smithies and Duesenberry demonstrated that, in the long run, consumption is a linear (proportional) function of income. Smithies emphasized, however, that during the midcentury, a tendency has

[44]The parentheses are used to indicate that neither Keynes, nor the simplified Keynesian model that has dominated Anglo-American texts explicitly recognize time periods; thus the general statement $C=f(Y)$ |consumption is a function of national income| attempts to express a general relationship and is not identical with the more precise formulation $C_t=f(Y_t)$. In order to test this relationship or to use it as an equation in a Keynesian model, period identification is necessary (see also footnote 45).

[45]There existed, of course, ample empirical work in the literature that was common knowledge, and did not require specific references, such as, for instance, the German economic statistician Ernst Engel's (1821-1896) work on workers' consumption patterns (Engel's "Iron Law of Wages" is named after Ernst Engel, *not* Marx's friend and collaborator Friedrich Engels). Moreover, on occasion Keynes took specific issue with the empirical work of the Australian, Colin Clark, and the American, Simon Kuznets (cf. *The General Theory*, pp. 102-104). Still there is little empirical data in Keynes' writings, nor did he seem to feel a particular need for such support. In his reponse to his critics in "The General Theory of Employment," (*Quarterly Journal of Economics*, Vol. 51 (1936-1937), Keynes complains about "traditional theory's" neglect of consumption-expenditures, and restates his case. "People's propensity to spend is influenced by many factors, such as the distribution of income, their normal attitude to the future and...by the rate of interest. But in the main *the prevailing psychological law seems to be that when aggregate income increases, consumption expenditures will also increase but to a somewhat lesser extent"* (*op. cit.*, p. 214, our italics). Note, no empirical reference; a mere restatement of an intuitive reasonable relationship.

[46]An excellent survey of empirical consumption-investment studies in Ronald Botkin's "Keynesian Economic Concepts: Consumption Functions, Investment Functions and 'The Multiplier,' " in Sidney Weintraub, ed., *Modern Economic Thought* (Philadelphia: University of Pennsylvania Press, 1976).

[47]Arthur Smithies, "Forecasting Postwar Demand," *Econometrica*, Vol. 13, (January 1945), and James S. Duesenberry, *Income, Saving, and the Theory of Consumer Behavior* (Cambridge: Harvard University Press, 1949). Duesenberry based his analysis on the following empirical findings: The 1869-1929 aggregate savings and income time series presented by S. Kuznets, the Department of Commerce aggregate savings and income data published since 1929, and two budget studies for the period 1935-1936 and 1941-1942; see Duesenberry, *op. cit.*, pp. 1-3.

existed for consumption to increase in respect to income, both relatively and absolutely; urbanization, availability and importance of
new consumer goods, expansion of consumer credit, and structural
changes in the population, all these factors combine to challenge the
Keynesian view of society's propensity to consume.

Duesenberry agreed that individual (and aggregate) consumption
depended on current income [i.e., $C_t = f(Y_t)$], but concluded from
his investigations that several other factors, disregarded by Keynes,
also played a significant role. Specifically, Duesenberry considered
the change in income over a time period to be a significant factor.[48]
Increases in income may prompt initially a more than proportional
"catch up" increase in spending before settling down to a socially and
psychologically determined consumption/saving level. Over the long
run Duesenberry characterized savings behavior as follows:[49]

1. In periods of steadily rising income the aggregate savings ratio
   tends to be *independent* of income.
2. The savings ratio will be affected by changes in *interest rates,
   income expectations,* the distribution of income, the rate of
   growth of income, and the age distribution of the population.
3. On balance changes in these variables have not been sufficiently
   large to have had much effect on the savings ratio.
4. Over the trade cycle the savings ratio is dependent on the *ratio
   of current income to previous peak income.*
5. The effect of . . . (Duesenberry's savings postulates) taken together
   can be expressed by the equation $S_t/Y_t = 0.25 \ Y_t/Y_0 - 0.196$

Where S_t = current saving
        Y_t = current disposable income
and Y_0 = previous peak disposable income

[Duesenberry's postulates are as follows:

i. In periods of steadily rising income the savings/income ratio is
   constant.
ii. In periods of depression the savings/income ratio depends on
    current income and previous peak income.]

[48]Cf. Duesenberry, *op. cit.,* Chs. III and IV, esp. pp. 48-68.
[49]*Ibid.,* p. 111. Italics are ours, and stress deviations from Keynesian model.

6. The . . . (two postulates just stated) are consistent with all available data.

Duesenberry's long-run consumption function is a straight line with a slope of .9,[50] intersected by different possible short-run consumption functions (see diagram 1). Curves I, II, III, and 1, 2, 3, depend on structural and behavioral characteristics of specific trade-cycles and, respectively, "values of consumption in periods when Y_t/Y_O is substantially above 1."[51] Trade cycles move consumption from the line *OB* to follow the various possible patterns shown on Figure 11.11; however, in each boom "the gains in productivity since the last boom are exploited. Income rises to a level above the last boom. When (in the subsequent recession) investment falls off, income and consumption

Figure **11.11**

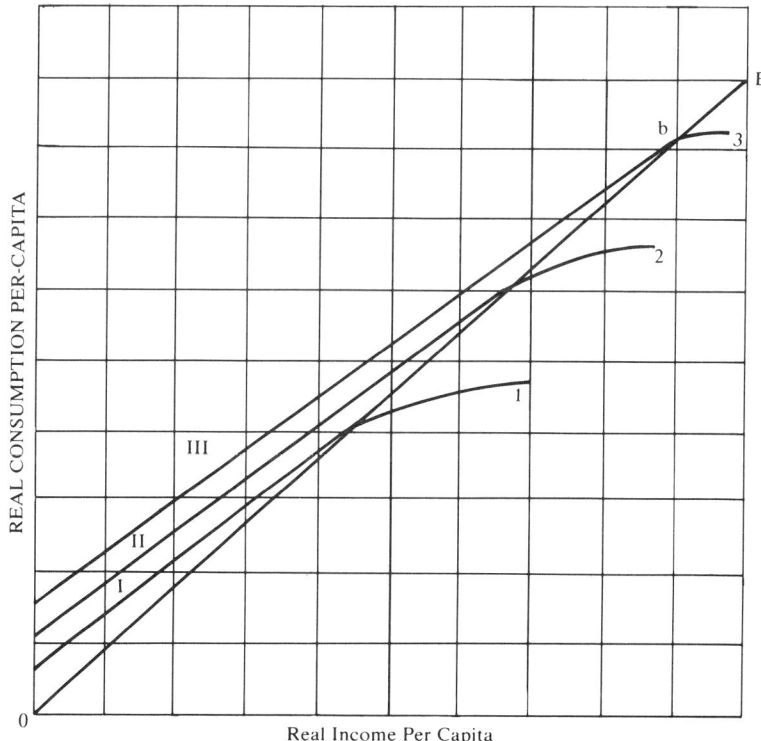

Source: Duesenberry, *op. cit.*, p. 114,
Diagram 1

[50]*Ibid.*, p. 111.
[51]*Ibid.*, p. 115.

decline, but not to the level of the previous depression."[52] Duesenberry postulates a "ratchet effect" in which the increasing short-run consumption function "keeps the economy from slipping back all the way and losing all the gains in income acquired during the preceding boom."[53]

The implications of Duesenberry's findings have only become fully recognized during the last decade. They not only throw doubt on Keynes' view of the economy, but, more importantly, completely destroy the need for excessive demand-encouraging, saving-discouraging legislation. It is Keynes as much as Domar and the "Keynesians" who are challenged by Duesenberry's conclusion that "the economy can absorb increases in productivity provided that a boom of sufficient magnitude occurs periodically . . . But it is important to recognize that the gap between actual and potential income does not need to widen progressively."[54]

Duesenberry's analysis of the complex saving/income relationship had not received the proper attention of Keynesian economists or Treasury bureaucrats. The "perverse" behavior of consumers during the 1970s in clinging to their established levels of living, despite all government fiscal and monetary policy efforts, has been a clear vindication of Duesenberry's work. If Duesenberry cast serious doubt on Keynes' consumption postulate, but failed to recommend alternative policies, Professor Friedman presented to the public a comprehensive program of monetary directives which were also based on his original analysis of empirical aggregate savings/investment data.[55]

FRIEDMAN'S PERMANENT INCOME HYPOTHESIS AND ITS
POLICY IMPLICATIONS

Friedman's view of the (long-run) saving/income relationship is closely associated with his approach to the demand for money.[56] Both

---

[52]*Ibid.*
[53]*Ibid.*
[54]Ibid. p. 116.
[55]Friedman used the same data used by Duesenberry: The Department of Commerce's aggregate savings and income series, published since 1929; S. Kuznets' savings and income data for the period 1869-1958 and the U.S. Bureau of Labor Statistics budget studies for 1935-1936 and 1941-42. The Kuznets' data showed a *long*-run constant consumption/income ratio of 88 percent (the source for Duesenberry's 90 percent long-run ratio). The budget studies, and the *annual* Department of Commerce data, provide some support for the Keynesian view that (in the short-run) the savings ratio increases with income and varies over the trade cycles, i.e., is reversible; Duesenberry's and Friedman's analyses emphasize the long-run relationships neglected by Keynes.
[56]Cf. Milton Friedman, *Studies in the Quantity Theory of Money* (Chicago: University of Chicago Press, 1956). The implications of Friedman's monetary theory are clearly expressed in his "The Role of Monetary Policy," *American Economic Review,*

the *real* demand for money and the long-run savings/investment ratio are quite stable, although the savings determinants are more complex. However, both these variables depend on the consumer's "permanent income," i.e., on the resources the individual household can expect to have at its disposal over a lifetime.

Friedman accepts the Keynesian definition that $Y = C + S$, i.e., that any income not spent during a time period is saved. Income, consumption (and hence, saving) are made up of a "permanent" and a "transitory" component (Yp and Cp, Yt and Ct). Permanent income is determined by the present value of a stream of *expected*, future receipts; the present value of this sum is, of course, determined by the individual household's discount rate; algebraically, we can represent this relationship by the equations.

(1) $Y = Y_p + Y_t; C = C_p + C_t$
(2) $Y_p/C_p = k$ or, better $C_p = kY_p$
(3) where $K = f(r, w, u)$

where

Y_p = permanent income $\qquad$ Y_t = transitory income
C_p = permanent consumption $\quad$ C_t = transitory consumption
r = rate of interest
w = ratio of wealth to income
u = propensity to consume; u varies, however, with respect to age and taste of the individual consumption unit.

The various temporary factors which affect Y_t and C_t, such as unexpected income or losses, are distributed randomly such that the expected value $E(Y_t) = E(C_t) = 0$.

Friedman used essentially the same data that had been available to Duesenberry and came to the very similar conclusion: (1) k has remained constant since 1897, and (2) the transitory components became less significant, the longer the time period under consideration. Although specific aspects of Duesenberry's and Friedman's saving theories are different, their main conclusion agrees: over the long run, consumption (or saving) is a constant proportion of income.

To the extent that Keynes was only concerned with short run consumption/saving behavior, the impact of Duesenberry's and Friedman's work on the Keynesian model is not immediately obvious. Duesen-

(March 1968), 58, pp. 1-17. Our discussion of Friedman's policy recommendations is taken from his *American Economic Review* contribution, referred to as "The Role."

berry, moreover, considered primarily the "welfare considerations" of his theory, and took issue with Keynesian policy recommendations only implicitly.[57] Friedman, however, made a major effort to spell out the policy implications of his consumption/saving analysis.

INTEREST RATES AND THE QUANTITY OF MONEY

Associated with a stable long-run consumption function is a similarly stable demand for real cash balances. This stability condemns the Keynesian fiscal-monetary policies to lower interest rates (and hence increase the marginal productivity of capital) by increasing the quantity of money. Friedman postulated that, after initial success, price increases would generate inflationary expectations which, in turn, would increase nominal interests to the point where the *real* interest (i.e., nominal interest less rate of inflation) would have returned to the level from which increases in the quantity of money had attempted to displace it. The exact process would take place in the following manner:[58] Increases in money supply, through central bank activities, will generate, initially, increased economic activity, income and spending, which, in turn, will lead to an increased demand for loanable funds and a higher liquidity preference by consumption units. Increased demand for loans and increased economic activity will also raise the price level unless there exist significant unemployed resources in the economy; the increased price level will reduce the real quantity of money (certainly with respect to the new level of economic activity), thus prompting interest rates to rise once more at least to their original *real* level. If the monetary expansion is long-lasting, or if the rate of increase in the money supply is particularly high, real and nominal rates of interest may rise beyong their original level because of heightened inflationary expectations. In the U.S. the periods 1972-73 and 1978-80 have seen precisely the type of developments postulated by Friedman. The Federal Reserve has been unable to "peg" the level of interest rates during this period, as Friedman expected.

If the central bank cannot displace interest rates from their "natural level" over the long run, neither can it use monetary policies to lower unemployment below its "natural level." Friedman adopted the neoclassical view that a given level of unemployment (or better, employment) is associated with a given structure of real wages, over

---

[57]Duesenberry, *op. cit.,* pp. 93 ff. and pp. 104 ff.
[58]Cf. Milton Friedman, "The Role of Monetary Policy," *op. cit.,* pp. 1-17.

the long run. Although in the short run, *unanticipated* inflation will increase economic activity and hence employment, the decrease in real money supply and consequent increase in interest rates will also tend to reestablish the "natural rate" of unemployment, which is compatible with the rate of capital formation and existing rate of technological innovations. Although Friedman did not stress this point in his "The Role of Monetary Policy," expectations of growing uncertainty, inflation, and lowered returns on investment could also drive down the rate of capital formation, innovation and employment.

Since monetary policy, over the long run, can have no beneficial effect on employment and the real interest rate, Friedman recommends that the monetary authorities concentrate on a stable policy that will eliminate uncertainty and prevent money from becoming a "destabilizing factor;" a publicly announced policy of increasing the monetary quantity, M_1 (currency and checking accounts in commercial banks) by a given quantity, say 3-5 percent, which is slightly above the secular rate of productivity growth.

THE PHILLIPS CURVE

The short-run and long-run trade-offs between inflation and unemployment have been a topic of research and controversy since World War II. Prof. Friedman's finding that, in the long run at least, no trade-off exists, had been a minority view for a long time, until the events of the 1970s strengthened his position. Much of the trade-off discussion centers around the so-called Phillips curve, and any treatment of post-Keynesian economics must deal with this topic.

In 1958 the British economist, A.W. Phillips, published a study on the relationship between unemployment and the rate of change of money wages, which showed a fairly close relationship between percent changes in wage-rates and unemployment, as shown on page 378.[59]

On the basis of the trade-off curve fitted to the data, Phillips concluded that, if war years are eliminated, given a secular productivity growth of 2 percent per annum, the money-wages relationship would be stabilized around 2.5 percent unemployed and a rate of wage increases equal to the rate of productivity growth. Phillips himself did not deal with the inflation phenomenon directly, but subsequently, economists and policy makers applying the "Phillips curve," equated

---

[59]A. W. Phillips, "The Relation between Unemployment and the Rate of Change of Money Wage Rates in the United Kingdom 1862-1957," *Economica*, 25, 1958, pp. 283-299.

Figure **11.12** 1861-1913

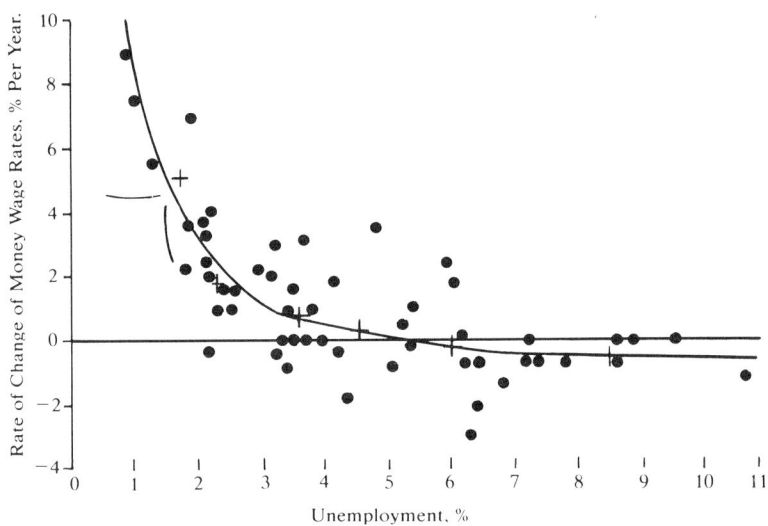

Source: A.W. Phillips, *op. cit.*, p. 285.

money-wage rate changes with price level changes. Implicit in the Phillips article was also the neoclassical assumption that wage increases in excess of productivity would cause unemployment; although Keynes himself would not have objected to this implication, the Keynesian policy makers quickly drew the more cheerful conclusion that the convex nature of the Phillips' curve clearly indicated that trade-offs among alternate rates of inflation and unemployment were attainable quite easily; i.e., a, say 2 percent, increase in inflation would decrease unemployment by, say 1 percent.

The stagflation of the 1970s has disproved the optimistic inter-pretation of the Phillips' curve rather than the actual work done by Phillips, Samuelson and others on the short-run wage-rate-unemploy-ment relationship. Friedman, of course, postulated that the long-run Phillips' curve is vertical, i.e., stable.[60]

[60]Empirical investigations by Paul Samuelson and Robert Solow ("Analytical Aspects of Anti-Inflation Policy," *American Economic Review, Papers and Proceedings,* 1, 1960) were much more pessimistic. To maintain unemployment at the 3 percent level would require an annual inflation rate of almost 50 percent (48.5 percent exactly). On the other hand, if wage increments exceeded productivity growth, 5-6 percent unem-ployment would persist.

THE "PERVERSE" CONSEQUENCES OF "RATIONAL EXPECTATIONS" AND "ADAPTIVE BEHAVIOR" FOR COUNTERCYCLICAL POLICY.

We have already noted Professor Friedman's analysis of the "perverse nature" of long-run interest rates; central bank policies to lower interest rates through expansion of the money supply actually lead to higher interest rates because the "rational" or sophisticated savers realize the inflationary nature of money supply growth and hence require a higher nominal return on their savings to maintain the "real" interest rate. The interest rate phenomenon, however, is merely a special case of "adaptive behavior" which nullifies government attempts to manage ("fine tune") the economy or to carry out social reforms. Innumerable examples exist to illustrate this point, but we shall cite only one.

The Johnson administration, belatedly, attempted to counter through higher taxes the inflationary consequences of massive social spending to create a "Great Society" in the midst of the Vietnam war. According to Keynes' notion of stable consumption/savings functions, the higher taxes ought to have resulted in lower spending and hence a decline in the overheated demand for labor and resources. The increased taxes, however, did not alter the inflationary expectations of consumers and businessmen who, quite rationally, reduced their savings and increased their borrowings in order to purchase consumer and producer goods *now,* rather than later when prices would be, and actually were, higher. Quite similarly, very high nominal interest rates of 14-18 percent during 1979 failed once more to reduce demand for loanable funds and depress consumer spending, since the American public *did not expect* inflation to subside; given this expectation, it made good sense to borrow and buy commodities now which would soon be more expensive, and repay with cheaper dollars later. In both examples, the expectations of the public prompted "adaptive behavior" which made both fiscal and monetary policy devices ineffective.

The inability of government officials and economists to predict the consequences of policy decisions has been noted since the days of Burke.

In our opinion, Professor Forrester and his group have formulated the "perverse behavior of complex organizations" most concisely during the 1970s;[61] the direct and indirect influence of the so-called

[61]Cf. Jay Forrester, "The Counterintuitive Behavior of Complex Systems," *Collected Papers of Jay W. Forrester* (Cambridge: MIT Press, 1975); *Industrial Dynamics*

"MIT group" on Congress and intellectuals has been noticeable, and
has been influential in the emergence of "sunset legislation," i.e., the
adoption of a law for a limited time period in order to assess its
intended and unintended consequences. The "MIT group" has been
less successful in gaining the attention of mainstream Anglo-American
economists.[62]

The ability of man and organizations to subvert policy decisions
through adaptive behavior has also been recognized by Professor
Herbert Simon and his former colleagues at Carnegie-Mellon University,[63] commonly referred to as the "Carnegie School." Although Simon,
Cyert and March had a considerable impact on both organization
theory and schools of management, the Carnegie School's "behavioral
economics" attracted considerably less attention among professional
economists, although, unlike the "Forrester group" they did publish in
mainstream journals.[64]

The Simon-Cyert-March concepts of adaptive behavior, organizational learning, and organizational slack present great analytical and
mathematical difficulties for orthodox models of the firm, and this
may have been one of the reasons for the economic profession's
neglect of "behavioral economics."[65]

MIT Press, 1961, *Urban Dynamics* (MIT Press, 1969), *World Dynamics* (MIT Press,
1971); also Donella H. Meadows, et al., *The Limits to Growth* (New York: New American Library, 1972).

[62]Interestingly, the Forrester group has gained considerable attention in the East
European countries; Professor Janos Kornai's *Anti-Equilibrium* (New York: American
Elsevier Publishing Co., 1971, especially Part IV) for instance, shows Forrester's
influence.

[63]An excellent survey of Simon's work is contained in his Nobel Prize lecture, delivered in Stockholm on December 8, 1978, and reprinted as "Rational Decision Making
in Business Organizations," *American Economic Review,* (September 1979). The "Carnegie School's" definitive book is R.M. Cyert and J.G. March, *A Behavioral Theory of
the Firm* (Englewood Cliffs, N.J.: Prentice-Hall, 1963).

[64]Note, for instance, Simon's "Theories of Decision Making in Economics and Behavioral Science," *American Economic Review* (June 1959), a truly seminal paper, or
his earlier paper "A Behavioral Model of Rational Choice," *Quarterly Journal of
Economics* (February 1959), which anticipated much of current "Rational Expectation
Theory," although Simon has stressed the practical "behavioral" limitations of current
"rational" expectation theory (cf. "Rational Decision Making in Business Organizations," *op. cit.,* p. 505.

[65]"Organizational slack" implies that a firm may command excess resources which
are not compatible with "maximizing behavior." Since the firm may operate very far
from any optimum, the slack serves as a buffer between the environment and the firm's
decisions. *Responses to environmental events can no longer be predicted simply by
analyzing the "requirements of the situation," but depend on the specific decision
processes that the firm employs.* However well this characteristic of a business firm
model corresponds to reality, it reduces the attractiveness of the model for many

The major lesson of the MIT and Carnegie schools, for the purpose of macroeconomics, has been the difficulty of correctly anticipating the short- and, especially, the long-run consequences of policy decisions. This phenomenon had already been anticipated in Keynes' seminal 1937 article, "The General Theory of Employment."[66] The changing nature of the businessman's expectations, which adapt themselves quickly to new information and events, seem to make anything but the shortest of short-run planning impossible. At least this was the conclusion of various economists during the 1960s and 1970s who have been called the "Rational Expectation School." Although significant differences exist within this group, there is sufficient agreement among them, however, to discuss them as a group.

THE RATIONAL EXPECTATION SCHOOL

The inability of economic policy to cope with the stagflation problems of the 1970s has drawn attention to the "rational expectation" economists who postulated that Keynesian policies are bound to fail in the long run because of the "implausibility" of being able to fool all the workers all the time. "Workers and firms . . . would wish to bargain about real (not money) wages, aware of inflation. Accordingly the natural rate of unemployment...would be inflation proof."[67]

Although the Rational Expectation School launched an effective attack on Keynesian policies, its aims are much more ambitious. Drawing on the Austrian theory of expectation, the rational (neo-Austrian) expectation theory intended to "reconstruct equilibrium economics, given uncertainty."[68]

---

economists, who are reluctant to give up the process-independent predictions of classical theory. (H. Simon, "Rational Decision Making in Business Organizations," *op. cit.*, p. 509, our italics.)

[66]J.M. Keynes, "The General Theory of Employment," *op. cit.* We have already discussed the significance of this important article on p. 318.

[67]Brian Kantor, "Rational Expectation and Economic Thought," *Journal of Economic Literature* (December 1979), p. 1423. Kantor's article provides an excellent survey of the emergence of the Rational Expectation School.

[68]*Ibid.*, p. 1423. The revival of the "Austrian School of Economics" has brought with it a confusing overuse of the term "Austrian." The "classical" Austrian school consists, of course, of the late 19th century economists von Menger, von Wiesner and von Böhm-Bawerk. The longevity of their most prominent students, von Mises and von Hayek—who is still alive and productive at a ripe biblical age—prevented the term "Neo-Austrian" from being affixed to them or their immediate associates. We shall use this term, however, to classify the works of the von Mises students, I.M. Kirzner, Ludwig Lachman, etc., and their journal. The current center of "Austrian Economics" has been the United States, and specifically New York University's Graduate School of Business Administration, where von Mises taught the last 30 years of his life, until 1976.

The specific impact of a well-defined process of rational expectations was first developed by John Muth in two relatively little known articles in 1960 and 1961.[69] Ironically, as Professor Simon remarked,[70] Muth was prompted to develop a rational expectation theory through an applied research project on developing a decision rule for smoothing employment-production levels, jointly undertaken with Professors Holt, Modigliani and Simon.[71] The methodology developed appeared to Simon and Modigliani as a simplified behavioral decision mechanism which would "satisfice" existing explicit and specific constraints;[72] Muth, on the other hand, perceived in the analytical mechanism generated by this study "a (general) paradigm for rational behavior under uncertainty,"[73] that would improve economic analysis since traditional "dynamic economic models do not assume enough rationality . . . Expectations, since they are *informed predictions* of future events, are essentially the same as the predictions of the relevant economic theory."[74]

We share Professor Simon's misgiving about the operational value of a theory whose classical Austrian assumptions—e.g., profit maximization—seem to be empirically unsupportable, especially since little attempt has been made by Muth et al. to include the known facts about decision processes in their work. On the other hand, the work of Muth and, later on, Sargent, Lucas, Prescott and others did provide the basis for a devastating critique of the operational assumptions that had been the basis for Keynesian stabilization policies.[75]

The relative newness of the "Rational Expectation Theory" and the lack of sufficient empirical evidence preclude a discussion of the

[69]John F. Muth, "Optimal Properties of Exponentially Weighted Forecasts," *Journal of the American Statistical Association* (June 1960), and "Rational Expectations and the Theory of Price Movements," *Econometrica* (July 1961).

[70]H.A. Simon, "Rational Decision Making," *op. cit.,* p. 505.

[71]C.C. Holt, F. Modigliani, J.F. Muth, and H.A. Simon, *Planning Production, Inventories and Work Force* (Englewood Cliffs, N.J.: Prentice-Hall, 1960).

[72]"Whereas economic man maximizes--selects the best alternative from among all those available to him, his cousin, administrative man, satisfices—looks for a course of action that is satisfactory or 'good enough'". From H.A. Simon, *Administrative Behavior,* (New York: Free Press, Third Edition, 1976), p. xxix.

[73]H.A. Simon, "Rational Decison Making," *op. cit.,* p. 505.

[74]J.F. Muth, "Rational Expectations and the Theory of Price Movements," *op. cit.,* p. 316.

[75]See, for instance, R.E. Lucas, "Expectations and the Neutrality of Money," *Journal of Economic Theory* (April 1972), and "An Equilibrium Model of the Business Cycle," *Journal of Political Economics* (December 1975). Also, see T.J. Sargent, "Rational Expectations, the Real Rate of Interest and the Natural Rate of Unemployment," *Brookings Papers on Economic Activity,* 1973, Vol. II.

possible merits of the constructive aspects of this school. There is little doubt, however, that the rational expectation theory, along with most of the other post-Keynesian concepts developed during the last twenty years, seriously undermines the case for Keynesian or quasi-Keynesian policies (i.e., the adulteration of Keynesian policies perpetrated by decision makers during political pressure).

The status of economics during the last quarter of the twentieth century is quite similar to its state during the 1930s; a high level of theoretical refinement and sophisticated tools which have little apparent operational value and seem to be based on incorrect assumptions. We hope, however, that schools of economics such as the Carnegie or MIT groups, which take a broader behavioral view of an empirically verifiable political economy, may set the directions for a new "post-Keynesian" revolution which will give us the operational tool for the next three decades.

BIBLIOGRAPHY

This Bibliography lists most of the original sources that serious students might want to study, and, in addition, we list several especially worthwhile secondary sources, which will reward scholars and laymen alike.

A History of Economic Doctrine by Gide and Rist is an especially charming and venerable book which gives a picture of the development of economic analysis as viewed by two sophisticated Gallic scholars who received their training at the turn of the century. Their treatment of the French Utopian Socialists, the Physiocrats, and J. B. Say is the next best thing to reading these writers in the original (in the case of the Utopians, probably better).

Lewis Haney's *History of Economic Thought,* the standard work before World War II, presents an unusual personal viewpoint and is especially perceptive in its treatment of Malthus, the Mercantilists, and the Kameralists. It also has an impressive bibliography of Kameralists' writings, though not all of the books quoted by Haney can be found in American libraries.

Eric Roll's *The History of Economic Thought,* especially in its first edition, gives a very detailed analysis of the classical economists from a Marxian point of view. His treatment of Marx in the third edition is also worth reading.

Finally, Schumpeter's *History of Economic Analysis,* although written mostly for serious students of economics, is such a superb intellectual *tour de force* that everyone interested in economics should have glanced through it at one time or another. His *Capitalism, Socialism and Democracy,* written thirty years ago, is as topical as today's newspaper and a *must,* along with Orwell's *1984* and Huxley's *Brave New World,* for anyone who wants to understand the dominant forces of our time.

Books

Allen, F. L., *Only Yesterday,* New York & London, Harper & Row, 1931.

Allen, R.G.D., *Mathematical Analysis for Economists.* London, Macmillan, 1938.

Allen, R. G. D., *Mathematical Economics,* London, Macmillan, 1957.

Ashley, W. J., *An Introduction to English Economic History and Theory: Part I, The Middle Ages,* New York, Putnam, 1910.

Ashton, T. S., *The Industrial Revolution 1760-1830,* New York, Oxford University Press, 1955.

Ashworth, William, *An Economic History of England, 1870-1939,* London, Methuen, 1960.

Baumol, W., *Economic Theory and Operations Analysis,* 2d ed., Englewood Cliffs, N.J., Prentice-Hall, 1965.

Beales, H. L., *The Industrial Revolution,* London, Cass, 1958.

Beer, Samuel H., ed., *The Communist Manifesto,* New York, Appleton-Century-Crofts, 1955.

Bell, John F., *A History of Economic Thought,* New York, Ronald Press, 1953.

Bellman, R., *Adaptive Control Processes — A Guided Tour,* Princeton, N.J., Princeton University Press, 1961.

Bellman, R., *Dynamic Programming,* Princeton, N.J.: Princeton University Press, 1962.

Bellman, R. and S. Dreyfus, *Applied Dynamic Programming,* Princeton, N.J., Princeton University Press, 1962.

Bentham, J., *The Works of J. Bentham,* New York, Russell & Russell, 1962.

Berington, H., *Nineteen Million Elephants and Other Poems,* Boston, Houghton Mifflin, 1950.

Blanc, Louis, *L'organisation du Travail,* Paris, Au bureau de la societe de l'industrielle fraternelle, 1839.

Blaug, M., *Economic Theory in Retrospect,* Homewood, Ill., Richard D. Irwin, 1962.

Böhm-Bawerk, Eugen von, *Karl Marx and the Close of His System,* New York, A. M. Kelley, 1949

Brems, Hans, *Output, Employment and Growth,* New York, Harper and Row, 1959.

Buckley, W., ed., *Modern Systems Research for the Behavioral Scientist,* Chicago, Aldine, 1968.

Burmeister, E. and A. R. Dobnell, *Mathematical Theories of Economic Growth,* New York, Macmillan, 1970.

Burns, E., *A Handbook of Marxism,* New York, International Publishers, 1935.

Byerly, W. E., *Introduction to the Calculus of Variation,* Cambridge, Mass., Harvard University Press, 1917.

Chandler, A. D., Jr., S. Bruchey, and L. Galambos, eds., *The Changing Economic Order: Readings in American Business and Economic History,* New York, Harcourt Brace Jovanovich, 1968.

Chenery, H. B. and P. G. Clark, *Interindustry Economics,* New York, John Wiley, 1959.

Cole, Charles W., *Colbert and a Century of French Mercantilism,* New York, Columbia University Press, 1939.

Cole, G. D. H., *The Life of Robert Owen,* 3d ed., Hamden, Conn., Archon Books, 1966.

Coulton, G. G., *Social Life in Britain: From fhe Conquest to the Reformation,* Cambridge, England, Cambridge University Press, 1919.

Cournot, A. A., *Researches into the Mathematical Principles of fhe Theory of Wealth,* tr. by N. T. Bacon, 2d ed., New York, A. M. Kelley, 1927.

Crankshaw, Edward, *The Fall of the House of Habsburg,* New York, Viking Press, 1968.

Daire, M. Eugene, ed., *Oeuvres de Turgot,* Paris, Guillaumin, 1844.

Dantzig, George D., *Linear Programming and Extensions,* Princeton, N.J., Princeton University Press, 1963.

Deane, P., *The First Industrial Revolution,* Cambridge, England, Cambridge University Press, 1965.

Dicey, A., *Lectures on the Relation between Law and Public Opinion in England During the Nineteenth Century,* London, Macmillan, 1905.

Dobbs, M., *Political Economy and Capitalism,* Westport, Conn., Greenwood, 1937.

Dorfman, Joseph, *Thorstein Veblen and His America,* New York, Viking Press, 1935.

Dorfman, Robert, Paul Samuelson, and Robert Solow, *Linear Programming and Economic Analysis,* New York, McGraw-Hill, 1958.

Duesenberry, James S., *Income, Saving and the Theory of Consumer Behavior,* Cambridge, Mass., Harvard University Press, 1949.

Duffus, R. L., *The Innocents at Cedro: A Memoir of Thorstein Veblen and Some Others,* New York, Macmillan, 1944.

Durkheim, Emile, *Le Socialisme: sa definition, ses debut, la doctrine saint-simonienne,* Paris, F. Alcan, 1928.

Elgerd, O. I., *Control Systems Theory,* New York, McGraw-Hill, 1967.

Elliott, W. Y., *The Political Economy of American Foreign Policy,* New York, Holt, Rinehart and Winston, 1955.

Engels, Friedrich, *The Condition of the Working Class in England,* trans. & ed., W. 0. Henderson & W. H. Chaloner, New York, Macmillan, 1958.

Ernle, R. E. P., *English Farming Past and Present,* 3d ed:, London and New York, Longmans, Green, 1922.

Fechner, G. T., *Element der Psycho-Physik,* Leipzig, Breitkopf und Hartel, 1860.

Fox, S. H., *Fundamentals of Numerical Analysis,* New York, Rowe Press, 1963.

Friedman, Milton, *Monetary vs. Fiscal Policy,* New York, W. W. Norton, 1969.

Friedman, Milton, *A Program for Monetary Stability,* New York, Fordham University Press, 1959.

Friedman, Milton, *A Theory of the Consumption Function,* Princeton, N.J., Princeton University Press, 1957.

Friedman, Milton and Anna J. Schwarz, *A Monetary History of the United States, 1867-1960,* Princeton, N. J., Princeton University Press, 1963.

Galbraith, J. K., *The Affluent Society,* Boston, Houghton Mifflin, 1958.

Galbraith, J. K., *American Capitalism: The Concept of Countervailing Power,* Boston, Houghton Mifflin, 1952.

Galbraith, J. K., *The New Industrial State,* Boston, Houghton Mifflin, 1967.

Gale, David, *The Theory of Linear Economic Models,* New York, McGraw-Hill, 1960.

Gide, C. and C. Rist, *A History of Economic Doctrine,* trans. R. Richards, Boston, D. C. Heath, n.d.

Hadley, G., *Linear Algebra,* Reading, Mass., Addison-Wesley, 1961.

Halevy, E., *The Growth of Philosophical Radicalism,* trans. Mary Morris, New York, Macmillan, 1928.

Hammond, J. L. and B., *The Rise of Modern Industry,* 5th ed., London, Methuen & Co., 1937.

Hancock, H., *Theory of Maximum and Minimum,* Boston, Ginn & Co., 1917.

Haney, Lewis H., *History of Economic Thought,* 4th ed., New York, Macmillan, 1949.

Hansen, Alvin H., *Fiscal Policy and Business Cycles,* New York, W. W. Norton, 1941.

Hansen, Alvin H., *Full Recovery or Stagnation?,* New York, Norton, 1938.

Harris, Seymour, ed., *American Economic History,* New York, McGraw-Hill, 1961.

Harrod, R. F., *The Life of John Maynard Keynes,* New York, Harcourt Brace Jovanovich, 1951.

Hatomaka, M., *Testing the Workability of Input-Output Analysis,* Princeton, N.J., 1957 (mimeographed).

Hayek, F. A. von, *Road to Serfdom,* Chicago, University of Chicago Press, 1944.

Hayek, F. A. von, ed., *Collectivist Economic Planning,* London, G. Routledge & Sons, Ltd., 1947.

Hecksher, Eli F., *Mercantilism,* trans. M. Shapiro, 2 vols., London, G. Allen & Unwin, Ltd., 1935.

Hillier, Frederick and Gerald Lieberman, *Introduction to Operations Research,* San Francisco, Holden-Day, 1967.

Holroyd, Michael, *Lytton Strachey, A Critical Biography,* New York, Holt, Rinehart and Winston, 1968, 2 vols.

Homans, G. C. and C. P. Curtis, *An Introduction to Pareto,* New York, Knopf, 1934.

Hughes, Jonathan R., *The Vital Few,* Boston, Houghton Mifflin, 1965.

Hughes, H. Stuart, *Consciousness and Society,* New York, Knopf, 1958.

Intrilligator, M. D., *Mathematical Optimization and Economic Theory,* Englewood Cliffs, N.J., Prentice-Hall, 1971.

Jevons, Stanley, *The Coal Question, An Inquiry Concerning the Progress of the Nation & the Probable Exhaustion of Our Coal-Mines,* London, Kelley, 1906.

Jevons, W. S., *Theory of Political Economy (1871),* reprinted New York, court Brace Jovanovich, 1920.

Kaplan, W., *Ordinary Differential Equations,* Reading, Mass., Addison-Wesley, 1962.

Karlin, S., *Mathematical Methods and Theory in Games, Programming and Economics, I, II,* Reading, Mass., Addison-Wesley, 1959.

Keynes, J. M., *The Economic Consequences of the Peace,* New York, Harcourt Brace Jovanovich, 1920.

Keynes, J. M., *The End of Laissez-Faire,* London, L. & V. Woolf, 1926.

Keynes, J. M., *Essays in Biography,* London, R. Hart-Davis, 1951.

Keynes, J. M., *The General Theory of Employment, Interest and Money,* London, Macmillan, 1946.

Keynes, J. M., *How to Pay for the War,* New York, Harcourt Brace Jovanovich, 1940.

Keynes, J. M., *A Treatise on Money,* 2 vols., London & New York, Harcourt Brace Jovanovich, 1930.

Keynes, J. M., *Two Memoirs,* London & New York, A. M. Kelley, 1949.

Koopman, T. C., ed., *Activity Analysis of Production and Allocation,* New York, John Wiley, 1951.

Lancaster, Kevin, *Mathematical Economics,* New York, Macmillan, 1968.

Landes, D., *Unbound Prometheus: Technological Change and Industrial Development in Western Europe from 1750 to the Present,* Cambridge, England, Cambridge University Press, 1969.

Lekachman, Robert, *The Age of Keynes,* New York, Random House, 1966.

Lekachman, R., ed., *Keynes's General Theory: Reports of Three Decades,* New York, St. Martins Press, 1964.

Leontief, W., *The Structure of the American Economy,* 1919-1935, 2d ed., New York, Oxford University Press.

Leontief, W., et al., *Studies in the Structure of the American Economy,* New York, Oxford University Press, 1953.

Lerner, Max, *The Portable Veblen,* New York, Viking Press, 1948.

List, F., *National System of Political Economy,* trans. by G. A. Matile, Philadelphia, J. P. Lippincott, 1856.

Locke, John, *Two Treatises of Government,* Cambridge, England, Cambridge University Press, 1960.

Lundberg, Eric, *Studies in the Theory of Economic Expansion,* New York, Kelley & Millman, 1955.

McCormick, Donald, *The Mask of Merlin,* New York, Holt, Rinehart and Winston, 1963.

McCulloch, J. R., *Principles of Political Economy,* London, A. Murray and Son, 1870.

McLeod, H. D., *Elements of Political Economy*, London, Longmans, Green, 1858.

Malthus, T. R., *Principles of Political Economy Considered with a View to their Practical Application*, London, W. Pickering, 1836 (1936).

Mantoux, P., *The Industrial Revolution in the Eighteenth Century*, rev. ed., trans. Margery Vernon, London, Jonathan Cape, 1957.

Marshall, Alfred, *Principles of Economics*, 8th ed., London, Macmillan, 1946.

Marx, Karl, *Capital*, Moscow, Foreign Languages Publishing House, 1957.

Marx, Karl, *The Communist Manifesto*, ed. by D. Ryazanoff (pseud.), New York, Russell & Rusell, 1963.

Marx, Karl, *Das Kapital, Kritik der politischen oekonomie*, Hrsg. von Friedrich Engels, Hamburg, O. Meissner, 1880-1894.

Mehring, Franz, *Karl Marx, the Story of His Life*, tr. Edward Fitzgerald, New York, Covici, Friede, 1935.

Meier, G. and R. Baldwin, *Economic Development: Theory, History, Policy*, New York, Wiley, 1957.

Menger, A., *The Right to the Whole Produce of Labor*, New York and London, Macmillan, 1899.

Mill, James, *Elements of Political Economy*, 3d ed., London, H. G. Bohn, 1844.

Mill, James, *The History of British India*, New York, Chelsea House, 1968.

Mill, J. S., *Autobiography of John Stuart Mill*, New York, Columbia University Press, 1924.

Mill, J. S., *Principles of Political Economy*, 2 vols., London and New York, The Roxburghe Press, 1900.

Mills, C. Wright, *White Collar*, New York, Oxford University Press, 1951.

Moore, G. E., *Principia Ethica*, Cambridge, England, Cambridge University Press, 1922.

Morgenstern, Oscar, ed., *Economic Activity Analysis*, New York, John Wiley, 1954.

Morishima, M., *Equilibrium, Stability of Growth*, Oxford, Clarendon Press, 1964.

Mun, Thomas, *A Discourse of Trade: From England unto the East-Indies, 1621*, New York, The Facsimile text society, 1930.

Mun, Thomas, *England's Treasure by Forraign Trade, 1664*, New York and London, n.p., 1895.

Myrdal, Gunnar, *Monetary Equilibrium*, London, William Hodge, 1923.

Neümann, J. von, and Oscar Morgenstern, *Theory of Games and Economic Behavior*, Princeton, Princeton University Press, 1947.

Neusel, Alfred, *List und Marx*, n.p., 1928.

Novack, David E. and Robert Lekachman, eds., *Development and Society*, New York, St. Martins Press, 1964.

Origo, Iris, *The Merchant of Prato*, New York, Knopf, 1957.

Oser, *The Evolution of Economic Thought*, New York, Harcourt Brace Jovanovich, 1963.

Pareto, V., *Manuale di Economica Politica*, Milan, Societa Editrice Liberia, 1906.

Pareto, V., *Les Systemes Socialistes*, Paris, V. Giard & E. Briere, 1903.

Pareto, V ., *Tratto di Sociologia Generale,* Florence, G . Bera, 1916.

Pollard, Sidney, *The Development of the British Economy,* 1914-1950, London, E. Arnold, 1962.

Pontryagin, L. S., et al., *The Mathematical Theory of Optimal Processes* (trans. by K. L. Trirogoff), New York, Interscience, 1962.

Pyle, J. P., *The Life of James J. Hill,* 2 vols., Garden City, N.Y., Doubleday, 1917.

Riesman, David, *Thorstein Veblen: A Critical Interpretation,* New York, Scribner, 1953.

Robertson, D. H., *Essays in Monetary Theory,* London, P. S. King & Staples, 1940.

Robinson, Joan, *The Accumulation of Capital,* London, Macmillan, 1956.

Robinson, Joan, *Essay on Marxian Economics,* London, Macmillan, 1942.

Roll, Eric, *The History of Economic Thought,* 3d ed., Englewood Cliffs, N.J., Prentice-Hall, 1957.

Roosevelt, F. D., *The Public Papers and Addresses of Franklin D. Roosevelt,* New York, Random House, 1938.

Ross, J. B., and M. M. McLaughlin, *The Portable Medieval Reader,* New York, Viking Press, 1949.

Saint Simon, Henri, Comte de, *Selected Writings,* ed. and trans. F. M. H. Markham, "First Extract from the Organizer," Oxford, R. Blackwell, 1952.

Samuelson, Paul, *Economics, an Introductory Analysis,* New York, McGraw-Hill, 1970.

Say, J. B., *A Treatise on Political Economy,* trans. from the 4th ed. of the French, Philadelphia, Grigg & Elliot, 1836.

Schlaifer, R., *Probability and Statistics for Business Decisions,* New York, McGraw-Hill, 1959.

Schmoller, Gustav von, *The Mercantile System and Its Historical Significance,* New York and London, Macmillan, 1897.

Schumpeter, J., *Business Cycles, A Theoretical, Historical, and Statistical Analysis of the Capitalist Process,* New York, McGraw-Hill, 1939.

Schumpeter, J., *Capitalism, Socialism and Democracy,* New York, Harper & Row, 1941.

Schumpeter, J., *History of Economic Analysis,* New York, Oxford University Press, 1954.

Schumpeter, J., *Theory of Economic Development,* Leipzig, Duncker & Humbolt, 1912, and Cambridge, Harvard University Press, 1934.

Seligman, B. B., *Main Currents in Modern Economics,* New York, Free Press, 1962.

Seligman, E. R. A., *Essays in Economics,* New York, Macmillan, 1925.

Sen, J. S. R., *The Economics of Sir James Steuart,* Cambridge, Mass., Harvard University Press, 1957.

Shackle, G. L. S., *The Years of High Theory,* Cambridge, England, Cambridge University Press, 1967.

Shawcross, William, *Dubcek,* London, Weidenfeld and Nicolson, 1970.

Sloan, Alfred P., Jr., *My Years with General Motors,* New York, Double-day, 1964.

Smith, Adam, *An Inquiry into the Nature and Causes of the Wealth of Nations* (Modern Library edition), New York, Random House, 1937.

Smith, Adam, *The Theory of Moral Sentiments,* London, T. Cadell and W. Davies, 1804.

Sraffa, Pierro, *Production of Commodities by Means of Commodities, Prelude to a Critique of Economic Theory,* Cambridge, England, Cambridge University Press, 1960.

Sraffa, Pierro, ed., *The Works and Correspondence of David Ricardo,* Cambridge, England, Cambridge University Press, 1953.

Stigler, George J., *Production and Distribution Theory,* New York, Macmillan, 1946.

Strachey, Lytton, *Eminent Victorians: Cardinal Manning, Florence Nightingale, Dr. Arnold, General Gordon,* New York, Putnam, 1918.

Studenski, Paul and Herman Krooss, *Financial History of the United States,* New York, McGraw-Hill, 1962.

Svennilson, S., *Growth and Stagnation in the European Economy,* Geneva, United Nations Economic Commission for Europe, 1954.

Sweezey, P. M., *The Theory of Capitalist Development,* New York, Oxford University Press, 1942.

Tawney, R. H., *Religion and the Rise of Capitalism,* New York, Harcourt Brace Jovanovich, 1926.

Taylor, A. E., *Advanced Calculus,* Boston, Ginn, 1955.

Toynbee, A., *Lectures on the Industrial Revolution,* New York, Humboldt Publishing Co., 1884.

Tustin, A., *The Mechanism of Economic Systems,* London, Wm. Heineman, Ltd., 1957.

Usher, A. P., *An Introduction to the Industrial History of England,* Boston, Houghton Mifflin, 1920.

Vandermoulen, D. C., *Linear Economic Theory,* Englewood Cliffs, N.J., Prentice-Hall, 1971.

Veblen, T., *Imperial Germany, and the Industrial Revolution,* New York, The Viking Press, 1939.

Veblen, T., *The Instinct of Workmanship,* New York, B. W. Heubsch, 1914.

Veblen, T., *The Place of Science in Modern Civilization,* New York, B. W. Huebsch, 1930.

Veblen, T., *Theory of Business Enterprise,* New York, Scribner, 1904.

Veblen, T., *Theory of the Leisure Class,* New York, Macmillan, 1899.

Vickers, D., *Studies in the Theory of Money,* Philadelphia, Chilton Book Co., 1959.

Wall, J. F., *Andrew Carnegie,* New York, Oxford University Press, 1970.

Walras, Leon, *Elements of Pure Economics,* tr. William Jaffe, Homewood, Ill., Irwin, 1954.

Webb, Sidney & Beatrice, *History of Trade Unionism,* rev. ed. New York, Longmans, Green, 1920.

Weber, M., *The Protestant Ethic and the Spirit of Capitalism,* trans. Talcott Parsons, New York, Scribner, 1958.

Yan, C., *Introduction to Input-Output Economics,* New York, Holt, Rinehart and Winston, 1969.

Periodicals

Arrow, K. J. and Gerard Debreu, "Existence of an Equilibrium for a Competitive Economy," *Econometrica, 22,* (1954), 265-290.

Blaug, M., "Myth of the old poor law and the making of the new," *Journal of Economic History, 23,* (June, 1963), 151-184.

Burns, A. E., "Economic Research and the Keynesian Thinking of Our Times," National Bureau of Economic Research, *Annual Report,* 1946, vol. 26, 1-38.

Chandler, Alfred D., Jr., "The Beginnings of 'Big Business' in American Industry," *Business History Review, 33,* no. 1 (Spring, 1959).

Darlington, C. D., "The Origin of Darwinism," *Scientific American, 200,* (May, 1959), 60-66.

De Roover, Raymond, "The Concept of the Just Price: Theory and Economic Policy," *Journal of Economic History, 12,* (1958), 418-434.

Domar, E. D., "Capital Expansion, Rate of Growth and Employment," *Econometrica, 14,* (1946), 137-147.

Dorfman, R., "An Economic Interpretation of Optimal Control Theory," *American Economic Review, 59,* no. 5, (December, 1969), 817-831.

Ezekiel, M., "The Cobweb Theorem," *Quarterly Journal of Economics, 52,* (1938), 255-280.

Fussell, George E., " 'High Farming' in East Midlands and East Anglia, 1840-1880," *Economic Geography, 27,* (January, 1951), 72-89.

Hansen, Alvin H., "Growth or Stagnation in the American Economy," *Review of Economics and Statistics, 26,* no. 54, (November, 1954), 409-414.

Harcourt, G. C., "Some Cambridge Controversies in the Theory of Capital," *The Journal of Economic Literature,* (June, 1959), 369ff.

Keynes, J. M., "The General Theory of Employment," *Quarterly Journal of Economics, 51* (February, 1937), 209-223.

Langer, William, "The Next Assignment," *American Historical Review, 63,* no. 1 (January, 1958), 283-304.

McKenzie, L. W., "On Equilibrium in Graham's Model of World Trade," *Econometrica, 22,* (1954), 147-161.

McKenzie, L. A., "On the Existence of a General Equilibrium for a Competitive Market," *Econometrica, 27,* (1959), 54-71.

Menger, Karl, *Ergebnisse Eines Mathematischen Kolloquiums,* no, 6, 12-20, 1933-1934.

Menger, Karl, *Ergebnisse Eines Mathematischen Kolloquiums,* no. 7, 1-6, 1934-1935.

Neümann, J. von, "A Model of General Economic Equilibrium," *Review of Economic Studies, 13,* no. 33 (1945-1946), 1-9.

Neümann, J. von, "Uber Ein Ökonomisches Gleichungssystem . . ." *Ergebnisse Eines Mathematischen Kolloquiums,* no. 8, (1937), 73-83.

Parsons, Talcott, "The Motivation of Economic Activities," *Canadian Journal of Economics and Political Science, 6,* (1940), 187-202.

Phillips, A. W., "Stabilization Policy in a Closed Economy," *Economic Journal, 64,* (1954), 290-323.

Raskob, J. J., with Samuel Crowther, "Everybody Ought to be Rich," *Ladies Home Journal* (August, 1929).

Ricci, V., "Pareto and Pure Economics," *Review of Economic Studies,* (October, 1933).

Rothschild, K. W., "Some Recent Trends in the Literature of German Economics," *American Economic Review Supplement, 54,* (March, 1964).

Samuelson, Paul, "Wages and Interest: A Dissection of Marxian Economic Models," *American Economic Review,* (December, 1957), 884-912.

Seligman, E. R. A., "On Some Neglected British Economists," *Economic Journal, 13,* (1903), 46-54.

Simon, H. A., "Theories of Decision-Making in Economics and Behavioral Science," *American Economic Review, 49,* (June, 1959).

Stigler, George, "The Development of Utility Theory," *Journal of Political Economy,* 1950.

Suits, Daniel B., "Forecasting and Analysis with an Econometric Model," *American Economic Review,* (March, 1962), 104-132.

Veblen, T., "Economics as an Evolutionary Science," *Quarterly Journal of Economics,* 12(July, 1898).

Viner, Jacob, "Power versus Plenty as Objectives of Foreign Policy in the Seventeenth and Eighteenth Centuries," *World Politics, 1,* no. 1, (October, 1948), 1-29.

Viner, J., "The Utility Concept in Value Theory and Its Critics," *Journal of Political Economy,* 1925.

Wald, A., "Über Einige Gleichungssystem der Mathematischen Ökonomie," *Zeitschrift Für Nationalökonomie, 7,* (1936), 637-670. [The English translation appeared in *Econometrica, 19,* (1951), 368-403.

INDEX